The Women
of City Point,
Virginia, 1864–1865

The Women of City Point, Virginia, 1864–1865

Stories of Life and Work in the Union Occupation Headquarters

JEANNE MARIE CHRISTIE

McFarland & Company, Inc., Publishers
Jefferson, North Carolina

LIBRARY OF CONGRESS CATALOGUING-IN-PUBLICATION DATA

Names: Christie, Jeanne Marie, 1944– author.
Title: The Women of City Point, Virginia, 1864–1865 : Stories of Life and Work in the Union Occupation Headquarters / Jeanne Marie Christie.
Description: Jefferson, North Carolina : McFarland & Company, Inc., Publishers, 2020 | Includes bibliographical references and index.
Identifiers: LCCN 2019058726 | ISBN 9781476678771 (paperback : acid free paper) ∞
ISBN 9781476637341 (ebook)
Subjects: LCSH: United States—History—Civil War, 1861-1865—Women. | Virginia—History—Civil War, 1861-1865—Women. | City Point (Hopewell, Va.)—History, Military—19th century. | Women and war—United States—History—19th century.
Classification: LCC E628 .C48 2020 | DDC 973.7/81082—dc23
LC record available at https://lccn.loc.gov/2019058726

BRITISH LIBRARY CATALOGUING DATA ARE AVAILABLE

ISBN (print) 978-1-4766-7877-1
ISBN (ebook) 978-1-4766-3734-1

© 2020 Jeanne Marie Christie. All rights reserved

No part of this book may be reproduced or transmitted in any form or by any means, electronic or mechanical, including photocopying or recording, or by any information storage and retrieval system, without permission in writing from the publisher.

Front cover image of General Rufus Ingalls and group in City Point, Virginia 1865 (Library of Congress)

Printed in the United States of America

McFarland & Company, Inc., Publishers
 Box 611, Jefferson, North Carolina 28640
  www.mcfarlandpub.com

To the women, past and present, who believed in the
concept uttered by President John F. Kennedy:
"Ask not what your country can do for you,
but what you can do for your country."
It is my hope that future women will believe in this, too.

Table of Contents

Acknowledgments	viii
Preface	1
1. "Sisters, Sisters"	5
2. Women Within the Safeguard	12
3. Nameless No More: Contraband Women	22
4. Government Nurses	34
5. Independent Nurses	55
6. Women of the United States Christian Commission (USCC): Prayers and Dinner	72
7. Women of the United States Sanitary Commission (USSC): The Art of Networking	92
8. State Agents: Logistics, Supplies and Catfights	114
9. A Funny Thing Happened on the Way to the Front: Incidents of Harassment and Humor	126
10. Officers' Wives: Parties and Swishing Silks	140
11. Homeward Bound Journey	153
Appendix: Weather for 1864–1865	233
Chapter Notes	240
Bibliography	255
Index	265

Acknowledgments

Although many names have been lost over time, I would like to acknowledge the kindness of various friends who shared information and periodic research with me—and they have been numerous. I wish to thank Sarah Carolan, who read and re-read assorted versions of this book. Her continued patience, suggestions and support helped make the completion possible. Specifically, I wish to thank James Blankenship and Danielle Nelson, who were with the National Park Service (NPS) at City Point while I was conducting my research and believed in the quest. The unit has now been closed and merged with the Petersburg Battlefield Park. Although I did not know Park Ranger Emmanuel Dabney at the time, he has been a significant resource at the Petersburg National Battlefield Park. There were many others, but I wish to thank some of the founding members of the Society for Women of the Civil War (SWCW): Eileen Conklin, DeAnn Blanton, Betsy Estilow, Juanita Leisch, Marie Melcorie, and Katie Teriney. They were kind enough to include me in the establishment of the SWCW. Their interest and encouragement continued to stimulate my resolve to tell the ladies' stories. The organization also provided a network of newer members who offered wonderful suggestions about my research and shared a spreadsheet of "nurses" who served during the Civil War.

Additional thanks go to the Daughters of the Confederacy, specifically Miss Dorothy Hudson (now deceased) and the headquarters staff who were open to my research desire and helped me ferret out various concepts. The Beth Ahabah Museum provided me with total access to their archives and the Museum of the Confederacy in Richmond offered many new suggestions. Thanks also go too Diane Reid and members of the Godfrey Genealogical Library in Middletown, Connecticut; the Dewitt Library; the Tioga County Historical Society; the New York Public Library; the New Haven Historical Society; and Yale University, specifically William Massa Jr., manuscript archivist at the Yale University Library. Additional helpers were Francis Pollard and Dale Kostelney, Janet Schwarz, Joe Robertson, Liz Gusher and Ed Reid, and Jamison Davies at the Virginia Historical Society, now the Virginia Museum of History and Culture. Owed thanks are Phyllis Young at the Library of Virginia; Jay Daly at the Wood Memorial Library; Jessica Powers of Historic Hopewell Foundation; and Jean and James Mecklin of Hopewell, Virginia, who opened their private collections to me. Helen Wannel, researcher at the Iowa Historical Society, helped me discover "Aunt Becky's" real family history. The Manuscript Division at William L. Clements Library at the University of Michigan held helpful resources, as did the Western Michigan University Civil War Collection. Dianne Hassan, research specialist at the Danbury Museum and Historical Society taught me many secrets of discovering past histories. John Stanton, Laurie Verge, Jane Singer and D.W. Gaddy with the Surratt Society encouraged me to find the real Sarah Slater, who wandered in and out of City Point, and to discover the truth about her relationship with Judah P. Benjamin. The Manhattanville College Library staff allowed me to explore the library stacks for many assorted histories; and the Western Connecticut University staff, specifically Russell Gladstone, Joan Reitz, Veronica Kenansis, Aura Lippincott, Brian Stevens, Annmarie DiCesare, and Angie Staino-Zavatkay, allowed me to bring part of the original exhibit into the library and kept badgering me to tell the story of these women and helped me when I was mired in mud. In closing, I need to thank several Vietnam War veterans who have offered suggestions and support and believed in the quest. Specifically, Nellie Coakley, Joan Garvert, and Grace O'Brian, who graciously allowed me to test nursing questions and procedural issues I suspected were true based on my hospital exposure. In addition, Doug Bradley, Frank Barry, Bernie Edelman, and Art Wiknik, Jr., I love you all and just knowing you saw the connections between the past and the war we all knew helped keep me on track and going.

There are many others, such as Carol and Ted Nichols, Tim Flynn, Jim Caccavo, and Jim Conway, who have listened to my passionate stories and prodded me to finish the book. I would stop and start writing with each of six different family moves but many individuals just kept asking me when I would compile what I had learned. I appreciate every single one of them. Without their interest, this book would never have been assembled and completed. I hope the research-based stories and fragmented pieces of the women's "homeward bound journey" inspires others to expand the knowledge and information about women who survived the Civil War.

Preface

City Point, Virginia, was a small town near the city of Petersburg that served as General Grant's headquarters during the siege of Petersburg. It became one of the busiest ports in the world during those months.

The following chapters are constructed like presentations to a group of curious visitors about the devotion that bonded the women and the military soldiers at City Point, Virginia, during its Union occupation from June of 1864 until the end of the war in the late spring of 1865. Much of the research emerged from the questions people have asked, such as "Where did the women go?" and "What did they do after the war?" Over time and with much research, I developed a personal commitment to tell the "dead ladies" stories. This book is about the many diverse women who came to work as "caregivers," state and organizational representatives; it also covers the wives, local individuals, and a mixed bag of "visitors" at City Point during that time. The information herein reveals the women's frustration, anger, empathy, compassion and even humor while at City Point. By defining their roles and illuminating their tasks, a new understanding of what the women really did while at City Point emerges and helps connect them with generations of women across multiple wars throughout time.

The initial research began when the internet was just becoming an everyday tool. I was a speaker with a peripatetic forum about Vietnam experiences in the state of Connecticut. A fellow veteran of Vietnam, Joseph Mariani, who was part of the group and knew of my interest in stories of women in war, inspired my quest by gifting me Frank Moore's *Woman and the War*. When I opened the book, the hair on my arms started to rise. I knew these women—I knew the sights, the sounds and smells that my proverbial sisters encountered. I knew their stories were like the experiences of so many women who had been in other wars. Neither Joe nor I had an idea of where the journey would go or how long it would last.

After my service in the Vietnam War, I became acutely aware of invasions and the impact of occupation life. I lost good friends and witnessed the changes in the local people's homeland and culture. When I moved to Virginia, being a Yankee, I quickly understood the unique perspective of the ladies of the area. At that point in time, I was creatively resolving long-distance schooling while conducting independent research on several women. The citizens of Richmond shared their values and viewpoints and I respected them. As an illustration, at one specific event in Richmond, the community stood up and sang "Dixie" with intense meaning and heart. I was dumbstruck with the similar depth of passion and meaning I had felt and witnessed in Vietnam when the servicemen stood up one night and sang "God Bless America." Thus, my insight into their lives and history gained me greater depth of understanding.

Eventually, I wandered into City Point as a tourist and started asking about the women that had been there. Later, when I served as a volunteer researcher for the National Park Service (NPS) at the City Point unit, life was never dull. Those of us on duty never knew what surprises would come through the door in terms of old letters, photos, and stories. Every day was an adventure and I learned a significant amount about the location and the individuals who had lived there. I also learned that the basic military facts ("men and maps") were known by historians, armchair historians and visitors, but very few people knew about the many women who had come to the City Point area when General Grant displaced many citizens and occupied the area during his siege on Petersburg. In fact, the NPS staff only knew of about twelve women at the time who had been at City Point. Therefore, I focused on the lives of the women who had been there and eventually presented a lecture and exhibit at the location where their contributions could be felt as they broke through barriers.

My original research began with a computer, primitive by today's standards, and pencil and paper. As the internet expanded, so did my research possibilities and results. Moving around the country provided me with opportunities to visit various historical societies and conduct searches for old letters and diaries of those who had been at City Point. One thing led to another. The internet evolved, and recently, genealogy sites have provided much information, although the information continues to be refined. Old newspapers and books have provided significant data, and more recent editions of books and the internet have provided other resources.

Realizing I could not research every woman who had served in one capacity or another during the Civil War, I focused in on the ones I knew. That group expanded rapidly and became intertwined with the women in the area and those who just came to see what was going on. There are so many wonderful stories and so many wonderful women during that period of history. As a result, the Society for Women and the Civil War (SWCW) has begun a database of the many women who actively were engaged during the Civil War, primarily those serving as some form of caregiver but also those fulfilling other capacities. However, my research allowed me to see not just a "nurse" but different types of nurses, and then different types of jobs the women engaged in. Sometimes this created a gender-bending culture that inspired and led many into women's movements like Suffrage and eventually toward advocating for the 19th Amendment. The Civil War women shared many commonalities with other women in other wars and in other generations past and present. Looking at these women and what they did, what they learned, and where they went after their year in a war zone provides stepping-stones that have previously been missing. The ladies of City Point illuminate the stones, and their contributions are felt today when women break through social, cultural, and even gender barriers.

An assumption is often made about women who served with or in the military: that they must have been nurses. In reality, there were many occupations that women fulfilled. This book shows the different roles and diverse groups the women engaged with. At the beginning is a brief history of the are to help illuminate the norms that prevailed at the time and that made it difficult to for change to happen. The first couple of chapters develop a portrait of the local ladies, both white and African American, and bring light to the problems they encountered. The following chapters delineate the various types of nurses, the organizational agents and representatives, the officers' wives, and a host of the visitors that made life interesting for those in the area.

Death and life during the war and in the war zone were constant. Illness and disease prevailed on all levels. How the women coped with these conditions provides an understanding of the toughness they developed. These women broke barriers and changed standards of acceptability. Nursing, for example, emerged as a noble profession with multiple duties.

When research allowed, the question of what happened to the women was addressed, providing a long "homeward bound" look at the impact that one year had on the women, be it in a civilian or military context. Life was changed, they were changed and all of them learned a great deal about the world around them. Participating in the war was their million-dollar education.

Over the past decade I have gathered primarily qualitative research material. Some of the primary sources were mixed with diaries and letters and secondary sources such as somebody writing about the women, like Frank Moore, or old newspapers. Initially I tracked contextual concepts and patterns, not knowing if they would be fruitful. Several proved to be very minor, not bearing significant information or insight, while others were very helpful. Two helpful examples are the work schedules and the weather during the year from June of 1864 to April of 1865. Secondary sources were derived from speaking with individuals who knew the local history, and speaking with women who had served in various capacities with the past and current military. To answer questions of triage priority, a brief survey was conducted among the women who visited the City Point area in the mid-1990s, in addition to consulting contemporary literature.

While conducting the research I uncovered many images of the now long-lost women. The photos were often grainy and unusable for print and from old sources such as newspapers or period books. I have, however, listed the locations and citations of those images after each chapter's notes so others may see what the women really looked like. Additionally, I know there are several types of learners, so when relevant I have included a citation to help the visual learner understand the contextual situation more fully. On occasion, stories have been written by the press about the woman and I certainly hope the reader will take the time to read what others have said about the ladies and help bring them back to life.

It should be noted that biases of the 1860s do emerge in period sources, but it is not my intention to provoke more bias. The terminology has been kept true to the time to represent the cultural norms and standards of the period. At times even I had difficulties reading the way citizens in 1864 wrote about one another. As a result, the insensitive language of 1864–1865 context stands intact, providing insight into the situation and lives of the women while at City Point.

There are both old and new works published about the "nurses," such as *Women of the War* by Frank Moore, *In Hospital and Camp* by Harold Elk Strubling, *Women on the Civil War Battlefront* by Richard H. Hall, *All the Daring of the Soldiers* by Elizabeth D. Leonard, and *Our Eldest and Last Civil War Nurses* by Jay S. Hoar. A hospital transport diary is found in *Shadowing Grant* by Stephen J. Recker. There are state-specific books about Civil War women such as *Maryland Women in the Civil War* by Claudia Floyd and *A Vast Army of Women: Maine's Uncounted Forces in the American Civil War* by Lynda Sudlow, and there are reprinted diaries from some of the women, such as *Reminiscences of an Army Nurse During the Civil War* by Adelaide Smith, *South After Gettysburg* by Cornelia Hancock (edited by Henrietta Stratton Jaquette), *Under the Guns* by Annie Wittenmyer, and *A Woman's War Record, 1861–1865* by Septima Collis. Roles of nurses have been addressed in *Women at the Front* and *This Birthplace of Souls* by Jane E. Schultz. However, nobody has delineated their roles. *The Women of Gettysburg 1863* by Eileen Conklin is location-specific, but once more nobody has specifically looked at City Point. No other author has addressed the impact of life in this war zone for these women. However, a common thread of experiences in all the books remains the same across the wars and across time.

1

"Sisters, Sisters"

Most people would agree that within any family there are both physical and psychological differences among siblings. Children ask one another, "If you are my sister, why do you look so different?" or "Why am I the tallest or shortest one in the family?" In the 1952 movie *White Christmas*, there is a song that provides a glimpse into the difference of sisters. The song "Sisters, Sisters" elicits smiles because the listeners recognize their own idiosyncrasies in the lyrics. For example, "she wears the dress and I stay home" typifies differences within a family. This diversity can be seen across all groups, not just families. Looking at the generic pool of women who were involved in the Civil War shows the same type of diversity. These women were a "family" who had differences amongst themselves and it was these differences that helped change the way women were perceived. Due to the wide range of situations faced by the women in City Point, Virginia during the occupation, there needs to be some clarifications. The clarifications set the stage for a deeper understanding of the changing cultural norms that these women helped precipitate. Primary excerpts from various sources help establish the standard of pre-war behavior that can be contrasted to wartime and postwar experiences faced by these women in the chapters that follow.

This chapter is divided into four sections: a general introduction about women in war; a brief historical introduction to Virginia to provide context; a discussion of the acceptable cultural norms for women of the period; and a section setting the stage for a discussion of life in 1864–1865.

Women in War

In every generation, men and women play a multitude of gender-specific roles. During periods of upheaval and war, women are forced into non-traditional roles, such as becoming an ammunition factory worker, while men are occupied with combat. This helps establish new goals and norms for their peers and succeeding generations. These newly empowered women emerge as a significant force that helps change the societal context and their culture at large.

During the "War of Northern Aggression," better known as the Civil War, women on both sides cast aside their cultural norms and took part in the war efforts. Based on primary and secondary research, this text focuses primarily on the lives of the women in the greater Richmond, City Point and Petersburg areas of Virginia during the war years. This includes Chesterfield, Prince George and Dinwiddie county. The war lasted four grueling years, from 1861 to the surrender in April of 1865. The dominant year of focus here, though, is the last year of the war. Occasionally, examples from 1861 and 1862 illustrate a perspective but not as often as was found during 1864 and 1865. This research examines northern or "Yankee" women separately from southern women's experiences. Although the southern women shared similarities in their daily lives, the differences of enduring and defending their homes provides a counterbalance with the Yankee women of the occupation. Much of the information on the northern women was from May and June 1864, when the Army of the Potomac invaded the area. Although it is hard to generalize one woman's life experiences to represent that of a collective group of women, many individualized experiences were shared to provide a broad concept of daily events. A look at the safeguard groups separately illustrates the different hardships they each encountered, but familiar concepts help to form one protective experience. Familiar historic stories always make interesting reading, but the bits and pieces of the unknown lives discussed in the second section of this research makes for a richer contextual history. The information is fascinating and perhaps interesting enough to inspire future research. It is the author's hope that new information will continue to be discovered and provide a greater identity to the previously overlooked "Dead Ladies Society." The new awareness will enhance the personal histories and hopefully resolve some of the lost pieces.

Brief Historical Context of the Virginia Area

The population of early Virginia was comprised predominantly of Anglican landowners who focused on farming rather than on trading and commerce. Due to the geographic layout of the seacoast communities during the early period of Virginia history, the state lacked a large port city that collected commercial business skills in one single place. As a result, women in this early cultural context were restricted to family farms or plantations and this position dominated their primary social and cultural lives. Dialogue, protocol, and social communication for women were supplemented by the other residents in the plantation areas, as well as the church parish.[1] Anglican laws pertaining to voting, citizenship and the holding of office discriminated against individuals in the Baptist, Presbyterian, and Jewish faiths, so communities were not diverse. Life in general was controlled by founding norms and small circles of families.

During the next one hundred years, the American population grew. Cities and towns began to develop all over Virginia. Frequently, they emerged from the merchant or trading and commerce class. In some cases, the new wealth exceeded that of the plantation owners, but their heritage was considered of less social rank. Lower still on the social and cultural pecking order were the skilled laborers, artisans, and any individual who was a recent immigrant perhaps unable to speak the language and with little or no relevant skills. However, despite traditional opinions, the "melting pot" enriched the overall culture in Virginia, creating fierce devotion to a state that had become prominent in American historical development.

By the 1850s it was desirable to call Virginia home. Citizens were proud of their political heritage. Seven presidents—Washington, Jefferson, Madison, Monroe, Harrison, Tyler, and Taylor—hailed from Virginia. Although the identity of the state had become strong, women remained tightly controlled by their restrictive culture.[2] One visitor to the state, Jonathan Boucher, noted that women from the Virginia area were "allegedly mindless and shallow, [and] yet in general good housewives; and good mothers as any in the world."[3] While young men were schooled in law and politics, the young women were educated mainly on deportment.

Prior to the war in 1860, the general area of City Point offered a host of professions. Farming was prevalent, but because of the proximity to the James River, there were also water-related professions such as sailing and working as ship hands, lighthouse keepers, and fishermen. The trades included shoemakers, coopers, woodcutters, saw millers, brick masons, wagoners, and seamstresses. There were also lawyers, a doctor, a sheriff, a court clerk and handful of merchants. They were primarily men's jobs because women were expected to remain at home and care for the children.

Acceptable Cultural Norms for Women of the Period

According to some men of the period, "The truth is the average man prefers mental repose rather than mental titillation [and] the companionship of a woman."[4] Women of the pre-war period were viewed as being physically inferior. Medical textbooks described women as having bones small and smooth. Women's shoulder blades and knee joints were not fit for carrying heavy loads or marching and their muscles were less compact than men's. Women's brains were considered lighter in weight, with blood flowing to the sensory portions of the body, rather than to the brain for cognition. Women were yielding, irresolute, and timid at times of danger. They were considered dependent, sympathetic, and impulsive. Given to social tattling, women could not be trusted with sensitive information. But most of all female duties were considered of value "at home" and not of value in the outside world.[5] As a result, proper, well-bred members of the same family never argued in public. A lady was always judged by the character of her associates when out in public or even within her private life, and thus this provided a challenge to the women who served as nurses just a few years later. Etiquette of the period focused on a young woman's communication skills, such as properly recognizing and greeting members of the community, polite social "tattling," visitation rules and protocol, correspondence, and when to use and how to use calling cards. Conversation was a difficult art to be conquered. The conversations were to be designed so that the young lady did not need to say something unique but rather would be able to extend the remarks of others and be attentive and pleasing to those around her. As an example, when a guest came to visit and entered a sitting room, the lady would rise and offer the guest a seat and then specifically congratulate them on their arrival and express the pleasure the visit brought to her. She then inquired about her guest's journey. A hostess needed to possess sufficient information to provide an account of how an item came into the home and where it had been acquired. Knowledge of appropriate geography in a private context as well as cultural knowledge was very important. Public manners for the ladies were equally as specific. She never offered to shake the hand of a person that she had met for the first time. Handshaking was only to transpire after a third meeting and never with a gentleman unless she was very intimate.

Behavior and manners were restricted and rigid for any young lady of the time. Social etiquette dictated a young woman's dress not only by color and style, but appropriate fashion for each occasion such as for balls and dancing parties, musical engagements, and even the inevitable funerals.[6] Her perfect order and exquisite neatness provided a cultural elegance that identified who she was and where she had come from in terms of her family's background. These verbal and nonverbal cues carried over into her social experiences as well.[7]

William Flagenheimer provides a charming illustration of the behavior and demeanor appropriate for such a young lady when he met his future wife at a dancing school ball. The young lady was Miss Rosa Cohn who had gone to Baltimore to visit her relatives. She was then about 15 years of age, her hair was jet black, wavy and beautiful, and she wore it in beautiful long curls. "She was a great attraction in the ballroom, especially since she was exceedingly modest with a quiet and unassuming and extremely lady-like demeanor. I almost adored her from the first introduction I obtained to her. She was the ideal of a proper lady to me."[8] The public manners Rosa displayed indicated sophistication and social etiquette that defined her status in life. William understood the dynamics and assumed that every proper young woman had to know such manners that should be applied at gatherings in the ballroom, at the dinner table, and during courtship. Their culturally regulated courtship would eventually lead them to marriage and their next acceptable stage. During the next stage of life, young women were to have command of the appropriate terminology and behavior when directing servants or raising children.

A woman's duty as she approached her late teens and early twenties was to marry and establish a home. This included the management of the help. Old established families had slaves or hired help. Many members of the community hired slaves daily, weekly, monthly and yearly from their owners who were among the social friendship caste. Daily life required shopping for and preparing three meals a day and this task often became the responsibility of a trusted slave or help. More menial tasks, such as doing the laundry and pressing and storing the clean clothes, required a great deal of time and was a job for a slave or indentured person. To complicate these jobs, the weather could often be uncooperative. When it was wet, mud was dragged into homes and splashed on clothing. If it was dry, the dust invaded every open window and clung to clean wash that had been hung outside to dry. Less affluent women often found their tasks shared among the family members, or specific tasks became a greatly reduced priority. Work was work, and survival in the new land often meant that a poor community housewife would spend her days washing, pressing, cooking, and cleaning for others only to return to her own home at the end of a long hard day.

The next feminine stage was conceiving, bearing, raising, and educating the children. Women were expected to be sterling role models not only for their households but the community at large. Their husbands (private sphere) and community (public sphere) demanded high levels of quality and commitment from the women. The task of motherhood was viewed as the guardianship of a child's early life. During those early formative years, it was believed influences caused the character of a young child to become set. Proper women never raised their voice in public and never went out in public alone. This would change greatly during the war years. Women were to manage with delicate control for ironclad results. The symbiotic relationship was privately and publicly reinforced.

Another cultural expectation was the social education of their children. Teaching the mannerisms of polite diplomatic behavior and fashionable bearing in society was significant to young ladies and young children in general. Children required constant attention and supervision. Children, when properly brought up, were never permitted to say "I won't" or "I will," but were instructed to be tempered by expressing "I do not want to" or "I do want to," especially to their parents. If circumstances prevented academic success, the children needed to be provided with social and communication skills. Mothers were viewed as having a powerful influence over the welfare of future generations but both parents needed to agree on a personal philosophy on general education. "During the first eight to ten years of [a child's] existence," the academically astute woman was seen to guide the destinies of the mind. As the rulers with the velvet gloves, they had an outlet for their own social repression, and some derived great pleasure from their children. The tacit cultural education to wait on the wants of the young and to teach respect by being respectful was the woman's domain. "When a mother greets her child with smiles and addresses him [or her] with mildness and affection, she is teaching chords of sweet harmony."[9]

The restrictive Anglo-Saxon culture defined women's roles and controlled feminine actions and attitudes, but that was about to change. The desire to help in a patriotic manner was very strong during the war years but lurking in the background was "a desire to escape" the cultural norms and standards.[10] Each generation that confronted such conflicts challenged the patriarchal control that confined women to parlors and polite conversations. Many upper- and middle-class women sought the opportunity to escape. They too wanted to help in the war effort and sought out options that might not have been available to them even two years prior to the start of the war.

Setting the Stage for the Women's Invasion

A few general points need clarification when explaining the women of the Civil War. First, the women who survived their war experiences were forever changed. Their unique viewpoint allowed them to challenge their sense of community and their perceived understanding of what their country required from them. Although many returned to their former households or familiar duties, they were different after the war on many levels and were worldlier and wiser. They had a sense of confidence that allowed them to survive the challenges of their new, changing societies. Second, their daily tasks assumed new meanings and complexities. The independence they had to assume during the war morphed into a new persona and standards of what was acceptable postwar. Many developed a "can-do" spirit to ask questions and stimulate dialogues that would previously had been forbidden. Third, the national crisis in cultural, environmental and political structure provided diverse opportunities for women. Women saw and heard things that occurred during the occupation of General Grant's army at City Point. These incidents, based on historical facts and personal letters, diaries, and memoirs, provide a kaleidoscope of understanding about the lives and roles of the many women who occupied the same military location as nurses, caregivers, Christian and Sanitary Commission representatives, state agents and more.

Women who had previously served as slaves had significant access to the lives of those they served and excellent opportunity to observe daily activities in the City Point area. A fourth point is that women learned to cope with various forms of oppression. Harassment and abuse were consistent factors in the lives of women. Based on the need to survive, the women developed appropriate identities and developed their powers of observation. Finally, stereotyping of positive and negative situations and behaviors took place in all contexts. As an illustration, not all slaveowners were as cruel as some were. Not all slaves wanted to leave their homes and not all Yankees were evil. On the other hand, many slaves were treated poorly and inhumanely and did want to escape to freedom. For example, Miss Cornelia Hancock confronted many examples of negative treatment while working in Washington. One former slave came into her hospital with his master's name branded on his forehead. Others were so weak they could barely carry their young children and often dropped them. Another had come north with all the devices used to control him, including a whip that could be used by a young child and a three-pronged iron collar he had been unable to remove from around his neck.[11] Like the slaves, soldiers, regardless of the side they served on, were similar in their construction of negative and positive stereotypes in the 1864–1865 war zone. There were many good, honest men from both the north and south. War was and will always be a nasty game with winners and losers on both sides, and consequences that extended to their friends and families back home. The ghosts of those stereotypes continue to influence generations of men and women even today.

2

Women Within the Safeguard

When General Grant moved across the James River to begin the siege on Petersburg, he deemed the land in and around his headquarters, located in the village of City Point, to be part of the safeguard area. Within this area was City Point, Bermuda Hundred, Point of Rocks and the Petersburg area about nine miles away. City Point was founded around 1613 but was only technically called City Point after 1703, with the area of Hopewell connecting to the Eppes properties.

General Butler brought the Army of the James to Bermuda Hundred on the Appomattox River and confiscated Reverend John Strachan's home for his surgeons, who would work in the field hospital. About the same time, General Grant set up headquarters at City Point where the Appomattox met the James River at the former home of Dr. Eppes (sometimes spelled Epps). Although Dr. Eppes owned three properties, his residence, or "plantation," was known as Appomattox Manor. At first a tent was erected for the general, but before long, trees were cut down and a log cabin was built right outside the manor house on the tip overlooking the James River.

Not only was General Grant's headquarters and the Army of the Potomac there, but also a massive hospital complex was located there. The Depot Hospital was developed at City Point, and another hospital complex was just across the Appomattox River, north of the plantation at Bermuda Hundred at the Point of Rocks. The two locations were close enough that the female nurses and caregivers in one location could walk or take a transport to the other without significant difficulties. Petersburg was about nine miles away and more of a walk, but there were many local residents within that area. Many of those residents were women and small children due to men being away fighting for the Confederacy.

As diverse as the composition of the area was in terms of its residents, so were the women's individual stories. This chapter provides a look at several of the southern women who remained at home to care for a wounded family member or look after the homestead. Not only did they have to contend with having their families torn apart by the war, but in December of 1864, General Grant ordered all citizens living within five miles of the rear lines to move to another location. If the families opted not to do so, they faced imprisonment or the potential for military movements and invasion, plus the confiscation of the limited supplies they had. Several of the ladies, such as Mrs. Baylor, Botts,[1] Richardson, Robertson, Birchett, Talbot, and even Mrs. Hatcher and her daughters, despite some having a house guard, had real safety concerns because the "Order" offering protection for residents within the safeguard area had been issued and occasionally rescinded, only to be reissued.[2]

It was a confusing time, and nobody felt totally safe. As an illustration, Mrs. Birchett lived in her home with her wounded husband, surviving on greens and cornbread,[3] while young Emma Wood Richardson left the Hampton, Virginia, area in the early part of the war to seek refuge at Weston Manor with elder Mrs. Mary Nelson at City Point. However, by 1864, the Nelson house was close enough to incoming shells that the family sought other options. Eventually, Emma Wood Richardson and family were told that General Sheridan needed her home and she had to relocate. This happened over and over to the women who chose to stay in their homes. However, the very first incident was a difficult one, demonstrating what the southern ladies would have to endure and the courage they had.

City Point was an area with lots of activity. It was an exchange location for POWs, and several southern women who had become prisoners were released at City Point. Several female spies roamed the area, seeking places they could safely spend a night, and there were southern families with their children who were simply trying to get out of the war zone to reach a safe place.[4] Finally, the chapter concludes with a short story about the only known "house of ill repute" during the occupation.

It All Started in June

It was early in June 1864 when people heard about Mrs. Stiles' predicament. The weather was getting hot but was still pleasant, with a breeze coming off the James and Appomattox rivers. Although the south had been at war for three years, being out in the country allowed residents to grow a few crops that would help sustain them during the desperate times. Dr. Eppes and his family had left their plantation, Appomattox Manor, and headed to a safe location in Petersburg.[5] The slaves on the plantation had split up, with some going to find the Yankees while others went either to Petersburg or stayed in the area. Although there had been cannon fire in 1862, the cannonading had not started yet toward Petersburg, so you could still hear a few birds in the trees. However, folks knew the military was approaching because the air had grown quiet and there were fewer and fewer birds around.

Mrs. Stiles lived only a few miles away from Appomattox Manor, down by the Prince George Courthouse, but the news about her unpleasant incident spread like wildfire in the City Point area. Some Yankee companies had come across the river to set up their headquarters. They marched in with all the noise and the clanking and clinking of their equipment. The horses and wagons made the already dusty ground even worse. The residents could hear the soldiers talking about Mrs. Stiles. Of course, the slaves working for the incoming military had access to the story as well, and the news traveled fast. Each day presented more information of Mrs. Stiles' feminine courage and the abusive, ungentlemanly Yankee behavior.

Mrs. Mary Stiles' husband, Benjamin, had joined the Confederacy and gone off to fight the Yankees, so Mary had asked her cousin, Miss Lucy William, to come live with her and her two young children. Lucy resided a quarter of a mile from the courthouse but technically had no place to go when the military came into the area, so she accepted the offer and lived in Mary's home for safety and security. On occasion, the two ladies would visit and stay with Lucy's mother in another location but always returned to the Stiles house. In truth there were some nice Yankees, but the general perception of their cruelty created fear and terror among isolated southern women. The rumor that the evil Yankees would come in and tear homes apart often prevailed. Yankees stole anything worthwhile and took what they wanted, and what they couldn't take, they destroyed. Life during the war years was difficult but when the Yankees invaded a home, life was almost unbearable. Since the women feared the Yankees coming to their homes, they would often sleep in the woods with any animals or valuables they might have.

On June 18, several Yankee soldiers came to Mary's house. Mary and Lucy tried to be confident, but they were afraid and huddled the children around them for protection and waited for the Yankee soldiers to leave. The story about what transpired ended up in a court-martial trial that lasted for three days. According to the court-martial:

> The men came to the house around 3:00 pm on the first visit of the day of the violation. They wanted to know if she had any potatoes to sell? [Mary] said No. Later that same day, they came back about dark with coffee and sugar. They wanted her to make some [coffee]. She did.[6]

The coffee and sugar issues were important facts but that was not the whole story. Mary said she was home with the children and her cousin and the men asked her to have some coffee but she refused. Posing as concerned soldiers, they asked Mary if she had a safeguard or protection for her home like Mrs.

Hatcher. She said she did not have one, so, "Geary and Gordon told her they would remain and do so." The women were told to get a mattress and put it in the hall. Mary and her cousin went and got a mattress and did as the soldiers requested, and Mary and Lucy retired to their bedroom with the children. Distrusting and fearing the soldiers, they locked the door for their own security.

On the second day of the court-martial, the story changed a bit. Apparently, the questions were re-asked and this time the women said the men had approached the first time to see if they could buy some corn. When Mary said they had none they called her a "damned rich secessionist" (i.e., a southern woman). Later they asked Mary if she "had any meat to sell." Mary said she "had meat to eat but none to sell." From their choice of words, there was another intention in the meaning, although that was not even considered by Mary. When the men occupied her hallway, they set up their sleeping blankets. Mary, Lucy, and the children went into their bedroom and locked the door but they didn't change into their sleeping attire because they were very nervous about the situation. After they had gone to bed and had slept for about an hour, one of the soldiers knocked on the door asking for water. Being a good southern lady, Mary got up and opened the door to get them some water. The men grabbed Mary and dragged her to their bedding. Terrified and fearing the worst, Lucy quickly tried to close the door and lock it to protect the children and for her own protection. One soldier held Mary's arms so she couldn't get away while the other tore off her skirt and raped her. When they were finished with their violent act, they allowed her to take her skirt and return to her bedroom. She said, "I'd rather be dead, I wish he would have shot me." After the incident, the soldiers packed up their things as if nothing had happened and went back to their camp, leaving the distraught women and the household to deal with their trauma.

Mary and her cousin were very upset. She had not only been violated, but her honor and integrity had been compromised. Vexed over what to do, Mary thought about the options. She had lost her husband to "the cause," she had limited food and supplies for her family, and now she had been violated by the Yankees. The only real course of action was to try and speak with the commanding officer in the area. Unsure if the commanding officer would even listen to a Secesh woman, as they called her, Mary decided to uphold her own standard with dignity and propriety. While Lucy stayed with the children, Mary walked unescorted through all the dust that was flying up from the military wagons and marching men. She walked silently, knowing that she was being observed by many of the soldiers and heard their chatter and occasional biased comments. She walked with determination all the way to the provost marshal's office near Camp Jones on the Jerusalem Road and waited to speak with him. Explaining anything to a superior person was a demeaning act, but Mary knew she had to say something. Fortunately, Provost Marshal Marsena

Patrick listened to her story and said he would investigate it. In truth, Mary was not certain he would do anything because she was a woman of the safeguard area and her husband was a Confederate soldier. Still, there was something in the provost marshal's demeanor that allowed Mary to hope he would investigate.

Illustrating stark differences from the soldiers' behavior, the provost marshal did investigate the alleged violation. When he started to ask questions about the incident, Provost Marshal Patrick had limited difficulty in locating the men. "The leader could not keep away from the spot, after the crime, and was the first to speak of it as an outrage, before any other person knew of it. He was arrested and to make his own story good, he had to tell of his comrade."[7] Two men were heard talking about their conquests, and charges were brought against them. Ranson S. Gordon and Daniel Geary of the 72nd New York Volunteers were charged with the rape and pleaded not guilty to the charges. They had witnesses to attest to their story, but during the court-martial the witnesses could add nothing to help Gordon and Geary. Mary and Lucy both had to testify and were cross-examined by the court-martial board. One question they were asked repeatedly was, "Why didn't you yell?" Mary and Lucy could not believe the question even came up, because the house was a half mile away from the next house. Who would have heard them?

The deliberation with the board continued for three exhausting days. The rumors that the men might be hanged swirled around the area like flies on spoiled food. Newspapermen started coming into the area to watch the impending, gruesome event. The telegraph men became the reporters' immediate friends because the reporters could get the news out quickly when anything happened. Finally, the soldiers were found guilty of the violation. The sentence was death by hanging.

Mary not only had to contend with the initial harassment and then the rape, but she had to struggle with the legal and ethical ramifications. Taking the life of another individual was not easy even for some of the soldiers, but for a woman, who was at the wrong place at the wrong time, it was very complex and difficult. According to the provost marshal, local Army Chaplain Rammel went to talk with Mary at her home to find out if she was willing to live with the guilt of these men being hanged. Mary's reply was a firm "yes."

On July 15, 1864, the two soldiers, Ranson S. Gordon and Daniel Geary, faced their fate. On the morning of the execution, according to the provost marshal, "The 68th and 114th soon came into position and then the guard with the condemned wagon, with their ministers. They mounted the scaffold and the Order of the Court and the Sentence" was carried out.[8] The clergy talked with them a few moments and at their request, Ramson said for them, that they died hoping for mercy through Jesus Christ and acknowledged the justice of the sentence about to be executed. Rammel made a short prayer and both clergymen took leave of the condemned and left the scaffold. The feet were tied, the eyes bandaged, the ropes adjusted, the tap of the drum and the drop fell. Scarcely a convulsion, both being killed instantly. They hung, perhaps, 5 minutes, when [Provost Marshal Patrick] remounted the scaffold.[9]

The provost marshal stood on the platform with the men hanging beneath his feet and warned all those who were in the area against such acts of violence. Mr. H.F. Parker was one of the onlookers and said, "they were hung for the crime of 'Rape' committed on the person of Mary E. Stiles in Prince George County Virginia on or about the 10th of June." He had gone to see the hanging to satisfy "his morbid curiosity" and admitted that even though he had seen a lot of dying while in the Army, "he didn't want to see another man hung."[10] Finally, Colonel Collis cut the bodies down and the corpses were placed in wooden boxes and taken to the embalmer before being escorted back home with Geary's brother.[11]

In another instance, there was a soldier charged but released because he had exchanged sugar and coffee for the consensual act. On July 2, 1864, charges were made from women on the north side of the James and were investigated by Colonel Sharpe, but nothing transpired from the allegations.[12] The situation of a white woman having the courage to complain about her mistreatment was in stark contrast to the reality of what many slave women had to endure. Generations of mulatto children bore witness to the women who had been violated by men of a different class and race. Many military and local folks were upset over the Gordon and Geary hangings—locals because they knew one of their neighbors had been violated; and military men were upset that they had to hang two otherwise useful soldiers. A typical opinion was offered by Mr. Parker, who thought about the situation and said, "These two were hung, their time was out since the act was committed."

The hanging was not the end of Mrs. Stiles' story. Concerned about how she would handle the reality of the situation, Provost Marshal Patrick rode over to her house on Friday, September 2, and "asked about her welfare. She said they were very little molested, as they ha[d] a Safe Guard—and she [wa]s now 'All Right.'"[13] The news about such an incident travelled throughout the military and finally reached Mary's husband Benjamin. Hearing of all the troubles and trauma poor Mary and Lucy faced, Benjamin could no longer stand the isolation and approached the provost marshal on March 9, 1865. Mrs. Stiles had previously written several letters, including one to the provost marshal, pleading to have permission for Benjamin to come through the Union lines to see and be with his wife. As a concerned and caring family man, the provost marshal tried to help her deal with her trauma by letting her husband come into the safeguard.[14] By the next month, the war was over, confirming that the provost marshal had made the right decision on behalf of Mary and Benjamin.

That was the introduction to how frightening life in the safeguard at City

Point could be, and what potentially lay ahead when dealing with the military. With each day, more and more soldiers arrived. The place rapidly filled up with all sorts of noisy animals, soldiers, and their equipment. Each day, more and more slaves flooded into the area as refugees to seek the dream of freedom. Many sought out the Yankees for protection, food, and employment. Previously enslaved women, who often had domestic skills such as sewing, cooking, and doing laundry, saw an opportunity and sought work within the military post. Knowing how to listen and develop strong memories for instruction made up for their limited literacy. Plus, they offered cooking, clean laundry, and some fine sewing to those who needed help. Standing up for one's own rights and challenging the men, like Mrs. Stiles did, however, was not part of the occupation culture for most of these women.

As difficult as the experience of dealing with the Yankees was for Mrs. Stiles, Miss Mary Catherine Wiseman had a Yankee experience that was just the opposite.[15] Similar to the Stiles, Williams, and Eppes families, the Wiseman family had resided in the area prior to the war. Catherine Wiseman was young and polite to many of the people who occupied her home territory and took the oath of allegiance on September 22, 1864. However, not having access to the pumped water at the hospital, the residents of City Point had to go to the local well up on the bluff to get water. One day while going to the well, Catherine caught the eye of a young soldier, Fred Belch, who was camped near the waterfront. The two began to speak to one another. Before long he was totally smitten and began to think about his new acquaintance in a more permanent way. It seemed he had fallen in love with Catherine and she began to share his feelings. When the war ended, the soldiers were marched off to return home. Typically, the wartime connections would end, and most men would never be seen or heard from again.

Fred went back his hometown of Philadelphia, where he was mustered out of the military. However, he did not forget the delightful young lady from City Point. Shortly thereafter he returned to City Point where he married Catherine in 1865. They remained in the area as it transitioned back to a quiet postwar location. Fred became the keeper of the lights on the James while Catherine became the mother to their six children.[16] Several other Wiseman family members went back to farming or shop-keeping while Fred and Catherine moved into a charming house that remains in the current town of Hopewell, Virginia.

Exchange Point and Spies

City Point was an exchange location for POWs, and several southern women who had become prisoners were released at City Point. Mrs. Levy, age 33, and Miss Bidgood, age 44, were both from Richmond and had gone north to visit family members but without a pass. Mrs. Levy was married to a merchant in Richmond and Miss Bidgood might have been the wife of a gentleman with the Jackson Hospital.[17] Heading north was not a problem. The problem arose when they tried to return to Virginia and had to cross through federal lines. Most sentries were suspicious of large bags and parcels, especially ones heading south. To the sentries at the checkpoints it appeared that the "ladies' baggage" was a bit excessive and the contents were filled with contraband goods. As a result, the women were arrested and sent to Old Carrol (Old Capitol) Prison. After several months of incarceration, they were granted leave and allowed to go through the lines. However, they were permitted to do so with only the clothes on their backs. Their point of departure brought them to City Point, where they could then take a flag-of-truce boat back up the river to Richmond.[18] The trip through the lines for these women, without any baggage, seemed to cause confusion not only for the travelers on the transports with them but for the military as well.

Another woman, Mrs. Martin, had been a POW who had been released, but transportation to her home in Mobile, Alabama, was not immediately available. She was discovered and caught in no man's land while at City Point. She claimed she was trying to return to the south, however, the military was not quite sure how to get her home without significant problems. Always pleasant, she had to remain in limbo until they could find safe passage and transport for her. Having a woman reside in limbo caused significant accommodation problems. If the women stayed with the nurses, they could have a place to sleep but not necessarily have access to a mess hall. Staying with other organizations might provide better accommodations but those opportunities remained limited. Eating at local establishments required a male guard and money. She could diplomatically socialize but could not go into the hospital to speak with Confederate soldiers. Life could get complicated when a woman found herself in the position of exchange at City Point. Fortunately, Mrs. Martin was able to head home.

In January this awkward accommodation situation transpired again with a woman (not a former POW) who had remained at City Point for some time while trying to go north. She was finally granted a presidential pass, provided with an escort, Captain Oliver, and headed north on board the *Silver Star*.[19]

The transient population at City Point also included several female spies who roamed the area. For example, Mrs. Nettie Slater was a charming spy and double agent working for Judah P. Benjamin who came through City Point on the Flag-of-Truce boat. Without the slightest hesitation, she declared to the provost marshal that she was the daughter of Mrs. Baylor, who lived in the area, and the wife of Mr. Slater. However, she turned out not to be the daughter of Mrs. Baylor though she was the wife of Rowan Slater, a Confederate soldier from North Carolina. After her brief and charming encounter with the provost marshal, she moved on to "see Mrs. Baylor" and circled around to board a transport heading north to New York and then on to Canada to the Alban Raiders.

Mrs. Slater was polished and slick. Not all spies were. A dubious individual was spotted sporting the eagle of a colonel and appeared very anxious to get on a boat headed to Washington. The person's slight figure and lack of masculine hair created suspicion, and she was discovered to be a Rebel spy.[20] Once more, accommodation was difficult for the women and the military who had to deal with them.

There were women from southern families, such as Mrs. Morley, who were simply trying to reach a safe place and get out of the war zone. Another group consisted of three large families of women and children who had arrived at City Point to seek refuge.[21] Similarly, there was a southern woman who appeared on board the *Colyer* with her six children.[22] The question was where to billet the women and her children. Should they stay at City Point or were they to reside with a local safeguard family until passage could be arranged? The Talbot family had two young ladies who were noticed by the military plus an unnamed group of seven "secesh women" in the safeguard area. This mixture of southern ladies always caused suspicion and warranted concern from the Union forces, although no charges were brought against any of these groups.

Local Hotel and Strumpet

The following is a short account about the area's only known "house of ill repute" during the occupation. When the Union Army moved into the City Point area, accommodations for visitors were extremely difficult. It was not uncommon to find people sleeping on the docks or on top of boxes or under tables. If a visitor was lucky and could find an accommodation, it was usually only a tent, because there were no hotels in the area. One enterprising southern lady decided to change all that.

Clara Haxall Grundy was known to have previously resided on Cary Street in Richmond where, according to Mary Chestnut, she entertained many an officer.[23] Her success as a hostess was not always appreciated by some of the ladies in the area and they had a particularly unflattering name for Mrs. Grundy. Similar to camp followers and spies, intelligence gatherers were nothing new to the military situation. Gathering secrets and information meant you had to be close to where the military was. Like the city of Richmond, City Point provided easy access to men with military and transportation information.

The local residents were always suspicious of strange women coming into the area. A host of ladies sailing into and out of the location and nurses on some of the transports confronted and struggled with the slanted perception of dubious women's work. Locals generally saw the women as prostitutes or strumpets.[24] Technically, "strumpets" were those who stood about or walked the streets to attract lonely men and were nothing new, especially in a war.[25] Although we do not know any of their names, strumpets were found on some of the boats tied up at the docks or moving out in the river or going to and from northern ports.

Clara C. Huxhall Grundy was not one of the women on the boats, but was connected to a place where people might stay, such as a hotel. In 1862, the Maltby House hotel concept was conceived in New York as a place for men to gather. The idea grew, and the hotel eventually developed into a fashionable facility in Baltimore.[26] Having no fashionable accommodations at City Point other than the eating tent known as the Metropolitan Hotel, the USSC often found themselves in search of a place to house people; sometimes men, but especially ladies. Men sometimes bedded on the hard ground, but some women were given a spare bed with the nurses, while others, like Miss Dix, found herself sleeping on a shipping box in a supply tent. With such complications it was time for a hotel.

When the Maltby House in Baltimore decided to expand their facilities to City Point in October 1864, an opportunity presented itself for the talented hostess to not only earn an income, but to gather intelligence information for the Confederacy. Because men were oblivious to her real role, they talked freely as if the ladies were simply guests in the area. The City Point Maltby Hotel was a wood-framed building constructed in a T shape that offered sleeping quarters for 150 people. There were also two large dining rooms for both soldiers and non-military individuals. The cost of a meal was one dollar, with lodging another dollar.[27] Tea tables for the ladies and gentlemen of the area were available, however, the "tea" was not always of a variety everyone enjoyed. Not pleased with the behavior of the hotel's clientele, Aunt Becky openly called Madam Grundy a strumpet.[28] In addition, Miss Smith noted that Mrs. Grundy had also offered to have the nurses stop in for tea, but the perceptions of the hotel clientele made any woman sipping tea with Madam Grundy subject to gossip.[29] There is no physical record of Madam Grundy owning property in City Point, but the reputation of her serving as hostess in the area prevailed and she was good at accomplishing her goal of gathering information.

With each passing week, life at City Point grew more exciting. In the next chapters, several stories of the contraband women and nurses are revealed.

3

Nameless No More
Contraband Women

This chapter extends a bit of the cultural and social background of the women of City Point, including several former slave women, then called contraband women. These women lived in the safeguard area and several held jobs that provided an income. Despite their new emerging identity, most of the women's true names remain unknown. They were simply called "Aunty" or "Hannah." Just like the white southern women, their lives changed greatly with the war. They faced the daily hardships of the war, but residing in the safeguard provided them with new opportunities to become educated and highly skilled. These women also found opportunity for greater social, cultural, and political mobility when the situations arose, becoming role models for the younger generation.

Fleeing from their former owners to the perceived land of milk and honey, some former slave women ended up in the City Point area, where they found a more supportive community and employment. Harriet Jackson worked as the chief cook on the steamer *Prince Albert,* and Mary Jones worked as a servant for officers in the Ninth Corps.[1] Women known as "Hannah," "Aunty" Cook, and "Aunty" Miranda were employed by Union soldiers and Yankee women during the occupation. There is a good probability that Martha Batte and Sally Rives, among others, took jobs with the military or visiting individuals because they lived in the area and were established washerwomen, while a more elusive name such as P. Hamblin was listed as a seamstress. Others, who remain nameless, provide insight into their lives and communities they lived in. On the railroad map of the City Point area, one can see "contraband quarters" near the Engineers Corps, but many more were housed in other locations in the area. Census records, historical documentation and diaries allow these women to emerge from the historical fog to create more of an understanding of the contraband community and their roles during the occupation at City Point.

Contrabands and Community

The term "contraband" is often attributed to General Butler. However, according to the *Official Records of the Union and Confederate Armies*, General Butler's written statements and communications with the War Department requesting guidance on the issue of "fugitive slaves" did not use the actual term "contraband." On the other hand, the Army (and Congress) determined that the military would not return the fugitive slaves who went to Union lines and classified them as "contraband." The term was commonly used by the United States' military to describe a new status.[2] The government used contrabands as laborers, cooks, and laundry workers to support Union efforts and soon began to pay limited and often sporadic wages for their work. As a result, former slaves established camps near Union forces. The Army helped support and educate refugees and USCT soldiers, as well as supporting organizations such as the Contraband Relief Society and the Freedman's Bureau, while the Freedman's Relief Association operated heavily in the Mississippi valley and New Orleans.[3] Although a direct link to the organizations at City Point remains elusive, several visitors, like Mrs. Swisshelm and Dr. and Mrs. Breed from D.C. were connected with the relief organizations and came to City Point to see what was going on. The likelihood is that some form of the organizations existed at City Point in 1864 when there was a significant influx of contrabands.

Prior to the war, in Prince George's County where City Point is located (contemporary town of Hopewell), there were 4,997 slaves listed in the census records. Of that total, there were sixty-five slave holders who each controlled twenty or more slaves, or about 56% of the county total. Some plantations (or farms) housed between 100 and 153 slaves.[4] The Eppes plantation, a major household in City Point, had 130 slaves.[5] When the war came, many owners simply moved their slaves into the Carolinas, Georgia or Louisiana, rather than freeing them.

According to Anna Holstein, the wife of Reverend Holstein, the contrabands arrived in large numbers and looked as if they had left in a hurry. They appeared to take items they thought would be most useful. As an illustration:

> One with a bed upon his shoulders; another with a box as large as he was, many of the women carrying cooking utensils, a little fellow, of six or eight wearing a gentleman's jacket.... The young girls wore flounced silk dresses, evidently confiscated from their misses's wardrobe.[6]

With the significant influx to the area of the contrabands, their livestock, and any household items they could bring, a problem arose over what to do with everyone. Provost Marshal Marsena Patrick issued an order that all black women entering the Union lines would be sent to the large Depot Hospital complex, where they were to work in the laundries. The men were hired as teamsters, dock hands and some eventually served as soldiers.[7] Along with their new freedom, finding food in the war-torn land where even the birds had disappeared was a major concern. General Order No. 30 of January 25, 1864, stated:

> The following is hereby established as the ration for issue by the Subsistence Department to all adult refugees and to the adult colored persona commonly called "contrabands," when they are not employed at labor by the Government, and who may have no means of subsisting themselves, viz: Ten ounces of pork or bacon, or one pound of fresh beef, one pound of corn-meal five times a week; and one pound of flour or soft bread, or twelve ounces of hard bread, twice a week: and to every hundred rations ten pounds of beans, peas, or hominy; eight pounds of sugar; two quarts of vinegar; eight ounces of adamantine or star candles; two pounds of soap; two pounds of salt; and fifteen pounds of potatoes, when practicable. The children under fourteen years of age half ration will be issued; and to women and children, roasted rye coffee at a rate of ten pounds or tea at a rate of fifteen ounces to every ration.[8]

With their perceived freedom, supply of food, and the opportunity for employment, life could provide some semblance of normalcy for those who had lost everything. Life looked hopeful with each passing day. With the sense of normalcy came a form of balance back into their lives, and they relished the changes.

Less than twenty miles away, life for individuals in Richmond was not as forgiving. According to author Jack Trammel, Shockoe Bottom in Richmond had more than sixty-nine slave dealers and auction houses that played a major role in the history of slavery in the United States, serving as the second-largest slave trading center in the country, second only to New Orleans.[9] Some slaves were devoted to their owners, like Eliza Page,[10] who carefully watched over her mistress Sara Pryor and the children. Others sought creative improvement in their personal lives. Hannah Lynch,[11] who ran a small fruit stand, was punished for reselling apples. Martha, slave of Mrs. Macarthy, was charged with being a runaway[12]; Catherine, slave of Mrs. Voss,[13] and Henrietta, slave of Mr. Gary,[14] were caught stealing items and all were whipped twenty-five to thirty times for their behavior. A freed mulatto woman, Mary Bradley,[15] dared to have an unlawful assembly of twenty-five negroes fiddling, dancing, loud laughing and talking. Another freed black woman, Martha Henley,[16] wore apparel from Miss Richardson and also received the punishment of lashes. Free or still enslaved, life was sometimes harsh and there was a desire to leave the area and head those few miles to City Point, where they would be subjected to the more liberal Union rules and regulations.

One of the rules from General Grant indicated that in the occupied Union area the contrabands were to be put to work at various jobs. Many people were needed in the large laundry facility at the Depot Complex. This was exceedingly difficult at first due to the hot and dry weather, and the complex had no flowing water. In a few short weeks with help from the U.S. Christian Commission's donation of pumps, water was piped up from the river to help with the laundry and keep the dust down, and also to maintain personal cleanliness. Several laundry buildings were then constructed. The structures allowed washed sheets and clothing to be dried inside, away from the blowing dust, and provided a place to iron items and repair them before being returned to the owners. Wash day was always Monday and the laundry facility was maintained by 160 contraband individuals. The buildings were two stories high, 200 feet by 40 feet, with a 40-foot engine house attached at one side. Working in the laundry facility meant also having a warm place during the winter because quarters were on the upper level of the building.[17] However, not all the hired contrabands knew how to organize their tasks, and on occasion, women like Sophronia Bucklin had to teach the men and women how to sequentially sort and accomplish the daily laundry tasks.[18] Just learning a system improved the quality of their work and made their new lives much easier and less overwhelming. It also provided an opportunity to develop some supervisory skills for those who assumed the leadership of the groups and enhanced their community.

Roles of Women During the Occupation

Up until the war, teaching a slave how to read or write was against the law in the south, although there were some who privately taught slaves to read. The plantation mistresses knew they were challenging the law but felt strongly enough to provide basic education when possible. When northern women such as Helen Gilson from Boston arrived at City Point, she set out to help the former slaves learn to read and write. The desire to improve the contrabands' lot in life was intense. Primary education rooms or schools were set up for those who had had a difficult life. The pupils ranged in age from youngsters to older adults. Miss Gilson noted that she would have twenty contrabands with significant desire to learn around her in the evening hours. Reading that had been forbidden was now a skill they could learn and use. With the powerful ability to read, the contrabands could also step outside of their personal comfort zones and become intelligence gatherers. Sliding back through the Confederate lines was relatively easy for the contrabands. Confederates assumed a slave could not read, so correspondence papers and orders were unguarded. This provided a perfect opportunity for the contrabands to gather information. One perfect example was Mary Bowser, who posed as a slow-witted house slave at the home of Jeff Davis in Richmond. She gathered information and passed it on to her Union sources.[19]

Miss Gilson focus was not on intelligence gathering; rather she focused more on their individual Christian development and would "teach some of them their letters" and attempt to simplify Biblical passages about being good and pure. Her students also sang and prayed with her. However, a lack of technical literacy meant that many contrabands had developed excellent memories for construction, animal husbandry, and agricultural skills, plus the necessary skills to remember and recreate recipes that were often complex and required a variety of cooking techniques. In addition, it meant that they had to maintain the ability to remember details they would hear and to be able to transfer the information to another person, like a reporter. Likewise, taking care of others or nursing those who were ill or those who had been whipped or injured became an asset and those with these skills flourished during the war. Several women who demonstrated those skills were Eppes family members, as well as a woman whose name was Harriet Jackson.

Like laundry skills, domestic caregiving was another prime option for the women. As an illustration, Georgiana worked with her husband for General Grant. Diley James worked in the Quartermaster Department and Nancy and Rachel served as personal servants for several officers' wives. One local resident who knew the housekeeping situation quite well was Paulina Eppes. Paulina was born in 1848 on the Appomattox plantation and was one of the 130 slaves Dr. Richard Eppes had owned prior to the occupation.[20] Paulina's father was one of Richard Eppes' most trusted slaves, James Madison Ruffin, and Paulina's mother was Harriett Ruffin. As a relatively compassionate, religious man, Richard Eppes felt his slaves should be baptized. Many of the children were baptized at St. John's church in City Point.[21] Along with Paulina, James and Harriet had several other children: James (1850); Agnes (1851); John (1853); Samuel (1855); and Indianna (1858), so she had brothers and sisters around her.[22] During the occupation of City Point, many former slaves left the area, but Paulina had housekeeping skills and worked as a domestic servant for some of the higher-ranking officers in the confiscated area. Consistently steady in her duties and mindful of her unique position of knowing a great deal about the area and the families there, she maintained her knowledge base but kept a low profile and listened carefully. Having access to what the households offered, she lived a relatively comfortable year during the occupation. Taking advantage of the new possibilities offered by the government and the Freedman Bureau around 1870, Paulina expanded her skill base and learned to read and write. The 1880 census indicates that Harriett Ruffin, Paulina's mother, was also a domestic servant. A decade later Paulina was listed as a chamber maid and had earned enough money to rent a house on her own in the area. When the war was over, Paulina married Henry, who was a sailor, and they had several children. One daughter, Mary Elizabeth, died tragically of poisoning at age eleven in 1882. Henry died of consumption in 1889. In 1939, Paulina Eppes, at age 90, became a vocal history advocate when she completed a WPA interview.[23]

Related to Paulina was Susan Slaughter (b. 1813), wife of Steward Slaughter (b. 1817). Unlike Paulina, Susan left the area during the war and moved a short distance away to Hampton, Virginia, with her husband. Steward waited on an officer and Susan probably served as a cook or as a house servant in the area. After the war in 1874, Susan joined her son, Richard Slaughter, at his wedding and returned to the general area of Hopewell.[24] Another "Aunty," known as Amy Slaughter (sometimes called Nancy Lewis), resided at another of the Eppes' family homes near Bailey Creek during the war. Aunty was old enough to have "had double children, but had none."[25] Just two miles from City Point proper, Bailey's Creek was occupied by Sheridan's Cavalry, so laundresses, cooks, and servants would have been needed and "Aunty" would have served in one of those roles.[26]

Harriett Jackson was not related to the former Eppes slaves but was another example of how women could survive. Harriet was a mulatto and former slave and had been a nurse to General Fitzhugh Lee when he was a child. By 1865, she was a middle-aged woman working as the chief cook on board the steamer *Prince Albert*. On the 12th of April 1865, she was working on board with several other freed women when a group of captured Confederate officers were loaded onto the steamer. One very weary but sincere officer, Lucien Hall, had carried a small boiler that someone had handed him on his forced march to City Point. At first, he sat quietly resting and observed the actions of individuals on board. Shortly thereafter he decided to approach the kitchen area to see if he might get some water and boil it for coffee. Harriet was the person he felt had the most authority among the contrabands. At first, Harriet was terse with him, but he started to speak in a respectful manner and they started to engage in polite conversation. Before long they were comparing notes and gathering news. Harriet eventually asked if he knew General Fitzhugh Lee. Lucien said he did, and Harriett revealed that she had served as his nurse when the general had been a child. After several more moments Harriet shooed the other contraband women away with other tasks while she took Lucien's boiler and made him some coffee.

As a woman who was now in control, she was confident enough to defy the military authorities and gave food to the Confederate prisoner. He was deeply touched by her kindness and compassion and remembered her enough to write her name and the incident into history.[27] Not from City Point, Harriet probably returned to her own home in the Fairfax, Virginia, area when the war concluded.

Subtle control was also evident in an incident not at City Point but in close proximity. A U.S. Christian Commission (USCC) minister was trying to assist some wounded soldiers and was denied food and drink for them by a white woman. Not totally understanding her anger, he was very frustrated. Shortly thereafter he was approached by an elderly black woman: "She was lame and could hardly walk under the weight of two large baskets." She told him that she "was a slave and my husband [wa]s a slave, and my children [we]re slaves." However, she had something to give the wounded and wondered if the minister would consider taking the items. She talked about her moral and religious commitment to help others, and explained how she would knit socks at night by the fire so somebody's feet could be warm. She then proceeded to pull out a "paper of tea" and offered to give it to the USCC man. Next came some fruit and garden items she had preserved. In total disbelief, the Christian Commission man was stunned by her generosity for the wounded and offered to pay her. True to her generous nature, she did not want the money but just wanted to know she had made a difference in the soldiers' lives in some small measure. Like Lucien Hall, he was deeply touched and paid her by saying many times, "God Bless you Aunty." Perhaps he learned that beauty and kindness could be found where he least expected, and he wrote about it to share with future generations.[28]

Although these examples are limited, there are other stories from the Yankee women who occupied the area that shine a light on other women. It should be noted that according to the 1870 census after the war, aggregated communities of many of the freed slaves developed and thrived in the area. Instead of escaping and abandoning their wartime residences, they became proactive and developed a profession. Only nine miles away from City Point, Petersburg had had a significant freed community prior to the war,[29] and many returned. As an example, Amanda Marshall, Susan Branch, Amanda Bragg, and Mary Johnson all found work as "domestic servants" after the war in the area. In addition, several Hannahs appear as cooks in the local area of City Point. During the period of occupation there were Hannah Randolph; Hannah Walker, connected to the Rives family; and elderly Hannah Eppes. Nurses wrote about their Hannahs, but it's impossible to know which individuals they were writing about. Nevertheless, contrabands provided a wide range of exposure to the Yankee women while at City Point. Specifically, three stories by Cornelia Hancock, Adelaide Smith and Sarah Palmer allow us to better understand the lives as they discovered a new awareness of the plight of the contraband women.

Cornelia Hancock, a Quaker from New Jersey, had invested in the Civil War at Gettysburg. Some of her first exposure to the refugee and freed slave problems came when she started her hospital work. She noted how the "lame, halt, and blind" had often been the ones who escaped from slavery. She saw women who had no feet because they had been frozen and then amputated, severely restricting their ability to get around. Others were so weary they could hardly move. Even though Cornelia had seen wounds and scars on the battlefield, she was not prepared for the magnitude and nature of scars the former slaves bore. Two different slaves came from Louisiana and had the name of their master burned into their foreheads. She was shocked that neck and ankle irons were still worn. They had no way to remove them when they escaped.[30]

Attached to the hospital, Cornelia noted that the women were often used as cooks in the kitchen and maintained a unique ability to help her procure what she needed. In turn, Cornelia provided them with clothing whenever she could but was mystified as to why she never saw them wearing the clothing. She said when she gave out the clothing it was like "pouring water through a sieve"[31] because the clothing disappeared quickly and was never seen on the women she worked with. Obviously, the influx of less fortunate people who needed clothing more than the women who were gifted it was to blame, and the community of freed slaves watched out for their own.

At one point Cornelia was befriended by a woman known as "Aunt Hannah" who tried to share a red scarf with her. Aunt Hannah demonstrated how to wear the scarf around her head, but Cornelia thought that the scarf looked better as a wall decoration. Aunt Hannah just shook her head trying to understand her new friend. Cornelia knew Aunt Hannah had a vested interest in Richmond and often spoke about how the end of the war would bring changes. Although Cornelia did not remain in the area long enough after the war to find the answer, she surmised that Aunt Hannah had family members in the area and that they would all be in touch with the war's end.

One relationship between a contraband woman and Cornelia was quite enlightening to others. On July 10, 1864, a woman and a young boy began working for Cornelia Hancock. At the time, protocol required a contraband to always address a white woman by her proper title of Miss or Mrs. or Mrs. (with her husband's rank such as Major or General), but this former slave called Cornelia "Honey" and resided with her in the tent with her child. Having a contraband in the tent was not that unusual, but to those around her it was shocking that the mother and child were sleeping in a regular bed. The new rumor surprised and amazed many of the women in camp. Comfortable with the situation, Cornelia referred to her as a "Perfect Old Slave."

Next, another Hannah story. The abilities of a contraband were not always limited to cooking and cleaning. There were several Hannahs that appeared on Dr. Richard Eppes' list of slaves prior to the war. One was Hannah Slaughter, age fifty-six, who was known to have stayed in the area when the Union forces came.[32] It is not known if the Hannah of this story was Hannah Slaughter or the young Hannah Corn, who would have been about fourteen, or another woman who moved into the area whose name was also Hannah.

"Hannah" was a contraband woman that independent nurse and eventual state agent Adelaide Smith hired, even though she thought Hannah was "rather incompetent" on the domestic front. Hannah had apparently helped in one of the kitchens of New Jersey, Pennsylvania, or even New York state agents, and that was good enough for Miss Smith. More than a cook and house servant, Hannah became an excellent source of support when Adelaide arranged one of the few legal weddings on the base during the year of occupation.

The wedding was between Major Eden and Annie Bain in February of 1865. Annie had found lodging with Miss Smith and her associates. After three months of deliberation and frustration, Miss Smith decided she should arrange a covert operation. Hannah became critical to the operation. She became the eyes and ears of the wedding plot, recording and recalling information to Adelaide. When the actual day arrived, Hannah was on high alert. Nothing and nobody got past her. As the wedding hour approached, she made sure the situation looked "absolutely normal," so nobody would suspect a bride, groom, Methodist minister, and wedding party were gathering. Once inside their selected location, Hannah stood sentry at the door. After the ceremony, she was invited to come inside and celebrate.[33]

"Aunty" was another nameless contraband who was important enough to be identified by what she wore. Like many others, she had a bright red turban and a white apron over her clothing that gave her definition, and like Hannah, she stayed with Adelaide Smith after the 2nd Corps Hospital left. Like Cornelia Hancock did, though still considered a cultural taboo to many outside observers, Adelaide allowed Aunty to sleep in a regular bed and not on the floor. Aunty and Hannah may have been related or just friends in the community and may be in a photograph of Miss Smith in front of her eventual log cabin. From all indications, this "Aunty" remained at City Point after the war ended.

Finally, a story from "Aunt Becky" about her experience with a deceased former slave woman. Sarah Palmer, known as Aunt Becky, was from upstate New York and had not been around individuals of color before she joined a regiment and went off to war as a nurse. She was often curious and amused about the nameless contrabands she had contact with as she moved south with the military. At City Point she learned a lot about the contrabands who lived in the Virginia area. Her comments were often filled with curiosity as she opened her mind to another culture and another way of life.

Aunt Becky exhibited her curiosity when she noted:

> We had a laundry established by the river-side where colored people did the washing for the hospital and for us. It was quite amusing to go down to the river and watch the gambols of the little darkies, whose fathers and mothers worked over the wash trough.... They were a careless, happy set, as they lolled by the river and enjoyed themselves in camp. Their prayer meetings often ended with dancing and song, in which negro element was exhibited in its perfection. They had many privileges, good rations—sometimes better that our own men and were under far less restraints.[34]

Intrigued by a culture she had not before known, Aunt Becky also wrote:

> I went one night to look upon the corpse of an old wrinkled woman who had died, one of their own numbers, over whose table remain the moans of loud lamentation resounded. Naught belonging to the deceased could ever be used by a single blood relation, and her scanty possessions were soon scattered amongst the group of sym-

pathizing friends around. She looked very calm in her last sleep; the slave could no more fetter in that land—that blessed country from which no tinge of Africa's hue can debar the uprising spirit. Those boney hands had done their work on plantations, and in the planter's kitchen, and those dimmed eyes had looked upon the deliverers as they broke the bondage of her people.[35]

Psychologically challenged by the war around her and philosophically challenged about slavery, she added, "She could well lie down in peace, while children and grandchildren were left to solve the problems of newly found liberty."[36] Who the woman was is lost to history; however, an Eliza Bonnett was listed as a colored woman amongst the many graves in the area.

Before moving on to the nurses, three relevant references need to be briefly mentioned. First, "Old Aunty Cook." Two headstrong ladies, Miss Bain from England and Miss Smith from New York, went to visit the officers in the Dutch Gap area one day. As a newly freed member of the area, Old Aunty Cook had been hired by the officers stationed in the area. She was a skilled and creative cook and made tasty meals for the men and their guests. Having experienced "good cooking" before the two women met Old Aunty Cook, they were surprised and impressed with her culinary abilities.[37]

Then there was "Aunty Miranda" who worked with Mrs. General Collis (Septima) during the winter of 1864. Uninterested and unable to maintain a home under occupation conditions, Mrs. Collis sought help. Who else would be an acceptable asset other than a woman who had worked in a plantation with responsibility and sense of order? Aunty Miranda was an older woman whom Mrs. Collis found living in the area and then hired. According to Mrs. Collis, "she was an excellent cook and maid," thus relieving Mrs. Collis of mundane duties and allowing the general's wife to socialize with other officers' wives. In photographs of Miss Smith in front of the Collis quarters, one can see several of the contraband women.[38]

Finally, a story about "one excited old woman." Having been raised as slaves put the contraband women in unique positions at times. They cared about people, yet they wanted their freedom. This was evident when a black woman was watching Confederate prisoners being marched into City Point after the battle of Hatchers Run. The men were being driven along like cattle, their captors showing little regard for their wounds or their physical condition. The woman, either having been a slave or perhaps one of the freed women of Petersburg, recognized some of the men and gestured in an excited way to the prisoners. Her gestures let the captured men know she would let their families know they were alive and she could reveal where they were headed. Once more, using a skill that did not require reading or writing but acute verbal and nonverbal communication, women provided valuable assistance to the soldiers.[39]

These stories and illustrations help identify the nameless women who served as the underpinning of the City Point culture. The information about their communities, some of their roles and their experiences demonstrate how the women who preceded us were responsible for the welfare and understanding of the generations that would follow. Among Civil War pensions, there are a few freed and contraband women nurses recognized, such as Emma Stephenson,[40] Susie King Taylor and Harriet Tubman, but for the most part, the women who served as nurses volunteered to help with the sick and wounded.

The Commissioner of Revenue listed deaths in 1864. Among the contraband population, diseases such as chicken pox, measels, whooping cough, diptheria, dysentary, pneumonia, bowel and lung problems, and various fevers prevailed. Many of the illnesses were ones a woman may have experienced in her own family prior to the war. So, they came into the hospital having some knowledge, but what they were not prepared for was the same problem novice white nurses experienced, and that was the mass casualities component. Once more, the women learned from one another, and from empathetic nurses like Miss Gilson and Miss Bucklin, about how to organize a ward with wounded soldiers. The nurses had learned how to treat minor injuries, such as by pouring water over a wound,[41] but now they had to learn how to deal with massive numbers of sick and wounded. Always willing to learn from a good role model like Miss Gilson, they learned to provide structure to their caregiving process. In addition, they gained nursing knowledge about how to listen to the soldiers' breathing. Instead of avoiding eye contact, the new nurses now paid attention to the soldiers' eyes and body language as a way to communicate. Nurses who could write gathered names and information. Some probably wrote letters for the wounded. One has to remember there were significant USCT in the area and one hospital was dedicated to the contrabands. As the wards filled with more sick and wounded, more woman stepped in to help. The sound of music was medicine, and like their white sisters, the black women used their voices in song. Reporters noted that they would frequently hear the voices of the contrabands singing religious hymns. At times it was mournful but very rhythmic and moving, and at other times the singers were praising heaven. The swinging to and fro of even a wounded soldier helped serve as medicine. Frequently a female voice would rise above the others and you knew that the contraband nurses were doing what their sisters did.

The community around the area of City Point and Point of Rocks provided some stability for the contrabands, slave or former slave. They were happy with their freedom but they yearned for more. They had begun to transition into new roles and new attitudes, so the occupation year was a growth experience. One woman, Celia, worked in the laundry at Point of Rocks and got married[42] during the year. Happy occasions did happen even in those difficult situations. A real high point was whenever President Lincoln came into the area. Everyone was pleased, and the contrabands were very excited and happy. They believed in his compassion and positive attitude for them. When the declaration came that the war was over, many citizens and soldiers were jubilant.

Although more names should be known and more last names need to be connected, the different levels of the community began to emerge. Additional fragments of information are listed in the last section of the book and perhaps shed light on the situation for readers.

4

Government Nurses

Every woman identified as either a "nurse" or "matron" was a unique individual with a story all her own. The next two chapters examine several women with battlefield experience and employment promises, and several who worked with caregiving organizations, yet they were all considered nurses. Women like Mrs. Barlow, Mrs. Lee, and Mrs. Farnham, for example, were battle-tested and savvy and had come to City Point from other locations as part of the military. Other women, like Helen Gilson, Adelaide Smith, and Cornelia Hancock, were independent contract nurses who also had battlefield experience and worked with the USSC. Like sisters in a family, they each thought the Army needed her specific nursing skills and each thought she had the perfect solution for how to care for the sick and wounded.

Nurses like Mrs. Laura Newman and Mrs. Amanda Farnham may have gone in and out of the hospital complex but primarily went to the front with their husbands' units. Other nurses such as Aunt Becky and Sophronia Bucklin joined the government "Dix" nurses and remained at the City Point hospital complex. Independent or contract nurses also stayed in the City Point area, where the doctors that had hired them stayed. Other women from the USSC Hospital Transport service included Misses Case, Hood, Harriette Sharpless, and Reifsnyder, plus Rebecca Gray and Maria Hall (see the USSC chapter). There were also various other government and independent nurses located right across the Appomattox River at Point of Rocks. They had a different hospital complex but learned to work around many of the same rules and regulations and performed many of the same duties. The two hospital areas and the diverse groups of women were occasionally able to socialize with one another, but to generalize what and who a nurse was remains difficult.

As previously noted, there were many women who came into City Point during the occupation of the Army of the Potomac from 1864 to 1865. Some came in June, while others came later during the year. Some stayed for a short time and others were there the whole time with the military. The general assumption was that women who came were "nurses" or "matrons" because they took care of the soldiers in one way or another. Although they appeared to know what they were doing medically and organizationally, many had learned their caregiving skills through the on-the-job experiences. Reporters from the *New York Times* described nurses as those who were regularly enrolled as hospital assistants. Walt Whitman, who was a male nurse during the Civil War, explained to a reporter about the value of a woman nurse: "Moving among the men, or through the ward, a hearty, healthy, clean, and strong person ... full of humanity and love, sending out invisible constant currents, therefore does immense good to the sick and wounded."[1]

Some stayed a long time and were truly helpful, while others seemed to float from location to location without clearly defined roles. The most often overlooked caregiver/nurse was the "general nurse." She was perceived to be a nurse, but was really the wife, mother, or sister who came to take care of loved ones and simply stayed on. All the women were extremely busy with feeding and bathing the wounded, listening and talking to the soldiers, plus writing letters for the dying and for the families of the deceased soldiers. The women brought a touch of sanity to a highly stressful situation and served as a reminder of the soldiers' lives back home. In addition to the general nurses, there were "ward nurses" who were convalescing soldiers not ready to go back to their units. A unit also had a "general orderly," "ward steward," like a pharmacist, or "ward master." These were always men who had specific duties and did not always appreciate having the women in the wards.

The background and experiences of the women were as different as they were as individuals. These women had a level of respect for one another even when they didn't agree. A war zone breeds a survivalist mentality. Many nurses had large networks of friends and associates at home as well as in the military whom they could ask for help or supplies when they needed them. However, they had enemies they needed to avoid in order to get their jobs done as well. As Miss Hancock said about being a nurse with the military, "There never was a place where you have stronger friends or more violent enemies."[2]

City Point Hospital Complex

Prior to the war, the generic area that was City Point had focused on farming and was very quiet. The small village adjacent to the Eppes plantation was known as Hopewell. At Hopewell, there was a railroad that went down to Petersburg and connected to Richmond and several old docks for the boats that sailed up the James River. Overnight, though, the sleepy village of Hopewell and City Point was transformed. During the war, most soldiers' supplies came from their families and organizations back home via boat. City Point became a very large quartermaster supply depot with 125,000 men, 65,000 animals, and eight different docks for the boats, along with the hospitals.[3] Suddenly, the area buzzed from the first bugle calls at dawn until the last sounds of "Taps" at night. The Depot Hospital started on the former property of Dr. Eppes and began with 18 tents in mid-June, but grew quickly to 1,200 tents.[4] As fall approached, the military cut down trees to make log cabins to help keep the patients warm, but some patients still had to live in the tents. The local well could barely keep up, so two big steam pumps took water from the river and pumped it up to the hospital, making life easier for everyone.[5] In addition, there were several natural springs that provided cooking and drinking water to some of the local residents. In total, there were seven hospitals in the City Point area. The largest was the Depot Hospital, with laundries, bakeries, dispensaries, assorted kitchens, mess halls and officers' quarters. It covered 200 acres and was able to care for 10,000 patients. It was a huge complex of 90 cabins and 12,000 individual tents.[6] There were four corps included in the Depot complex: the 2nd Corps with 20 wards of 100 patients each; the 5th Corps for a short time; the 6th Corps before they left for the Shenandoah Valley; the 9th Corps, which included the Corp d'Afrique that had 12 wards from June until December when they moved to the Army of the James; and the Cavalry Corps. If you were not military and you didn't go through the Depot Hospital you could go to one of three other hospitals—the Post Hospital, the Engineers Hospital, or the Pest Hospital. Civilians used the Railroad Hospital, the Wagon Train (or Teamsters) Hospital, and the fourth was the Government Employees' Hospital. There was always confusion about who was in which hospital and people often would have to look through several hospitals to find a particular individual. Plus, there always was the confusion of people and soldiers coming in and going out of the area to be buried, returned to duty or sent north on a hospital transport steamer. The hospital resembled a nest of ants, with the ants all scurrying in and out of the anthill with their food. It looked like confusion, but they seemed to get their tasks done.

The first tents went up in mid-June. Miss Bucklin described how fourteen anxious and weary nurses came to the area on June 19. She described how the officers got one tent and the nurses got another. The nurses had carried their own blankets, so they spread them on the floor of the tent and used their valises as pillows. In the morning they still had not had anything to eat when one of the doctors found a barrel of pork and three loaves of moldy bread. Some of the men fabricated a dining table which was a well-used and stained stretcher that had "considerable use." The food was prepared by a cook and set out for them to share but nobody had utensils, so they ate with their hands and passed the one existing coffee cup around so everyone having breakfast in their group could have some coffee. No sooner had they finished the humble first meal when they heard the call, "the wounded are coming," and everyone kicked into high gear.[7]

In June and July, the temperature in the area was generally quite hot and humid. Fighting was close to Petersburg so there was still some grass and growing crops in the City Point area and local residents were more tolerant of the heat than newcomers. New residents had learned to live with the heat (and humidity and mosquitos) and did their tasks accordingly during the day.[8] As soon as the Union forces started marching into the area, their wagons killed the grass and crops, and the ground turned to dust. The marching men made lots of dust that flew everywhere. In fact, when the 9th Corps came in during June, they marched along the roadway and a plume of dust hung over them like a cloud[9] and was a good six inches deep.[10] Local residents were surprised when they saw women walking with the soldiers. The wagons were full, and some of the women who were walking had pots and pans hanging from their knapsacks.[11] Within a few short weeks, the military had water pumped up from the river to reduce the dust and prevent it from covering the wounded patients. However, as dusty as it was when dry, when it was wet it became mud. The mud was worse than the dust and six inches deep in places. It stuck to the feet like cement. Some locations quickly cut down trees to make corduroy walkways with the trees lined up next to each other and then covered with dirt. But the extremely bumpy road gave some of the women, like Miss Hancock, headaches.[12] However, the transportation options were to ride a horse or mule, walk, or ride in a wagon. Regardless of which option one selected, the mud oozed through the tree cords and splashed and splattered all over everything. Newcomer soldiers and women were angry about the mud being splashed on them by passing wagons or sticking to their feet but they realized they had to learn to adjust to the local conditions.

Two of the Battle-Tested

During this era, modesty when speaking about personal qualities and attributes was a feminine characteristic that controlled the way the women conversed about one another.[13] The experienced ladies knew and understood the communication protocol and used it when they worked for other agencies, such as the United States Sanitary Commission (USSC) or Ladies' Aid Societies. With one group they talked in a more modest, subservient role, and with other organizations, they spoke in more of a supervisory role. One role required more civilian chatter while the other required more military talk.

For some women it was difficult and frustrating to have to use both. As an illustration, Mrs. Mary W. Lee (no connection to Robert E. Lee) came from Philadelphia via Great Britain. She had a son who served with the 72nd Pennsylvania Regiment[14] and she had been through numerous battles, helping whenever and wherever she could. Mrs. Lee served as a mother to the soldiers and mentor to the novice women she liked. She liked the young nurse named

Miss Hancock. Perhaps it was a consistent belief that she had to be near the action to provide the most good that made others sometimes think she was a bit too assertive. Regardless of what they thought of her, Mrs. Lee was a woman who got things done and she never waited for others to pontificate about what needed to be done. Not only did she work like a galley slave,[15] she loved to cook, especially when it came to large groups of soldiers. If she didn't have what a recipe required, she was clever enough to improvise and make something very tasty out of almost nothing. According to Miss Hancock, they always saw her making a new batch of something for the soldiers.[16] She was proud of her ability to make things and had a great reputation. When hunger plagued her wounded soldiers, Mrs. Lee would either go and get food or spend her own money to purchase food from the sutlers that had supplies,[17] and often the purchases came at a higher price.

Many of the nurses and matrons talked about how some of the women had a patient who was fading away and how they managed to find a small portion of something special, be it medicine or nourishment to keep them alive. Mrs. Lee told one of the stories. She had a young man in her care who had grown very weak and was not able to keep anything in his stomach. Mrs. Lee thought and thought about what she might get him to eat. While she was sorting through some of the supplies that had been sent to her, she found a small portion of Indian meal.[18] Indian meal is finely ground corn that some people call cornmeal. According to the Wittenmyer cookbook, during 1864-1865, Indian meal was made as a pudding by either boiling or baking the meal with sweet milk. At City Point, the luxury kitchen had sugar or molasses that they added for sweetness. A few local plantations also had a spice they called "ginger" that could be added for extra flavor. True to her nature, she procured a little of the spice and made a sweet ginger mush. Once the mixture was cooked, Mrs. Lee humbly approached the dying soldier and convinced him that that the milky mush would be easy for him to eat and that it would taste good. She made up a small portion of it at first and spoon fed him so he could swallow it without any real effort. In just a few days, her motherly success had blossomed and she was able to get him to eat more foods. Eventually, the soldier recovered and went back home. This experience leaves one to wonder, was it the special food she made for the soldier or was it the special attention she gave the soldier? Maybe it was a combination of both.

When a family member came down to nurse their wounded soldier or claim their loved one's body, Mrs. Lee was empathetic and tried to help them. She had integrity, determination, and internal strength, so the soldiers and officers did not want to argue with her. In fact, many of the women were equally determined not to be pushed around by rules and regulations or by the men and often stated their positions without saying much. Their demeanor said a great deal about who they were and what they knew. This is how Miss Hancock was. Maybe the emerging "no nonsense" attitude of her new novice colleague impressed Mrs. Lee and helped in Miss Hancock's development into a strong woman like her mentor. Maybe it was the fact that Mrs. Lee and Miss Hancock's mothers were community friends back home.[19] Regardless, Mrs. Lee was a steady and reliable person who could be counted on to provide the best care possible when the battles raged around her. She was, as the men would say, someone who had been tested under fire and just continued to do her job.

Another lady who comes to mind when one thinks of the personification of a nurse is Mrs. Arabella Griffith Barlow. She was the wife of Major General Francis A. Barlow of the 61st New York Infantry. Like Mrs. Lee, she had been at multiple battles before reaching City Point. She was devoted to her husband, the soldiers, and the cause, and would do whatever needed to be done. She actually was associated with the United States Sanitary Commission (USSC), but everyone called her a nurse. She spent a great deal of her time with the 2nd Corps hospital. With the familiar pattern shown by Mrs. Lee, Mrs. Barlow worked, and worked, and worked, and then worked some more. She finally reached the point of exhaustion and had to head home to regain her health. When she returned home, she was unable to recover from her illness and exhaustion and passed away, having given all to her country.

Government, or Dix Nurses

Government nurses were called "Dix nurses" because they had been recruited and hired by Miss Dorothea Dix, who had been authorized by the Union to form a nurse department. According to Miss Dix, the nurses had several strict rules. They could not be young nor pretty and they needed to be almost like a nun. They were to stay with their own group and withstand many difficult hours and work situations. Following a surgeon's or commander's order was imperative. They were never to question the authority in a medical situation, and regardless of their feelings, they had to obey the military regulations.

There was, however, a great deal of variety among the ladies, although they tended to be plain in appearance and wore similar cotton dresses. One woman, Mrs. Amanda Farnham, wore a bloomer outfit, but overall they were very respectful to the military commanders and their rules and regulations. Mindfulness to duty was the most important quality. In some regards, the Dix nurses were considered "mere machines, incapable of thought, and unworthy of any attention beyond requiring them to be obedient, without questioning whenever their rights were infringed upon."[20] It was a difficult role for anyone, let alone a woman who had left home to help others.

For many of the women at City Point, especially the nurses and matrons, the work was never-ending and very lonely. As Aunt Becky noted, "After my rounds I sit here lonely, hardly knowing what to do with myself to pass the time of day."[21] The rule of only socializing with other nurses made life difficult, and when depressed or saddened by a loss, she noted, "We nurses should be insensible to anything only the performance of our strict duty—should have no heart to enter into the feelings of far-away friends—should stile all humanity in our souls, and be deaf, dumb, and blind."[22] Needless to say, the life of a government nurse left much to be desired by the ladies who really cared. Their internal conflict challenged their professionalism. However, they learned to deal with difficult situations by struggling to maintain their composure while tears ran from their eyes.[23]

Another demand of the government nurses was to deal with the ghastliness of wounds as well as obeying orders. They dared not to talk back when they disagreed with a doctor's prescription. They averted their eyes so they would not make eye contact that might be seen to challenge the doctor. The ability to be around so many sick, wounded, and dying took all the energy they had at times. The smells of the wounded, burned, and dying were initially difficult to cope with. As Miss Bucklin put it, "Wounds and suffering became a habitual sight, the absorbing nature of the hospital labor gradually hardened [my] nerves to the strength of steel."[24] Although not identified as depression or PTSD then, being unhappy and feeling less than optimistic about the situations among the women was not uncommon and was mentioned in the stories of Aunt Becky, Miss Bucklin, Miss Hancock and others. Soldiers and the contrabands would watch them as they would retreat into their tents and hear them as they cried with exhaustion and sadness. Somehow, the women managed to return to their duties, try to smile, "and cheat their own attitudes into cheerfulness"[25] towards those they had to care for.

Government nurses received $12 per month for their work. If, however, a nurse was a higher ranked matron, she received $16 per month. Surgeon Edward Dalton was the Depot Director and had control over the whole hospital. In contrast, Army surgeons earned the grand amount of $165 per month while the assistant surgeons earned between $100 and $130 per month. A contract surgeon earned a more reasonable amount of between $30 and $50 per month. Regular military pay went to the stewards, who were like warrant officer pharmacists, then the ward masters who took care of the sanitary conditions, and finally the nurses and poor recovering soldiers, who received only their regular military pay.

If an observer watched the activities in the hospital ward on a normal day, they would begin to feel the regulated routine of the government nurse. When compared to a day when the casualties began to pour in, a different image emerges. For example:

4. Government Nurses

Routine Schedule in the Hospital

Five o'clock a.m.—Bugle call in the summer, six o'clock in the winter. Get up, pour some water in the basin, and wash my face

Six o'clock a.m.—Say my morning prayers and write an entry into my personal diary. Write a letter for the mail boat to take at 1000 and then open the flap to let fresh air into the tent.

Six forty-five a.m.—Go to the kitchen and get some breakfast. Joke, coax, and command the food to be brought out of the kitchens for the soldiers.

Seven o'clock a.m.—Short staff meeting with the supervisor or surgeon for the daily review of the program. Make note of any special patients and where they are in the ward. Three times a day we feed 600 men. Breakfast is served in the wards, the ambulatory go to the mess tent. We start feeding the low diet cases.

Eight o'clock a.m.—Remove any of the breakfast trays that are left. Begin checking the bed linen. See who might need new clothing. Make sure the information gets to the matron. Working on one section of the ward, start washing the patients' hands and face, comb their hair.

Nine o'clock a.m.—If it is a sunny day get some of the men outside. Start changing the dressings that must be done three times a day. Those with maggots need extra care.

Ten o'clock a.m.—Three hours after starting it is time for a tea break. The mail boat is in with news.

Eleven o'clock a.m.—Two hours later the first changing of dressings is almost finished. Time to start the ambulatory patients back out for their dinner [lunch].

Twelve o'clock noon—Start feeding the low diet patients, hand feed those who cannot feed themselves.

Twelve thirty p.m.—Trays that are left need to be picked up.

Twelve forty-five p.m.—Get a quick dinner.

One o'clock p.m.—It is time to start cleaning the dressings again. Those with the most severe wounds are attended to first. Stand by a bed at the last moment of life, receiving his last message for his wife and child. Cover his face when he expires and cut a lock of his hair if requested.

Two o'clock p.m.—Continue dressing changes. Give those who need special low diet meals extra stimulants. The passenger steamer and some mail comes in at two. Softly smile at those who did not receive any mail because their hope has faded. Help the families who have come looking for their soldier.

Three o'clock p.m.—Finish the dressings and read to a soldier.

Four o'clock p.m.—Finish up any last dressings and get ready for the supper meal.

Five o'clock p.m.—Start bringing in the food for the special diet cases and start feeding those who need special help. Get the ambulatory out to the mess tent.

Five thirty o'clock p.m.—Start changing the dressings again.

Six o'clock p.m.—Some dressings can hold for a while longer so they can wait. Play a round of checkers with a wounded man then start working on the paperwork for the next day. Make sure I have the correct names and units written down in my notebook.

Seven o'clock p.m.—One of the patients is fading rapidly. Hold him until he dies.

Eight o'clock p.m.—Finish with the dressings.

Eight thirty o'clock p.m.—Nurses can leave the wards and get something light to eat.

Nine o'clock p.m.—Lights out. Go to bed and try and get some sleep.

Ten o'clock p.m.—Taps during the winter, eleven o'clock during the summer. If one considers the normal day busy all one needs to do is look at what transpired on a day when mass casualties came in.

Chaos Schedule

Five o'clock a.m.—Bugle call and we hear the cannons and know casualties will be coming in. Wash face quickly, pull back hair and try and get some breakfast if available. Make a quick check on the ward. See if there any spare beds.

Six o'clock a.m.—Ambulances start coming in at daylight, bringing the waves of slaughter. Check on the transport schedule and go over who is going "out," get his supplies [personal effects] ready for the boat departure. Do some triage and try to find places to put new soldiers.

Seven o'clock a.m.—Get the men who are going "out" loaded on the transports. It takes two hours to fill one boat. All was in a hurry and confusion. Try and find some paper to write a dying man's name for his family and his last words. Supervise the removal of old soiled linens, get stewards and male nurses to clean the incoming.

Eight o'clock a.m.—The men have wounds, illness of chronic diarrhea, fevers ... they are emaciated. Famished for food ... the soldiers behave more like ravenous wolves than human beings. Get food to those who can take it but be careful of those who had been starving. Some men still moving in and out of the area.

Nine o'clock a.m.—Start feeding the ravenous men. The wounded have no beds and the dust is just pouring over them.
Nine thirty o'clock a.m.—A boat arrives with 300 and the sound of the drum call the stretcher bearers in line. All who can rush to the landing.
Ten o'clock a.m.—Remove blood clotted and stiffened woolen garments from the ghastly wounds. The wounded just keep coming in. Some have maggots in their wounds.
Eleven o'clock a.m.—Find supplies for the incoming and start washing their face and hands. Empty the basin of the dirty, bloody water. Somebody has got to start getting food into the low diet patients.
Twelve o'clock noon—Stop and run for a doctor ... a man's artery has just started bleeding. Just as one set gets comfortable another set comes in and we start all over again.
One o'clock p.m.—Continue to bring in the supplies for the wounded, find extra beds and facilities for the overflow. The scent of blood and discharge is awful. Go outside and get some clean air.
Two o'clock p.m.—The hospital is filled, the ground is covered with wounded, the length of a line and the cook house, on the table, under the table, everywhere.
Three o'clock p.m.—Continue feeding liquids to the newest batch of wounded. A wounded soldier is very excited ... get morphine to calm him down.
Four o'clock p.m.—The stream pours in ... bloody and ghastly. Get some new supplies out for those who are able to be moved, washed and changed. Start logging the wounded in. Keep working, there is little time to dwell on death, get anyone standing around to provide extra help.
Five o'clock p.m.—Find beds for the incoming and clear any who may have been stable enough to move to another ward. The earlier scenes are repeated again and again. The nurses are so hungry. We have had no time to eat all day.
Six o'clock p.m.—Hand feed the men who can't eat on their own and start feeding the low diet patients. After they eat, log them in and move them to a new ward. Start preparing a list of those who need to be sent out on tomorrow's transport as soon as they are bathed. Send orderly out to get passes.
Seven o'clock p.m.—Clean up any of the food that is left, start washing faces again, write emergency letters. Make sure names are correct. Offer stimulants to those who can take them. I am hungry too but nobody has come to relieve me.
Eight o'clock p.m.—We are losing men so fast from the pains of

amputation. The smell of the wounds and the groans of agony are awful. Some are so serious they do not see us moving around. Make sure the latest to come in have clean clothes and sheets, start changing the filthy old dressings. Get someone to throw old bandages with maggots away.

Nine o'clock p.m.—Wash face and hands of the latest, offer liquids to those who need them. Write more emergency letters for the dying men. Cover their face as they expire.

Ten o'clock p.m.—Offer food and liquid to the low diet patients. Make sure the ward masters and stewards are set for the evening hours. I am very tired ... I can hardly stand upon my feet.

Eleven o'clock p.m.—I know what it means to be so tired that you could be shot and not know it. Exhausted, I fall asleep with the wounded and dying so close to the tent.[26]

Mrs. Amanda Farnham

One battle-tested Dix nurse was Amanda Colburn Farnham. She had come down from Vermont in 1861 with her brother's regiment, the 3rd Vermont.[27] Like the other women, she was a hard worker. However, she was also a clever and resourceful woman who had worked during the Peninsula Campaign in Virginia, Gettysburg, Antietam, Fredericksburg, and Cold Harbor before coming to City Point. She was always trying to find a better way to do something and no doubt would have made a great general. Watching the carnage and chaos and seeing the continuous waste of filthy and often torn clothes, Mrs. Farnham decided there had to be an alternate solution to supplying her troops with replacement clothing.

The soldiers were always running out of clothing due to the item wearing out or being thrown away and burned due to all the gore, holes and lice. Having lice was a real issue, and even the ladies in the hospitals had the crawling pests in their hair, clothes, on their tent roofs and floors. They were everywhere, and people tried to "endure them with the heroism of martyrdom."[28] The Yankee soldiers often called them "graybacks," like small confederates. Sometimes the "grays" reached the size of kernels of wheat or even corn, especially when they got into the seams and folds of the clothing. When people said they were "knitting," it did not mean the same type of knitting ladies did when making socks or mittens. It meant removing the graybacks.

What was so unique about Mrs. Farnham was that she saw a simple solution to a massive problem and helped change lives. One day, while on the other side of the James River at Cold Harbor, Mrs. Farnham had the bright idea to take the filthy clothing before it was destroyed and wash it. Like a diplomatic general, she ordered the contrabands to get some big pots. Next, she had the pots filled with boiling water. People around her thought she was a bit crazy because she threw all the clothes in the pots and simply boiled them. She figured if boiling killed things when cooking then it might kill lice. Afterwards, the clothes were dried and reused. It was a great moment of practical application by a woman. After the first batch worked for killing the lice and cleaning the clothing, she did more boiling of the wash and taught all the contrabands that worked with her to do the same. This resulted in the whole laundry system changing. Clothing that had been so difficult to obtain became easier to get, and many soldiers had better protection from the rain and bad weather because they had clothing on hand instead of having to wait for supplies to reach them.

When General Grant moved into the City Point area, Mrs. Farnham came with the regiment for a short period of time in 1864. However, about August 21, the 6th Corps moved toward the Shenandoah Valley and she went with them. Later, around the 4th or 5th of December, she returned to City Point[29] before heading back home.

Miss Sophronia Bucklin

Miss Sophronia Bucklin had passed the plain and subdued appearance test that Miss Dix required of her applicants. She was devoted to her duty and stayed within the norms of the job, so she was in all practical sense a good government nurse. In fact, she did exactly what was required of her without a questioning look, even if it was cleaning dishes,[30] and absorbed the difficulties she faced with her own sense of commitment to the cause.[31]

Sophronia started out in the Washington area hospitals when the ghastly wounds met her head-on and challenged her initial ability to remain a nurse.[32] Like many of the other women, she had headed south for different battles and was at White House Landing before arriving at City Point. She behaved in the prescribed Dix nurse manner of sticking to a "little knot" of nurses and remaining aloof from the other people around her, especially the state agents, commission people and other nurses.[33] The expression she used was that governmental nurses were like soldiers because they "sat wearily about in our thoughts" while "work went on without cessation."[34]

Government nurses were not permitted in the kitchens for cooking of meals for the soldiers and relied on the Sanitary and Christian Commissions to fulfill those needs.[35] Besides, as a Dix nurse, Sophronia had no stove to work with thanks to a very difficult doctor. She explained the responsibilities she faced:

> Duties were to give medicine; distribute the food on the plates at the scullery; distribute meals to the appropriate patients; comb heads and wash faces of those unable to

do so; see everything about their beds and clothing was in the right condition; prepare what delicacies [she] could procure and dress wounds.[36] [In addition] she would bandage slight wounds and administer drinks of raspberry vinegar and lemon syrup.[37]

Without kitchen access and a personal stove, she had difficulties fulfilling the preparation of delicacies that were part of her job, which frustrated her. Miss Bucklin had several run-ins with the more unorthodox Mrs. Holstein, who was attached to the USSC. Mrs. Holstein had an official role and served as a constant "friend" to Dr. Burmeister, who was quite surly and disorganized.[38] The power struggle Sophronia had with Dr. Burmeister over access to the simple stove and the right to cook delicacies made the lives of many of the soldiers more difficult. It wasn't until Dr. Burmeister was reassigned and a new doctor, Dr. Hammonds, came in that Miss Bucklin was finally able to get a Silby stove so she could prepare some delicacies without the USSC or the interference of Mrs. Holstein.

After getting over her initial trauma of seeing such terrible wounds, especially those filled with maggots, and hearing the moans and groans of the injured and dying, Miss Bucklin became a hardened Dix nurse. She said the wounds and suffering became a habitual sight, although the magnitude of the incoming wounded often surprised her.[39] As regular as her pocket watch, Miss Bucklin started at 0700 and ended at half past eight in the evening.[40] Before long, the regularity of her hospital duties and routine tasks suited her schedule and she began to feel like a methodical housekeeper.[41] However, she had a personal challenge. Some of the other ladies, such as Mrs. Collis and Miss Hancock, were plagued by the constant cannonading sound, and Sophronia was extremely sensitive to, and never got over, the sounds of the men when they were in conscious or unconscious pain. Their pain bothered her, and she indicated she had an elevated stress level whenever she talked to the people around her. She frequently mentioned how the groans continued to echo in her head.[42]

Although the Dix nurses had access to laundry facilities and meals, there was a privacy concern Sophronia shared with other nurses. As regular as the bugle calls, Miss Bucklin washed her clothes on Monday in a basin and hung what she dared out on her tent lines to dry.[43] She hung her wet personal items inside her tent to reduce the potential for theft and the ensuing wild stories about how a soldier might have acquired the item. Dining in the mess tents also brought constant scrutiny. When she dined with the officers, they gossiped and invaded her personal and psychological space. At times she found some of them interesting to talk with, but there were other times when she just needed her own personal space. She figured out that having a stove in her quarters provided a much-needed respite. The women had some regular and personal housekeeping or organizational behaviors when they were in their own quarters, such as growing a few flowers or writing letters every week until they went home, but for the most part it was a regulated routine.

Lastly, though Miss Bucklin was regulated by hospital rules and at times seemed almost indifferent to some of the greater needs of those around her, she did have great compassion for others. One evening, Miss Bucklin was going to help another woman who had taken up residence near her tent and who was in physical distress. Gathering wood for the woman's fire and then water and camphor, Miss Bucklin set out to help. After she got the necessary things, she went to get the doctor. Despite the distressed woman's need for some form of care, the doctor told Miss Bucklin not to help anymore and let the woman's family come and get her. As a result of the command, Miss Bucklin absorbed her own feeling of compassion and took her leave. She followed orders and left the woman alone without the wood, water and camphor.[44]

Many of those serving had a very deep sense of empathy for the mothers and wives who came to pick up the dead sons or husbands, but they too understood the rules. On a regular basis, many women came to nurse their almost dead son or husband back to a point where they could take them home. Some came and devotedly picked the worms out of their son's or husband's wounds. Others stood guard over their loved ones until they opened their eyes for the last time. The soldier made eye contact or perhaps even said a name, then died. The wives or mothers withdrew in somber solace knowing that they had been together at the very last moment of life.[45]

One particular mother stayed for four months until she could find her son who had died. Miss Bucklin was touched by the way the woman had the putrid, decaying body removed from the grave and prepared for the trip back home.[46] When a deceased soldier was taken on board a transport, the guards and other soldiers offered a salute out of respect and understanding. Though it did not bring the soldier back to life, the honor and respect provided the family members a feeling of warmth to know there loved one died as a brave soldier.[47]

As a collective caregiving group, these determined women had integrity and compassion that helped them endure the hardships of being in the war zone. They had sacrificed their families and in some cases their health. As a controlled group, they brought order to the insane moments of chaos.

Sarah Palmer, aka "Aunt Becky"

Dix nurse Sarah Palmer, or "Aunt Becky" as was her nickname, had a bit more gumption than Miss Bucklin when something needed to be done. There are many stories about Aunt Becky. It is hard to just focus on one or two, but quickly one sees that even though she was a Dix nurse she was quite similar to and yet very different from Miss Bucklin. Raised in Binghamton, New York, she was the only girl in a house of ten boys. Aunt Becky had thick skin. As the only daughter she was soft, but she was also pragmatic, and she was funny at times. Her biggest asset was that she loved her soldiers and was totally devoted to them. Aunt Becky was a unique, wiry character filled with integrity and determination. When people asked her why she had joined the 9th Corps as chief matron under Dr. W.E. Johnson, she said it was because of her favorite nephew. That may have been her overt reason, but nobody ever saw him, although people knew Aunt Becky had two brothers who were stationed around the City Point/Petersburg area. One brother was at the front near Petersburg and would come through City Point and stop to see her. In 9th Corps she was with troops from Iowa, New York, Michigan, Wisconsin, and Pennsylvania, and called all the soldiers "her boys."

It is hard to understand why she left her two little girls, Alice and Belle, with a family member back home when she joined the war in 1862, but her sense of protecting others was likely a strong factor. Like several of the other women, Aunt Becky went through battles like Fredericksburg, Rapidan, Wilderness, Spotsylvania Court House, Ni and Po Rivers, and Cold Harbor, before she came to City Point. True of the government nurse requirements, she was not young nor particularly attractive. A very practical woman, she arrived with only two dresses in her valise, a little black hat, and a very large pair of leather shoes that were three sizes larger than she needed. She said it was "so she wouldn't get blisters while marching from one place to another."[48] Her dresses looked like a stripped mattress because they were made out of bed ticking. She wore one and washed the other, then wore that one until it got dirty, then switched to the clean one. She was a very down-to-earth person and was not concerned about fashion like some of the ladies. She had come to help the soldiers and kept her focus. When she had any spare moments, she enjoyed the rare opportunity to be with a few of the other nurses.[49] However, most of her free time was consumed writing letters for "her boys" while in her tent. Her quarters were basic. In her tent she had a bed, dresser, chair, a couple of boxes, and a shelf for special items. However, in contrast to Miss Bucklin, Aunt Becky had a stove right from the start of her tour at City Point and some type of covering for the floor. Although bothered by the constant cannonading noise, she found the infestation of mice that nibbled at her possessions during the night to be the most frustrating, often to the point of tears. There were so many mice that scurried around while she was trying to read or write letters that they drove her to distraction. She even tried to kill them using a sword she had acquired. Sometimes at night they crawled over her face and "invaded her space."[50]

As a Dix nurse, her job was to distribute foods. Aunt Becky was very concerned about what and how much the boys ate. Her preoccupation with their diets started with a bad experience shortly after she had joined the regiment. A trunk had been delivered to the regiment by a Sanitary Commission man, and inside the trunk, among many other items, was a cake. The cake had turned rancid, but a very hungry soldier ate the cake, got sick, and died. From that point on, Aunt Becky was extremely careful about the food her boys ate. In fact, she became a bit of a crazy mother figure, fussing about the food they would get. She often hung around the high and low diet kitchens, waiting for someone's back to be turned so she could cook or take food. One day she even burned her dress while cooking between two stoves. Since she had a scorch mark on one dress, people could tell when she changed her dresses.

When Aunt Becky saw a soldier who was in need of some special care, she did a version of Mrs. Lee's creative trick. Aunt Becky had a big, old cloak from the campaign marches. Instead of opening her purse and using her own money, she would throw the cloak over her shoulders and hide chunks of dried beef, basins of custards, tins of milk, chunks of butter and any other items she could find.[51] Even though Dix nurses were not to be in the kitchen, Aunt Becky often was. The chief cook openly hated the "calicos" (women) and frequently got so angry that he would kick convalescing soldiers. Regardless of his behavior and her anger towards him, the cloak trick continued. If the weather was cold, the cloak was a logical garment, but when the weather was warm, the staff knew what she was up to and looked the other way. When the soldiers saw her walk back into the wards with her cloak on, their eyes would light up knowing there were surprises coming just for them.

A compassionate woman, Aunt Becky knew her boys by name. She knew their needs and wants and tried to always watch out for them. She openly called them "her boys." She took excellent care of each of them by making sure their faces were washed and their hair was combed. The boys deeply cared about her even to the point of stretching the truth at times when bending a regulation.

As much as Aunty Becky understood her boys, she didn't understand the contrabands. Having been raised in rural New York, she had not been exposed to slaves before the war and used to watch them for amusement. She called them her "sable" people. According to Aunt Becky, the initial experience at City Point was not what one might call an "inviting place" for white people because there were so many former slaves who had come into the area to escape.[52] The slaves wanted freedom, food, and protection, and they wanted work. Although a few could read and write, they had other life skills that they had learned while working on the plantations. As a result of their past experiences, they filled many of the jobs around the military units, primarily cooking and washing. The nurses and the women and men from organizations hired them as well.[53]

As a matron, seeing that the sheets were stripped and getting clean clothes for the wounded required Aunt Becky to work with the laundry. The laundry was one place the "sable" people spent a lot of time. The facility started out as a small space but by the end of the year, when the weather started to get cold, the military had built a two-story building. It was a long building, about twenty feet by fifty feet, so the wet sheets and pillowcases could dry during bad weather.[54] The military allowed the contraband families that worked in the laundry to live upstairs where it was warm and comfortable. In addition to the long laundry house, there was a big, four-horsepower steam engine that brought water up from the river for the laundry and to the soldiers so they could bathe and wash themselves when they were able. Although Aunt Becky was very tolerant of her boys' misbehaviors, she lost her nurse's composure when any of the "sables" got injured or hurt around her. She felt that her boys moaned and groaned because they had traumatic injuries or severe illnesses from the war, but she had little patience when the "sable" boys howled and made a fuss at what she perceived was nothing. Aunt Becky displayed a strong bias because she believed the boys she cared for had been through so much more and they didn't complain like that.[55] As a result, she tended to ignore the "sables" like they didn't exist, and wouldn't call them contrabands.

Her bias continued with a particularly volatile incident. One day a young black man was parading down the street with his girlfriend. One of the naïve young hospital ward nurses decided to tease him about the way he was strutting about with the girl. The male ward nurse made some sweet-sounding noises to mimic the black man. In a split second the enraged contraband "sprung upon him, opened his jack knife, and with the ferocity of a savage cut the ward nurses throat from ear to ear." The wound was not deep enough to kill him and the man recovered, but the contraband was secretly taken to Washington by his friends before any revenge could take place from the soldiers.[56] Her bias from that situation and being aware of the rumors about how black soldiers who were fighting for the Union would kill any rebel soldier they found,[57] had Aunt Becky keeping her distance from the contrabands.

Complexities of life and survival were ongoing issues that required obedience and duty to regulations for the nurses in the hospitals and tolerance for difficult situations, especially in the case of the Dix nurses who could not just leave. By March of 1865, she was

> Tired of the noise; tired of the tongues which, talk, talk, talk at the supper table; tired of having my house invaded at all hours of the day and evening; tired of the Virginia mud; tired of trying to be happy, and tired of everything. I see the same old camp—the tents, the barracks; the same figures clad in blue ... I wish I could go home.[58]

One of her own brothers passed through City Point on his way home on a furlough, but as a government nurse, she had to remain. Aunt Becky did not manage to get away until the end of the war and often wondered if her daughters still remembered her.[59] Another aspect she could not escape was "the smell of the wounded," festering gangrene, the dead, and the dying, especially on the sultry, windless, humid days, when "the stench was almost enough to make you feel sick to your stomach."[60] Along with the smells came the big, black, and shiny green flies that buzzed around the wounds, laying eggs. The wounds and the latrine situation were hothouses for the flies even though the trenches around the hospital area were treated with lime. The latrines were covered but the open and untreated wounds had to be cleaned regularly. The women hardened their nerves to the smells and vileness. For new nurses or other uninjured people in the wards, one trick was to draw their nostrils in to minimize the impact until they learned to block out the smells.

Aunt Becky was very aware of the process of dying but maintained her utmost integrity for the dead. Death was an accepted result at City Point. There were regulations and specific procedures before a soldier was buried or sent to his family (see USSC on burial procedure). When a soldier knew he was dying and wanted to be buried in a box instead of just being put in the ground, Aunt Becky was his champion. She was passionate about assisting in a dying soldier's final wish. Soldiers, with their last breath, would ask her to be placed in a coffin, or if she would write a note to his family:

> How could I with hold a promise asked by those dying lips? God only knew how keen my anguish was, when I saw death stealing away the sense of those men. Who were dear to my soul, and I knew I could move heaven and earth to grant the dying request of a soldier, and I promised that his body should not lie in an uncoffined grave.[61]

As a Dix nurse, she had to be very respectful to rank and regulations but when Aunt Becky found that one of her protected boys had been thrown on the dead wagon and taken off to the graveyard, this cut into her soul. She purposefully marched up to the chaplain and demanded her charge be placed in a box. Her anger and determination surprised everyone, and a guard was placed on "her boy" until she could find some wood for a crude box. When the box was constructed, Aunt Becky compassionately combed the deceased soldier's hair, and washed his face, wrapped the body in a sheet, and had him placed in the box. The box was then buried in the soil of Virginia, like so many others. However, Aunt Becky had kept her promise.

Aunt Becky's integrity held when it came to other issues with the men, and they knew it. Unlike Miss Bucklin, she challenged the Dix nurses' system to circumnavigate the problems. As the year rolled on, the whole military complex developed organized chaos and logistical routines such as when the transports would be unloaded or loaded with the wounded. Soldiers with any money were easy prey for unscrupulous doctors who looked for opportunities like the sutlers who took poor soldiers' money. In fact, the next story made many smile at Aunt Becky's behavior when they saw what happened from the bluffs above the docks.

When the 13th Regiment started to send in large numbers of casualties, soldiers who had been in the hospital had to be moved out of the ward to other locations in order to free up the cots. One of the boys had given Aunt Becky his money for safekeeping because he trusted her and knew he would get the money back. When he was ordered on board of the *State of Maine* transport headed for Washington, he did not have time to contact her, and she found out after they had moved him to the landing. True to her nature, Aunt Becky stopped what she was doing and walked over to the landing. She stomped and flopped along in her big shoes and went right up to the surgeon who was standing on the plank between the transport and the shore. He was nasty and very gruff and fluffed himself up like a peacock and told Aunt Becky she could not go on board unless she had a special order. She didn't have an order but she did have a soldier's money and her determination. The surgeon then held out his hands to Aunt Becky and gestured for her to give him the money and he would give it to the soldier. Aunt Becky knew this surgeon's reputation and did not trust him. As unique and sinewy as she was, she had learned to play a few of the games while with the military. She made a minor comment to him and then turned as if to give up the battle. As soon as the surgeon turned to talk to another person, Aunt Becky dashed up the plank, past the guard and onto the transport where she found her soldier and gave him the money. Normally a controlled Dix nurse, every once in a while Aunt Becky would go against the regulations. This was one moment when she stole the show from a surgeon. As she left the plank, she graciously thanked the surgeon and commented about how comfortable the soldier looked. With great anger and lungs full of very hot wind and intimidation, the surgeon looked at Aunt Becky and demanded to know if she had gone on board. Adding a bit more salt to the wound, Aunt Becky said she had and again smiled graciously. Fit to be tied, the surgeon demanded to know if she had other orders. Aunt Becky commented, "only verbal ones." Then Aunt Becky turned like a visitor or dignified lady would, swishing her dress as if it was made of silk and clomped off in her big shoes, leaving the surgeon red-faced with anger and embarrassment that a woman had undone his authority. Everyone seeing the show turned back to their work and laughed and smiled about what Aunt Becky had accomplished. Her promise to the soldier was kept and his money was returned and she was quite pleased with herself.

Although the rules and regulations were always good to revert to when needed, they needed a bit of flexibility from time to time. As an illustration, each day a sergeant from one of the units issued orders for the day. The orders were not handwritten but printed on a printing press at City Point. The orders had to do with the sanitary store that were going to be available and what the diet rations would be for the day. As a Dix nurse, Aunt Becky had to conform to regulations and she understood that being with the military, everything was done in a regimented way. Her knowledge served her well as the year went on. One day she was standing in an office where requisitions were issued and several were laid on the table next to her. Understanding the necessity of the paperwork and fearing very limited retribution, she cared more about the soldiers in her care. Several pieces of the valuable papers slipped off the table into her pocket[62] where they could be delivered at a more useful location and time.

One incident that rattled her was when a 13-year-old drummer boy from a Rhode Island regiment came into the ward and continued to bleed from his lung. Although Aunt Becky had grown accustomed to the moans of soldiers, this young man called for his mother. The drummer boy worried that his mother would be alone if he died because his father had passed away and he thought only of her. Perhaps it was her own children that she missed but something about the young man affected her. He asked if she would write to his mother and she agreed to do so. Quite a while after the young boy had passed and been buried, Aunt Becky received a letter in return for the mother. As she read the letter, her Dix nurse façade crumbled, and she shed tears for him that were difficult to stop.[63]

Aunt Becky was a good but common person. She wanted to be called the "common nurse for the common soldier." That is all she ever wanted to be and that was exactly what she was.[64] She was often angry with the military style of justice toward the soldiers but held her tongue when there were executions and overt punishment and physical abuse on the soldiers.[65] She became sad and depressed when her boys started to go home. She cried and worried that nobody would ever remember her,[66] but in fact they did, and always invited her to their reunions. After the war she returned to her children and married a former soldier. Nevertheless, those who met her remembered quite a bit about her for she was a unique and devoted government nurse.

Mrs. Charlotte McKay

Certainly not the last of the good government nurses was Mrs. Charlotte McKay, who served at the Cavalry Corps Hospital at City Point with her assistants Mrs. Ehler and Mrs. Spaulding. Like Mrs. Lee, she had previous experience and personified "mother" to many of the sick and wounded. Like Aunt Becky, she was a religious lady who showed significant bravery when difficulties confronted her, and like Aunt Becky, she stood up for what she believed was right. Because of their beliefs, the two were also very closely connected to the USCC. Mrs. McKay had a beautiful voice and loved to sing songs in the ward or in the USCC chapel.

Mrs. McKay shared many common themes with the other nurses. She had the experience, she was aware of the cannonading, and it was not uncommon to have the men comment to Mrs. McKay about how her hands "feel like my mother's."[67] One story about her motherliness pertains to a young soldier who came to her tent one day seeking Mrs. Spaulding. However, Mrs. Spaulding had just left the tent and was headed in another direction. Mrs. McKay asked why he was looking for her and he said that Mrs. Spaulding was his mother. Kicking into high motion, she then pointed to the direction Mrs. Spaulding had gone, and the young soldier started off to find her. In a few minutes, Mrs. Spaulding got word from a sentry that her son was looking for her and she turned around and headed back to the tent. When the two found one another, there was a joyous, tearful embrace. Having not seen one another for over two years, they talked and covered much territory and shared much news. Eventually the young soldier had to leave. As he was parting with his own mother, Mrs. McKay slipped him a bundle. Inside were shirts, drawers, socks, handkerchiefs, towels, canned milk, tomatoes, peaches, tea, and tobacco. Then she wrapped a large, colorful handkerchief around the whole thing and, like a good mother, reminded him that on a cold night of picket duty, he could wrap it around his neck to stay warm.[68] Once a mother, always a mother.

Mrs. McKay had many great experiences and connections with the Corps. They adored her and were constantly trying to please her. With the soldiers' youthful innocence, they made her cut paper pictures to hang on her walls. Even rebel soldiers carved items and rings for her so she might remember them.[69] She was their hero, and like so many of the nurses, they remembered her.

There were countless other nurses who deserve to be mentioned. In addition to the government nurses, there were the women with the United States Sanitary Commission who worked on the hospital transports removing the wounded to northern hospitals. There were also "independent nurses" or private contract nurses like Miss Gilson, Miss Adelaide Smith, and Miss Cornelia Hancock. They are presented in the next chapter. Each had their own way of operating within the military rules and regulations. Each left her mark on the history of City Point.

5

Independent Nurses

Independent nurses were women who, unlike government nurses, worked for a specific doctor or were contracted by a specific group or military unit. Unlike the government nurses, they could be young and attractive. Their attire was a washable cotton dress similar to the government nurses' and they followed a similar hospital schedule. For the most part they followed the rules and regulations of each location but had more opportunities to leave the hospital complex and explore the local area. With this sense of independence and freedom, many were confident and would get quite impertinent when they found themselves under restrictions or being bullied or pushed around by doctors, and even local residents. Independent nurses were not restricted only in what the military supplied and often made sure they received necessary supplies from home. Often these women would be bartering or swapping supplies and goods with others outside of their wards to round out their daily needs. With their extended network and supplies, they could go into the kitchens and cook if need be. This flexibility and freedom differentiated them from the "Dix" nurses, yet people misunderstood their role and called them "a nurse." Below we examine three independent nurses, Miss Gilson, Miss Smith, Miss Hancock, and two daughters of the regiment who acted as nurses when needed.

Miss Helen Louise Gilson

Miss Gilson was a legendary member of the 3rd Army Corps. She was dubbed the "Florence Nightingale of the Army of the Potomac" by the *Philadelphia Inquirer* right after the war.[1] Prior to the war, she was a Boston schoolteacher, but when the conflict began, she followed her uncle, the former mayor of Chelsea, Massachusetts, Mr. Fay, who was with the USSC. At first, she tried to join the Dix nurses because she was well-connected, but she was rejected because she was too young. She found admittance with the USSC and quickly learned the art of caregiving on a hospital transport, but never felt as if she had all the answers and shrank from any notoriety.[2] Consequently, she became an independent nurse. Like other battle-hardened ladies, she went to Gettysburg, Antietam, Fredericksburg, Chancellorsville, White House Landing, and City Point. She often worked with Mrs. Husbands, who was a great mentor for her.

If being in war embodied chaos, Miss Gilson personified soothing sanity. In the hospital, she would speak in a calm, subdued, soothing voice, and often sing like a "petition for peace" as she went through the wards.[3] Earlier in the war, she developed a significant ability for speaking to the newly freed former slaves and explaining to them in a digestible language how their nascent freedom would be different from the lives they had previously known.[4] In turn, their fear and intimidation evaporated, and they trusted her. She became the person to go to when answers were needed. She was a personal mentor to many.

At City Point, Miss Gilson became a charismatic leader. Instead of indifference and a "you should have known better" attitude, she used positive suggestions and accolades for her subordinates. The soldiers and staff aspired to be the recipient of her praise. In some of her wards, the soldiers tried to display their competitive "ingenuity" to make their ward the best through their attention to cleanliness and even making paper decorations.[5] Even though she exuded a sweetness, her word was law. When she ran the diet kitchen, it was with structured discipline and not haphazard cooking. Respect for her was always at the forefront of others' minds, yet she was approachable and kind toward them. It was estimated that her kitchen fed up to 900 men, and she did so with soothing grace and dignity.[6]

As the war dragged on and battles around City Point transpired, there were significant numbers of black soldiers who were wounded or ill with typhoid and other fevers. Miss Gilson was not hesitant around those who were different, unlike Aunt Becky. She had a holistic approach that she applied to all the sick and wounded, as opposed to nurses who only cared for men in their specific corps. She believed her job was to care for needy and neglected soldiers regardless of who they were or where they came from. As mentioned previously, the almost nonexistent hospital area for the contrabands and USCT was appalling. Many of the men were in very serious condition from wounds, fevers, or general lack of medical attention, and infection was a major factor in the death of many. Applying her previous successful communication experiences with the freed slaves, she accepted the challenge of working with them at a time when most people didn't want to help. If the volunteer hospital workers had no training, she would train them and demonstrate how to be a good nurse. All her regular coworkers thought she was crazy and at great risk for contracting their illnesses and dying. Her solution was pragmatic. First, she spoke with Major General Burnside and explained the situation and laid out a practical solution. Then, she used grace and dignity to organize the facilities for the Colored Hospital, including women of color to serve as nurses. She also established a special diet kitchen. The two components became known as the Corps d'Afrique Hospital. Once more in the kitchen, her spiritual beauty and eloquence allowed people to understand what was needed and how to proceed. She taught the women and men the organizational skills they needed.[7] Her magic as a caregiver etched kindness and compassion in the hearts of all who knew her. Her vision extended beyond her hospital as well, and when there was extra food, she made sure the families of those in the hospital were not forgotten.

Miss Gilson's soothing quality was enhanced when she would sing and play the organ in the small chapel. Several compared her to a spirit from another world. Her hymns consoled those who were considerably troubled and those who were delirious from fever. When she sang in the wards she was like a magnet because she would automatically draw voices from the men around her. One favorite song was "Just before the Battle, Mother." The men would try to sit up or rise up on an elbow if they could, and many would wipe tears from their eyes.[8] Not only did songs draw emotions from the battle-hardened soldiers, but it was not uncommon to have men brought to tears when she recited a psalm or read a scripture.[9] Her voice had a magical quality about it. Similar to her ability to transcend language with the freed slave, she transcended the distance for the soldiers who were melancholy about home.[10] By listening to them, and letting them speak about their homes, she reduced their psychological wounds of homesickness as well as their physical wounds. She was a gifted soul to those she worked with and was respected by all those who came in contact with her during the war.

After the war, she remained in the area to help with the Freedman's school in Richmond. Her calming and soothing qualities continued to prevail. Her respect for others was fondly exhibited when she participated during Memorial Day honoring those who had fallen for the Confederacy. While in Richmond, she met and married. Eventually, she returned to Massachusetts for the birth of her first child and died during childbirth.

Miss Adelaide Smith

Another independent nurse who came from a large city was Miss Adelaide Smith. She had grown up with her family near New York City. Her father ran a business on Bedford Avenue in Brooklyn. The Naval Hospital was close to their home, so the war touched them with each incoming load of wounded or sick soldiers. Her mother helped in the war relief efforts by sending young Adelaide back and forth with pails of soup her mother had made for the soldiers in the hospital.

In New York and the surrounding areas, there was a great effort to seek local help when the transport ships would discharge their cargo of sick and wounded soldiers. Men from New York and New Jersey regiments were frequently taken to Park Barracks, while the wounded and sick from New England were sent on to other hospitals.[11] The Park Barracks Association was a group of wealthy ladies who supplied the soldiers with food and clothing and acted like a Ladies' Aid Society with one exception: they were not organized. Each lady had her own feelings about how to care for the soldiers. Vexed by these differences in opinions, several of the ladies had heard about a young woman named Adelaide Smith, and her ability to be a very good organizer.

As a result of her reputation, she was recruited to take charge of the diet kitchen at Fort Wood on Bedloe's Island. Of all the tasks Miss Smith had to do in this job, cooking for the sick and wounded was the easiest part. Working to keep the peace and putting one logical system of distribution in place while dealing with all the various ladies' opinions was the real challenge. Similar to the way a mother sorts out the truth amongst squabbling children, Miss Smith started to make sense of the personalities and the many supplies that came to the hospital. Like Mrs. Farnham, Miss Smith developed a systematic and very organized way of doing things. First, she set to work making piles of clothing and food donations. Then she categorized and inventoried each pile so she knew exactly what she had and where it was located. Next, she made lists for the doctors to identify what they needed for certain wounded soldiers, then streamlined the request process. Around the time she left for war zone hospital work, there were a lot of changes transpiring in the military hospitals. In addition, the Manhattan Sanitary Fair was taking York City by storm and the excitement of helping the soldiers spread to many of the women in the area.

Miss Smith was single, thirty-three years old, and attractive when she went to Virginia. She had not survived numerous military battles like other nurses had, but she had hospital experience. How she ended up going down to the City Point area remains a vague speculation. She had been a secretary for the Mission of Masons organization in New York around the time of the big Sanitary Fair[12] and heard about the opportunity or read about the organization in the paper.

However, someone from the Mission of Masons promised employment at Point of Rocks next to the City Point area. The belief was that with the Mission of Masons organization, she would be a nurse and replacement for Miss Clara Barton. She was told she would "mitigate the suffering ... and provide relief for the sick and wounded." Furthermore, "more than thirty nurses were in the field and [the organization was] making preparations still further to extend the usefulness."[13]

To reassure her, she was informed that she would have a badge for protection in case she was ever captured by the enemy. Apparently, other women, like Miss Ney, Miss Dunbar, and Miss Edson, believed the same story and came down to the area as well. They had, however, been recruited by snake-oil salespersons back home who said they represented an organization that really did not exist in the war zone. When Miss Smith and Miss Dunbar sailed out of New York with earnest intentions, they each had a pass from General Butler, and they wore a Mission of Masons patch for identification and protection. On the same ship with Miss Dunbar and Miss Smith were several other women. However, two other women were interested in a more lucrative profession and preferred to associate with the soldiers in another manner.

When preparing for their adventure, the women recruited by the Mission of Masons had been told not to pack much because everything would be furnished in Virginia. As a result, Miss Ney, Miss Dunbar, and Miss Edson were having a difficult time dealing with their limited supplies. Furthermore, Miss Sarah Edson found that the financial promise had been broken and her funds used for other gains. She was so angry that she actually filed a complaint with the Advisory Committee in New York.[14]

True to her nature, Miss Smith had not listened to the orders and had packed abundant clothes, supplies, and money. Thus, she was able to survive in City Point quite nicely. When she got to Point of Rocks on the opposite side of the Appomattox River and realized there was no legitimate work and that she would not be replacing Clara Barton, she was quite angry. She ripped off the Mission of Masons patch, but still kept the pass that allowed her some flexibility until she found work as an independent nurse and made accommodations with some of her traveling colleagues to go back home.

While at Point of Rocks, Miss Smith experienced a situation similar to ones that other nurses had had with a special patient. During the day, she would walk through the hospital wards looking at the soldiers' faces and body positions. She would listen to where the men chattered or where there was silence and she would listen for their breathing pattern. By doing so, she could quickly assess certain health aspects and individual needs without taking many steps or speaking to the patients. She noticed if they looked at her or tracked her as she walked through the ward. She also noted if they attempted to speak with her or if they mentally drifted off into another world. If the intensity of the odor was strong from rotting flesh and infections, she knew gangrene had begun. She payed attention to the moans and groans. Were they regular or did they have a unique pace? She intuitively knew there was a different situation with each pattern. As an independent nurse, her normal course was to focus her energy on the soldiers who needed the most attention. Sometimes added attention came from a doctor or male ward nurse, with a gesture or nod of the head. Mostly she was busy enough with her regular tasks that she might walk past a patient, assuming they were sleeping or did not need her help. Such was the case for one sad, young boy who had run away from home and joined the 37th New Jersey regiment. She had passed by him on several occasions until one time he finally caught her attention with his pathetic pale skin and inability to move. He was gravely sick. When she stopped to speak with him, she found he was unable to eat unless the food tasted like something his mother had made. Like the other ladies who could cook, Miss Smith thought about a good recipe and made up something that would pass for his mother's cooking. Miss Smith's special trick was that she used a small silver, not tin, cup, a real spoon, not the military issue, and served the food with a fabric napkin. She pretended the food was like his mother's and fed him tiny spoonsful. Gradually, the young soldier regained his strength and she was able to convince the main surgeon, Dr. Porter, to allow her to have the young soldier serve as her orderly. As an orderly, he could walk out of the ward, and she allowed him to sleep in her quarters while she was on duty during the day. This special option to get away from all the other wounded and sick and to breathe the fresh air improved his mindset. Seeing his improvement, her compassion inspired her to negotiate a bed for him on a hospital transport headed home, where he could recuperate fully.

Miss Clara Barton went in and out of various locations with the military units during the war. At one point, Miss Barton returned to Point of Rocks to take supplies out to the front. Quite frustrated and angry about having been such a fool believing that she could "replace" Clara Barton, Miss Smith knew the time to leave had come. As a result, she headed over to City Point, where she reconnected with Miss Ney and Miss Dunbar, who had had previous grievances with the Mission of Masons as well. These ladies were now working on Agency Row with the Maine agents. Self-assured about her ability and recognized among her close peers, Adelaide found a job working in the depot hospital as an independent nurse. However, this was not without problems.

Being a well-composed young woman, and coming from the big city of New York, Miss Smith's appearance was very important to her. Unlike Aunt Becky and some of the government nurses, who had only the bare necessities, she brought a wardrobe and various accoutrements to make her life comfortable. Shortly after she got to her own quarters in City Point, she hired Hannah, one of the former slaves in the area, to personally work for her. Former slaves and contraband were culturally and politically not permitted to call a white person by their first name. It always had to be Miss, Mrs., Mr., or if in the military, their rank. Hannah addressed Adelaide as Miss Smith. The two women developed a good relationship and watched out for one another. In addition, having Hannah as her servant elevated Adelaide socially, and she liked the status. Plus, the appearance of a personal servant made her stand apart from the government nurses.

City savvy and sophisticated, Adelaide had thought about what she would need for her wardrobe before she went to Virginia. In her trunks she had her own equestrian outfit to wear when she could get a horse to ride, as well as other dresses. Miss Smith was very particular about having various dresses to wear, but that meant that multiple aprons were imperative while working in the hospital wards. Like many of the ladies in the camp, she stuck to the habit of having her laundry washed on Mondays.[15] An expert organizer whose skills were only enhanced by the war, she was very careful to instruct Hannah about what items needed to be cleaned by hand and which were to be taken to the laundry and then picked up when dry. Similar to some of the other independent nurses and wives, she also hired contraband seamstresses to maintain her wardrobe and when possible make new dresses. Having somebody else do the sewing meant that she had time to grow a garden with things like carrots, peas and flowers during the warm weather, and she could network and socialize. These options made the ladies more attractive than the government nurses in general, and their lodging was more attractive.

Unlike the government nurse who may or may not get a relief shift, when Miss Smith was off duty, she was often talking to different state agents, riding, or visiting with the people around her and gathering new supplies.[16] One issue she had to address on a regular basis was a problem of socializing or not socializing with the officers and dealing with their various forms of harassment. Networking with individuals who could help was agreeable and strategically valuable, but the officers often just wasted her time unless she needed something from them.

Confident as Miss Smith appeared, she used to talk about how she was often "annoyed by the calls of the officers, who had little to occupy their time, could not understand how it was possible for us to be too tired to entertain them."[17] During holiday time, for example, she said there were up to twelve men for every two women in the mess halls. All the men were trying to get the women's attention. The misplaced attention was flattering and frustrating at the same time, and she said she "felt like a piece of meat being thrown to hungry dogs."[18] But then the holiday spirit—with delicacies and letters from home, plus decorations in the ward and in the camp—seemed to create a mood that made many feel better.

Miss Dix understood how an attractive woman could divert attention and cause problems in the masculine world of the military. An eye-catching woman, Miss Smith was busy and popular. In just one week, she counted forty-five visits from officers who had come from the front or from Grant's and the Hospital Headquarters. The officers came to visit when they had nothing better to fill their time and interrupted her from the noble task of writing letters home for all the soldiers in the ward who could not write for themselves. She often tried to ignore the visiting officers by keeping her eyes down on the paper as she continued to write, and tried not to engage in their conversations with anything more than a polite response. Some of the officers, thinking they had the right, never seemed to get the hint that she was busy and that she didn't want their company. Some came into her tent laughing and joking like silly schoolboys.

However, others did get the message and left, allowing her to have treasured moments of personal space. One story about Miss Smith and some of the problems with men may sound familiar to some of the other women's stories.

> One evening I was very tired and three officers slightly under the influence of liquor, annoyed me greatly. At taps I said significantly "it's taps, gentleman!" "That does not concern us," one replied, "we can stay as long as we wish." "General Grant himself could not stay in my tent after taps," I retorted indignantly. They made no move to go, however, I arose and simply pointing to the tent opening, declined any reply to their remarks.[19]

As an illustration of her preferred independence during her free time, Miss Smith and a visitor, Miss Bain, arranged a small trip upriver to see the Dutch Gap. The Dutch Gap was an engineered channel that had been cut through a narrow section of the twists and turns on the James River. When completed, it greatly reduced the time needed to go to or from Richmond. Having been created by engineers, it was a curiosity that many people wanted to see. If nothing exciting happened, it was a lovely outing. However, it could be a dangerous situation because the rebel sharpshooters had access to the opposite shore.

On this particular occasion, the attractive, single ladies had been invited for Thanksgiving dinner aboard the USS *Onondaga* that was anchored opposite of the Dutch Gap. To travel the approximate eight miles, the women arranged to have two men from the Corps d'Afrique escort them in an ambulance that could transport them over the bumpy corduroy roads. When they arrived, they found ten or twelve officers in their full dress uniforms waiting for them. This was challenging for Miss Bain, so she chattered about regular activities with the officers and about her major friend. Miss Smith had more appropriate social skills and talked about hospital life and what was happening on the post.

After dinner, the officers cordially invited the women to tour the upper level of the ship. Then they suggested getting into a rowboat to cross the rest of the river and tour the gap. The rowboat landed on the shore and the guests were helped out. With both sides of the channel being so close to one another, shots and shells passed overhead, but with no apparent or imminent danger. Before long, one of the officers started dancing around the ladies by moving from side to side. At first this appeared silly, but then he explained that he was trying to protect them from sniper bullets. Until that moment the women had not considered how close they were to the rebels hiding in the bushes. Shortly thereafter, one of the "rebs" yelled, "better take those ladies away."

Like working in the fever ward, the woman were still oblivious to the danger they were in. The ladies climbed a hill to get a better view of the digging that was still going on when a shell screamed overhead and exploded nearby. The officers grabbed the women by their hands and pulled them into a gopher hole that was used for bomb protection.

The tour of the gopher hole had not been part of their planned event, but it certainly was illuminating. After all, the gopher hole had a wooden floor and roof to prevent the earth from caving in and also served as a mess, with a cook having prepared a meal of biscuits as well as presenting a container of peppermint sticks. The table had been set with a real tablecloth, tin plates, cups and two tined forks, indicating premeditated thought on the part of the officers. The firing outside continued and blocked the rowboat's safe return. In addition, it was getting late. Finally, Adelaide spoke to one of the officers, and he offered to keep them safe if they wanted to stay in the gopher hole overnight. Without much of a second thought, the two women said they would "rather risk the shells and drowning." Propriety being first on their minds, the women demanded to re-cross the area in the rowboat. Feeling like novice soldiers in battle, they were frightened beyond their composure. However, they made it to the other shore, clambered out of the rowboat and made a wild, unladylike dash for the ambulance that had been hidden in the woods, waiting for them. When they finally returned to the hospital complex, they promised to not be so independent the next time they received a dinner invitation.[20] The two women realized that perhaps the government nurses were protected for a reason.

The year at City Point for Miss Smith was an educational one. She had started with limited hospital experience but quickly learned a great deal about being in the war zone. She also learned a great deal about working with others, especially the men in the military, and parleyed those life skills when organizing New York suffragettes after the war.

Miss Cornelia Hancock, a younger woman from New Jersey, presented a strong contrast to Miss Smith's accomplishments, self-confidence, and sometimes almost brash New Yorker manners. Both had courage and individual dignity that some of the other nurses shared, but Miss Hancock came from a different philosophical background.

Miss Cornelia Hancock

Miss Cornelia Hancock was unmarried, twenty-five years old, and from southern New Jersey. As a Quaker, she believed in her own God-given ability and destination. Her brother and male relatives had gone to war and she felt she needed to do the same. Her sister, Ellen, had married Dr. Henry Child from the Philadelphia area, so Miss Hancock convinced the doctor to let her know when she could go to work in the war. When Gettysburg began, Dr. Child notified Miss Hancock that her help was needed, and she went off to war for her first lessons in very raw, dirty, and gory hospital work.

A baptism of fire is an expression that fit Miss Hancock's experience. Cornelia started her nursing career by finding herself at Gettysburg with the 2nd Corps doing whatever she could wherever she was needed. Like Mrs. Lee, she did what she felt had to be done and learned a great deal while doing it: "Nobody had time to give orders or ask."[21] She learned to help the emotionally and physically wounded either survive the experience or die with some sense of self-dignity. She discovered how to feed many desperate mouths with almost nothing. She survived the traumas of the "overpowering, awful stench of gaping wounds that announced the unburied,"[22] which strengthened her fortitude. She had a feminine practical sense that blended with the tough skin of someone who had witnessed such terrible scenes. After Gettysburg, she moved to Washington, where she worked in the contraband hospital and reconfirmed her abolitionist upbringing. Unsatisfied with these more mundane tasks after having witnessed serious combat caregiving, she did what many of the other women had done and traveled with the military units. First, she went to Brandy Station where she met the love of her life, Dr. Dudley, then on to the Wilderness, White House Landing, and finally to City Point. Her true combat nursing experiences were quite dramatic and different in comparison to Miss Smith's initial managerial ones.

Miss Smith had Hannah as her helper and housekeeper, while other ladies had personal servants with them. Government nurses had to do their own work. Miss Hancock was more aligned with Miss Smith and had several women working for her. One was vivandière Bridget Deavers from Michigan, who worked for her as helper and housekeeper when Bridget had been forced back from the front by the military command. The employer/employee relationship between the two women was strong. However, Miss Hancock had a more traditional relationship with those who worked with her than some other women did. Miss Hancock always seemed annoyed but smiled kindly when one the contrabands called her the informal "honey."[23] She understood it was a term of endearment because she was a young lady and they were not trying to make fun of her, but it still perturbed her.

Perhaps it was her family and Quaker background that made her more tolerant or perhaps it was her baptism by fire that made her sensitive to those in need. Cornelia employed a few contraband children who also helped her. She understood their situation after she saw the plight of many abused, sick, and lame contrabands while she was working in Washington. Miss Hancock had several issues that bothered her throughout her experiences at City Point. One was the sidesaddle issue, because the saddles were hard to attain. Another was a young doctor from Yale, and a third one was the constant noise in the war zone.

Like Adelaide Smith, Miss Hancock was a young, fashionable, and private young lady. Unlike the Dix nurses and more like Adelaide, she was very concerned about her attire. She was most put out when gossip swirled around about where she got her clothes. To quell the rumors, she had a local tailor sew for her. Her mother regularly sent supplies and fabric from home, and like Miss Smith, she had her own riding attire. When she needed clothing repairs, she used the local tailor. He was a soldier from one of the wards and she explained that he "has been putting two skirts together and tomorrow I am to have a ride on Lieutenant Fogg's horse."[24] She knew exactly what her goals were and how to get what she wanted. Being able to keep up with the dignitaries and wives was important to Miss Hancock. One morning, she watched "two ladies riding on horseback"[25] but also made sure she was observed riding by her peers. A much better rider than Adelaide Smith and several of the other ladies or officers' wives, she flaunted her skill. Even though riding in a war zone was not what a good nurse should be focused on, the experience provided pleasure instead of danger. Trusting her family, Cornelia often wrote about her passion, such as, "I do like to ride on horseback and do it every day."[26] She was even adventurous enough to try riding a mule: "I took a ride upon a mule [I] had been given by one of Sheridan's cavalry."[27] Her friends told her that was not dignified and not what a proper lady should do, so she returned the mule.

The military did not allow much room for nurses' personal items. Many had to carry what they needed, and that greatly restricted what they could bring. Saddles provided by the military were abundant for the cavalry and soldiers' horses. Sidesaddles for ladies to use were few and very far between. Young women had to locate or obtain their own sidesaddles whenever and wherever they could. Cornelia was obsessed with the possession of a sidesaddle. According to the social norms of the time, a lady could not just go out and get a sidesaddle. Cornelia had to network long and hard to have her friend Dr. Dudley, or some of her Sanitary Commission friends, procure a sidesaddle for her. Bending a rule of ownership, Miss Hancock overtly verbalized her desire as, "There was a splendid side saddle that I wanted to confiscate."[28] In contrast to a government nurse, when she saw something she wanted or needed, she exerted her personal power to obtain the item. She flaunted that the "Sanitary Commission made me a present of a sidesaddle, one a Secesh had to leave behind: it is not a very splendid one."[29]

Confident about being correct in accepting what had been left behind, she wrote to her family when the sidesaddle was confiscated for her. The ownership remained vague, so people around her heard how angry Cornelia was at then having "her saddle" confiscated by another woman. She always wondered if Mrs. Farnham had taken the saddle when the 6th Corps went to the Shenandoah Valley. Miss Hancock wrote to her family and friends about how she was "inconvenienced very much by having lent my saddle to a lady in the Cavalry Corps who has skedaddled with it in her possession to the Shenandoah."[30] Miss Hancock's mother wrote back that she was most concerned about her daughter's love for adventure as opposed to being a serious caregiver.

As an independent nurse, Cornelia had significant flexibility with the way she thought, acted, and worked. Utilizing her freedom and employing the art of getting what she wanted was just part of Cornelia's charm. She occasionally journaled about what went on in her daily personal space and expressed how frustrating it could be. Miss Hancock likely started as a jack-of-all-trades before she ended up as an independent contract nurse with Dr. Aikens. She worked at whatever task was needed. By the end of the war, she had shifted from caregiving roles and grown comfortably into the role of diet kitchen manager. When her residential foe, Mrs. Holstein, finally left, Miss Hancock took over completely as the manager of the new diet kitchen. Now as a woman in control as opposed to a more submissive Dix nurse, she exercised her jurisdiction over the system. The new kitchen measured 72 feet by 20 feet, had a new tin stove and was full of shiny, big pots.[31] Cooking and cooperation among the agents and organizations was necessary if anything was to get done. Trading favors and swapping supplies became a common practice and the food improved in both quality and quantity. For Cornelia, nursing shifted from working in a ward to that of food provisions for the soul, and the soldiers loved the extra care. In every hospital, there was a fund that accrued from the sick not using all their legal rations which, if properly managed, supplied the sick with an occasional luxury. "Twice [she gave] ice cream to [her] patients"[32] by utilizing part of the fund. In addition, the Medical Purveyors boat was another source for delicacies. When Cornelia couldn't find what she needed through the military, she would search to fill the deficiencies supplied by the Sanitary and Christian Commission and Purveyors' boat.

As a government nurse, Aunt Becky had a basic tent with plenty of mice to share in her quarters. In contrast, Cornelia's personal space included very comfortable accommodations while at City Point. Instead of just one tent, she had two tents put together that provided a sense of privacy and personal identity. One part served as her private dining area while the other was for her private quarters. Even though she designated a "dining" area in her own tent, she found she occasionally had to dine in the mess halls among many men, but she learned to cope with the noise and confusion while feeling like she was on display.[33] Once more in contrast to a government nurse's living space, her quarters had a wood floor, two beds, four chairs, and even linen sheets. Part of the time, she had Bridget Deavers from the Michigan regiments living with her when General Grant forbade women at the front. Bridget helped keep everything spotless.[34] In turn, for the housekeeping service, Cornelia provided Bridget with newer and clean clothing solicited from her mother and friends at home. Living in the tents was just a way of life in the summer, but by fall of 1864, the military had started to construct log cabins for the winter, making the women's accommodation more comfortable.

As previously mentioned, Miss Hancock was a young lady who cared about her image—like Miss Smith—and most if not all the women had problems with the officers. She would pontificate about male visitors, "I think there have been many over from the regiments round: their sole purpose seeming to be to see a lady."³⁵ Cornelia also knew "there [wa]s no danger from anything in the army, except an unsophisticated individual might possibly have their affections trifled with."³⁶ However, sometimes it became personal for the women. Next to the sidesaddle obsession, Miss Hancock was extremely fond of a young assistant surgeon, Dr. Dudley, who had graduated from Yale Medical School.³⁷ Validating Miss Dix's fear about having an attractive young woman as a nurse with the military, Miss Hancock met the young doctor while at Brandy Station when he had been wounded. Young Dr. Dudley was quite a catch and Cornelia was an attractive young lady who was very interested in him beyond his medical skills. Their relationship developed in depth and had some complications that reduced her focus from her job as caregiver.

Although Dr. Dudley did not ride in from the front on a regular basis to see her, he was discreetly around the area and they exchanged notes and letters when they could not be together. Those around them felt the energy when they were in each other's presence. At times he even requested her to pursue an option that any government nurse would have found exceedingly difficult to do, and that was to take leave and visit him. Miss Hancock always tried to be coy and would fuss about him. Not only did she write letters home for her patients, but she extended the boundaries and wrote to Dr. Dudley's family. In return, she received mail from Dr. Dudley's sister Nellie³⁸ and his mother, so the relationship had considerable depth that complicated everything.

The doctor shared a familiar connection with the nurses in that he was a good officer and he cared a lot about his men. For example, when the battle of Hatchers Run ended, Dr. Dudley chose to remain with the wounded and ended up becoming a prisoner of war and was taken to Libby Prison in Richmond. With her beloved doctor as a POW, when she listened to the stories from former prisoners, it made work in the wards difficult. Cornelia had heard about how challenging life was and started to lose her professional psychological control. Like caring for those who were going to die, she couldn't do much about his situation but carried on the best she could. Still, she overtly worried about what everyone else would say because, as Aunt Becky said, "the gossiping of neighbors is hardly confined to the women."³⁹

Advised by others to get a new focus once Dr. Dudley was captured, Miss Hancock began to concentrate on her abolitionist views that she had developed while in Washington. For example, she elevated the status of the contrabands to the "freemen" and became their advocate. Similar to many of the nurses, Cornelia had a strong sense of human dignity and ethics. Those she worked with seemed to sense her conviction and respected her for her beliefs and strengths. With her energy back on nursing, Miss Hancock fussed more about the sights and putrid smells of the wounded. "A wounded man is a sad sight but the saddest yet are the sights in the hospital now, cases of chronic diarrhea, men emaciated to a skeleton and blacker than a mulatto. Oh! How awful it is, they are very much more trouble to care for than the wounded, they are full of notions, and have no appetite."[40] Miss Hancock did not have the same empathy as other women, and didn't pull out special utensils or make special treats for patients like Mrs. Lee and Miss Smith did, but she made sure she talked with them and tried to address their concerns.

Moreover, the constant noise of the cannons booming[41] got to Cornelia as it did many of the other nurses. Perhaps it was a reaction to her early experiences at Gettysburg with all the terrible destruction. Perhaps it was a reaction to all the burned bodies she saw and smelled at the Wilderness. Perhaps it was the loss of her dear friends. Whatever the trauma was, she could not hide her feelings when the cannons boomed. She identified them as "belching double venom"[42] or "thunderbolts running riot."[43] Her colorful description of the incessant noise was perceptive insight into how she hated the machines of war and all the death and destruction war represented and how it affected her soul deeply. Following the pattern of many other nurses, she became traumatized on multiple levels and the complexities of losing someone special while in the war zone took its toll.

The independent nurses were like the government nurses in many ways. One thing they had in common was their awe and pleasure when President Lincoln came to City Point and went through the hospital wards. Regardless of their rank or organizational status, the nurses all remembered his high hat, bony hands, and how he would bend forward to speak with each soldier he met. His overt and utter compassion for the humble soldier became a memorable moment for the men and the women. Furthermore, he exuded a message of love for those who had done so much for their country.[44] It was a moment and message none of them ever forgot.[45]

In addition to the government and independent nurses, there were other women who were also dubbed nurses. Some of the woman worked in the wards from time to time, but for the most part they were attached to the United States Sanitary Commission (USSC), and their experiences and routines on board transports are detailed in Chapter 7. It should also be noted that under the generic umbrella of being a nurse, there were several other women who provided caregiving but were called the *vivandières*.

Vivandières

Finally, a brief look at two women who exceeded general caregiving norms. They were not hospital nurses and they weren't wives, but were very independent and made a significant impact. Called "daughters of the regiment," or vivandières, they were gutsy, bold, courageous women who were devoted to a specific regiment and provided immediate caregiving during a battle. The tradition of being a vivandière historically in America goes back to the American Revolution when wives would follow their husbands into battle and offer spirits or fluids along with medical care when it was needed. Periodically, they were even called "camp followers" because some offered cooking and laundry services for the soldiers, although that term changed as wars went on. During the Civil War, it was not unusual for daughters, sisters, and wives to become involved with the units their father or brothers were in. They marched in their parades and served as providers of good will to boost morale. If they went off to the war and followed their father, brothers, or husbands, it was a difficult and risky obligation. Most of their names are lost to history or were never documented officially, although a few are periodically mentioned. They are Augusta Foster with the 2nd Maine regiment,[46] Kady Brownell with the 1st Rhode Island infantry,[47] Eliza Wilson from the 5th Wisconsin regiment,[48] and Virginia Hall, who served with the Philadelphia Fire Zouaves.[49] As the war progressed, these women reverted to less challenging military roles and assumed more domestic nursing ones. However, in Michigan at the start of the war, it is believed that nineteen women enlisted with the 2nd Michigan regiment. Annie Etheridge with the 3rd Michigan Infantry and Bridget Deavers with 1st Michigan Cavalry are known to have been in the City Point area around 1864–1865.

Some wives, such as Laura Newman, went to the front with their husband. One wife, who remains nameless (see the second section of Homeward Bound Journey) went to the front at Petersburg with her husband, died, and was buried amongst the many soldiers' graves in the City Point area. However, these brave women never participated as actively as Annie Etheridge and Bridget Deavers.

The vivandières' attire was very practical. Some wore bloomer-styled clothing and carried a weapon, while others, like Bridget and Annie, wore skirts. Their task was to help the wounded when on the battlefield and encourage the men to fight when the battle raged around them. They were very much at home on the back of a horse and would have put the well-attired "equestrian" ladies to shame. The vivandières were present at the beginning of the war and stayed until the end. If soldiers could list all the battles they had been in, Annie and Bridget could probably list more. As the fall season approached in 1864, General Grant ordered that all women were to be removed from the front. That impacted some, while other women, like Laura Newman, failed to comply with the order until the need to return to the post became absolutely necessary. Or they refused orders and stayed with their unit. Bridget, however, complied and went to City Point.

Bridget Deavers

Bridget came to the United States from Ireland in 1849 at the age of eleven. When the war started, she was attached to the 1st Michigan Cavalry as their mascot or daughter of the regiment and stayed the course.[50] Periodically, she would come into City Point and interact with some of the other women. One story that built her notoriety was bringing in Captain Whitney from Company B when he had been wounded at the Battle of Five Forks. Somehow Bridget managed to get the wounded captain over the back of her horse, then rode with him into City Point. Unfortunately, the wounds he sustained were too significant and the ride too difficult and the captain died later, but many people heard the story and admired Bridget's concern and tenacity for trying to save her captain.

Bridget cared about her boys and worked as a liaison with the USSC and USCC. When the organizations needed to locate a soldier or needed information about a soldier, the representatives went to Bridget first. She knew every man in the cavalry unit. She provided excellent healthcare for her regiment while they were moving from location to location. She listened carefully to each of them, she knew each of their names, their likes and dislikes. She paid specific attention to their wants and needs and when offered supplies she took only what would be needed for her specific soldiers. Furthermore, she had a sense of their moral and religious construction and was always available for them when they needed to speak with someone.[51] At one point, Bridget was given money to spend and to do something "nice for herself." Instead of spending the money on clothes, travel, or food, or replacing her beloved pony, she shared the money with her soldiers. Sharing what she had with her "friends and her brothers" and making others happy—that was doing something nice for herself.[52]

When the order came from General Grant for women to leave the front, Bridget complied and went into City Point. She and found quarters with Cornelia Hancock in 2nd Corps, replacing the contraband help. One day, Bridget was in the tent when General Barlow stopped in to visit Cornelia. The general stepped into the tent and commented about how clean everything was. Cornelia just smiled and mentioned that Bridget was her housekeeper and made sure the floors had been scrubbed clean on a regular basis. Bridget's reputation for her personal appearance and need for order also prevailed in the kitchens. According to Aunt Becky, Bridget's brawny arms made sure all unpainted shelves and tables were snowy white with her scrubbing.[53] Unafraid of difficult tasks, she was willing to scrub and polish the area to make sure it was better than before.[54]

When the war ended, Bridget went with her units and was alleged to have continued on elsewhere. Despite no real records of Bridget, there are several clues. Some suggest she married another soldier, or perhaps she raised a family, or perhaps she just remained like an ephemeral ghost in the hearts and minds of 1st Michigan Cavalry and its history.

Annie Etheridge

At only five feet, three inches tall, Annie Etheridge was a petite woman who was attached to the 3rd Michigan Infantry as a vivandière at sixteen years of age. However, she had also worked on the hospital transport boats with Amy Bradley, so she had some practical nursing skills and was nicknamed the "little Sergeant in Petticoats" by Amy.[55] Respected and well-liked by others, she could sweet talk the City Point Commission women into riding miles to deliver the desperately needed supplies to her Michigan units.

Annie was an excellent rider. On the field of battle, it was not uncommon for her to ride into the battle with coffee inside her canteen to help give the wounded a boost and to retrieve wounded soldiers. Even at her petite height, she was given several captured rebels to turn in.[56]

At Chancellorsville, she was on her favorite roan pony when her boys started to retreat, so, acting as a guide and cheerleader, she reminded them they had good range and that they could win.[57] Acts such as those endeared Annie to her regiment. While at Petersburg, she remained true to her regiment and cared for any of the soldiers who sustained injuries during battle. With her caregiving activities close to the action, Annie's skirts frequently became pierced by bullets, offering evidence of her battle time. As the year progressed, the clothing situation grew worse and she started to look like she was attired in a ribbon skirt. Finally, being convinced by her boys and General Grant, she came in from the field. She was in dire need of clothing. Her female friends on the post tried to help her acquire badly needed replacements. Like a contraband would, Annie gathered a little of this and a little of that but she did not care about her appearance, only her soldiers. From Cornelia, she received a couple of skirts and brown stockings, while a few of the nurses provided her with a corset and threads to hold the sides tight.[58] When she had extra items, she put them in a box for future need or the conclusion of the war. Her only focus was to get back to her regiment where she could care for the sick and wounded.

The vivandières were never formally trained in nursing other than by life experiences. The instinct for offering care while under fire was in their nature. Like the government nurse and the independent nurses, these women came with the intent to stay the course of the war. However, they also were savvy enough to know when they needed help, and felt comfortable reaching out to others, like the commission women and state agents, for assistance for themselves and their soldiers.

6

Women of the United States Christian Commission (USCC)
Prayers and Dinner

The next two chapters may seem like a detour, but the background information will help in understanding the roles of the women who came to work with the Christian and Sanitary Commissions. The United States Christian Commission (USCC) was founded on November 16, 1861, with a concept that sick and dying soldiers needed prayers to fulfill their potential sense of immortality. The organization was an offshoot of the multi-denominational New York City YMCA, representing several religious groups.[1] The services of the USCC ended in 1866. It was predominantly a male-focused organization with very limited opportunities for women.

Headquarters for the USCC were located in Philadelphia, with George H. Stuart serving as the chairman. Recruitment locations varied for the delegates, but larger cities such as Boston, New York, Chicago, Pittsburgh, Cincinnati, and Baltimore provided the majority of individuals, while Philadelphia dominated in recruiting representatives. Christian Commission personnel came from a mix of diverse evangelical religious and social-based groups. For example, Unitarian groups came from Springfield, Massachusetts, while the state of New York sent Presbyterian ministers. The representatives also brought their various agendas. Reverend Sanborne arrived from New York with revenue[2] while Connecticut USCC members solicited in the press with an appeal to their citizens by explaining:

> The work among our soldiers is now very pressing. Let such good men and true—whether ministers or laymen—who feel that they have a fitness for this work, call upon Reverend Henry Powers, at the rooms of the Ladies' Soldiers' Aid Association, and they will be [considered for] commission in due form.[3]

More succinctly, one delegate wrote that they were not to "trespass on others grounds." They were to attend to all wards, distribute stoves, and be systematic and quiet while they worked.[4] From the beginning, they provided diverse backgrounds and community support systems.

The Christian Commission, like the Sanitary Commission, had branch locations around the states and many local groups under each of the branch divisions. They solicited for funds around the country with New England, Eastern, and Central divisions often emerging on top. A few representatives came from California from the group known as the Pacific Christian Commission. When not collaborating with the Sanitary Commission, the USCC had their own fundraising efforts and contributed personnel and thousands of dollars to help the benevolent and charitable cause.[5] The Pacific branch in San Francisco had significant wealth that generously contributed to the cash flow, with over $20,000 in gold for the USCC.[6] The Pacific Commission also offered the Central Commission delegates who were willing to leave California for the war zones to help with the psychological and spiritual support of the soldiers and their families.[7] With significant monies, the organization could purchase new items like equipment for the major installation of the various Army units, or smaller supplies to help[8] feed or clothe soldiers.

Orders affecting City Point came from George H. Stuart out of Philadelphia, where Stuart oversaw the extensive supplies that often needed to be sent quickly. One incident of rapid delivery came when the diet kitchen at the Point of Rocks needed help. Initially, the kitchen had no chimney to vent the cooking smoke, which made breathing difficult. It only had dirt floors and was usable only when the weather was dry. When the head matron, Mrs. Annie Wittenmyer, saw the situation, she was appalled. According to her report, she saw the kitchen and the food that looked like "swill buckets" and "slop." With permission from the surgeon in charge, she contacted President Stuart, and within a day, an order had been given to send supplies down to alleviate the situation.[9]

Although not all supplies are listed here, by September of 1864 the USCC delegates had access to food and supplies that regularly went to City Point from Philadelphia and Baltimore. For example, they were sent:

240 cans of veal	519 lbs. of tea	94 bottles of fruit syrup
960 cans of beef	16 lbs. of spices	498 bottles of brandy
1,848 cans of turkey	98 lbs. gelatin	889 bottles of cherry
645 lbs. cured fish	4,829 lbs. Farina	1,077 galls blackberry cordial
2,743 lbs. beef-tea jelly	14 barrels dried apricots	wine
3,246 cans of peaches	14 barrels dried apples	27 bottles of port
4,988 cans tomatoes	395 lbs. chocolate	671 bay rum

1,332 cans cherries	681 lbs. sugar	4,800 tonic pills
240 cans of plums	50 lbs. flour	5 lbs. chloroform
3,202 cans of jelly	4 boxes cheese	12 bottles alcohol
980 lbs. coffee	54 bottles catsup	25 bottles Camphor
443 lbs. butter	149 boxes of hospital supplies	

In addition to food supplies, they sent:

3,664 shirts	2,000 crutch heads	16 brooms
1,142 socks	1,933 housewives (kits)	3,744 pencils
75 pairs of shoes	1,672 combs	11 gross of pens
2,348 suspenders	480 lbs. soap	24 slates
147 quilts	12 canes	676 pen holders
453 towels	20 pages of pins	168 quarts ink
2,668 rolls of bandages	183,000 envelopes	24 feeding cups
160 arm slings	754 reams of writing paper	156 boxes of matches
324 crutches[10]		

As City Point expanded, the Christian Commission sent 13 wagons and 60 horses to help transport the supplies to the various units.[11] In addition to smaller supplies, large supplies were sent. One came in the form of a coffee wagon that could go directly out to the incoming wounded.[12] Actively seeking ways to assist the Army of the Potomac, the USCC also coordinated the purchase and installation of a steam hose engine (no. 4) from the Baltimore Fire Department that provided City Point with water to keep the dust and dirt at a tolerable level[13] in the busy, hot months of July and August.[14] In late July, the USCC also presented the Army of the Potomac with a cooking wagon that was similar to the coffee wagon and could be moved to various locations.[15]

More relevant and necessary supplies came from other locations and were often requested by the commanders or the delegates who worked with the specific military units. Rubber blankets for the soldiers in the trenches in front of Petersburg were a constant request.[16] The rubber blankets were very helpful to the soldiers but also to the women who were in the area, especially while in tents. As an example, when accommodations were just changing from tents to log cabins, the women's quarters had a roof of pine branches to block out the sun during the day and chill at night. However, one evening a heavy storm blew in and everything got wet. Their beds, clothing, and supplies were all soaked and most were ruined. Undaunted by the situation, Mrs. Jones and Miss Noyes sought out the supply of rubber blankets and placed them over the items they could salvage and wrapped the blankets around themselves. When daylight came, another request was sent to USCC president for lumber to finish the roofs of the quarters.[17]

Other supplies arranged by the commission came from a variety of locations. For example, on August 4, 1864, the schooner *Charlotte Shaw* left Boston and was headed to City Point loaded with ice, vegetables and sanitary stores,[18] while Utica, New York, sent eight barrels of assorted supplies to the USCC City Point.[19] Larger cities like New York, Springfield, Massachusetts, and Rochester, New York,[20] plus many lesser towns such as Enfield, Connecticut,[21] also sent supplies. While some towns provided goods and materials, others simply provided money. Each month the incoming sources of revenue were tallied and published for greater transparency and to encourage a competitive desire. Less competitive towns offered lesser amounts. In February of 1865, West Winstead, Connecticut, raised $252 while Plattsburg, New York, raised $180 to support the soldiers and the war. Humble Patterson, New Jersey, submitted a modest $39.[22]

Frequent areas of conflict that emerged within the commission were public relations and the disbursement of money. The sanitary fairs organized by the USSC were widely recognized and raised considerable amounts of money for the war effort; however, fundraising agents for the USCC found their own niche among their diverse populations and continued to bring additional funds for the soldiers. One continuous call was for financial donations, but also rags that could be used for bandages, as well as fruits and cordials.[23] Local fundraising and making supplies was viewed as part of the woman's domain. Members of the Ladies Christian Commission back home found items to make to add to the haversacks. A simple rectangular-shaped sewing kit called a "housewife" or a "needle album"[24] was regularly needed. Consequently, the USCC would gather the ladies together in a town or even the children in Sunday school and provide direction on how to construct a sewing kit. The kits were often made out of strong calico fabric or similar materials and contained needles, yarn, and a thimble for mending clothing. They held up with significant use and they were often filled with a small note to the soldier and the maker's post office address, so the soldier could write a note back.[25]

Regardless of where delegates came from, their preliminary focus for the USCC was on benevolence and management of the spiritual welfare tasks rather than the intense labor required to maintain the caregivers in the war zone.[26] Delegates were divided into three general tasks: field, hospital, and battleground work.[27] In a slight name change, the battleground volunteer representatives were occasionally called "minute men" because they appeared immediately following a serious battle, did the best they could to triage, and then returned home, allowing other groups to come in and assist with the dead and wounded.[28] This rapid strike force often caused confusion among those who did not understand their specific battleground purpose.

Fundamentally, the USCC was a male-based organization which staffed various facilities or locations. At the start, women were only permitted to organize supplies and events and help with the fundraising. The women were always subservient volunteers. In 1862, the board of the USCC realized that the aspects of care required the greater intervention of a few select women. Among the roster of 5,000 USCC delegates named between 1862 and 1865, there were only thirty-four women delegates recognized and listed, primarily from Chicago and St. Louis. This does not mean that they were the only women serving with the USCC. Reverend Moss, for instance, provided a list of about eighty-seven female diet kitchen managers in his annals of the Christian Commission.[29] Although not common, several of the women delegates died from illness while working for the USCC during the war years[30] but none of these women were listed at either City Point or Point of Rocks.

While in a war zone, male delegates wore a small metal badge on their left breast pocket to identify them. The decision to become a delegate for either laymen, doctors, or ministers was difficult. For one, they had to be physically fit to endure the movements of the army and the shifting battles.[31] Women representing the USCC wore a fabric badge that resembled an open Bible sewn on their attire. They, too, had to be healthy enough to endure the war zone. Their stay was shorter, however, as they remained with the diet kitchen for only six weeks.

Like the variations among the citizens, military, and nurses at City Point, members of the Christian Commission had their own distinct personalities, rules, and regulations from the other commissions. Their unique primary objective significantly set them apart from the United States Sanitary Commission (USSC). First and foremost, they were on a religious mission[32] to preach the gospel and distribute religious tracts. Next, as opposed to the long-term commitment the USSC made, the Christian Commission delegates paid one dollar to join and then volunteered without pay for six weeks at a time. With careful planning, when the local delegates returned, they were able to schedule the fourth Sabbath of each month for meetings to focus on the support of the military. These returning delegates learned how to persuade their audiences at home to contribute to the cause by painting vivid pictures about the agony of the wounded and bloody scenes they had encountered while being at a battle site. Such descriptions were designed to overtly move their audiences into supporting the cause by contrasting their safe and comfortable lives with the horrors of life in the war zone.[33]

In general, the members of the USCC were more reserved and complacent than the more aggressive Sanitary Commission or state agents. As mentioned before, the duties the men encountered were either battleground, special relief/ field or hospital in focus. For example, one soldier wrote:

> One day I fell wounded. I dragged myself to a bush concealed from the enemy and I lay there. Night came on. I think I must have died before morning, if no help had

come. It grew very late, and there was no appearance of assistance. At last I heard a sound; there might be help in the distance. I tried to call out, but my voice was [too] weak; it went by a short way. A light came near to me. I summoned all my energies and raised my voice to its highest pitch. Directly I saw a lantern approaching. Soon a man's voice asked what was the matter?. I told him I was dreadfully wounded. He set the lantern down and started off for assistance.[34]

The person who had found the soldier was a member of the USCC doing his field work. He went back and retrieved a wagon to load the wounded soldier on. The soldier survived because of the USCC delegate's field work. After the incident, the soldier wrote, "I owe my life to them."

An example of the special relief given by the USCC could be seen when examining why delegates joined the USCC. Compassion for others was a consistent theme for the USCC representatives. More specifically, an awareness of a need and the amount of compassion involved was illustrated by the behavior of one USCC delegate on a train heading across Pennsylvania. A woman traveling with her frail, injured soldier husband who was leaning heavily upon her was noticed by a member of the USCC. The soldier appeared to be exhausted and could not sit alone. His wife had tears streaming down her face. The USCC delegate noticed the couple and engaged in conversation with the wife and asked if he could help. At first, he traded places with the wife to provide her with a bit of relief, and when they reached the next stop, he switched places again and got off the train. A few moments later, the representative returned with food and drink for the couple with hopes of reviving the soldier and his weary wife. The delegate stayed with the couple until they reached a point where their paths went in different directions. He again left the train and came back with tickets for the couple's belongings that he had checked on to their final destination. Then the delegate helped carry the weary and injured soldier over to the next train before saying farewell. People observing the incidents were deeply touched by the humble kindness that personified the image of the compassion for which the USCC stood.[35]

Another example was from a woman from Chicopee Falls, Massachusetts, who was on her way from Baltimore to Washington on board a steamer. In this instance, it was a delegate and his wife helping a soldier. According to the woman, the delegate on the boat made a point of speaking with everyone he could engage in conversation. He finally went below deck and found a very sick soldier who had not had any food for several days and was in a difficult condition. The delegate quickly enlisted his wife, who directed the steward on the boat to make some cracker gruel (like grits) from their limited personal supplies. She delivered the gruel to the ill soldier and the food was enough to sustain the soldier so he was able to walk off the boat when they docked.[36]

Another aspect of relief provided at City Point was a chapel and library or reading room near the hospital, as well as accommodation tents for the staff.

The facilities became the center of their community. The original chapel was thirty by twenty feet, with a canvas fly that went over the frame.[37] The USCC flag was flown over the structure so patients and other individuals would know where they were. However, the tent was also used for the wounded if need be. At times, the incoming wounded were so abundant in the USCC tent that identifying the soldiers who had just come in was difficult. The flexible housing was not uncommon when the battles began. The staff would vacate their tents during the day for the wounded and share the ground under tent awnings for sleeping quarters.[38]

After a short period of time, a wooden framed chapel with a tarred roof was built for the USCC at City Point for a quiet place to pray, dream, or just regroup and even learn to read. The relief it provided also became a blessing for individuals like Aunt Becky because it became a place to listen to prayers and singing so she might forget the sounds of the wounded.[39] Some of the soldiers "went to the CC library and read a while" and others talked with the chaplain that was on duty. The "dime novel" was created and satisfied immediate needs; however, most books were religious in nature and just as popular at the time. One excited soldier noted that he had found a copy of the popular book by Victor Hugo called *Les Misérables*.[40] Another officer, Captain Langdon, wrote to the USCC on behalf of his soldiers about their wish to read. He said that his soldiers were not beggars but books or reading material would help them pass the hours in the trenches because they could not get to the reading room. The captain said that at a previous location, the gentlemen and ladies affiliated with the USCC sent three boxes of reading materials. He asked for books and papers that they could read and pass from one to another. In response, the commission asked for materials from the public; it could be old or new, sent to USCC to get them to the troops. Further, books could be left at the local Savings Bank or the Commercial Bank for the Christian Commission.[41]

Relief also came in the hospital work that engaged both men and women. At the onset of the war, chaplains were on short supply, so various chaplains were recruited for the USCC to provide burial- related issues. When they were not preparing a sermon and had available time, they were allowed to move around to the various locations, seeking soldiers who needed spiritual assistance.

Men, such as delegate John Gerrigan from New Jersey, delegate D.C.H. Whitmore of Fitchburg, Massachusetts, Rev. A.L. Pratt of Bradford, Vermont, Rev. J.K. McLean of Framingham, Massachusetts, and Rev. S.L. Bowler of Orono, Maine, all served at City Point.[42] They combined special relief efforts with their hospital tasks. Serving as chaplains and delegates, they helped with burials, the incoming bloody hospital trains from the front and running the religious programs at the post. They also had difficult letters to write to critically wounded soldiers' families, explaining the injuries and probability of death.[43] One example of the difficulty involved a soldier who passed away around 1100 hours. By 1700 hours (five o'clock), the body had been removed and sent to the embalmer. At 2200 hours (ten o'clock) in the evening, as the delegate was writing difficult correspondence, there was a knock on his door. A man came in and asked about the soldier who had died. When the delegate asked why he wanted to know, the man at the door said he was the deceased soldier's brother and that he had brought the deceased man's wife with him. Upset over what to do, the brother only knew he could not tell the wife what had happened to her husband. The delegate remembered his obligation to the USCC and said to the brother, "our duty [i]s to see the wife and deliver to her the messages and tokens of dying love of her husband and speak the words of comfort in the name of the Lord."[44] For the chaplains and delegates it became an all too familiar task.

Working at City Point in public relations were chaplains and professional delegates such as Reverend B. Roberts of Rochester, New York,[45] and academic scholar Dr. Farnham of Syracuse, New York.[46] Others like "S.T." served as a special agent and wrote public relations information for the newspapers about the experiences of the commission. Special Agent J.M. Stevenson and five other delegates drove a four-horse wagon to the front filled with papers, books, and "delicacies" to distribute to the soldiers. Together their task was to get along with one another for the time they were there and remain focused on the general goal of the USCC.

Seeking other ways to preach and console soldiers, delegate John Gerrigan set up a schedule for prayer meetings on Wednesday and Sunday evenings. Saturday was filled with Bible classes, and on Friday he offered classes and general religious meetings to anyone who wanted to come. When the soldiers could not reach him at the post, he would try to get out to the units to speak and convert the soldiers.[47] Others tried to hold at least three prayer meetings each week and two or three services on Sunday and if possible a meeting every night.[48] Not only were the delegates to hold religious meetings, they were to establish good public relations in accordance with the tenets of the USCC.

The delegates had subtle and overt duties they were responsible for. In general, they were sent to military locations where they could establish friendly associations with the army officers. Reminiscent of the delegate on the train, they were to display kindness, courtesy, and respect to all the command members of the Army of the Potomac. When not setting up and delivering a sermon or passing out Bibles and religious tracts, the delegates were to visit with the soldiers and save their souls. However, one can see there was minimum opportunity for women's interaction other than cooking and occasionally singing at a church meeting.

In September of 1864, for example, the Philadelphia headquarters, sent "twenty-five delegates and two hundred and seven boxes of battle-field store, for the relief of the army"[49] with supplies to have been distributed between the "Special Relief" efforts and the "Hospital Delegates." Even though they were provided with supplies, most delegates found the magnitude of the destruction and reality of the war initially shocking. When returning on a hospital car, one male caregiver wrote about how his first experience changed his life:

> Imagine a car a little wider than the ordinary one, placed on springs, and having on each side three tiers of berths or cots, suspended by rubber bands. These cots are so arranged as to yield to the motion of the cars, thereby, avoiding the jolting experience even on the best kept roads. I didn't stop to investigate the plan of the car then, for I saw before me, on either hand, a long line of soldiers shot in almost every conceivable manner, their wounds fresh from the battle-field and all were patient and quiet; not a groan or complaint escaped them, though I saw some faces twisted into strange contortions with the agony of their wounds. I commenced distributing my oranges right and left but soon realized the smallness of my basket and the largeness of the demand, and sadly passed by all but the worst cases. In the third car that we entered we found the colonel, lieutenant-colonel and adjutant of the 28th Ohio, all severely wounded. We stopped and talked for a while. Mindful of the motto of the commission to give "aid and comfort," I tried a little sympathy on them, "Poor fellows!" "No indeed," said they. "We did suffer riding twenty miles"—it wouldn't have been over fourteen or fifteen, but a shattered limb or a ball in ones' side lengthens the miles astonishingly—"in those horrid ambulances to the cars." "We cried last night like children, some of us," said the lieutenant, "but we're all right now. This hospital train is a jolly thing. It goes like a cradle." Seeing my sympathy wasted, I tried another tack. "Did you know that Sherman was in Dalton?" "No!" cried the colonel, and all the men who could rose themselves up and stared at me with eager questioning eyes. "Is that so?" "Yes," I replied, "It is true." "Then I don't care for this little wound," said one fellow sapping his right leg, which was pierced and torn from a Minnie ball. Brave me! How I longed to take our whole North and pour out its wealth and luxury at their feet. A little further on in the car I chanced to look down on an eighteen or nineteen-year old; hair tossed back from his white brow; long brown lashes lying on his cheek; face as delicate and refined as a girl's. I spoke to him and he opened his eyes but could not answer me. I held an orange before him, and he looked a yes; so I cut a hole in it and squeezed some of the juice into his mouth. It seemed to revive him a little, after sitting a short time I left him. Soon after they carried him out on a stretcher—poor fellow. He was dying when I last saw him. And I could but think of his mother and sisters, who would have given worlds to stand beside him as I did. By this time it was growing dark, my oranges had given out, and we were sadly in the way; we left to be haunted many a day by the horrible pictures we had seen on our first visit to a hospital car.[50]

As a final task, the male delegates and chaplains came when a soldier died in the hospital. They were expected to serve as a witness of the death.[51] The promise of salvation for those in harm's way, who had not heard God's word or had lost their way, was foremost. When life failed, it was the male delegate who logged in the deceased information and facilitated the burial[52] with rough headboards marking the name and location of graves. Serving as chaplains, the USCC delegates covered the burials at the four large City Point cemeteries and corps hospitals. They also said prayers for bereaved friends and family when soldiers were interred. The task was to say prayers for the deceased while standing graveside before the soldiers fired a salute over the grave. The delegate remained a moment, while the order for "right face, forward march" was given.[53] With a brief pause, the delegate would move on to the next ceremony. This was a difficult task but one the chaplains and ministers shared because of their previous religious backgrounds. While at City Point, these men had a lot to manage both physically and emotionally.

Women's Roles with USCC

Like Miss Dix's requirement for the nurses, the USCC women needed to be almost nun-like in their deportment. Their limited time in service and religious mission required them to be subservient to the surgeon in charge, the greater heavenly power, and the internal organization of the units they served. Mrs. Wittenmyer noted, "Women who enter the service of the Christian Commission should be impelled by the highest and holiest motives—should be influenced wholly by love to God and humanity."[54]

One of the initial requirements for the Christian Commission women who were delegates was that the location they were sent to would provide them with at least one large kitchen, two storerooms and two sleeping areas. Although the delegates' quarters were in separate tents, they were generally clustered in the USCC designated area. However, male delegates would periodically be embedded with a unit while the women would be billeted next to or near a corps kitchen or facilities for other women.[55]

At City Point, the USCC faced the General Hospital. There were four levels or rows of facilities, starting with four buildings across the front. The reading room for the soldiers was on one end and the chapel on the other end. In between the reading room and chapel was a post office and workspace for the delegates and a storeroom separated by a pathway. In the second row, there were two large tents that could accommodate twenty-four beds with the office of the field agent and the office of the individual relief in between. Again, there was a separate pathway. Behind that row was the cooking tent, which was fifty feet by twenty feet in size. To the side of the cooking tent, the USCC had pitched a dining tent where individuals could sit down and have a meal.

The female delegates worked behind the cooking tent. They had a tent to sleep in and several tents that were nine feet in length for other accommodations and supplies. To the opposite side of the women's sleeping tent was the stable for their horses. When camps were initially set up, they pitched tents to accommodate the needs of the military and hospitals. As soon as reasonable, trees were cut down and rocks gathered for chimneys and the construction of log buildings began. Mrs. McKay noted that the USCC building had a large kitchen, storeroom, a reception room and then an area for sleeping quarters.[56]

Like the male delegates, the women who joined the USCC were generally from affluent homes and they were not paid for their service. They were not trained as nurses and had only basic household and healthcare abilities. Ill prepared for what they would be exposed to during their short stay, one female delegate noted, "What a sight met my eyes. I had seen soldiers many times, bright, well dressed, healthy looking soldiers, but ... this motley crowd on the wharf ... half clad, wan, neglected-looking creatures.... My heart died within me. I shrank back from all the sickening sights. Now I realized what my work was, and I broke down and cried like a woman, not an army nurse."[57] These Christian Commission women were almost always confined to a hospital environment, where they were respected and seen as patriotic ladies.[58] Technically, they were classified in two levels; either the more supervisory role of a matron, or the more hands-on role of a manager of the special diet kitchens.

Few actually considered themselves nurses even though they wore calico attire and spent time in the wards. Engaging the wounded required special inner strength and some had previous exposure to the plight of those less fortunate at home. At City Point, the scale was magnified. If and when the Christian Commission women worked in the wards, they were to always bring kind Christian words to those around them and speak with a positive consciousness regardless of the situation. On one occasion, one of the women saw two critically injured patients and knew they would not survive their wounds for very long. As she approached them, she asked what she might do for them and then added, "Poor boy, I hope you have learned to look toward your savior for comfort, for you need his love sorely." One of the soldiers replied he was a Catholic, so she opened the Bible she was carrying and read passages to him to try and comfort him. When she paused, he asked to have her write his name in the book, so he could take it with him. Before long the doctors and other nurses were bustling around his bed as she silently said another prayer and quietly walked away.[59] Among the duties needed was an innate ability to provide a touch of home to the patients, be it with a smile, delivery of food, a soft voice, a prayer, or even bringing simple flowers into the wards.

Like the other caregivers, the USCC recognized the comfort and value of correspondence to and from home. Letter-writing for a sick or wounded soldier was encouraged while working in a hospital. As an example, one dying soldier in 1864 asked the representative to write a letter home for him to his wife.

> My Dear Wife:
>
> I am sick—low with diarrhea; I don't expect to get well. But I feel that I am going to a better world, I feel prepared to die; and hope and trust and pray you will meet me in heaven. Bid farewell to Catherine and David for me. If you live to raise the children, raise them to the religion of the Bible. Religion seems more precious and

valuable to me now than ever before. If you choose, come and take my remains home. All is bright and clear. "My title is clear to mansions in the skies."
That God may abundantly bless you and the children is my prayer.

                        Farewell.
                        Your Affectionate husband.[60]

One difficulty for the women when in a ward was that they might have to sit on another soldier's bed to write letters for a wounded soldier if a chair was not convenient. Simple as the act might seem, the novice Christian Commission women first had to get authorization from a doctor to sit on a bed.[61] Justifiably, the doctors did not want a woman relocating an equally ill soldier or causing more pain and injury to a wounded soldier. The whole process consumed time and created awareness of the complexities in the wards.

The regimented USCC women had limited options for jobs and tasks but primarily were expected to serve in the kitchens. Their specific organizational rules permitted them to have a tea break and allowed visiting the wards only after the doctors had made their rounds. It was imperative to get along with everyone and respect the military command, especially the strict commands of the surgeons. They were never to question or doubt the surgeons' requests. The women serving with the Christian Commission had to keep a record book which was open to inspection at any time. In kitchen work, there was more red tape. They had to track weekly incidents and file monthly reports to Mrs. Wittenmyer. In addition, one of the requirements was that they were expected to attend prayer meetings in the evening and sing with the congregation regardless of how tired they were or how they felt.

Whether they were exhausted, ill, or distraught over the day's events, the stipulation of singing was used to reinforce thoughts of the soldiers' homes and invoke Sunday school lessons.[62] A woman's soft melodic voice was considered a soothing power or resource that others could engage in. Instruments were often difficult to locate in the war zone, but the human voice was always available and very desired. After the delegates held their meeting in the chapel or even in the wards, they would start by encouraging the soldiers to sing a prayer. Often when the women started singing the situation changed, and the pain of the day melted away. Reverend McCabe noticed that even when out in a forward area, the sound of a song such as "The Battle Hymn of the Republic" or the "Doxology" would float through the air and bring peace to the minds of those who heard it.[63] Most often, the songs that were familiar cast a fascinating spell over the soldiers. Songs that touched the heart of the sorrowing soldiers were represented by "Tenting on the Old Camp Ground," "Just Before the Battle," "When this Cruel War Is Over," and more heroic ones such as "The Battle Cry of Freedom," "Tramp, Tramp, Tramp," and "Marching Through Georgia."[64] Of course, the ever-popular songs like "Yankee Doodle" and "John Brown's Body" remained in constant demand. Classic songs were the "Battle Prayer," "The Girl

I Left Behind," "The Union Wagon," "Close His Eyes His Work Is Done," "Soldiers' Tears," "Mother Is the Battle Over,"[65] "Cottage of the Dear Ones Left at Home," and for fun, "I'm Going to Fight Mit Siegle."[66]

Mrs. Wittenmyer noticed that when one of her delegates had a good voice, the wounded were lifted by hearing a song. A surprise to some of the women was the reaction to a newer song that had grown in popularity during the war. The new song was called "Let Me Kiss Him for His Mother." It was very popular in the Army, especially when sung by the women of the commissions, and even more so when they could add a special emphasis to the line "Kiss me for my wife."[67] Those around the USCC area looked forward to the point in the day when singing would begin because it brought a release of the daily tensions and transported the singer and the listener to another time and place. The universal appeal of song was infectious, and once members started singing, they would sometimes hear cooks or the contrabands joining in while standing in the background.[68] The shared positive commonalities of singing and music was opposite a negative reality of dealing with the trauma of a war zone.

Trauma of the Situation

The battle-tested ladies who had served in multiple battle locations had developed a tough skin, but for the USCC women, this was often their first exposure to war, and it was shocking. Even the toughened nurses who had to deal with the magnitude of illness, injury and destruction had the added stress of operating under exacting military discipline. Women like Mrs. Holstein, a minister's wife, had no choice but to accept the sounds and sights and smells of the wounded versus the joy experienced when singing.[69] Throughout the year, the cannons could be heard by everyone in the area. With every battle, the incessant sounds of the incoming wagons brought more moans and groans, and when they heard excessive cannonading the women knew a difficult and sickening scene was about to begin. Another sound they heard that sent chills down their spines was the solemn drum rolls which indicated an execution was going to transpire.[70] In January, a large group of people walked or rode to a designated area and formed a three-sided square as Newel W. Root (aka George Harris) was shot for desertion. In March, deserters and bounty jumpers, such as William T. Griffin (aka George Bolter), were shot on the heights above the complex.[71]

This form of music bore a whole new meaning. The "whole mournful" death march was played by the band as the doomed man walked to the fatal spot and empty coffin.[72] The drum's consistent solemn tone found the women listening with a deep ache in their hearts for the moment when they heard the muskets fire and they then prayed for his soul. The former soldier who faced this fate received spiritual consultations from a chaplain before being executed, but the sound of the chilling drumroll for the women was difficult to forget. The trauma the members of the USCC observed and felt when they heard an execution was just as real as the magnitude of the wounded they observed, and left just as large an impression.

Feeling guilty about surviving so much disaster and death was a common struggle for the women. For the spiritually minded USCC women, this psychological struggle left them feeling guilty that they could not do more for the soldiers. For a nurse, the feeling of being burnt out and suffering from depression[73] was very real and sometimes the women were found crying because of the mournful sounds: "It seems almost sometimes as if I could not bear it any longer."[74] However, different from the other soldiers and women, members of the Christian Commission arrived with a benevolent feeling toward the enemy and a mindset that helped them focus on their task.

Tension among the different personalities and backgrounds of the delegates was typical of the tension between the two commission organizations. Conflict between the USCC and USSC did transpire, but the two groups generally stayed out of one another's way or politely invested in a more holistic attitude. One real point of contention, especially among the women, however, was when another kind of drumroll was played, indicating the arrival of mass casualties. With limited warning, hundreds of casualties poured in suddenly on wagon trains or rail cars and required immediate attention from everyone. Triage had a very different sequence for the organizational groups of women. Some women tried to wash the blood and grime off the wounded. State agents tried to get the soldier's name, rank, and unit. The women of the USCC felt compelled to pray with each solider before any other action was taken. This assortment of priorities in the moment of crisis caused problems. In reality, the benevolent USCC women were following orders stated in their contracts they originally signed. Their procedures, protocol, obligation, and chain of command had been carefully outlined. One specific clause discussed battlefield-related triage and stated, "If dying, point them with prayer to Jesus, and give them a Christian burial,"[75] validating and justifying their actions. Due to their benevolent role, it was not uncommon to have wounded incoming soldiers trust them with the few private possessions and money they had. The soldiers had full confidence that the Christian Commission personnel would see that their families were given the money or possessions should something happen to the soldiers.[76]

Fortunately, this benevolent attitude was enhanced by their willingness to help the contrabands. Coming from northern states that were more sympathetic to the plight of the escaped slaves, many of the Christian Commission delegates were willing to help the contrabands while at City Point. In February, one delegate wrote that there were schools for the colored troops and the men were very attentive but materials were limited,[77] so a request for a Bible and tracts was made. The USCC members were not alone in their sympathy towards the contraband soldiers. Many of the nurses shared this same feeling.

As part of his public relations campaign, a delegate known as S.D.T. wrote to make others aware of the Christian connection with the contrabands. He explained that there was a headquarters for the freedmen and that some of the corps had schools for them. In addition, he noted that at least three of the USCC delegates were acting as teachers and the students were very anxious to learn. "In only three weeks the contrabands could learn their Testaments." Other books published by the Tract Society offered the students a chance to perform simple writing. Delegate S.D.T. also used more amusing benevolent examples in his column to the citizens back home. He said, "A negro [soldier] the other day came in to have me write a letter for him. He had the night before, while out on picket, hailed a reb to exchange hardtack and tobacco with him. They met, and the rebel was his former master."[78] The letter-writing promoted a positive image about the usefulness of the USCC for the downtrodden. The campaign of benevolence was effective, and in April they received $1,000 from a Miss Blydenburg of Durham, New Hampshire, for "charitable and philanthropic purpose connected to the anti-slavery position."[79]

The Diet Kitchens

The women in the diet kitchens wore badges that looked like an open book or open Bible and they were generally sequestered within the kitchen domain. Occasionally, when the number of wounded was not too overwhelming, the women had free moments to interact with the soldiers. It was carefully stipulated to happen only after the rounds had been made. Most interactions with the men were related to food needs, but one non-food-related experience was when the women went into the wards to help make decorative paper ribbons ahead of President Lincoln arriving at City Point. Much to the soldiers' surprise and almost delight, when the president, Mrs. Lincoln, and several senators came through the wards, the paper banners were so low that the president's hat tore many of them to shreds.[80]

Mrs. Annie Wittenmyer was the matron in charge of the kitchens at City Point. She was deeply trusted by the soldiers and General Grant. However, she challenged officers and surgeons when she confidently offered a pragmatic perspective on nutritional healthcare. Like the battle-tested nurses, her knowledge came from her past experiences. She was deeply religious, so working with the USCC women in the diet kitchens was natural. Carefully crafting her vision, she parlayed her concepts into a powerful general superintendent role supported by Surgeon General Barnes and President Lincoln.[81] Mrs. Wittenmyer's organization and research helped establish a standard for the nutrition guideline of the diet kitchens throughout the war. Together, the members of the USCC formed a collective voice and this added to the uniqueness of the City Point complex.

Mrs. Annie Wittenmyer was both a prominent and dominant name at City Point and Point of Rocks. To add to the story of her achievements, here is some insight into her background. Born in 1827 in Sandy Spring, Ohio, Annie married a wealthy older man who made her life comfortable. In 1850, they moved to Keokuk, Iowa, where she opened a school for children who could not otherwise afford to attend school. Shortly thereafter, she opened a Sunday school and recruited others to help those in need with clothing donations and learning how to read and write. When the war started, she worked with the Soldier's Aid Society and eventually became a state agent for Iowa as well as being in charge of the diet kitchens. She commanded the response of military and lay people alike, and the normally headstrong surgeons learned to listen to her.[82] In 1862, she received a special general pass from Secretary of War Stanton.

> Order Number 362 from the War Department. Permission to visit the United States General Hospitals within the lines of the several Military Departments of the United Stated, for the purpose of superintending the preparation of food in the Special Diet Kitchens of the same, is hereby granted to Mrs. Annie Wittenmyer, Special Agent of the United States Christian Commission, and such ladies as she may deem proper to employ, by request of the United States surgeons. The Quartermasters' Department will furnish the necessary transportation.[83]

Coming into the war with this administrative background, Mrs. Wittenmyer offered organized structure that many of the surgeons lacked. When she first arrived at the new Point of Rocks camp, she was disgusted with what she saw. Pots and kettles were black from overuse and lack of cleaning. Food was at best bland or what might be termed "mystery meat." The servings were poured into cups that had been dragged from battle to battle and some men grew ill from thinking about what they had to eat. Convinced of her own abilities and knowing she had backers, she confronted the surgeon in charge. When he asked her how she liked his facilities, she told him how awful they were. Furthermore, she said she could have it all turned around in just a week. The challenge was accepted by the surgeon and the race was on.

As stated earlier, Mrs. Wittenmyer immediately got in touch with the chairman of USCC in Philadelphia with a list of supplies and the equipment she needed. She then sent a telegraph to her two most trusted friends, Mrs. Jones and Miss Noyes, and told them to come to the area. By the time they arrived, the kitchen had almost completely been transformed, a change which also included teaching the help how to use the new supplies and equipment. The women began serving better-tasting, nutritious food, much to the surprise and delight of the soldiers. Shortly thereafter, Mrs. Grant heard about the transformation and began sharing these stories with her husband. To put the transformation rumors to rest, General Grant decided he would make his own inspection. The general and two aides took off their military uniforms and put on civilian clothes and slouch hats and went to the new kitchen. They were shocked at the efficiency and surprised at the quality of the food. General Grant noted that even his food was not of the same quality. He returned to City Point and within a short span of time the USCC kitchen at City Point was also offering the quality fare he had experienced under Mrs. Wittenmyer.

Diet kitchen duties required organizational skill and strict adherence to the surgeon's rules, but the many short-term responsibilities required other skills. As an independent nurse, Miss Cornelia Hancock wrote to her mother about her negative feeling regarding the Commission. Not understanding the rules and regulations of the Christian Commission, Cornelia felt the USCC was not well organized and did things in a sporadic manner.[84] However, Cornelia thought the USCC offered a better service to the incoming wounded right after a battle. When the boat whistle would call them forward and it was not the case of mass causalities approaching, the caregivers would go out with milk punch for the soldiers and hot coffee. The women of the Christian Commission also offered tea and hot toast.

Two women who worked in Mrs. Wittenmyer's kitchens at City Point were Mrs. Ella Cole, of Medway, Massachusetts, and Miss Jennie Pitkins, of Hartford, Connecticut. Although little is known about them, they personified the rules and regulations established by the USCC. By experience, Mrs. Cole had been with USCC diet kitchens in a previous location so she probably was the matron in charge, while Miss Pitkins was most likely the manager of the kitchen. They had seven white soldiers and three contrabands at their disposal to do the actual cooking.[85] Mrs. Fannie Hazen, from Cambridge, Massachusetts, was another USCC member who also worked in the diet kitchens and provided any assistance she could within the rules and regulations,[86] but the limitations sometimes frustrated her. There were other related duties not fully described nor always approved that an occasional USCC lady might find herself doing. According to Miss Bucklin, "One woman employed by the USCC, took a team [and wagon] and scoured the country round for solid things which only a farmer usually possesses in plenty (fowl, eggs, milk and butter)."[87] Although food produced from the kitchen was edible, fresh food made life even better.

City Point did maintain a large military bakery and the bread that it provided was a staple for the Union forces. One favorite trick was to send the smell of fresh bread into the ranks of the enemy who were sometimes a short distance away. As a result of this large facility, the women of the CC did not have to worry about bread shortages. Coffee, tea, milk punch, lemonade and crackers were other familiar items supplied by the military, but there were many food combinations the soldier cooks did not consider. The women in the diet kitchens tried to communicate new recipes and better combinations to the soldier

6. Women of the United States Christian Commission (USCC)

cooks. Educating the cooks on how to make something new on a mass scale was always a challenge. The complex issue of no longer using family proportions became an experiment for the diet kitchen managers. What follows are some examples from Mrs. Wittenmyer's recipe book:

Coffee
Have the water boiling, and just before the coffee is to be served, add one pound of ground coffee to every gallon of water: stir well, and boil briskly for fifteen minutes; set the kettle off the stove, pour into a pint of cold water, and allow to settle. Sugar and milk to suit taste. When eggs can be obtained, one egg to each pint of ground coffee, beaten and stirred in, will make the coffee very clear.[88]

CSA Substitute for Coffee
Take sound ripe acorns, wash them while in the shell, dry them, and parch until they open, take the shell off, roast with a little bacon fat, and you will have a splendid cup of coffee.

Beef Tea
Mince four pounds beef very fine, and pour over it one pint of water. Boil it hard for five minutes, skim the mixture well and pour it through a colander. When perfectly cold, strain the liquid and season the liquid with salt.

Apple Pie
Cover the bottom of your pudding pan with a crust as made below; add a single layer of pared sliced apples, with sufficient sugar to sweeten, and add a little lemon. Alternate the layers until the pan is full; bake in a moderate heat and serve with a sauce.

Crust
Pare and boil and thoroughly mash a sufficient quantity of Irish potatoes. To every two pounds of potatoes add one spoonful of sweet butter or lard, a little salt and enough flour to make a dough, which can be handled and used as ordinary pie crust. When potatoes cannot be obtained, well boiled rice, thoroughly crushed and made into a paste, with butter and flour added, will be found as an excellent substitute, and is very nice for drop dumplings.[89]

Just over the line the Confederates made another form of apple pie.

CSA Apple Pie Without Apples
To one small bowl of crackers, that have been soaked until no hard parts remain, add one teaspoonful of tartaric acid, sweeten to your taste, add some butter, and a very little nutmeg.

While their crust was made with potatoes as well, it lacked a few items.

Boil six good-sized mealy potatoes, and mash them fine, add salt, a spoonful of butter, and two of water, while they are hot, then work in flour enough for making a paste to roll out, or put in two or three spoonfuls of cream, and no butter or water. This is a good crust for hot pies or dumplings.

Oysters Fritters
Thicken two quarts of milk or water with sifted flour. So as to make a tolerably think paste; add a little salt, and half teaspoon of soda, dissolved in a cup of sour milk; add

four eggs well beaten. To each quart of batter, add one pint of oysters, and some salt and pepper. Bake on a hot griddle, greased with butter.[90]

CSA Oyster Fritters

Take young green corn, grate it in a dish; to one pint of this add one egg, well beaten, a small teacup of flour, two or three tablespoonsful of butter, some salt and pepper, mix them all together.

Florence Nightingale was a strong advocate on the beneficial value of milk on the sick or wounded soldiers. "Milk and the preparations from the milk are the most important articles of food for the sick."[91] As a result, Annie Wittenmyer promoted the same belief and milk punch was often served in the hospitals.

Milk Punch

Beat an egg until very light: stir into a pint of milk; add brandy, sugar, and nutmeg.

There was always a chicken cooking someplace on the hospital complex— food for the soul. Of course, the chicken may not have always been legally acquired.

Aunt Becky had a favorite member of the USCC who always said, "Blessing on You,"[92] and he became a favorite delegate among the nurses and women in the area due to his attitude toward the wounded and those in need. The Christian Commission may not have always had a pot boiling with a chicken in it, but they had tins of chicken and crackers. When the "blessing on you" contributions or extra food were shared with a meal of chicken and crackers, the soldiers felt doubly blessed. At other times, the USCC members were considered a blessing when they provided coffee, crackers and bologna sausages to the weary staff who had labored for hours on end.

There were also special times when the USCC kitchens used tins of ham for meals. One nurse had been promised a tin of ham for her soldiers but found the hams were still on a barge. Realizing the disappointment of not having ham to eat and not wanting to break a promise to her soldiers, one of the CC members went on board the barge to get a ham. The diet kitchen cooked the ham and then sliced it and brought a plate of ham with crackers for the nurses and soldiers.[93]

However, as controlled in their rigid duties as the diet kitchen women were, they were all still just human beings and they sometimes found a decision made by others to not be wise and sometimes even dangerous. For instance, on January 14, a party of friends, including some of the members of the USCC, went on a ride to Dutch Gap. They crossed on a pontoon bridge and drove about six miles up the James River to Aiken's Landing. After lunch they boarded a small steam "torpedo-boat" and headed to the gap, running the "gauntlet of the guns of the Howlett's House battery and the sharp shooters waiting along the banks." When they got to the Gap, they walked about and

6. Women of the United States Christian Commission (USCC)   91

then boarded the small boat again. They returned without being fired upon but they realized how lucky they were for not taking fire[94] because several members of the Sanitary Commission had been fired upon and several people had been killed on a similar voyage.[95]

Together, all the benevolent and self-sacrificing men and woman of the USCC worked at City Point to make a difference in the lives of the soldiers and the staff aiding the soldiers. They may have only been there for a short period of time and they may not have been appreciated by everyone, especially for their focus and rules. But their contribution was important. Regardless of their roles, they added significantly to the supplies and equipment and morale that was life at City Point.[96]

7

Women of the United States Sanitary Commission (USSC)
The Art of Networking

There is considerable information about the United States Sanitary Commission (USSC), but many may not realize the organization served both the Union and the Confederacy. Most of the work of the Sanitary Commission, however, was with the Union military or in the Union states. The following information is a bit of a bypass but will help explain the very different roles of the Christian Commission and Sanitary Commission staff members while at City Point.

Like a well-organized machine and the nascent American Red Cross, the USSC was known for their members' ability to motivate people and organize communities. Imagine the concept of a supply train. The USSC and the USCC worked closely on one end of the community while the state agents were more concerned with the technical supply end while at the front. Although any woman seen in the wards was dubbed a "nurse," the role of the Sanitary women was quite different from the other women working at City Point and very different from the limited Christian Commission (USCC) women's roles. The geographic location of City Point made the facility one of the larger depots for USSC supplies and materials. As opposed to the male-dominated Christian Commission, the Sanitary Commission had both men and women working at various locations, specifically in the supply and relief departments. Although they might occasionally cross paths, the USSC men and the women had different job-related tasks. Ironically, the hierarchy of the organization was all men, yet the seal of the USSC used a personification of a female caregiver. This mixed message provides some insight into the internal problems of the organization and why it started to change from the onset of the war.

At the onset of the war, the Sanitary Commission had a lot to learn, but by 1864 and 1865 they had honed their business into an effective machine that

7. Women of the United States Sanitary Commission (USSC) 93

coordinated military movements with the kind donations from many men and women, primarily from the union states. Dubbed by some as the "inseparable branch of the Army"[1] or Lincoln's Fifth Wheel,[2] the development of the complex organization is a fascinating story all unto itself. Several sources explain and elaborate on the diversity of the USSC, such as *Civil War Sisterhood* by J.A. Giesberg[3] and *Defending the Union* by J.T. Censer[4] or older resources such as the *United States Sanitary Commission Compiled from Documents and Private Papers* of 1863, or *Hospital Life in the Army of the Potomac* by W.H. Reed,[5] along with various collections in historical societies, such as the New York Public Library and the Open Library. Regardless of the resource, most readers and researchers would concur that the USSC grew from the merger with the Women's Central Association, various relief organizations, and the early male-based Sanitary Commission. The origins were in 1861 when Dr. Bellows established the USSC as an organization designed to alleviate the ignorance of maintaining health and to develop a sense of discipline within the disaster of war. Frederick Olmstead was their first CEO, but many "branch women" ran the logistical supply organizations around the Union and gave the women a sense of voice.

The USSC was an interesting blend of personalities and was not as regulated as the Christian Commission. First, it had a large aggregated national organization as opposed to the often locally focused religious groups. The representatives were not short-term volunteers like the Christian Commission ones were, but were salaried employees, earning between fifty to one hundred dollars a month. Members wore multiple hats, shifting gears from one group to another as the need required and even working as nurses if need be. This led to some confusion of roles and responsibilities. The structure of the organization allowed for skillful networking to accomplish a task while the members were serving at City Point. However, outsiders were often confused who was with what organization. As an illustration there were logistical supply anxieties, such as transportation of soldiers to and from the hospitals, and the USSC stepped in to assist. Also, several very determined women would arrange to get soldiers back pay from the military in those cases.

Logistics and Supplies

The USSC had large depots in Boston; New York; Philadelphia; Frederick and Annapolis, Maryland; Harpers Ferry; Chicago; and Louisville. Depots were also in New Bern, Beaufort, New Orleans, and City Point. The smaller aid or relief societies would gather materials and send supplies on to the depots that served as gathering points. The Commission worked with the community liaisons, shipping materials where they were needed.

A chaotic beginning at the start of the war evolved into an organized and powerful socio-political machine that offered a feeling of home that was not a priority for the government. Hackett wrote about the "home connection" regarding such useful items as notes that conveyed a message: "Blankets, shirts, and other gifts sent to the Sanitary Commission for the soldiers, show the thought and feeling of home." Or, "This blanket was carried by Milly Aldrich (who is ninety-three years old), down hill and up hill, one and a half miles, to be given to a soldier." A demonstrative connection pinned on a bed quilt: "My son is in the Army. Whoever is made for this warm quilt, which I have worked on for six days and the greater part of six nights, let him remember his own mother's love." Yet another note on a pair of socks said, "These stockings were knit by a little girl five years old, and she is going to knit some more, for her mother says it will help some poor soldier."[6]

The public relations touch of home offered an opportunity to connect citizens across the country and allowed them to bond with the soldiers who had left their homes, regardless of the side they represented. Citizens in one part of the country had limited knowledge of other parts of the country, so upon request the USSC offered information about a location. As the weather progressed into winter, requests for wool socks and wool mittens increased. Although a perception might be that Virginia was warmer than New England, the citizens needed regular reminders that their soldiers were often without adequate clothing and that soldiers could not make their own cold weather items. It was imperative that the soldiers receive the home front's assistance, and good public relations helped.

When the USSC vocalized the soldiers' specific needs, they knew that it emotionally connected civilians with the military and the Sanitary Commission openly recruited communities to give all they could. The Commission then coordinated the shipping of the items to locations where there were specific needs from representatives in the field, military requests, or knowledge of general need. In a subtly competitive manner, the newspapers listed what various organizations and communities were sending the USSC. As an illustration, in Bridgeport, Connecticut, on June 10, 1864, the local Ladies' Aid Society sent to Philadelphia depot:

> 38 pairs of slippers; 6 pounds of lint; 1 dressing gown; 8 handkerchiefs; 12 pillow ticks; 5 shirts; 3 pair of drawers; 2 pounds of slippery elm; 2 pounds of ground flaxseed; 4 bottles of current and 3 bottles of quince jelly; 2 cans of preserved quince; 2 quarts of bay rum, and 2 quarts of spirit of camphor; 7 papers of corn starch; 6 pounds of ginger snaps; 14 pounds of dried apples; 10 pounds of dried blackberries; 4 pounds of prunes; 2 dozen lemons; 2 bottles of pickles; 1 package of old linens; cotton; and bandages.[7]

In just a few short weeks, another request was posted in the Bridgeport paper for the "comfort for the soldiers" asking that children help with the drying and preserving of fruits. The premise was that every child was old enough to gather or pick fruit and was encouraged to do so for the wounded hospital patients. The child's parents or housekeepers were then encouraged to put up the fruit in a transportable way, such as canning or drying it. In a "call for citizens," all who were available to help were enlisted to participate in the task.[8] The cost of the sugar and the transportation was often covered by the local Ladies' Aid Society, but individuals were needed to put up the fruit. When a sufficient quantity was gathered, a major collection group such as the USSC was called in to coordinate the storage and delivery.[9] Another example was a call to make currant syrup, so cooking and drying instructions for currants was published in the newspaper.[10] The article stated that citizens could also use cherries and blackberries if they did not have currants, and advised the citizens that syrups or preserves would be appreciated for the invalids. Localities were encouraged to send local fruits. Closer to Virginia, blackberries were readily available so the USSC: "Appeal to the good people of your state to secure as nearly as possible every remaining blackberry for hospital use."[11] Furthermore, the USSC, working with Ladies' Aid Societies, advised people how to put the fruit up and how to pack it for shipping. Brandy and cordials were particularly needed. Understanding that all economic levels of society were being touched by the war, recipes were included "because people generally are not supposed to know so well how to make it."[12] Once more, these items were uniting the touch of home with the solider fighting the war. As mentioned before, the items were sent to depots around the area, and City Point happened to be one of the larger depots for goods and services with the Army of the Potomac. Along with the supplies came additional help in the way of doctors and nurses[13] to the large facility.

One critical aspect of the Sanitary Commission was the fundraising arm. This provided revenue while also creating public awareness in the local communities. One group might arrange a dancing party,[14] but more often communities arranged Sanitary Fairs in the large cities like New York, Philadelphia, and Chicago, raising thousands of dollars to support the procurement of supplies for the military. The Sanitary Commission also provided needed cash for transportation home for some soldiers or a family member. Raising money became a creative and efficient skill. At the Brooklyn/Long Island fair, for example, the community published a paper called *The Drum Beat* to help raise money. The paper was professionally illustrated and edited with works of popular artists, authors, and poets.[15] Often staffed by prominent social do-gooders in the community, local fairs allowed individuals to donate or purchase items and feel as though they had helped maintain the coffers of the Commission for the benefit of the soldiers and had brought awareness to local residents.

According to USSC representative William Howell Reed, at City Point there were houses, sutlers shops, markets, clothing shops, shanties, saloons, hotels and places to get ambrotype pictures taken. The location also had commissaries as well as old plantation type homes, chapels, and many tents and log cabins. On post, the military had constructed facilities such as a wash house, bakeries, and organization housing groups.[16] The location of City Point offered many services to the military and in turn, City Point had many diverse individuals who frequented the area. As sophisticated as the description of City Point sounds, it was another reality when visitors appeared on the scene. Often, they found no protection from the weather, no accommodations other than the open wharf or riverbank to sleep on, and food that was excessively priced at one dollar for "undrinkable coffee and some uneatable ham and eggs."[17] Some visitors were satisfied with these conditions but others were not. The viewpoint was totally in the eye of the beholder.

At City Point, the USSC Relief Department had a designated reading room on Agency Row for recovering, sick, or wounded soldiers who could walk to the cabin. In the room, the men could read a book or newspaper and had paper and pencils or maybe a pen to write a letter home to their family. When the soldiers could not afford postage for their letters home the USSC frequently provided the means to send a letter.[18]

The USSC also provided a skilled representative who, like the more powerful state agent, would help with back pay or family coordination concerns, plus they had transport boats and in-ward assistance. These tasks could be done by either a man or a woman. When the representatives went through the wards to see soldiers who could not get up and walk to the reading room, they always took paper and pencils to hand out to the soldiers, and a few had some small change such as a nickel to give to soldiers who had lost everything, just to make them feel more secure.[19] The connective bridge the Sanitary Commission members provided with home was priceless.

> Occupation is a great thing, and quite as important to the tone and heart of an army as hard bread and bacon ... would you believe ... that many poor fellow in this army ... has literally died to go home: died of the terrible, unsatisfied longing, homesickness. That it lies at the heart of many diseases bearing a learned name.... It is languor, debility, low fever, loss of appetite, sleeplessness, death; and yet through the sadness of it all they call Nostalgia. The loved ones at home have something to answer for in this business.... And it pains me to think that one man has let his life slip out of grasp, too weak to hold it, just because his dearest friends did not send him a prescription once a week—the price of a three cent stamp—a letter from home.[20]

Not only did the USSC try to help with postage and back or missing pay, but they also established and maintained good public relationships. Good relationships between the USSC and the military reaffirmed the organization's usefulness not only to the soldiers but to families back home. Public relations fell to Mr. J.R. Hamilton, who wrote for the newspapers on a regular basis and dispelled myths and rumors with every story. Another aspect that involved public relations was an issue concerning pensions and bounties. Under the umbrella of the Special Relief Department, the Sanitary Commission agents were prepared to help guard, shelter, and feed the sick, discharged, and disabled when they were in trouble.²¹ This of course required significant knowledge of who was in charge of what area and what was the best way to gain access to needed records or endorsements. To aid in the process, a small guide given to many soldiers called "The Soldier's Friend" offered ten precise points and provided structure for what was to be done in order to get assistance.

> **First:** To provide the sick men of the newly arrived regiments medicine, food, and care, as impossible for them to receive in the midst of the confusion....
> **Second:** To furnish suitable food, lodging, care, and assistance to men who are honorably discharged ... who are delayed in obtaining their pay.
> **Third:** To communicate with distant regiments on behalf of discharged men, whose disabilities or descriptive list, on which to draw pay, proves to be defective....
> **Fourth:** To act as the unpaid agent or attorney of the discharged soldiers who are too feeble or too utterly disabled to present their own claims at the Paymasters office.
> **Fifth:** To look into the condition of discharged men who assume to be without means to pay expenses of going to their homes....
> **Sixth:** To secure disabled soldiers railroad tickets at reduced rates, and through an agent at the railroad station, to see that these men are not robbed or imposed upon by sharpers.
> **Seventh:** To see that all men who are discharged and paid off do at once leave the city for their homes [to rescue them from evil companions].
> **Eighth:** To make them reasonably clean and comfortable, before they leave the city, such discharged men as are deficient in cleanliness and clothes.
> **Ninth:** To prepare to meet, at once with food or other aid, such as immediate necessities as arise when sick men arrive in the city....
> **Tenth:** To keep a watchful eye on all soldiers who are out of the hospitals, yet not in service, and give information to proper authorities, of such soldier as seem endeavoring to avoid duty or to desert from ranks.²²

Like any large organization, a structured and systematic approach to helping the soldier required basic recordkeeping, like name, rank, company, and regiment. In addition, any issue concerning back pay or monies drew unscrupulous individuals who were willing to "help" an unsuspecting soldier. Dubbed as villainous and "vicious," newspapers warned soldiers and citizens about being approached by such individuals.²³ At City Point, both men and women developed strong life skills as they worked with soldiers needing assistance. Furthermore, the USSC provided these services at no charge. As one can imagine in a situation of a vulnerable and sometimes confused soldier, illegal opportunities abounded and there were many hucksters and unscrupulous persons offering to help for a fee. Part of the ongoing public relations battle that the USSC fought was to convey the legitimacy of the Commission and the services they offered. One such example was a widow who was to receive her husband's bounty of one hundred dollars. She employed "an agent" (presumably from the Sanitary Commission) to obtain the money. The agent charged for every crossing of the river, charged to speak with her, charged for making the forms, charged for going to the Post Office, etc., until most of the bounty money was used. In reality, the agent was not a member of the USSC, but a scam artist. Another incident was when a soldier at Libby Prison in Richmond asked "an agent" to collect his pay. When the soldier finally received his pay, he had only thirty-eight dollars left of two hundred dollars.[24]

"The Soldier's Friend" guide was published in the *Sanitary Commission Bulletin* that was designed to unite many of the well-meaning health and welfare groups around the country. The *Bulletin* provided news about which agencies were sending supplies to the USSC and provided news from various locations. In 1864, just a few weeks apart:

> The steamer *Elizabeth* ... sailed from Philadelphia for City Point, VA with luxuries and necessaries for the soldiers from our Sanitary Commission. The cargo was valued at $45,000. The steamer has been in the service of the Commission for a long time.[25]

Returning to Philadelphia to resupply and head south again:

> The steamer *Elizabeth*, Captain Fowler, sailed from Philadelphia for City Point, with luxuries and necessaries for the soldiers from the Sanitary Commission. The cargo was valued at $25,000. The steamer has been in service of the commission for a long time.[26]

Not only did the *Bulletin* provide shipping information, but also it ran ads for services the soldiers might need on products such as prosthetics, insurance companies, and even poetry that could be recited and shared with others. The *Bulletin* was another connective thread from home for the small-business advertisers, their communities, and the readers.

As in any war, the USSC had supporters as well as detractors. W.H. Gay wrote about the nurses to his cousin Elizabeth in 1864. "I think you would wish yourself home again, not because you would not like it here. I think you would, but you must have very strong nerves if you could nurse in the hospital. To see suffering and dying of the wounded and mangled soldiers, it is hard to see them, although they are well taken care of as well as circumstances will admit."[27] Some, such as T.L. Seip, were more specific and posted their confirmation of the Sanitary Commission in the *Bulletin* by stating that the Commission had already helped the soldiers and "many lives had doubtless been saved by its operation, and untold misery alleviated."[28] There were those less pleased with the Commission's work. One such person noted, "Only doctors and Officers benefit[ed] from the commission supplies and ... the poor soldiers had to pay for items they received from the commission."[29]

Building Connections

Female USSC representatives were at their core still simply women. As a result of the cultural and gender biases of the time, they had a difficult political job, walking the line of a military taskmaster. Each corps had their own population of soldiers to protect. Each representative had to know what was going on with the units, who was missing what, and then how to best resolve the problem. The government and independent nurses, matrons, and doctors had very strong personal feelings about the USSC. Some loved the USSC, and some did not, but many gratefully accepted food and donations from both the USCC and the USSC to supplement what the government offered. City Point was a large depot, so when supplies arrived, the Sanitary Commission personnel had to write a letter of confirmation and gratitude to those who had sent the items regardless of the size. This took time but also provided the representatives the opportunity to sit in the reading room, where they were visible and could practice their public relations skills.

Being visible also meant soldiers and citizens could witness them going about their work. It was not uncommon for the Sanitary Commission women to directly ride out to the units to speak with the soldiers. As a Commission representative, she would have to arrange for a wagon or a horse like a state agent might do. If she rode a horse, she would try and locate a sidesaddle because proper women did not ride astride. Using a wagon required a driver. This logistical arrangement was easier than procuring a sidesaddle, plus they could carry more supplies, so the wagon was the most common mode of transportation.

Mr. Gay of the USSC in 2nd Corps talked about how he went "every other day to the hospital to distribute tobacco, pipes, writing material, needle and thread and helps write letter for the sick and wounded." In a letter to his female cousin, he suggested that if she wanted to do something for the war, she should consider becoming a nurse. He indicated a toughness was needed when working with the wounded and dying. He also insinuated that she should be able to ride well. He told about a woman in 2nd Corps nicknamed "Intrepid" because this lady rode "all over" helping the soldiers, and she was not afraid of the bullets "flying around [her] like bees."[30]

Dangers of having a horse or wagon get loose also needed to be considered, because horses bolting from fear was always a possibility. Danger of being shot and wounded was also always a worry. Rank and role offered no protection and the war zone dangers were indiscriminate. As an illustration, general superintendent of the USSC, Mr. Fay of Chelsea, was injured along with state agent Mrs. Spencer, when a Confederate bomb exploded on the wharf at City Point.[31]

On another note are the stories about various boating trips. One day a party of women in the hospital was invited, with several surgeons, to take a trip up the James River in the USSC boat. Everything was organized for promptness but the procrastination of one of the women caused all to be detained; when at length the women reached the wharf, there was only time to see the boat slowly steaming on its way with not more than eight or ten of the invited party on board. Disappointed and sadly vexed, they retraced their steps.[32]

Then there was a day the USSC staff took Aunt Becky out for a ride on one of the sailboats instead of going for a ride with horse and wagon. The change of atmosphere provided by the USSC was greatly appreciated by Aunt Becky. Good public relations experiences were always on the Commission's mind. However, danger prevailed. On another occasion, a "few ladies and USSC officers left at 1400 on a tugboat *Grover* so they could rest from their daily duties."[33] The group had decided to ride down to the Division Hospital where they had been invited by the USSC agents to sail on the river. The gesture was not uncommon, and Aunt Becky understood the opportunity was a moment of stolen "personal" time. For the women, it was delightful to be away from the wards and the soldiers who needed their constant attention. During the euphoric excitement of the ride, the group got too close to the guerrillas and a Mr. Wilson was shot and lived only a short time. The women on board were very excited to the point of near panic but survived the incident.[34]

On August 5, the USSC asked another group of women if they wanted to ride the supply boat up toward Richmond to Deep Bottom. The casual outing was on the *Sarah Brown* and came with a gunboat for protection. Their destination was another gunboat that blockaded the James River but was close enough for the passengers to see the outskirts of Richmond. The group passed the second gunboat without a problem just before the rebels fired thirteen rapid shots. The shots missed hitting almost everyone but did hit the boat. Second Engineer Hamlin of Brooklyn, New York, was killed outright. Mrs. Mayhew and Mary and Sarah Shaw were nearly hit and very frightened. Danger in the war zone had many ways of touching those who were there. Being very vigilant and observant were new life skill the women learned very quickly.

Transports

There were two distinct types of transports the USSC operated when it came to moving the wounded. First were the hospital transports that moved up and down the waterways. The boats ran to northern facilities and returned to City Point. The second was the improved railroad car used to bring soldiers in from the front. The railroad cars were quicker and less jarring than wagons.

Hospital Transports

As previous mentioned in the independent nurses chapter, USSC women worked on steamer transports like the *Connecticut* and *State of Maine*. These women were part of the "floating hospital nurses." The supply and transports boats were part of the USSC operations generally travelling to and from City

7. Women of the United States Sanitary Commission (USSC)

Point to Washington, Annapolis, Baltimore, and New York. By 1864, the boats had been reconfigured to accommodate wounded soldiers being sent north to various hospitals. Even with reconfiguration, there were problems, such as the rocking motion that made some people seasick, and snipers who often tried to pick off individuals on an open deck. Particularly difficult was that there was no way of compensating for the perils of winter when the boats faced the possibility of being damaged by the ice on the rivers.[35] With inclement weather, the boats could become disabled and could find themselves taking on water or running aground in Rebel territory. Making it onto a transport did not always mean the soldiers had reached safety.

The women who helped on the boats were hard-working and committed to caregiving. Although they provided liquids and some easily digestible food along with basic nursing, this was often under difficult conditions. In some instances, the wounded came straight from the field while others came from the hospital wards. However, the more difficult part of hospital transport work was being awakened in the dead of night when the steam whistle blew, waking the women and alerting everyone that life was about to be filled with chaos.

Transport ships were also used for prisoners who had been released from Libby Prison in Richmond and reached City Point via flag-of-truce boat. At City Point, the sick and wounded were triaged and when possible reloaded on a transport headed north to Annapolis or New York. Not everyone survived. For example, in January on one transport, two deaths were reported, while on another transport, four deaths were recorded. For some of those in critical condition, death was inevitable, so the women discreetly pulled a cloth over the deceased soldier's face when he expired.

One transported soldier said when he went on board, the beds were nicely made by the Woman's Council in Boston and "clean socks and a shirt laid out for me." The woman in charge asked if he wanted some soup or mild stimulants but all he wanted to do was wash and change his shirt because it was so dirty. The woman did not flinch at his filth but kindly said she would return with some soup and clean clothes that had come from a kind mother and sister back home.[36]

For large numbers of wounded, the USSC and sometimes the Christian Commission helped at the docks by providing feeding stations. Once the wounded were on board the transports it was the women's tasks to do the best they could for the soldiers and try to meet their needs. All of the women had multiple jobs. In a moment of necessity, the "nurse" helping the sick and wounded could have been a state agent traveling north, not a nurse. It should be noted that transports and ships had been coming to City Point even before the war, creating a strategic factor during the conflict. The James River allowed for oceangoing vessels to sail into the City Point docks to deliver their wares.

With such diverse traffic, crude gestures, jokes, and ungentlemanly behavior from soldiers and officers made it difficult for the women who were serving as legitimate nurses on the boats. Men, thinking about the strumpets offshore, would make wrongheaded assumptions about women on the transports. This often became a challenge to the women as they were trying to prove themselves legitimate in the war effort.

Some of the committed USSC women were Mrs. Fogg from Maine on the *Louisville*, her friend Mrs. Harris from Pennsylvania, and Miss Rebecca Gray on the *Vanderbilt*. There were also Miss Sharpless, Mrs. Case and Mrs. Hood on the *Connecticut*. As rosy as some of the soldiers' impressions were of the noble efforts of the female workers, the women sometimes had another experience entirely. Their stories frequently explain how they worked in difficult conditions. The difficulties would start when they checked in on the smelly, sick, disgustingly dirty, and very weak men. When they tried to give the wounded food or fluids on the decks, the rocking of the boats made feeding the soldiers exceedingly difficult. Being occasionally seasick themselves made feeding the outgoing men even worse. As previously indicated, the worst part was being awakened in the dead of night by the steam whistle, which meant mass incoming. When the boats arrived with injured, "the drum calls the stretcher bearers to fall into line and all who could appear at the landing" did so.[37]

When the women showed up at the dock, there were often men moving towards the transports while others were being unloaded from the transports. For the outgoing soldiers, several of the women stood in line and checked the men in. Each stretcher put on board required a name and home address from those who could speak. Someone numbered and stacked their knapsacks in piles. Their form of basic triage allowed for some men to be kept on deck while others who could stand the jostling movement were then lowered on their stretchers by ropes and pullies into the lower levels.[38] Loading of the wounded could take place at any time of day or night, especially when there were mass casualties. Depending on the location, weather conditions and time of day, some women held lanterns while the wounded were brought on board.[39] This was taxing work under normal conditions but more difficult during miserable weather conditions. At City Point the problem was often how to free up hospital beds when waves of mass casualties poured in. When this happened, many of the wounded who had been lying in a bed had to be "moved out." A pragmatic decision from a doctor clarified which wounded soldier would be taken by orderlies to the docks for transportation to a northern hospital and which incoming soldier from an inbound transport or the field would replace him. The casualties arrived in a filthy, disgusting state and overflowed the hospital capacities. Many, covered in the grime of the battlefield, needed to be cleaned off just to see who they were. It was not uncommon to have 250 men on board and to be on the transports for 36-hour journeys. Sometimes the nurses had

7. Women of the United States Sanitary Commission (USSC) 103

only "two basins with which to wash and dress their wounds, almost no supplies."[40] The lucky transports crews were the ones that had plenty of water, a stove, and a cook to help.

It was sometimes difficult to load the severely wounded because patients expired between the loading and unloading process. Miss Sharpless had a notable experience while she was chief nurse on the *Connecticut*. She was working on board when a young boy came in. He had been shot at the front in Petersburg. His eyes were closed and it was assumed he would not survive a necessary leg amputation, so someone had wrapped him in a blanket for burial. When he was finally loaded on board, he opened his eyes. Although his leg had been shattered and he was very weak, he was alive. Miss Sharpless considered the delicate situation and rigged a creative sling to keep his leg elevated while he was being transported to Washington. When they arrived in D.C., the young boy was moved to the hospital and placed on a water bed with a sling for six months until he was strong enough to use crutches. Once he recovered, his colonel showed respect and honor to the women when he asked the young soldier to take a sword that had been presented by his state's governor at Petersburg and carry it back to his governor to confirm the good medical care he had received.[41]

Miss Amy Bradley had started working earlier in the war and knew the difficulties of working on a transport, yet one particular experience left its mark. On one trip north, Miss Bradley befriended a Confederate prisoner from Mobile, Alabama, whose name was William A. Sewell. He had been shot in the wrist and arm and been placed on the floor along the side of the boat instead in a berth. Miss Bradley normally went up and down the rows of berths offering food and a kind greeting to the wounded. Like a regular nurse, she could see problems and hear the sounds they made or assessed their condition by the depth and pace of their breathing. She had finished her morning rounds when she noticed that the soldier lying on the floor had not eaten. As a caring individual, she stopped and bent down to speak with him despite the fact that he was an "enemy" soldier. She looked directly at him to show her concern. He said he was not hungry because he was in significant pain from his wounds. She quietly asked if the doctor had been to check him and he answered nobody had checked on him. Miss Bradley stood up and said she would be back. First, she got an orderly to remove his filthy boots and wash his feet off. Then she appeared with a basin of water to wash his face and hands. Still he did not want to eat so his tray was cleared away.

Several hours later the surgeon in charged pulled Miss Bradley aside and told her that there was considerable and "severe criticism" over her act of caring for the "reb." Furthermore, her loyalties could be challenged and she should expect angry behaviors from the staff. Shocked and stunned by the allegation, Amy Bradley could only say she believed that all the wounded needed care regardless of where they came from or where they were going. The surgeon warned her to leave him alone and only pay attention to the Union soldiers, but Amy insisted on treating everyone equally. Against orders and popular sentiment, she continued to offer care to the young Sewell. When they docked at Newport, he caught her attention before being taken off. With tears running down his cheeks, he thanked her profusely and said her act of kindness would never be forgotten. He added that because she had gone against the popular opinion, he would always think of Yankees in a different and more positive light. It was only a small battle that Miss Bradley had won but she felt like she had done something much more important.[42]

In addition to Miss Bradley, there was Miss Maria Hall from Wethersfield, Connecticut, and Mrs. Rebecca Gray from Brooklyn, New York, on the *Vanderbilt*. One of their coworkers was Mrs. John Harris. In June of 1864, she described the experience of bringing the wounded from a battle:

> Imagine a steamer of immense size, crowded from stem to stern and from hold to hold and hurricane deck with sick and wounded, principally wounded. Passageways, staterooms ... all the more filled; some with mattresses, some with blankets, others with straw, some in the death struggle, others nearing it; some already beyond human sympathy and help; some in their blood as they had been ... all hungry and thirsty. When we went aboard, the first cry we meet for our tea and bread. "For God's sake, give us bread," came from many of the wounded soldiers. Others shot in the face or neck begged for liquid food. With feelings of mixed character, shame, indignation, and sorrow blending, we turned away to see what resources we could muster to meet the demand.... [After scouring for supplies] in an incredible short time, we were back to our poor sufferers.[43]

The women on the *Vanderbilt* had a familiar pattern of duty. Others, like Miss. Willets and Mrs. Price, were in City Point on transport duty in July and followed the same pattern with their tasks. Together these Commission women represent a collective group of many, under the auspices of a nurse. Regardless of their affiliation, they illustrated their adaptability and courage to step forward for difficult duties. Based on research at City Point, if the women on the transports had to construct a daily log, it would very much resemble the following:

- Four o'clock in the morning. The steam whistle blows which means "get up!" The wounded are coming. We pull back our hair, splash our faces, and get dressed.
- Four thirty a.m. We are at our stations and are ready to work. Usually the men go to the deck level and work at checking the wounded in as they arrive. They record every name and the soldier's knapsack and any personal items and number them accordingly. The items are piled together for storage. Next, the wounded are placed on stretchers on the cargo platform, so they can be lowered below.

7. Women of the United States Sanitary Commission (USSC)

Our job begins as the wounded are lowered down to the women. Each time the cargo platform comes down, we need to take off a wounded man and escort him to a bunk or location where we have berths in the area. The wounded go lower, middle, upper. Whoever is available takes the next man to a berth, until they are all filled up. When thirty or forty soldiers are in place, two women start rounds with food and fluids. We simply take a bucket of beef tea, a couple tin cups and some bread and butter or crackers.

- Six thirty a.m. All are on board. We take a quick break to attend to personal needs, then drink coffee and eat bread and butter.
- Seven o'clock a.m. We check through the berths to make sure everyone has had some food. The seriously wounded can take only small portions, so we double check on them. If everyone is okay, and we have extra food, we go back and offer more until all the supplies are finished.
- Seven thirty a.m. After all the soldiers are fed, we start washing their hands and faces. For some, the mud and blood is caked on so heavily it will require half an hour just to see the face underneath. We continue working until tea time.
- Ten o'clock a.m. We have now been up six hours with little food and stimulants. We take a short break and have tea. After our tea, we recheck the serious cases. When we have soap available, we go through the cabins with soap. If not, we just offer beef tea again. Some of us stop for lunch break, while others curl up and get a quick nap. By one o'clock we are back at work.
- One o'clock p.m. We continue to hand-feed those who are seriously wounded. We try to write a letter for those who wish to have their families notified, but most are still not sure where they are or where they are going. The men that die before we get to shore have a sheet pulled over them. We have no other place to move them.
- Five o'clock p.m. We are informed that we are getting close to the docking area, so we start getting the wounded ready to be unloaded. Most of our work is just reassuring them that they will live, and that their knapsack and personal items will be with them. For some we need to tell them that a state agent or the Commission will help them. For those that are dying, we try to comfort them. Many are the days when we recite a Bible verse, hoping that they will make it to the hospital and the chaplains or the USCC agent. It has been over twelve hours since we started. We are tired, but still have work to do.
- Seven o'clock p.m. We have reached the docks, unloaded all the men. New hospital crews have come on board to help unload so

we start stripping the linens. We change the soiled ones, pick up anything that needs to be thrown out, and remake the beds.
- Nine o'clock p.m. Finally finished. We are too tired to eat. We find our beds and collapse, hopeful for a full night's sleep.[44]

With this difficult schedule, it is easy to understand why the women worked only periodically on a transport and at other times they worked in another Sanitary capacity. Some of the transports went to Fort Monroe, only a short distance away, while others sailed to Maryland or even further north to New York. When the boats returned to City Point, they brought eclectic and interesting individuals as well as devoted and distressed family members.

Although transport accidents were not overly common, the weather caused jostling problems, and wind enhanced the rolls and pitch of the boats. The rolling of the boats could also cause stomach problems. Additionally, transports were usually within range of the sharpshooters along the shore. However, the women were mainly preoccupied below deck, so snipers generally shot an officer or soldier. Odd accidents did transpire onboard, however. For example, Mrs. Fogg, who had served earlier at City Point, was serving in another location when she stepped through an open hatch while in Louisville, sustaining permanent injuries.[45]

There was another form of transportation the USSC was associated with—railroad cars. At the start of the war the ride to a hospital was excruciating, but by 1864 it had become more tolerable, and the men of the USSC generally were on board while the women assisted as the wounded were unloaded.

Railroad Car Transports

At the start of the occupation, wagons were still in use to bring in the wounded, but City Point had preexisting rail lines to Petersburg and up toward Richmond, so rail cars were used. The USSC helped plan the reconfiguration of the railroad cars to accommodate wounded soldiers. The cars had been adapted to go from the battlefront to the depot complex where the soldiers could be unloaded and evaluated. The cars no longer were filled with the wounded on the floor but had bunks that held stretchers. The stretchers acted as shock absorbers.

Having been a railroad hub to Richmond prior to the war, the newer cars were put to use at City Point. Although some men still did not survive the trip due to their injuries, the rail lines helped bring the wounded into the hospital more quickly and comfortably. As previously mentioned, when the rail cars started coming in, everyone went to help. For the Sanitary people, there was no time for being concerned about triage. They needed basic information first. This attitude caused other groups to consider the USSC harsh and abrupt, but the Commission staff had their priorities and had to accomplish their job. The increased use of the railcars to transport soldiers allowed large numbers of wounded to be moved into the hospital at one time, which created a wave that flooded the wards and required others to be moved to the transports.

Communication and Management Skills

The women who worked for the USSC had a difficult job navigating the political environment because they were always walking a line between pre-war cultural norms and the military management and taskmaster roles they were now required to assume. Each had their own population of soldiers to protect and each had to know what was going on with their units, in addition to keeping track of who was missing supplies and how best to resolve these problems. Although it was often forbidden by the military command to go out into the complex's larger area, it was not uncommon for the women to procure a "supply" wagon and ride out to the units so they could speak directly with the soldiers. If she rode a horse, a woman would try and locate a sidesaddle because proper women did not ride a horse astride and only the vivandières rode like the soldiers. The problem was, sidesaddles were next to impossible to procure. Officers' wives were the most probable resources, but they were not very approachable nor willing to let a stranger borrow their tack. As a result, a supply wagon was much easier to negotiate, and the women thus developed lifelong skills by adapting to touchy situations.

In earlier chapters, several battle-tested women were mentioned. Often women were called "nurse" or even perceived as a nurse when they really were nothing more than a woman offering some form of caregiving. The homelike perception was conveyed by their calico attire and admired by the wounded. It was not uncommon to have soldiers comment when the women touched their heads or washed their faces that their hands felt like their own mother. An old poem called "Is that Mother?" clarifies the connection between the ladies who went into the wards and the wounded soldiers.

> Is that mother bending o'er me,
> As she sang my cradle hymn,
> Kneeling there in tears before me?
> Say? My sight grows dim.
>
> Come she from homes lowly,
> Out among the northern hills,
> To her pet boy dying slowly,
> Of war battle wounds and ills?
>
> Mother! O, we bravely battled—
> Battled till the day was done;

> While the leaded hail storm rattled—
> Man to man gun to gun.
>
> But we failed—and I am dying—
> Dying in my boyhood years,
> There—no weeping-self-denying,
> Noble death demands no tears.
>
> Fold your arms again around me;
> Press again my aching head;
> Sing a lullaby you sang to me
> Kiss me mother, ere I'm dead.[46]

Commission women like Misses Murry, Reading, and Wilson were solid in their constitutions and managed difficult situations with personal integrity and pride. They understood what had to be done and had learned the most effective way to accomplish the established goal. It was not uncommon to find a civilian woman standing down on the docks who had come to locate a son or husband. Filled with sadness and utter frustration, she had no place to stay, no one to speak with, no knowledge of even where to begin. Her tears simply flowed uncontrollably. Seeing such an individual, the representatives tried to console her and find out who she was and who she was searching for. Once the basic information was gathered, they would try to provide the woman with food or refreshments and then worry about a humble accommodation for her. After allowing her to regain some composure, they would take the woman to the regimental hospital to see if they could locate her soldier. Best case scenario was he was still alive and desperately needed motherly care. Worst case was that he had passed away and was buried. If the latter, the USSC staff had to arrange for the body to be retrieved and prepared for burial back home. Accommodations and transportation back home generally were taken care of by the Commission, but the amount of time this effort consumed was considerable.

Other examples of the USSC women offer various perspectives. First is Mrs. Barlow, next is Mrs. Mary Morris Husbands, and to demonstrate a difference in style and composure, Mrs. Holstein. Mentioned briefly in the nurse section, Arabella Griffith Barlow was the wife of Major General Francis A. Barlow of the 61st New York Infantry. Mrs. Barlow was originally from New Jersey. After she finished school, she went to New York City where she met and married the "General" in 1861. She was thirty-seven and he was just twenty-five.[47] He was quickly promoted up the ranks and she reinforced his commitment and duty to the army by following him into battle.

Like Mrs. Lee and others, Arabella Barlow had been at Gettysburg and Fredericksburg, and then White House Landing, working primarily as a nurse before reaching City Point. Organizationally she was with the USSC, 2nd Corps hospital, but true to her nature of doing whatever was needed, she worked, and worked, and worked, and then worked some more. She would go through the

7. Women of the United States Sanitary Commission (USSC)   109

wards asking the wounded if they had what they needed. Her mind worked like a machine. Did they have enough blankets or pillows? Could she get them a clean shirt? Did they want paper and pencil to write a letter home? If they were sleeping or incapacitated, she looked to see what they had, and if she saw a need for items such as urinals and bedpans, tin cups or dippers, cushions or various wound support pillows, brushes and combs, spittoons and even spit cups,[48] she made sure they got them.

Serving consistently without a break and caring for so many soldiers, she grew exhausted. Exposed to the multitude of diseases, she was no longer unable to fight the germs. Quite ill, she left her husband and headed to Philadelphia to recover. Unfortunately, she had contracted typhus fever and died on the 24th of July.[49] The military sent her body north to her hometown of Somerville, New Jersey, where she was buried. Missing his companion and ardent supporter, the general soon met another young lady. According to Mrs. Colonel Daly, in less than a year he was considering marrying again,[50] and this was not well received. The loss of Arabella struck hard in the hearts of those who knew her. The gossip about her death flew around City Point from both the men and the women.[51]

Mrs. Husbands was often called the "Lady with the Apron" and was a woman the soldiers easily connected with. In fact, at the end of the war when the troops went into Richmond, soldiers saw her and yelled, "Hurrah for mother Husband."[52] Cleaver and very motherly, she was in fact a bit above the law because she was good at appropriating supplies and bargaining for a good trade when she really needed something special. She honed her leadership ability as a mentor to many of the young women who came to help, and she was admired for her apparent honesty and assistance when showing a novice how to become more efficient.

Mrs. Husbands' son and husband had both gone to war, so Mrs. Husbands left the local Ladies' Aid Society in Philadelphia to become a USSC matron. Filled with compassionate energy, she arrived at the City Point complex with many other women. Wearing dual hats, she continued to represent the strong and socially entrenched Philadelphia Ladies' Aid Society that represented the city of brotherly love as well as morphed her role into the official USSC liaison between the organizations, the nurses, and the military. She had significant political power, having previously served with military units, and quickly won respect and gratitude. When she took a stand for a soldier's pardon or commutation of a court-martial sentence, the ranking officers listened to her. The nurses knew she meant business and trusted her abilities, and as a result of this trust she moved in and out of the hospital complex with ease. One task that Mrs. Husbands did regularly was to go into 2nd Corps wards to see what the wounded or sick soldiers needed. However, Mrs. Husbands expanded on the caregiving process a bit. Her trusty apron became her signature trademark for handing out supplies.[53]

As opposed to the officers' wives and dignitaries, the women who worked for the USSC and USCC all wore simple, washable, calico attire. To keep these clothes clean, they wore easily washed aprons, saving a dress washing until later. Mrs. Husbands' concern for the soliders required a way to conceal and carry many supplies when she went through the ward. As a result, she constructed aprons with two very large and deep pockets on either side. When she would "visit" the supply room she would fill her pockets with as many of the socks, shirts, papers, pencils, and delicacies she could reasonably carry. Like a Santa pulling gifts from a sack, she would distribute supplies to the wounded in the wards. She was loved and admired by the observers, and the state agents loved to have her assistance. The soldiers trusted her with their last letter from home, their last bit of money, and if necessary, with their last breath.

Knowing so many were going to die required the USSC to be in charge of many difficult tasks. The "USSC superintended the burial of the dead" and gridded out the site with names. If you recall, Aunt Becky was most adamant that one of her soldiers was "properly" buried. According to protocol, burying the dead was a coordinated and regimented effort. The process was as follows: First, at the appointed time, an escort, drum corps, dead-cart, pallbearers, and the chaplain would assemble. Next, each deceased soldier received a dead salute, which was a three-fold rapping of the drums, a shouldering, and presentation of arms. Then the deceased were placed on the dead cart and covered with a flag. Next came a slow and solemn death march by the fife and drums as they headed to the graveyard.[54] After all the coffins or bodies were laid in the ground, a chaplain, such as Rev. Holstein, read a passage and made a few remarks.[55] If the chaplain had personal information about a man, he would try to add the information into his remarks before offering a closing prayer. Next, the escorts fired a three-gun volley over the graves before they left. Finally, as the group retired, the music would become more patriotic and upbeat. Any family members who may have shown up were consoled by a USSC or USCC representative. Eventually, the U.S. Sanitary Commission inserted in the fresh ground a wooden headboard with name, regiment and date of death, and the soldier's grave would be listed in a roster. When those tasks had been completed, a Sanitary Commission representative needed to resolve back pay and bounty issues. As an illustration, Corporal Myron Lake from the 109th New York Volunteers had been killed on June 17, 1864, before Petersburg. His remains had been taken care of and a burial taken place, but his financial records still had to be resolved. As part of the relief component for those who had died, the USSC pursued the information and by August 1, 1865, mailed a certificate with numbers verifying arrears of pay and bounty amounting to $143.58, which was sent to his father back in Ithaca, New York.[56] These aspects of the relief work required not only the preparation and burial of bodies, but the burial location and follow-up information for each family. It was detailed, time-consuming work and was performed by both women and men. Once, when the unpleasant but necessary exhumation of a deceased soldier transpired, the USSC community helped by purchasing a thirty-dollar metal case. They then obtained the appropriate permit from the surgeon in charge, verifying the proper burial location, and then coordinated the shipment home with Adams Express. The procedures around the dead always provided significant work for the various member of the USSC.

Mrs. Anna Holstein

As beloved and respected as Mrs. Husbands and Mrs. Barlow were, Mrs. Holstein had a difficult time representing the Sanitary Commission. Not everyone saw eye to eye. The USSC required tolerance from their members but sometimes issues caused a deep rift between them. Miss Bucklin, a Dix nurse, and Mrs. Holstein, who represented the USSC, were two ladies who could not find common ground. The nurses were different from the Commission ladies and state agents because they had specific rules and regulations they had to follow. In general, they all cared about the soldiers, but roles overlapped and opinions were often in conflict. Mrs. Anna Holstein was the wife of a preacher who worked at City Point and at Fortress Monroe. Mrs. Holstein had a variety of privileges through associations and social status she could call upon when needed. Accommodations were one situation where Mrs. Holstein pulled rank and lost significant respect among the other women at City Point. Her negative attitude about the fact she was to share her quarters with Miss Bucklin and others was not appreciated. When Mrs. Holstein refused to "tolerate" people invading her space, the nurses were surprised and resentful. She made the other women feel second-class and they never forgot it.

If you recall from Miss Hancock's kitchen concerns, it was sometimes difficult to work with Mrs. Holstein. Even though she was a preacher's wife and had served at Antietam, she had a problem with the sights of the wounded and the continuous flow of the mangled and bloody bodies. The stench of decaying flesh and the sounds of the moans and groans of the wounded took a toll on her patience. Her initial reaction about caring for the wounded was "one from which [she] she shrank instinctively,"[57] so engagement with the casualties was extremely difficult for her.

She came to City Point early on June 18, 1864, and got a full dose of field conditions right from the start. She worked in the 2nd Corps area of the hospital where the work of attending to the wounded was intense. While intently observing the casualties pouring in, she realized about one hundred soldiers were on the ground around her. The soldiers' last words of thanks were often more than she could bear under the reality of the situation, and the stress destroyed her composure. One early morning as she came out of her canvas tent, a humble soldier came feebly walking toward her, leaning on a comrade's shoulder. The soldier assumed she was a nurse and asked if she would dress his wound. The arm and the wound had not been touched since the first bandage had been placed on it in the field. Mrs. Holstein knew it would be putrid but had not been prepared for the creeping life that was now within the wound and even in the men's hair and beards. She instantly shrank back in repulsion but then decided she had no choice but to help, and started pulling the maggots out of the wound man's arm.[58]

Soon the incoming wagon trains started to increase, bringing more wounded into her area. Day changed to evening, but the constant care continued. Emotionally and physically exhausted, she tried to retire from the dead and wounded lying all around her quarters and withdraw to her tent. She was aware of her distant and apathetic perspective and noted, "How heartless it sounds to sleep under such circumstance."[59] The next day commenced at 0500, and she opened her tent flap and looked around only to see nothing but wounded, wounded, and more wounded men. She was desperate with every step she tried to take. Unfit for the rigors of her job for the Sanitary Commission, she was unable to do her job of feeding six hundred men. Innocent as that seemed, the work required her to offer food three times a day, not counting the stragglers who received a cup of soup, farina, or crackers as the need might be. She was not a nurse but noted in her diary:

> On June 20th 1st boat sent off today ... but others directly filled their places. Every train brings with it special interests; one man, as he was lifted to the ambulance, almost with his parting breath, gave his name, company and regiment, and then slept, to wake no more to pain and agony.[60]

Mrs. Holstein was overwhelmed by the magnitude of the wounded and soon opted to do other work. Her limited friends who had supported her were confronted with other relational and logistic problems, and before long, Mrs. Holstein was reassigned to less challenging jobs. In the meantime, her husband continued to bury the dead and started working towards the Williamsburg area. Anna became quite isolated without friends to support her. Overwhelmed with all the chaos, she sought work at other locations outside of the war zone but still with soldiers. Not surprisingly, the other women she had had to work with were not sad to see her move on.

In conclusion, by July of 1865, most members of the Sanitary Commission were on their way home. The vast majority of the USSC women were tough, gutsy, caring, well-organized women who knew how to get around much of the military red tape. They learned logistical operational skills that remained with them long after the war. Unlike the nurses, the women of the USSC had significant mobility in their management tasks and freely net-

7. Women of the United States Sanitary Commission (USSC) 113

worked not only at City Point but through their home communities. This provided them a certain level of responsibility beyond the role of the nurses. In addition, they worked relatively well with the men of the Commission and shared their responsibilities and duties. Indeed, they were a force to be reckoned with.

8

State Agents
Logistics, Supplies and Catfights

Many states, such as New York, Maine, and Indiana, had soldiers in the battles and campaigns around the City Point area. Each state with soldiers close to City Point sent official state agents to help their soldiers arrange leave, back pay, and to solve other logistical problems. In the election year of 1864, they also provided a service by getting ballots to and from the soldiers as they cast their vote for either the incumbent Lincoln or General McClelland in the presidential election. State agents were both men and women. The state agent women had jobs as political and logistics supply liaisons and had not come to be nurses. They were tough, well-connected, and they held their own when confronted by the men and military. This chapter tells the stories of agents networking and mentoring as well as one story of a major catfight that continued for months between two assertive, and at times aggressive, female state agents.

As a reminder, in City Point it was not unusual to see women moving around the area. If a bystander was personally unaware of each individual's role, it would be difficult to discern who was with which group or what task they were engaged in. To the newcomer, all women might be thought of as "nurses" because the location was a major hospital complex. Before long, however, it would be clear that all the women were different, in clothing, demeanor and status. Some, like Aunt Becky, were older and plain-looking while others, like Miss Hancock and Miss Smith, were younger and better dressed. Some were more extroverted, like the Sanitary Commission women, while others were subservient like the Christian Commission women. The women who worked with the soldiers in the hospitals and around the hospitals generally wore cotton dresses with aprons while dignitaries, visitors, and some of the officers' wives wore fancier silk attire. In contrast, contraband women primarily wore clothes that were less specialized because they wore whatever had been given to them. Sometimes they wore clothing that had been deemed unsuitable by others but cleaned and repaired for their own use. As a result of this adaptive skill of recycling, some of the contrabands had good working knowledge of how to remake a top or a skirt and they used this knowledge to develop professions as seamstresses. From the perspective of fashion, the wearing of mismatching tops and skirts was totally acceptable for them. However, contraband nurses often wore the more traditional calico attire and apron to blend in with the rest of the nurses.

After you, the bystander, noticed the women's varied appearances, you would realize that the business of all these women going to and from was due to the myriad of jobs they did. For example, the contrabands had clear roles and responsibilities and tried not to do someone else's job because it would get them in trouble. If you watched different groups of hospital women, you would soon figure out what their specific jobs were. They, too, were territorial. They tried not to cross the lines of the other women's jobs unless there were massive numbers of wounded, at which point all bets were off and everyone was recruited to assist.

In addition to the dress and role, some of them spoke with different accents. City Point had women agents from the states of Maine, New York, New Jersey, Delaware, Pennsylvania, Michigan, Indiana and Ohio. Even though they spoke with different geographic accents, they were all well-educated, which was especially important when they were asked to write letters home to the families of the wounded and deceased soldiers. In addition, the state agents could argue a cause like a seasoned lawyer and were confident and driven.

State agents' primary tasks were to protect and care for the personnel from their state. If two soldiers from different states were wounded and lying next to one another on the ground or on hospital cots, the agent would help the soldier from her state before offering aid to the other wounded man. Agents were political appointees, providing the individual with a lot of power to navigate the red tape and barriers they confronted on a regular basis. Although Mrs. Price from Pennsylvania had initiated a project of making shirts for the soldiers early in the war, it was her families' political connection that helped her become one of their agents.[1] Often, there was a primary agent and assistant agents to help accomplish all the tasks and complete all the details and arrangements. The state of New York, under His Excellency Horatio Seymour, sent fourteen agents[2] with rules and regulations to become role models for those around them. According to the state of New York:

> The state agent ... furnished relief to the sick, wounded, Furloughed and discharged soldiers of this state, while being transported to and from their homes: they ascertain the names and condition of all patients from this state in the army hospitals; kept a register of the same and furnished information to all who made inquiry concerning them, and thousands of relatives and friends obtained through them accurate information of fathers, husbands, brothers and sons in the service; they facilitated the

removal of bodies of deceased soldiers to their friends, when such action was desired, and later on, they also assisted the discharged soldier in obtaining arrearages in pay and bounty due them.[3]

Similar to way Commission workers received aid, state agent Mrs. Ruth Mayhew from Maine received many boxes and supplies, in her case from Portland. Mrs. Mayhew and the other member of the Maine Agency kept the supplies in a storeroom behind their regular tent. Skilled at her job, Mrs. Mayhew was very attentive while working, because she tried to talk to every soldier who went into the anteroom of the state agents' office. Mrs. Mayhew and some of the other workers would distribute:

> shirts ... a pair of socks or drawers ... a quilt ... a little farina ... tea and sugar to the soldiers. I used to watch her as she offered "Bowls of hot coffee and some other luxury, with a few words of motherly encouragement to the soldiers who [were] convalescents."[4]

Several representatives working with her at City Point included Miss Mary Dupee, Miss Rebecca Usher, and Mrs. Harriet Eaton.[5] These women made significant impacts to benefit their states soldiers' through the assistance and supplies they provided.

Another state agent, Mrs. Wheelock from Ionia, Michigan, noted how "ones daily duties were so similar, that an account of ones day's work would have been a fair specimen of every day's."[6] She was known by her associates as a list-maker and recorded the names of the soldiers in the wards and on the ambulance trains. She said:

> Michigan soldiers were scattered through all of these hospitals, and to find out and visit every one was no small task, it being almost a full days work.... After having gone the rounds once, and obtain[ing] a list of names of those I was to visit, the number of wards, and what each one needed, the work of supplying these wants would have been comparatively light, were it not for the changes which were constantly taking place by death, discharges, transfers, furloughs, new arrivals, and returns to duty, which were almost a daily occurrence.[7]

She used her excellent interpersonal skills to make the soldiers feel like they were special when she passed through the hospital wards. She developed a rhythm about her work in the wards by "stopping a few moments by the bedside of each Michigan patient, and telling them [she] had come with sanitary stores which had been sent by friends at home expressly for them."[8] She spoke in a soft, feminine voice and looked directly at the soldier so he felt that he was special. Her body language was confident and she was very credible in her response to the wounded or sick soldiers' requests. Her technique was effective, and the soldiers cared very much for her. For that brief moment of connection, the soldiers felt like she was their mother, sister, or special friend from back home. She always portrayed an outward sense of control even though she often felt like the situation was filled with chaos. As an illustration, one day she was working at an incoming ambulance train where she went quickly from one wounded soldier to another to get their name and regiment number. Her cotton dress was awfully dirty from the mud, dirt and blood of the men, but she calmly bent over each man, moving from one to another, listening and writing. Her professional facade was not impenetrable, however, she was rattled one day when she ran into a seriously wounded captain who touched her emotional chords. The gruesome, bloody, and grimy wounded soldier:

> Looked up with tearful eyes, and said: "Oh you are so kind, I don't know what to call you unless it be sister." "Very well," I replied. "I'll be your sister but tell me Captain, is there nothing more I can do for you before I go?" "If you would please write a few lines to mother. It will be so hard for mother, for she is a widow and I am her only son." Weak human nature was overcome, and I could only bow my head and weep.[9]

At the center of the Depot Hospital complex, a soldier or visitor could easily see the different states that had agencies because each had their own tent or cabin. Maine agents included Mrs. Johnson, Mrs. Sampson, Mrs. Eaton, and Mrs. Mayhew. Pennsylvania had Mr. Ritz, Mrs. Rebecca Price and Miss Sayles. Michigan sent Mrs. Wheelock and Mrs. Brainard to do much of the work for their state. Ohio had a gentleman in charge, and with him was his wife, who became very ill while helping at City Point. Indiana provided Mrs. Huron, and New Jersey had Dr. Hettie Painter and Captain Aaronson, while Delaware sent Mrs. Samples. Without much effort, the local groups all knew the women who claimed to be state agents from New York. They were Miss Ney, eventually Miss Smith, and the situational and politically powerful Mrs. Elmira Spencer, who had direct access to the agents' supply boat.

The various agencies' tents stretched in rows about half a mile long and looked much like a main street in a town. The Sanitary Commission[10] was at the far end of the street with Maine closest to the USSC, then Indiana, Ohio, and Pennsylvania, according to Miss Hancock. On the opposite side of the street were several divisions. Across from Maine was the First Division, across from Indiana and Ohio was the Second Division, and Third Division was across from the Pennsylvania agents. The other states followed suit. There were cooking tents between the rows. The front of each cooking tent faced the main street while the back of each cooking tent was open when the weather was good so the nurses could easily go back and forth to the wards.[11] Being so close to one another made life easier when the agents needed help from one another. However, the proximity also caused problems, as it was not a good situation when they didn't get along with one another.

One of the most respected agents in the area was Dr. Hettie Painter, who was representing New Jersey and sometimes Pennsylvania. Prior to the war, she was an unconventional doctor, which did not work in the military surgeries, so she periodically worked as a nurse. Although it is not documented, she probably shifted roles from an agent to that of a medical caregiver when she was needed out in the field. Like many of the people in this area, she helped the boys from New Jersey and Pennsylvania first but was known to help neighboring states' soldiers. She was a very kind, compassionate, Quaker woman who used her medical skills to attend to Miss Hetty Jones from Philadelphia when she became gravely ill from typhoid. Unfortunately, Miss Jones's condition accelerated, and she died while at City Point. Others, such as Mrs. Wheelock, also contacted typhoid fever. Mrs. Huron, the Indiana agent, almost died while at City Point but eventually pulled through. Having a female doctor on location was often very helpful for the women.

Dr. Painter was also an empathetic woman because she was a mother of a soldier in the area. Her seventeen-year-old son worked at one of the telegraph stations just a short ride from the hospital. Early in November of 1864, Dr. Painter took Miss Adelaide Smith, who was living in the back tent of the Maine Agency at the time, on a tour of the area and then to the telegraph station where Miss Smith got to meet Dr. Painter's son.[12] It had rained the night before, making the ground and roads very muddy, but the weather cleared and the roads began to dry out enough for passage. Dr. Painter secured a pass, a spring-less ambulance, and a knowledgeable driver, then picked up Miss Smith. Even though Adelaide had been at City Point for a while, they took a tour so Miss Smith could see and understand where things were because it was such a large area. They went out toward Broadway Landing, over toward Pocahontas Island, past the large signal tower and then toward Hatcher's plantation. Mr. Hatcher had sent all his slaves south so the Yankees couldn't free them, but some of his family remained at the homestead. Dr. Painter's son had set up his telegraph equipment inside one of the two-story slave cabins on the plantation and had hired a contraband by the name of George Washington to help him. Dr. Painter put George to work and they made an excellent meal of boiled potatoes and fried mutton chops. To finish the meal off in style, she made a cornstarch pudding.[13] It was a gastronomic treat for everyone.

The trip was quite a learning experience for Miss Smith. After leaving Hatcher's Plantation, Dr. Painter had the driver go near the area known as Dutch Gap. While there, they were mindful that shells and shots were a very real danger. Dr. Painter also told Miss Smith that the Yankees and the Rebels were stationed right across the river from each other and that they actually exchanged supplies by using the river current. To top the day off, Dr. Painter took Adelaide to meet a very important person around the Depot Hospital. It was not General Grant, or a fancy dignitary, but rather the doctor who did much of the embalming. According to Dr. Painter, the embalmer had significant control over many of the supplies and had access to moving "things" back north. They also had relationships with people not at the front. She felt it was important for the novice Miss Smith to learn about such matters and people.

Many individuals at City Point never went to the embalming tent where they laid out the dead in order to prepare them to be sent back home. There were actually several doctors who were certified as embalmers, but one in particular was Dr. Brunnel of the 9th Corps. There was also Dr. Brinton, and sometimes Mr. Wadsworth from New Jersey, and Dr. Dudley from the Connecticut regiments embalmed soldiers.[14] According to Dr. Painter, the embalmer was an important person to know, not only because they had access to the supplies, but because the embalmers understood human anatomy and learned about how the injuries killed the soldiers. Sometimes they had very interesting cases to work on and certainly many bodies to prepare for the ships to take them north. As a medical professional, Dr. Painter was not upset by the stop at this tent, but Miss Smith was. She had a hard time believing that anyone would have such a job, especially when they frequently had to recover bodies that had been buried and prepare them to go home. Like the soldiers and former slaves residing in the area, when surrounded by so much death and destruction, Dr. Painter taught Miss Smith that her personal feelings had to be put aside when a job had to be done. Dealing with death in a combat zone was part of the job. If you were going to survive the situation, you had to do what was necessary and dissociate one's feeling and emotions.

The Catfight

Soldiers fighting during war is expected, but two capable and educated women, on the same side, fighting each other was another issue. Even though Dr. Painter had sent a loud and clear message about controlling feelings, state agents and some of the women, like Miss Adelaide Smith, challenged one another on a regular basis for a multitude of professional and personal reasons. Miss Smith's attitude started with a misrepresentation of the organization of the Mission of Masons that she had been subjected to. The organization advertised and recruited individuals via well-placed ads or stories in the newspaper. The stories played on readers' emotions and emphasized a different perspective about the war reality. One ad said:

> In some degree to mitigate the suffering caused by the present war, by providing relief for the sick and wounded, and especially for those who have brother claim upon us…. Short of its history [the Mission of Masons] has already more than 30 nurses in the field and is making preparation still further to extend the usefulness. The nurses of the Mission all wear its badge for protection in case of capture by the enemy. Their benevolent labors are not limited entirely to the craft, but all sufferers, whether Mason or not, whether friend or foe, are recipients of their care. The Mason neither asks nor expects any lodging or chapel but is a voluntary association.

The article or ad would then announce: "Contributions of money may be sent to the Treasurer, Brother John W. Simmons, [an address was given] and supplies of provisions or clothing to...."[15]

The organization made many promises to those who might be interested in such an adventure. It sounded very patriotic and in line with Adelaide's ideals. As a result of such recruitment campaigns, Miss Smith put her badge on and headed south. As previously mentioned, she went to Point of Rocks first, only to find out the Mission did not operate in that location, so she then went to the City Point complex. Angered by the hoax, she was confident in finding work at the depot. Perhaps it was while Adelaide was searching for a connection that she met Mrs. Spencer, who represented New York. Being young and often outspoken, Miss Smith sometimes had problems with some of the men but that was to be expected. Her biggest problem was a woman she began to confront while trying to negotiate her own benefits. As a wife, Mrs. Spencer was not only a state agent but had access to the medical purveyors' boat, the *Planter*.

Mrs. Spencer was technically attached to the 147th New York Volunteers and was originally from Oswego, New York. She represented New York but helped the Maine state agents. She was experienced in dealing with difficult and stressed people and complex issues, so she was a very strong-willed woman who was not thrilled by the upstart. In August of 1864, Mrs. Spencer's position as state agent for New York became the topic of conversation and a window of opportunity for Adelaide.

The Depot Hospital complex was on the flat part of City Point. In addition to the medical facilities, there was the Quartermaster and Headquarters area and all the wharfs that went down a steep cliff to the river. The original sleepy City Point docks were old and rickety. Some individuals were afraid to go over the old docks because they creaked, and they sounded like enemies were hiding under them, just waiting to catch people. Once the military arrived, eight long piers were built to accommodate all the boats. The railroad cars came close to the wharf to load and unload supplies and soldiers.

It was an unbelievable mixture of boats, trains, wagons, supplies, and people, and it was always noisy with the animals and men adding to the sense of confusion. George Williams, a reporter for the *New York Times*, described the area as a mass of hospital tents, bakers, grocers, sutlers, and assorted establishments located on the high bluff.

> The wharfs were bigger than most because they accommodated schooners, steamers, and propeller type vessels. [The wharf is] over a thousand feet long, some eighty feet in width. This immense is built bodily over the water.... Upon the wharf stands a gigantic warehouse run up out of pine lumber, and shingled. In this warehouse is stored all the grains, and I saw piles of sacks of oats and corn large enough to fill the entire block of buildings.... Huge piles of blankets in cases turn toward the sky and

spread left and right.... Over at the "hay wharf," thousands of cavalry saddles, bridles, and other pieces of equine equipment: spare axles, wheels, tires, tongues, chains, and "bows"; handspikes and caissons, ammunition chest, trail ropes, and various other items.[16]

In other words, there was a substantial aggregation of supplies and war equipment constantly being offloaded at the dock and put on the trains to be sent to the front. On August 9 at 1130 hours, there was a massive explosion down on the wharfs. Everyone felt the ground shake. People miles away felt shockwaves and heard the noise and knew something awful had happened. One young soldier wrote in a letter to his local paper:

> There was a terrible accident occurred a short distance from our camp. A large barge loaded with ammunition was blown to atoms besides destroying a large amount [of] property on the shore near the scene of the accident. Many persons were buried in the ruins and a great many more were wounded with flying shells and timbers.[17]

One of the barges tied to the wharf that was loaded with ordnance supplies exploded due to an act of sabotage. The dock and supplies were there one minute and blown beyond recognition the next. Most of the dockhands were contrabands, who in one brief moment had been eliminated from this world. There was nothing left of the bodies or they had been blown into the river and were never found. The wharf was gone for a good 150 feet, and the barges that were around the area were simply gone; blown into a million splinters.[18]

Between forty-three to fifty-nine people were killed instantly and as many as 300 were unknown or missing. Many of the missing were contrabands who worked at the docks or people who had been wandering about when the explosion took place. Another newspaper account reported:

> There were five or six soldiers on guard on the vessel, and they with a number of idlers were occupied with fishing at the time. None of them have since been found. Of the large crowd of Negro laborers at work on the boat about 25 dead were found, and allowing for those blown overboard and missing, there were 50 killed. A number of instances of narrow escapes are related, many of which seem miraculous. Laborers are clearing away the rubbish at the landing, and it is said several barrels of human remains are found intermingled with the ruins, none of which can be identified.[19]

The post office and Adams Express offices were gone, along with all the packages and mail and people in the offices. Everything was just gone. The explosion was so powerful that the trees were stripped of all their leaves and the bare branches that were left were hung like seasonal decorations with mangled limbs and innards of humans. Several days later, the stench of rotting flesh and body parts was unbelievably difficult to adjust to. When looking down on the area from the cliff above, there was one spot that had been storing twenty tons of soap, candles, and flour; all had been melted into one massive lump. It was a wretched-looking pile of dough and one could only image what was mixed in with it. Though tragic, the massive blob was somewhat amusing to see.

The quartermaster's and government buildings high on the bluff above the wharfs were also blown to pieces from the explosion. A few officers up near the provost marshal's office were slightly injured from all the metal and wood flying through the air. Captain Scoville and Dr. Prentice were hit by some of the debris but not badly injured.[20] However, one soldier in the quartermaster building was blown 200 feet away from his office while his dog, which had been lying under his desk, was blown to bits and never found.

This single, brief incident created many new issues around the area. When the explosion transpired, Mrs. Spencer was out riding and was hit by some of the debris, which struck her in her corset. She ended up having problems with the wound and was unable to do her job effectively. That was when her private war with Miss Smith openly escalated.

As bad as the explosion was and as much as it added to the stench of the area, soldiers went over and picked up souvenirs. Private Freeman said he and his brother "Picked up something more than a hundred pounds of bullets in less than an hour. We also took a lot of broken shells, gun locks, bayonets, etc., which [Warren] shall improve the earliest in sending home."[21]

Gossip about the incident had it that one of the Negroes working for the quartermaster was unloading the barge and dropped one of the shells, setting off the explosion.[22] Part of the reason for the rumor was because many of the contrabands and their families who lived on the top of the bluff had sustained limited damage. Another reason was cultural bias from the soldiers and civilians. Collectively, they blamed slaves and contrabands for everything that went wrong because they were thought of as bumbling. The truth was that it was an act of terrorism by a Confederate Secret Service agent by the name of John Maxwell. He had placed a timing device in the barge that set off the firestorm. His justification was to stop Yankee supplies from being sent to the front and hopefully turn the tide of the war for the South.

The morning of the explosion, Mrs. Spencer and Reverend Van Ingen were in charge of agency No. 5 for the state of New York and were on horseback riding their daily route. When the explosion occurred, Mrs. Spencer was hit by the flying debris in her ribcage, but it did not pierce her corset. The impact of the injury, though, made it difficult for her to move around and do her job. Men's and women's tongues wagged about the dead and those who had been injured. Before long, those who were not her favorites began to talk about her incompetence at City Point after the incident. By the end of August, securing Mrs. Spencer's job became a real possibility in Miss Smith's mind. She wanted to be the replacement state agent and set her network into motion. Like most conflicts, there were opposing perspectives. Not everyone felt the same way about Mrs. Spencer. In fact, many members of the military at City Point liked

8. State Agents 123

and respected Mrs. Spencer and found Miss Smith abrasive. This mix of opinions made the political maneuvering sometimes complicated.

During Thanksgiving, Adelaide rode the back of the seasonal goodwill and started to make plans for her advancement after Christmas. She felt the time had come and started to make her move. First, Adelaide convinced herself and some of her close friends to promote and support her in a compassionate bid to take over for the suffering Mrs. Spencer. The action was meant to look like considerate empathy for an older injured woman. But like two cats fighting, there was a lot of yowling, subtle hissing, and staring one another down. When one cat thinks the other is conceding, they begin to make their territorial move. Adelaide found out that the first thing she had to do was gather documentation from City Point. She then had to travel north to Albany, New York, to meet with Governor Fenton. This task was not as easy as it appeared. Gaining local support meant she had to use all her political favors, so she sought out the two commission heads, Mr. Peek from the USSC and Mr. Houghton from the USCC. She diplomatically asked for assistance and planted the seed for them to write letters on her behalf. Mental manipulation merged with several other organizational experiences as she gained the needed credibility and built her case for becoming the new agent.

Her big opportunity came during the relatively quiet month of February at City Point. She was able to get a ticket on a transport that was going north. Her first stop was Fortress Monroe, and then she proceeded to Washington. In Washington, she was able to purchase a ticket on the afternoon train heading to New York City. When she got to New York, she headed home to her family in Brooklyn, where she collected warm winter clothes for the rest of her trip north to Albany.

While in New York, she told various stories that were then repeated to others as good gossip. Before long, her story about getting to Point of Rocks and then City Point became more negative. Obviously, she had no love for the Masonic Mission organization based in New York City and warned others about the fraudulent activities she had encountered. One of the people she told was Mr. J. De Cordova, who made a living out of telling stories as a speaker and author. He also saw a wonderful opportunity to take advantage of her profound frustration and anger. Deeply angered when she realized her story was being sensationalized and still deeply angered over the initial experience, she left the city for Albany, but felt relieved she had at least expressed her concerns to others about the experience.

From New York City, she took the New York Central train up along the Hudson River to Albany. At Troy, she stopped briefly to visit with one of her former patients' family, using a sleigh to cross the river because the ice was so thick. After an enjoyable meeting with the family, she headed to Albany to her meeting with the governor. When she arrived in Albany, it was the dead of winter. The hilly and steep streets were covered with ice, making walking quite difficult. Adelaide learned that the easiest way to navigate the streets was sliding down the hills. It was sometimes the least dignified way to travel, especially for a young woman, but fun for a child. Upon her arrival at the governor's office, she found him out of town. Once more, she was unhappy but undaunted, and waited three days for him to return. When she finally met with the governor, she presented her case to him with letters from the USSC and USCC and was granted a commission as a state agent from New York. Her instructions were to return south and meet with Mr. Morgan, who was in charge of the New York Agency in Washington. From Washington, she could catch a steamer back to City Point.

When she returned home, she found out that the Masonic Mission had once more used her as a foolhardy woman because of her willingness to provide a sensational story. Miss Smith was furious. Not only had her story gone around the rumor mills in New York, it had been placed in the paper with her name. The headline was "Fun for the Soldiers." The storyline was that Mr. De Cordova was going to deliver a humorous lecture that he called Miss Smith's surprise party. Intrigued, the local residents from New York wanted to hear the story. They went to the Cooper Institute to hear the speech.[23] Advertised as a fundraiser for sending reading material to the soldiers, they cleared $1,400. However, Mr. De Cordova misrepresented the benefit and spoke about the relief of the rebels in the Shenandoah Valley.[24] Absolutely beside herself with anger and embarrassment, Adelaide packed as quickly as she could and headed back to Virginia.

In the interim, Mrs. Spencer slowly gained her strength back and was able to forget the cat who seemed to always be ready for a fight. Although she never fully recovered, she was back at work performing her duties and riding around the post to see the soldiers from New York. When Adelaide arrived at the hospital complex, her supporters were excited for her and applauded the commission position she had obtained. Quite sure she was doing a good thing by becoming an agent, she arrived in early March, assuming she would take over for the recovering Mrs. Spencer. Wasting little time, she went to Mrs. Spencer's tent and showed her the letter from Governor Fenton. Confidently assertive, she announced, that she "would like to take possession in a few days."[25] The icy cold stare from Mrs. Spencer made the weather in Albany seem positively tropical. Mrs. Spencer was deeply entrenched in her position and heavily allied by her husband and friends who had control of the purveyors' medical supply boat. Mrs. Spencer had no plans to allow anyone to take over her position, let alone the arrogant young Adelaide. The relationship between the two had been fragile before the confrontation, but now they grew very distant and were difficult to be around. Although spring and then summer came and went, the ice never melted between the two. Aware that they were constantly being observed and were a source of gossip, the women managed to remain at City Point. Mrs. Spencer was quite savvy about dealing with difficult individuals, so she figured that they each could perform their agents' tasks but always at different locations. If one came into an area, the other simply moved out of the way. Each had a job to do and a responsibility to the soldiers from New York, but they never socialized together from that point on.

Finding herself the topic of gossip and a bit of a fool in the eyes of some of the military men, Miss Smith faded back into many of her previous tasks of being a caregiver. However, she loved to flaunt the fact she wore multiple hats and was also a New York state agent. She used her new political power whenever she felt she needed it, but left the war zone embarrassed by her foolish situation. The uncompromising strength of Mrs. Spencer was forever engraved in her memory. Many years later, the wound still festered when a bust of Mrs. Spencer was dedicated in the New York State Capitol in Albany. True to her persistent and somewhat aggressive nature, after the turn of the century, Adelaide decided to write a story about her wartime experiences and clarify for the record how successful she had been.

9

A Funny Thing Happened on the Way to the Front
Incidents of Harassment and Humor

Situational humor in a war zone is sometimes referred to as gallows humor. This bizarre behavior is a form of stress reduction that helps individuals cope with a difficult situation. To an outside observer, the humor may not seem very funny because the situations are often serious, and outsiders can't understand the innuendos and inside meanings that the participants use. That does not mean that the jokesters are not serious about what is happening, but they have learned, often via hindsight, that the glass can be half empty or half full. The psychological process is a critical one for switching from a negative to a positive mindset. The premise is that a person cannot laugh and cry at the same time, so being able to laugh is essential to survival, even when it may be bizarre, strange, or sometimes seem inappropriate.

Life in a war zone is filled with very sobering moments. Tragic, traumatic, and brutal events sometimes happen. Countless times an individual considers, "why I am doing this when I could be safe at home?" The women who went to City Point accepted the element of danger, the certainty of primitive living, and the putrid smells and pathetic sounds of the wounded and dying when they agreed to go there. To add to the stress, being a woman in the war zone meant that they were constantly "on duty" even when conducting mundane tasks such as eating, taking care of personal hygiene, or trying to do laundry. Women had to be constantly vigilant. In their limited world, they were always a subject of conversation for the men as well as other women. For some, like Mrs. Holstein with the USSC, it was too much and she went home. Strength and logic outwardly prevailed, and the women knew tears were not a public option. However, tears did fall in the privacy of their quarters. Hindsight helped but was only gained with time. Some of the incidents portrayed here were very serious, but after all was done, the woman's reactions and her ability to put the incident in perspective made the craziness laughable when she got together with friends. Hopefully you can at least smile.

Throughout the research for this book, small but amusing anecdotes were discovered and are used to bring this chapter to life. The various stories help readers visualize and understand the humor that helped maintain a sense of sanity during the insane time. Some of the women, like Adelaide Smith and Aunt Becky, had many funny incidents while with the Army of the Potomac. Other women were initially less insightful and more reserved, and their humor took longer to emerge. Short stories about practical jokes help us understand the fun the soldiers had with women in their midst. Sillier incidents of female misjudgment, such as thinking one could ride a horse, or going on a picnic when under fire, allow a glimpse into their own psyche and confining social norms. Like chicken soup for the soul, these moments of levity lasted a lifetime and provided for real personal growth and development.

Don't You Dare Pull My Pass

Passes to move around the area were extremely valuable commodities. Everyone forgets something at various points in their lives. Misplacing or not being able to locate your pass was a cause for great concern and stress but a lost pass did occasionally happen. Getting a new pass issued was possible, but red tape with rules and regulations bogged down the process and caused substantial delays in daily activities. On top of a lost pass, bored officers frequently had time to think about how they could mildly harass some of the women. As expected, the men particularly liked to focus on the women who would brush them off or pretend they were too busy for polite socialization. In reality, the brushing off was not always personal. The women were frequently just writing letters for the wounded, reorganizing supplies, or even helping with a deceased soldiers' arrangements for shipping north or burial. Adelaide Smith was one of the women who was often annoyed by the calls of the officers. Dubbed "the Colonel" by those around her, Adelaide let it be known that "they had little to occupy their time, and they could not understand how it was possible for us to be too tired to entertain them."[1] Even Cornelia Hancock felt a sense of danger when an individual in the Army, who was somewhat unsophisticated, had their affection played with.[2]

Walking the line between friendly and cooperative flirtation had to be done with care because women never knew what might transpire. On one particular occasion, Miss Smith had made an enemy among a group of young doctors and one decided to seek revenge. When the spiteful officer heard that she had lost her pass, he decided after his rebuffed evening he would push the unfortunate situation further. The smooth-talking doctor went to the provost marshal and managed to get a regulation passed saying that anyone without a pass must go to Washington.[3] Rumors and news always traveled quickly and friends knew Miss Smith was his target. She and her friends concocted a system of signals to alert her when he was headed her way. She skillfully would move from tent to tent so he could not locate her. Of course, this frustrated him even more, and it became an adult game of hide and seek. In the meantime, Miss Smith had her own counter force in motion and had her ally, Dr. Painter, use her influence with General Grant to get a new pass as soon as possible. Once a new pass was written and in hand, the real fun began. Miss Smith set her trap and sat in her tent writing while others watched and listened.

When the young doctor finally found her, he thought, "ah ha I have her," and gloated as he came into her tent. Playing the game, she was extremely polite and asked him to come in and sit down. Then she commenced chatting about trivial issues and totally occupied his time. He became more flustered and his face became flushed. Miss Smith then pushed the situation even further by bringing up her lost pass and asking him in her most coquettish voice what she should do. He was getting ready to burst forth with the regulation requiring her to leave, but she only let him take a breath before she innocently pulled out a piece of paper. The new pass upstaged him not only in reality but also in rank, having been signed by General Grant, giving her full privileges. With a moment of great embarrassment, he muttered and stuttered while in the background loud laughter broke out from those listening in the other tents in the area.[4] He was most embarrassed and stormed away, and she was quite pleased with herself.

People Say Humor Is When Something Happens to Another Person...

Several incidents come to mind when thinking about Aunt Becky. First, she was a unique, wiry, determined character filled with integrity, but she also had a quirky sense of humor and had been raised in a family of boys, so she understood the soldiers more than some of the other women. One day, she was at City Point heading out to an incoming hospital transport with several other nurses. The group of women were running late and rushed to get on board the transport. When they arrived, they found that the doctor in charge was out wooing other women and was not organized nor prepared for the number of returning soldiers. The women with Aunt Becky had brought along some bread and supplies, but not enough for the incoming soldiers, so the women realized they had to get food from the cooks. In the meantime, the cooks realized their authority figure was preoccupied and seized the moment to make quick money by charging the outrageous amount of ten cents for a pint of water. Upset at the lack of food, tea, or even basic coffee, Aunt Becky decided to take matters into her own hands. Like a circus clown, she stomped down to the male dominated kitchen space in her oversized shoes.

When she got to the kitchen, she was instantly given a very difficult time by the men running the facility. The cooks threw their arms in the air like an exploding bomb. They were in disbelief that she had dared to enter their domain and fluffed their feathers like roosters. They blocked her space, struck her arms and yelled at her, even going so far as to kill the fire for cooking. Undaunted by the fierce storm of ruthless cooks and experienced at holding her own, Aunt Becky simply sat down, defining her territory, and waited until the fire could be rekindled. To add to their anger, she indicated she might mention to the doctor that the cook had been making love to her, which encouraged him to leave with loathsome disgust after saying he would throw her overboard. When the fire started up, she got up, stomped around, and helped herself by making coffee with their expensive pints of water until she had a full pot. The cooks were greatly annoyed and exasperated beyond words. However, Aunt Becky was quite pleased with her accomplishment. With a full coffee pot in hand, she stomped back into the ward to pour the humble coffee into the soldiers' darkened cups, leaving the kitchen staff to readjust for their losses.[5]

Next was a wakeup technique that made many laugh and served as good gossip on the post. Aunt Becky was a very plain-looking woman and she knew it. She was not attractive or proper like many of the officer's wives. Although she was plain, she was appreciated and loved by many doctors and soldiers. At one point, a doctor feared for a patient he could not get to respond. The only medicine he could think of involved Aunt Becky. He figured he would ask her if she might help him encourage the soldier to survive. With a twinkle in her eye and up to the challenge, Aunt Becky approached the soldier's cot and said in almost a soft whisper, "I now have you." Then, she added that she was going to take him home to be her children's substitute father. The surprise of the visit and the shock of the message did the trick. The man slowly opened his very weary eyes, expressing a shocked look, and told her, "Madam I am a married man." Aunt Becky was quite pleased and smiled at her success in rallying the soldier. The doctor who was standing nearby laughed at her technique but was thrilled over having the soldier now aware of the situation he was in. Together they wondered if the soldier's wife would ever realize how loyal her husband had been.[6] However, married men were not always that honest. It was not uncommon to have soldiers write to ladies back home. Many of them were already married and just wanted female mail.[7] Only one was lucky enough to have Aunt Becky's wakeup touch.

Stealing My Purse

During the war, most of the women who were not officers' wives or dignitaries carried only the basic necessities with them when they traveled because they had to transport everything on their own. As a woman, you could not count on an ambulance or wagon being available when you needed one. In addition to their own belongings, many of the trusted women, like Misses Bucklin or Gilson, or Mrs. Mayhew, Mrs. Spencer, or Aunt Becky, carried money the soldiers had given them for safekeeping. When unscrupulous men figured out where there was an opportunity to steal valuables, the women became targets. In the following incident, there was not only potential money to steal but a case of wine, which was arguably even more valuable.

Dr. Hettie Painter had been at City Point for a while and had moved from her tent into a semi-log structure that had been brought to the area. It still had canvas portions as part of its construction. One evening, Dr. Painter had gone to bed to try and get a decent night's sleep. Her bedroom was quite modest with only a straw-filled, bunk-shaped bed, a dresser that was actually a packing box, and a former liquor cabinet with a small mirror on top of the box. To round out her furnishings, there was a chair made from a barrel and a case of medicinal wine. Someone had obviously been watching her movements, because shortly after she went to bed, an unknown hand slid under the canvas edge and was groping around for valuables. It seemed he knew where the valuables were, and the mysterious hand began to feel for items. Within moments, the hand ran into various solid items and made noises like the mice who were continually looking for food. Fortunately for Dr. Painter, her handbag was not where the thief had expected it to be and the wine that had been inside the box had been moved to another part of the tent. The noise of the fumbling was enough to wake Dr. Painter. Realizing she had an intruder, she quietly rolled out of her bunk and stood on the box to avoid the groping hand. Instead of hitting the hand with a heavy object, she took a deep breath, then began yelling at the top of her lungs. "Murderer, thieves, stop," she screamed, and then yelled in multiple directions, "help, help!" For a petite individual, her voice carried quite well and she woke up everyone sleeping in the tents around her. In a matter of seconds, the officers came to help, but the culprit had vanished like a puff of smoke, without any goodies. The only thing anyone could find was that the individual had lost one of his valuable boots as he ran away. However, those around her got a good laugh at the groping hand and the petite woman with a strong voice. Above all, they laughed at the intruder's lack of luck and were pleased the wine was still safe.[8]

Bugs in My Food

One has to remember that the men who joined the military were often younger than the women who cared for them, sometimes substantially younger. Among all these young boys were pranksters who behaved like children and proved true the expression "boys will be boys." Another Aunt Becky incident occurred when she first joined the 109th New York Regiment. Having a woman in their midst caused subtle hostility with the men and concern to some. They were frustrated because she was so practical-looking and because she was an older woman going with them. The young men felt as if she really didn't belong with the regiment, but they were also curious as to how tough she could be. As a result, some of the men decided to test Aunt Becky's strength when she joined the unit. Few realized Aunt Becky had eight brothers that had prepared her for what was to come.

During the course of five days, the chefs offered her interesting "gourmet" cooking. It started slowly, and after several days she noticed one very dirty rag being used for many things, including cooking her dinners. There was also a dirty pot of water being boiled for her coffee. Then one evening, dinner was a bowl of soup, which was not out of the ordinary. However, some of the men had made up a special bowl of cabbage soup just for her and managed to find a huge, big green worm as decoration that was quite alive and wiggled on the top of her soup. She looked at the worm and, not to be undone by the men, she ate around the large worm. When it had been cooked by the heat of the hot broth, she closed her eyes and swallowed it. Vexed but also mindful that she had volunteered to come with the regiment, she finally decided she had had enough of the hazing. With her oversized shoes on, she stomped out to the men in the ward and demanded better food. She having passed their test, a truce was declared and the men accepted her as their own. She was their protector and they became her boys and the relationship stayed that way until the day she died, although there were jokes about green worm soup.[9]

Hot Footin' It

Although winter in Virginia did not last as long a period compared to upper New York, Vermont or Maine, it could still be quite miserable. For anyone accustomed to a northern climate, they might say it was more like a long fall and early spring. Nevertheless, Virginia did get ice and snow. While temperatures in the early spring could still be cold at night, by late February, the trees began to blossom and the grass started turning green.

One day around this time, Miss Mary Blackmar went to visit and socialize with some of the other women. Enjoying a peaceful walk reduced the stress of being with the wounded. It was a good walk, but on her walk she found a young Confederate soldier who had been dumped by the road and was bleeding profusely. Mary quickly found some assistance and they got the young man to a cot, but they had nothing to stop the bleeding. As a compassionate person who ignored the side the soldier was fighting on, for the rest of that day and into the next she sat with her hand on the wound so he would not die. Finally, clots started to form, and a bandage held everything in check. Having had only brief catnaps during this period, she was tired beyond exhaustion, and she found her way back to her own tent. She was not only dog-tired, she was very cold, so she decided to use the trick others had taught her about heating up her bed.

In order to warm the bed and make life more comfortable, the women pulled a hot brick from the fire. Then they wrapped the brick in a blanket and placed it in their bed. Mary had done it before, so she wrapped the brick and placed in her bed. It was quite hot and warmed the bed quickly. However, being so tired, she didn't think anything about possible consequences. Mary got into bed thinking she would have a good night's sleep in her nice warm bed. The brick was so hot that it eventually caused the blanket to smoke and then burn. Smoke began to fill the tent and she slept on. Smoke seeped outside and began to signal a problem. Shortly after Mary fell asleep, her two roommates saw the billowing smoke and came to their tent. They quickly realized what the problem was. They woke Mary from her dead sleep to put out the fire. She was groggy and confused but quickly figured out why her roommates were making such a fuss. On a serious note, the fire burned Mary's feet, ankles and knees. She had blisters, but over time they all laughed about the night she tried to burn the place down. The good part of the story was that the soldier she stopped to help, survived.[10]

My Little Black Hat

Travelling with just one valise, Aunt Becky had only two dresses and her oversized shoes. According to the custom of the day, women wore hats and had one fashion accessory. Hers was a little black hat that she always wore to make her feel fashionable. In Virginia during the warm months, the sun beat down relentlessly and it got quite hot. Even though along the river there was a nice breeze, a short distance away from the river, the humidity could become difficult to cope with, particularly for a northerner. As mentioned in earlier chapters, when the troops poured in, the women in the area engaged in any activity that could help with making the wounded more comfortable. This particular day, Aunt Becky found herself no longer the fashion icon but acting as a cook in the open air, cooking over a fire, boiling chicken for broth. The heat of the fire got hotter and hotter and the intensity of the sun increased as the day went on. Never thinking to wear a fabric bonnet to provide shade, she instead wore her little black hat and focused on the task at hand. At first, she began to sway back and forth, and then she began to stagger. Soon she started to stagger about the fires and cooking pots like a drunken soldier. Before long she became unable to speak and then felt like she was blind from the glaring sun. Finally, she collapsed to the ground. Those who were initially around giggled a bit and thought Aunt Becky had been tasting the cordials, but then they realized her situation was serious, and she was having sunstroke. They all knew the humidity and heat were problems, but nobody thought about the black hat on her head. Fortunately, when she collapsed, she fell away from the fire, but her hat was still on. Seeing her on the ground, several men ran for help. Before long, Dr. Hays and several nurses came over to assist her and moved her to a shaded location where she could recover. The sunstroke was serious, but the fashion of the day became a matter to smile over. Once more, the gossip around the post added to the story, but after her collapse the women talked about the value of a light-colored bonnet verses a fashionable black hat.[11]

Soap?

Although there are several versions of this incident, the bottom line remains the same. In June of 1864, Dr. Mary Walker was confined at Castle Thunder in Richmond. Her release as a prisoner was arranged and the exchange point was established. General Grant used one of his boats to meet at a designated location near Turkey Bend to transfer her back to the Union side from the Confederacy. Another boat filled with USCC staff went along most of the way, but as they neared the area where General Hancock's troops were located, the rebels opened fire from the shore. Several shots were fired and missed the general's boat but hit the other boat with the USCC staff. A shell came through the cabin wall and passed over the heads of those aboard. Everyone screamed and fell off the benches and onto the floor. Several of the screamers then started to pray while others started to laugh about the serious situation. The real problem was that another shot had hit a barrel of liquid soap that was standing near the gangway and it was oozing all over the floor. Soap in the war zone was a bit of a luxury, but now excess soap slid all over the floor of the rocking boat and got on everyone's clothes. Nobody could stand up, and if they did, it wasn't for very long. When the boat finally pulled up to the dock, everyone slowly slid out and onto solid ground. They were covered in soap but still had to goods to deliver that they had brought along. The men on shore quickly learned about what had happened and why everyone looked ridiculous. Someone would occasionally say something about soap and everyone started to laugh. The captain of the boat was heard apologizing by saying, "yer can't get soap everywhar 'round heer." Even though some of the soap had been washed out of the cabin, the trip back to City Point remained almost as slick. When the rest of the Commission staff heard about the day's events, they all had a good laugh about everyone slipping and sliding around.[12]

You Want to Go for a Ride?

As mentioned earlier, horseback riding was one of the favorite pastimes for some of the women, and it was a desirable and significant skill. The women who could ride were a source of gossip and well aware of when another woman was out riding. Cornelia Hancock once noted, "There are two ladies out riding this morning."[13] Of course, women preferred to ride sidesaddle as genteel ladies, but there was only one saddle in camp and it was difficult to secure.[14] The Cavalry Corps converted two of their saddles for the ladies, but riding in them was quite uncomfortable, and the size of the horses made a difference. Squabbles over who had the sidesaddle or who could get the sidesaddle went on all year.

In order to go for a ride, the women went to one of the stables to borrow a horse from one of the officers or organizations. Then they could ride about the area. Riding attire was also critical. Cornelia Hancock sent a letter home to her mother to have a riding outfit sent down to her, and Miss Adelaide Smith arrived in the area with her own outfit. In sharp contrast to the fashionable outfits was Aunt Becky with her dress made of bed ticking.

Anyone familiar with horses knows they have to respond to a lot of non-verbal cues. The horse knows when you approach it how familiar you are with them. As an example, Mrs. Ord was an excellent rider and had full control over her horse. However, when a horse got a novice rider on its back, the horse would take off on the rider. Miss Smith was one of those persons who provided great entertainment around the area while riding past headquarters.

The incident is documented as follows. Being very assured of herself, Adelaide Smith decided she was going to look great in her riding attire and would look even more stunning on an elegant horse. She got into her riding attire and went to the stable and approached an orderly for assistance. She felt she knew how to ride but was unsure about how to tack up the horse, so she asked him to tack the horse up. Assuming everything was done in proper fashion, she had him lead the horse to a mounting block and got on. At first there were a few nice steps from the horse while she gathered the reins in her hands, but the horse quickly realized he could do as he pleased. In a few short minutes, Adelaide found the animal quite unmanageable as he started gallop. Barely able to hang on, she passed a hotel on the road where many officers were sitting. They smiled at first as she started to approach but then started to laugh at the streaming skirt fabric and ribbons, plus the look of sheer terror on her face. The horse then decided to gallop past General Grant's tent and jump over a pile of logs that were on the ground, nearly knocking over some soldiers who were standing nearby. Having total control over his rider, the horse suddenly stopped and lowered his head, making her rapidly lurch forward onto his neck and almost out of the saddle. A bit disheveled while hanging on for dear life, she realized that the elegant steed was standing in front of General Russell's open office window. Adelaide saw the general and graciously commented, "General, I didn't come here to see you because I wanted to, but because I couldn't help it." All those who had seen the ride broke out in great laughter. When an orderly finally grabbed the reins, he noticed the check rein had not been put on the horse, so he asked the general if she could ride another, more docile horse back to the stables.[15] For the next few days, her bones ached from the ride and she walked stiffly and slowly, which provided great amusement as the story was told over and over again.

In contrast to the general's elegant horse, Aunt Becky borrowed another colonel's horse. Colonel Catlin had gone north for official reasons and was trying to allow his horse time to recuperate and eat so he could put some weight back on. Having served the colonel during the war, the horse was very worn down and skinny. Some thought it the saddest-looking horse other than those who were to be slaughtered. The horse had a pronounced sway back, hip bones that protruded, and his ribs were easily counted. Instead of asking for a wagon which then required a driver, Aunt Becky thought she would use the horse and ride out to the front with supplies. Wearing one of her two ticking dresses and her fashionable little black hat, she properly asked an orderly to help her. This time, the problem was the dimensions of the horse. Not all saddles fit all horses, and the poor skinny horse was not compatible with the only saddle around. The horse filled his lungs with air as the saddle was placed on his back. Even though the saddle girth was tightened, and retightened by the orderly, when the horse exhaled the saddle started to slip. Aunt Becky mounted the horse and her weight was just enough to make the saddle slide downward. Several stops and attempts to retighten the girth helped, but it was a cautious ride.

When the soldiers saw the skinny horse with the not-so-attractive woman on it, it made them laugh. To add insult to injury, the horse was so famished that he wanted to stop every few steps and eat grass whenever he saw it. As a result, it was long ride to provide minimal supplies to the soldiers, but the event provided a lot of laughs along the way and great gossip for the men.[16]

Our Neighbors at Point of Rocks

The Army of the James Hospital was on the other side of the Appomattox River in a location known as Point of Rocks. Many of the women there were affiliated with the USCC and came from various locations. For example, there was Mrs. E.H. Jones, from Iowa Falls, Iowa, and Mrs. T.H. Potter, from Lawrenceville, Pennsylvania, and Miss Eunice Hardenbrook from Wyandott City, Kansas, in hospital kitchen number 1. Other ladies like Miss H.C. Flagg, from Hartford, Connecticut, and Mrs. E.M. Reeves from Sandusky, Ohio, were with the USCC kitchen number 3.[17] However, there were also Sanitary Commission women and nurses such as Mrs. Delia Fay, Cora King from Michigan, Lydia White from Washington and Susan Carrie Robinson from Haverhill, Massachusetts.

This random mix of women provided much needed diversity of opinions and outlooks. As a group, they often vexed the doctors because they did not behave or think like men. Generally, the officers and doctors felt that "the army is not the place for women anyway." Furthermore, the doctors felt "the women [were] sensitive creatures."[18] The doctors were often annoyed at the trouble women brought when they reported on the patients. Even more challenging was having only a few women among all the men, and they noted that three of the women were harassed by drunken cooks. The "most energetic" nurse of the group was Miss Joy. Formerly an actress and circus performer, she arrived at Point of Rocks from Boston as the wife of a Major Salm-Salm but kept her maiden name. Miss Joy decided that she and the other nurses were going to kiss President Lincoln when he came to visit their hospital.

Understanding that they could not rush right up to the president when he arrived, they decided to ask General Sickles if they could meet President Lincoln. This seemed like a logical request, so the general arranged to have them introduced at two o'clock in the afternoon. Quite pleased with their success at this appointment, the group of nurses went back to their quarters and changed for the occasion. They put on their best attire and then walked back to headquarters. When they got back to the general's office, they delicately indicated that they also wanted to kiss the president and asked if he thought it would be acceptable. A bit shocked but amused by their bold request, the general enthusiastically said it would be appropriate and only wished that he was the president so he could receive their kisses. The next hurdle was how to kiss a man who was so tall. The general said they should not worry and that the president "will accommodate himself." Eventually, the president entered headquarters and was greeted by the officers and General Sickles. He then announced to President Lincoln that he had a special request from some of the nurses. Each nurse was introduced to him, and after the introduction, each steeled her nerves and kissed the president, making everyone blush and laugh.[19]

Slightly Postwar "Humorous Yankee Alphabet"

Soldiers memorized and recalled poems and lyrics when they were marching or sitting around their camps. One woman walked around City Point constantly reciting a poem she had memorized. The mnemonics made reciting easier. Two months after the war, the soldiers adapted the alphabet that had been familiar previously into a version they preferred to recall with this postwar perspective based on the rebellion records:

9. A Funny Thing Happened on the Way to the Front 137

A   Stands for Andersonville—the ghastly monument of the most revolting outrage of the century.
B   Stands for Booth—let his memory be swallowed up in oblivion.
C   Stands for Canada—the asylum for skedaddlers, and the nest in which the traitors hatched their eggs of treason.
D   Stands for Davis—the most eminent low comedian, as a female character, of the age.
E   Stands for England—the enemy in our adversity sycophant on our prosperity. Music by the band sir. "Yankee Doodle."
F   Stands for Freedom—the bulwark of the nation.
G   Stands for Grant—the undertaker who officiated at the burial of the rebellion.
H   Stands for Hardee—the tactic couldn't save him.
I   Stands for Infamy—the spirit of treason.
J   Stands for Justice—give it to the traitors.
K   Stands for Kearsarge—for further particulars we use Winslow's Soothing Syrup.
L   Stands for Lincoln—we mourn his loss.
M   Stands for Mason—(more music by the hand; air, "There came to beach a Poor Exile," etc., etc.)
N   Stands for Nowhere—the present location of the CSA.
O   Stands for "Oh Dear, What Can the Matter Be?"—For answer to this question apply to Kirby Smith.
P   Stands for Peace—nobly won by the gallant soldiers of the Union.
Q   Stands for Quantrell—one of the gorillas in the rebel menagerie.
R   Stands for Rebellion—which is no longer able to stand for itself.
S   Stands for Sherman—he has friend and vindicator in Grant. "Nuf ced."
T   Stands for Treason—with a halter around its neck.
U   Stands for Union—"Now and forever, one and inseparable."
V   Stands for Victory—further explanation is unnecessary.
W   Stands for Washington—the nation is true to his memory.
X   Stands for Xtraditions—English papers please copy.
Y   Stands for Young America—who stands by the Union.
Z   Stands for Zodiac—the stars are all there, music by the band—
    The Star Spangled Banner O, long may it wave,
    O'er the land of the free, and the home of the brave.[20]

Another amusing phenomenon that would catch a passerby's ear was hearing the ways soldiers would adapt different prayers, poems, or sayings for their own group and situation. One Michigan infantry unit decided they would ask for their own prayer. It went something along the following lines: "Our

Father, who art in Washington; Uncle Abraham be they name; thy victory won; thy will be done at the South as at the North; Give us this day our daily ration of Crackers and Pork; and forgive our Quartermasters; for thine is the power. The soldiers and negroes, for the space of three years. Amen."[21]

Finally, Several Laughable Moments with General Grant

Focused on her way back home from duty in the south, one nurse, Matilda Morris, used her pass to head to the docks to board a boat she thought would take her back home. Protecting the dock was a young black man. As Matilda approached, the guard stopped her, and she pulled out the pass and was given permission to proceed but she was confused as to why she needed to board the general's boat. This dilemma of being on the general's boat didn't sink in for her because she was in a strange location and knew little about City Point or the boats that went in and out of there. As she was talking to the guard, a man in military uniform came aboard and sat down to read the newspaper. He finally asked if the guard was having a problem, to which the guard replied that this woman was on his boat. The man was General Grant and he smiled at the fact she had unknowingly headed to his boat. Like a gentlemanly Santa, he asked what the issue was, then using a nod of his head, he indicated it was okay for her to ride to City Point with him and instructed the orderly to make her comfortable while on board. At City Point, they each went their own direction, but Matilda certainly had a story to tell about riding with the general.[22]

On another occasion, the children of General Grant had come down from school to see their father. General Grant's manservant, William Barnes, often watched after the eldest son, Fred, when he came down to visit his father. Mrs. Grant normally lived in Burlington, New Jersey, with the children. Fred, who had been at school in Burlington, was on his Christmas holiday and wanted to go out on the river to shoot ducks. Still wearing his school uniform, neither Fred nor anyone around him gave second thought to the fact the uniform was gray and trimmed in black cord. Fred and the servant got in the boat and rowed out into the river with great anticipation of bagging a few ducks. Unfortunately, complacency of being at City Point and obliviousness to the war had set in. Before long, they passed a gunboat protecting the area. The staff on the gunboat had no clue that the general's son was down visiting his father and only saw two people in a boat and one in grey—so they fired a shot and told them to halt. Of course, the servant and Fred complied, but they had a difficult time convincing the gunboat crew that they were not Confederates but the general's family. The ironic part was that they were in sight of General Grant, and when it was all done they had a good laugh about wearing the color grey.[23]

Another funny tale from the general's adventures was a day in 1864 when a gaunt, very bony "Sanitary" man with a comical look on his face tried to reach the general's tent by scrambling through a hedgerow. He had figured the back-door way in to see the general might be more effective than the front door approach. Before long, he was stopped by a guard saying, "No Sanitary folks allowed inside." After negotiating various points, the man announced that he was President Lincoln and that he wanted to speak to the general. The guard then snapped to attention and allowed the strange-looking man to pass. Upon reaching the general's tent, any doubt was cast aside when the general instantly recognized him. It truly was President Lincoln. The president was then introduced to the general's staff and related his story that he had just arrived on the *Baltimore* with his son Tad and Assistant Secretary of the Navy Fox. To save time, President Lincoln thought the shortcut through the bushes would be an easier and quicker way to the general's quarters, but the story made everyone laugh.[24]

Finally, after many of the battles including Petersburg, there were many ill men who had been left lying about, waiting for exchanges. Being her normal self, Aunt Becky went to the quartermaster's office and "appropriated," with a quick elbow movement, fourteen exchange tickets. She then went back to where the men had been placed and tagged the most serious cases with an exchange ticket and had the men carried on board. The next morning, the doctor in charge came around and noticed there were individuals missing and asked about them. The reply was that they had been sent to Washington. Shocked by the actions, he asked by whose orders. The answer was of course, "Aunt Becky." Furious beyond control and threatening to discharge her and anyone in his path, he huffed and puffed and stormed off to find the general. He told his side of the story to General Grant and the general just started to laugh and said, "I have nothing to say, Aunt Becky outranks me." Even the general knew and understood his quirky and devoted nurse who was known as Aunt Becky.[25]

These stories show that even in the terrible situation of a war zone, laughter and levity existed as a way of coping and dealing. Humans have an inherent understanding that laughter is medicine for the soul and provides much-needed healing of the mind in difficult times. These women demonstrated that they were real people, dealing with real situations, and that even in the toughest times, resiliency is a skill that proves invaluable.

10

Officers' Wives
Parties and Swishing Silks

Life for this group of women was very different from that of the female caregivers. Although a few officers' wives and doctors' wives helped with the wounded in a caregiving role, for the most part these women embraced their responsibility of enhancing their husbands' careers, and stayed away from the hospitals. They devoted energy to the art of being seen while gathering information and gossiping about the other wives or dignitaries who visited City Point. Their attire consisted of fancy silks with hoops and customized riding attire, in stark contrast to the plain, hoopless, "calico" dresses worn by the caregivers. This chapter brings to light some of the officers' wives favorite pastimes and political maneuverings while at City Point.

One pastime was attending church services where they could be seen by the soldiers and officers as well as the other wives. The small, parasol-type umbrella that they carried to help shield them from the sun became an identifying and visible object in the church crowd. Sometimes those with good voices would sing, because songs helped spread joy and provided a touch of home among the group, just as songs did in the hospital wards.

Another pastime the officers' wives liked to engage in was touring. Mindful of being close to the battlefront, they remained at a respectful distance from the action and took fewer risks in their outings than the nurses and agents did. With every mini tour or even a major tour, such as going closer to the front, they were escorted. Seeing something new provided the women with an enhanced perspective and with information they could gossip about while socializing.

The other pastime they engaged in was the expected visitations or social calls to other wives and dignitaries. The protocol of their deportment remained similar to that of pre-war social calls back home. Like everything in the military and on the post, visitation protocol had rules and regulations. A wife had to be very mindful of her social obligations and status and the rank of her husband.

Stories about the officers' wives, such as Mrs. General Collis, Mrs. General

Grant, Mrs. Senator Harland and her daughter, Mrs. General Rawlins, Mrs. General Logan, Mrs. Admiral Porter, Mrs. Lincoln and Mrs. General Ord identify familiar themes. However, the visitors to City Point were a more eclectic group and came in greater variety. First, there was the endless stream of visits by dignitaries who often brought their wives and children along. There were the gawkers who arrived at City Point to see and be seen. They provided an interesting contrast to the women who resided with their husbands and gave both the resident men and women much to talk about. Although the women remain unknown, the well-known image of six women sitting on the steps of Appomattox Manor with Rufus Ingalls illustrates that there were numerous men and women who came to City Point.

In addition, there were the invited and the uninvited visitors. The invited visitors who came to visit City Point were generally politically connected and were provided with some form of accommodations. Men such as Surgeon General Barnes, Senator Wade, Honorable Judge Hooper and Secretary of War Stanton brought their wives and even some of their children.[1] They came to see the war zone firsthand and to make connections that would enhance their political and professional lives. Those who brought their children often invested in building alliances and associations with other families that would create social bridges that might last a lifetime. Having invited guests also meant that the officers' wives were expected to be gracious hostesses at social events in the evening hours.

Accommodations and meals were provided, and carriages arranged for the dignitaries. Few were willing to visit the hospitals, but in general they wanted to see or tour around the City Point facilities and several even approached the front. If a woman decided to see the front, she would normally do so in a carriage with an escort and was only taken close enough to view the area with binoculars. The men sometimes found it more thrilling to ride in an open train car to the front, but that meant their return trip was frequently filled with wounded men who were dirty and moaning.[2] With this limited access, the reality of the situation of war had an incomplete impact on them but often it made great firsthand news when they returned home. They could then tell others about what they had seen, or heard, and what they had experienced.

Women came prepared to change into several outfits during the day. In public, they wore silk dresses with hoops, while in private quarters they might wear a cotton dress with hoops. Some even brought a servant with them to help with the arduous daily tasks. There was little love lost between the social do-gooders and the hardworking nurses. Aunt Becky commented about the behavior of "swishing silks" and the disdain shown for the poor wounded soldiers as they toured a hospital ward: "One woman, leaning on the arm of a Congressman, noting what we lacked in our appointments." Aunt Becky "wondered if her jeweled fingers would shrink from the contact" with the poor wounded soldiers.³ In other words, there was little empathy for the sick and wounded from the women visitors who toured the wards.

Mrs. Mary Logan and Mrs. Daly

Mrs. Mary Logan was the wife of a former congressman from Illinois. In addition to her role as a congressional socialite, the military hierarchy provided structure for the command staff wives and they were expected to fulfill their social obligations. Mrs. Logan and her friend, Mrs. Daly, were two controlling ladies who constructed their own "correct" social circle at City Point. When together, the women talked about trivial issues, passing judgement on what should or should not be done and who should or should not do so. One of their dear friends was Mrs. Georgie (or Georgy) Patterson Porter, the wife of Admiral Porter; she was deemed a worthy social friend⁴ but was not always around. When she came to City Point, she would join in the activities of the two other women. Together, these ladies loved to organize parties and make arrangements for dancing in the evening hours where polite conversation was exercised. The women were also very skilled at selecting furniture and making comfortable arrangements for the guests.⁵ Naturally, this meant appropriating items from the local area. This was an occupied area, and confiscating items did not make the local residents happy. To maintain their good standing in the military community, Mrs. Logan periodically served as a "surrogate" mother to several of the officers' children who came down with their parents, thus allowing the parents to tour about. The situation provided a wonderful opportunity to gather more news and information from the children, who were encouraged to talk about various people or situations when asked.

Along with her own children, Mrs. Logan and her servants took care of the Grant children when they visited. She provided a safe, welcoming, and structured environment so the children would not be exposed to the difficulties around them nor get into mischief.⁶ Together, Mrs. Logan and Mrs. Daly set standards and influenced the lesser-ranking wives visiting City Point. Building long-term alliances with other officers and their families was also part of the learning experience for the younger members. For example, years later, one of the earlier associations became useful when the Logans' son married Elizabeth Porter, the daughter of Admiral Porter⁷; the husband went on to become a senator.

Mrs. Ann Harlan

Building connections among important people in City Point was the norm, but not all dignitary women came just to ascend the social ladder. A few, such as Mrs. Barlow, dared to provide nursing care. A few had more compassionate and public-spirited reasons to visit, like providing bread for the troops. Senator Harlan of Iowa, his wife Mrs. Ann Harlan, and their daughter Mary, came to visit with this public-spirited focus. While the other wives were "out and about" with each other, Mrs. Harlan was concerned about the soldiers and the contrabands. Recovering from the recent death of daughter Jessie, Mrs. Harlan refocused her personal life to worry about fresh bread for the soldiers. Prior to coming to City Point, she had placed a notice in the Washington, D.C., paper stating that she was using her personal steamboat to take supplies to the men in the Army of the Potomac. Among the supplies and materials, she included a simple request for fresh-baked bread. The response from the citizens of the area was so overwhelming that it prompted the president to establish baking ovens at City Point so the men could have fresh bread. As her social obligation, she was to oversee the project. These ovens proved to serve as a weapon against the poor and hungry enemy.

When Mrs. Harlan first arrived at City Point, she planned to check on her project and report the results to the president. City Point had constructed seven large commissary bakeries that turned out 100,000 loaves of fresh bread a day. There was nothing like the smell of fresh-baked bread, and while the bread was still hot it was put on the trains and shipped to the men in the field. The bread boosted the morale of the boys in blue, but the smell of the fresh bread caused misery for the starving Confederate troops who were often so close they could smell the bread.[8] Although she had not contemplated the double-edged sword, her bread ovens had made more of an impact than she initially realized.

Aware of her affluent social standing and connections, the exposure to proper social life at City Point presented another opportunity for Mrs. Harlan. Bringing her daughter Mary along with her on the trip allowed her daughter to meet many young officers. Eventually, Mary developed a strong relationship with one particular young man, Robert Todd Lincoln. In visiting City Point to check on the bread situation, the Harlans gained additional benefits from their efforts.

Mrs. Septima Collis

Social skills in the war zone also included being a supportive wife and gracious hostess when it came time for dinners. A southern woman by birth and upbringing, Mrs. Septima Collis had decided to side not with her southern birth state but with her state of matrimony.[9] She prided herself in her gracious social skills and her husband's rank and titles.

Mrs. General Collis had a large log cabin house and had hired several contraband women to work for her. While the "regular people" were eating basic foods, Septima relished in providing roasted oysters to her husband and the Grants, with white china plates and tablecloths at her dinners.[10] Financially comfortable, she made no bones about being able to get supplies from the local sutlers and the best northern markets. For example, she unapologetically announced to the other women that she would have access to turtles and fish from the James River. She enjoyed being heard and adored the attention of being visible. For Septima, public attention made her life interesting. At one point, her husband asked if she wanted to ride to the front with him so she could see the war firsthand. A good rider, she considered the invitation, but the reality of the booming cannons and the lightning flashes of the explosions made her hesitate. There were other, more appealing options. Instead, she preferred to set up dinners where she and her acquaintances could dine in comfort and engage in polite small talk. Not wanting to be bothered by the continued ugliness of war, before the war concluded she decided to turn her house over to Miss Adelaide Smith and move on to more comfortable accommodations elsewhere.

Mrs. Julia Grant

Despite City Point being the Union headquarters, Mrs. Julia Grant, wife of General Grant, did not always stay at City Point. She did visit regularly, however, while the children were in school in Burlington, New Jersey. As the wife of the commanding officer, she had many privileges available to her, but she had her hands full with obligations when at City Point. Assistance often came from those who might later wish a favor rather than those interested in authentic friendship. Mrs. Logan was one woman who provided such assistance with the children when they were at City Point, but the unique personalities of the women there provided a great deal of stress for Mrs. Grant. Understanding the social, political and cultural dynamics of the area, she tried to provide safe harbor for some of the command staff wives, in particular First Lady Mary Lincoln and Mrs. General Mary Rawlins. At the other end of the scale were several gawker women with strong personalities, like Miss Jane Swisshelm, Miss Annie Bain, and the "crazy old lady."

Mrs. Grant always tried to remain politically correct and calm. She served as a good role model for the other wives and was a gracious hostess for the many dignitaries who came to visit. When President Lincoln and his family arrived at City Point, she arranged a delightful ball that started at nine in the evening. As officers and their wives arrived, they were greeted and introduced to the various generals before they paid their respects to the president and his wife. At one point in the night, however, Mrs. Grant discovered that Mrs. Lincoln had disappeared. Mrs. Grant wondered what had happened. When she finally found Mrs. Lincoln and asked of her health, Mary Lincoln indicated that she needed to be excused because she had ridden in a carriage that day and was tossed about and the jolting had made her unhappy. Mrs. Lincoln was a difficult personality, but with much cajoling and sweetness, Mrs. Grant finally convinced Mrs. Lincoln to come back into the ball where they could sit in the rear of the salon. There they could observe and politely speak about the party members. The party lasted until midnight when everyone went back to their quarters and Mrs. Lincoln and Mrs. Grant could finally retire for the evening.[11] Mrs. Grant never knew what to expect but she did know she had to rise above it all and be the most gracious hostess she could be.

Mrs. Mary Hurlburt Rawlins

As with Septima Collis, there was a strong southern connection with Mrs. Grant and Mrs. Rawlins. Mary Hurlburt was born and raised in Danbury, Connecticut. This technically made her a Yankee. However, she had ventured forth as a young, impressionable woman to be a governess and personal tutor for the wealthy Lum family in Vicksburg, Mississippi. Life was very comfortable until the war started and began to challenge her life.

While in Vicksburg, she totally embraced the genteel southern way of life at the Lum household. When war broke out, Mary Hurlburt was so committed to the southern cause that she performed on the stage of the Apollo Hall[12] by wrapping herself in the Confederate flag and singing songs to help raise funds for the war effort. Eventually, the war reached Vicksburg, and Mary decided to stay with the Lum household even as the Union troops began to appropriate all the large homes in town. When General Grant arrived in Vicksburg, he set up his headquarters at the majestic Lum house. That meant his loyal companion, General Rawlins, and Mrs. Grant, were living at the Lum house as well. During this occupation, Mary was forced to live in another portion of the house. When General Rawlins saw her and found out who she was, he decided he was in love with her. Mary found his swarthy looks appealing and loved his dark eyes.

Having been a lawyer prior to the war, General Rawlins had a dominant personality and was earnest in his commitment to duty. As the military situation tightened, it became a requirement to appropriate all the horses and carriages in town. However, Mary needed a carriage to transport her into town, so she had to negotiate with General Rawlins. He had met his match. On the appointed hour, Mary got her carriage and thus started the relationship between the two. Observing the situation, Mrs. Grant's admiration and respect for Mary rapidly grew over the way she negotiated with General Rawlins. Long legal and philosophical discussions prevailed, and Mary was eventually swayed that she should consider returning to her roots.

Personal negotiations moved forward, but it took a while for General Rawlins to arrange safe passage north from Vicksburg to Danbury and then to City Point for Mary. It took even more convincing to get her to marry him, but she eventually consented. One thing motivating him was that he had lost his first wife and needed somebody to care for his family, especially his young daughter Emily. Mary was just the woman who could do so. Although Mary's social circles were limited to a few officers' wives and visitors while at City Point, Mrs. Grant approved of the marriage to General Rawlins and kept a watchful eye on both Mary and Emily. Mrs. Grant mentored Mary and made sure to introduce her to people who could assist her, while Mary became a surrogate governess, teacher, and mother until the end of the war.[13] The relationship between the Rawlins and Grants was so deep that when Mary needed a home after the death of General Rawlins, General Grant personally made all the arrangements for a home for them in Danbury, Connecticut.

Mrs. Mary Ord and the Ladies

Another social skill any fine young woman needed was the ability to ride sidesaddle. Not only did a ride in the cool morning air provide high visibility, but it provided a brief sense of freedom from the occasionally oppressive social and physical situation. According to Mrs. Daly,[14] proper ladies would rise at 0600 when it was cool, have their coffee or tea, get dressed, and then make social calls. Being a good equestrian was an efficient way to reach the other women who were not in close proximity. After tea or a social call, "a lady" would remount her horse and return to have lunch before dressing for afternoon calls. Later in the afternoon, the women were expected to rest and then dress and prepare for the evening social events. Being a good equestrian was a skill that demonstrated one's potential position and provided some freedom, but it also brought problems and caused headaches for Mrs. Grant.

First Lady Mary Lincoln was known to be a very jealous and difficult woman. She demanded total focus and obedience to her position as first lady. Mrs. Lincoln came to City Point on at least two occasions, and each time was fraught with problems, in part due to one really explosive moment with Mrs. Mary Ord.

Mrs. Ord was one of the excellent equestrians at City Point and was obviously the wife of General Ord. He was in charge of XVIII Corps area closer to the front, so she often rode along with him. When convenient, Mrs. General Griffins would also ride along with them. The pattern was nothing unusual and the two ladies felt totally comfortable in this role and enjoyed their outings with the generals.

Mrs. Lincoln, however, was not an equestrian and always insisted on a carriage. On this particular day, the entourage was to meet at a prearranged location to review the troops. The two highest-ranking women were Mrs. Lincoln and Mrs. Grant, and they selected a carriage to the designated location. However, as the group assembled, Mrs. Lincoln saw Mrs. Ord riding sidesaddle. That was insult because she was not in a similar carriage, but on horseback. Another and more significant breach of protocol was that she was riding ahead of the carriage. The final insult to Mrs. Lincoln was that Mrs. Ord was riding close to the president, who was also on a horse.

While riding along, Mrs. Lincoln boiled and seethed while Mrs. Grant chattered away, trying to flatter Mrs. Lincoln in order to reduce the tension. In reality, Mrs. Grant just wanted to leave the carriage and pretend the situation had never happened. Not knowing what had transpired inside the carriage or that she was offending anyone at all, Mrs. Ord innocently added to the escalating tension. Thinking she was being courteous and following protocol, she rode over to the carriage to speak with Mrs. Lincoln. Mrs. Ord had no idea she was in for a major firestorm. With the approaching gesture, Mrs. Lincoln blew her top and chewed out poor Mrs. Ord for all her missteps. Noticing a "hot situation" was in the works, young Major Steward rode over and tried to make a joke about Mrs. Ord's horse being headstrong. His attempt and comments only made matters worse and the vile tongue-lashing that commenced sent Mrs. Ord into tears. Mrs. Ord hung her head in shame. The gossip around the post flowed like hot butter, and the stories about the incident made history not only at City Point but in many newspapers. As a result, even the most confident socialite was never sure about her protocol when Mrs. Lincoln was around. The officers' wives liked the president and felt sorry for him. They did not understand how he dealt with such a volatile and difficult woman. The story about the incident created sympathy for both Mrs. Grant and Mrs. Ord.

The "Gawkers": Those Bothersome People

Not only did Mrs. Grant have to deal with the ladies and dignitaries, she also had to have a handle on less desirable people who arrived uninvited. The "fashionable rendezvous of sight-seers" arrived regularly, with scarcely one group leaving when another group would arrive.[15] While campaigning with General Grant, war correspondent Sylvanus Cadwallader dubbed the uninvited visitors to City Point as "gawkers." These men and women came to see what was going on and wandered in and among the tents seeking housing, food, facilities, and great gossip to return home with.[16] As one reporter noted, they:

> Swarm around the wharves, fill up the narrow avenues, that scarcely admit two men in passing between the long lines of six mule teams that stand in this city by the acre; plunge frantically across the road in front of your steed, wherever you ride, at the

imminent risk of your neck; ply everybody with ridiculous questions about the "military situation"; invade the privacy of every tent in reach; stand around every mess table they get in sight of at every meal time, like a pack of hungry dogs, until they are invited to eat or insulted into leaving; wander the place in every quarter, at all hours, sight-seeing, and especially infest the immediate vicinity of general headquarters. Here they congregate and flutter like silly moths around a candle, and may be seen at any hour of the day standing in rows or groups, staring and gaping at General Grant and staff, pointing out the different members of the latter to each other and seizing any unfortunate darkey belonging to headquarters that happens to pass within reach, and plying him with all manner of impertinent questions. "Does General Grant Smoke?" "Where's his sugar?" "Where does he sleep and eat?" "Where is his wife?" "What became of his son who accompanied him to Vicksburg?" "Which is Grant?" "Not that little man?"[17]

Generally speaking, they caused problems by adding to the already regular chaos and confusion. Other individuals chose to call them bloodthirsty or trespassers and the masses who arrived as thick as leaves. Never having experienced a war zone before, the visitors arrived on the boats without forethought and consideration of accommodations and provisions. One day, sixty women and children arrived aboard the steamer *City of New York*,[18] while on another day three hundred arrived.[19] As they left the boat, they did have to register, but they had really just come to satisfy their curiosity. For those who were not invited guests of the officers' wives, they had a difficult time trying to find a place to sleep and food to eat. The Sanitary Commission was frequently sought out to help find a place for these gawkers to sleep. With any luck, it could be a storage area filled with boxes that provided some shelter. Rooms simply were not available and sleeping on the hard ground or on the wharf or in the softer sand of the riverbed were other options for those who were not as lucky. Food was available "somewhere up on the hill where one could pay a dollar for a cup of undrinkable coffee and some uneatable ham and eggs, of extremely doubtful character."[20] If they had not brought sufficient money to purchase something to eat from the sutlers, that sustained the gawkers. If not, they wandered toward the mess tents and stood outside, hoping someone would donate food to them. If food was not passed around, they went hungry, making the return trip home the next day even more appealing. Not only was their arrival disruptive, but when they prepared to return, they caused significant confusion trying to get their passes stamped again. Squads of soldiers who were heading home formed lines. Armed guards controlled access to the transports and simply walking on board did not work. The gawkers, who were often tired and hungry, had to form their own lines, pay the return fare of seven dollars and fifty cents, and then get a pass before they could board.[21] Being a military installation, everything at City Point ran on time. For the gawkers, this was not so, making showing up on time to catch a boat sailing north another problem.[22] A missed boat meant they had to loiter for another day while becoming a bit more aware of the time and of the wounded soldiers being sent north. Having to wait was not a lot of fun.

The waiting process was stringent up until the end of the war, when passes to Washington and northern cities were no longer needed.[23] However, there were hordes of refugees still fleeing north and that made for very interesting conversations and experiences for the gawkers. As an illustration, one group of six southern refugees consisted of two parents and their three young daughters with an infant in the mother's arms. They had passed through General Butler's lines and were headed north. They were nervous because they were told the Yankees were wicked and "they were going to be killed" because that was what Yankees did to people of the south. As a result, the verbal and nonverbal informational exchange was very interesting.[24]

The responsibility of diplomatically dealing with gawkers once more fell upon Mrs. Grant. As the senior-ranking wife of the general, she had to help manage the gossip when a woman pushed the boundaries of acceptable behavior. One example was the case of Miss Jane Swisshelm, a noted feminist and antislavery advocate who had no intention of providing nursing care when she came to City Point. She had made several trips in conjunction with Dr. and Mrs. Breed, from Washington, D.C., because they were concerned about the treatment of the contrabands and freedmen groups. If they saw problems, their goal was to see what they could do for them. Independent nurse Miss Gilson (see Chapter 5) cared about the contrabands and was certainly someone Jane Swisshelm wanted to observe.

Virginia in the summer is quite hot and very humid. Accommodations, as previously stated, were sparse to non-existent for the gawkers. It was no exception for Miss Swisshelm, who wandered around talking to people to gather information and find accommodations. Before long, her clothing became quite dusty and sweat-soaked. Water and bathing were an issue, and a sponge bath with a used basin from the hospital just wouldn't resolve the problem for her. Neither would gathering water from one of the public wells.

Being an observer of the people around her and a liberal-thinking woman, she decided to do what many of the soldiers did. The good Reverend Sanborne from the USCC took a bath in the river every fourth day, so bathing in the river for her was logical.[25] The soldiers and men went down to the river in the early morning, removed their clothing and waded or swam in the river. This was normal and acceptable for the men but absolutely not appropriate for a woman. Yet, Jane Swisshelm needed some water. A pragmatic woman, she removed her shoes and stockings and went into the river. The water felt wonderful, so she removed a few of the outer pieces of clothing and washed them in the river. Those who saw her remove her clothing were shocked, but she proceeded as if the task were perfectly normal. She tried to dry a few of her items before putting them back on but nothing really helped. Like wildfire, the gossip about the incident spread through the camp and to the military staff. Mrs. Grant heard about the incident and tried to calm everyone down, doing damage control to no avail. Tongues wagged for a long time even after Miss Swisshelm returned north.[26]

Weddings in the War

In contrast to the peculiar Miss Swisshelm, Miss Annie Bain was one of the most successful gawkers. Some of the nurses, such as Miss Adelaide Smith, seemed to always invite attention from the men, but none of them offered their hands for marriage. Miss Cornelia Hancock pursed Dr. Dudley without success. Aunt Becky, on the other hand, had been married early and lost her husband but espoused about marital bliss, "If [husbands] sympathized with a wife as they ought, much of the misery of the household would be done away."[27] Annie Bain, however, was another story.

Miss Bain was an attractive blond woman from England whose focus at City Point was to secure a husband. She had a lot of pizzazz and was a quick talker with a lovely accent. When she arrived in the general area of Washington, she was unable to get a military pass to come to City Point to visit her "brother." Her alleged brother was Captain Robert C. Eden, a soldier at City Point. Undaunted by the military rules and regulations, Annie Bain used her feminine charm, and rolling tears, to talk her way through all the Union lines. When she arrived at City Point, her first task was to find a place to stay. After a bit of inquiring, she found a nurse who had a spare bed and would allow her to share quarters. That nurse was Miss Smith. Before long, the two women became good friends and were well-known as mischief makers. After three months of unsuccessfully trying to get to her "brother," an alleged suitor, to come visit her, Miss Bain became concerned. Miss Smith listened to the saga about how Miss Bain wanted to marry "her officer" but could not coordinate the event, let alone work around the military regulations.

Miss Smith decided that a covert operation was the only way. In the meantime, Captain Eden had been promoted to major, making his military obligations different. Adelaide contacted several of her associates and arranged a secret wedding. The wedding required permission from the military authorities on base, a minister, a wedding cake, wine, and of course a groom that had to be excused from his duty so he could be at the wedding location at a designated time and place.

This January caper included Chaplin Wakeman from the First Presbyterian Church of Allegany County, New York; Dr. Painter, listed as mother, from Camden, New Jersey; Miss Smith; Dr. Reverend Henry C. Houghton (USCC) from Jamaica Plains, Massachusetts; Miss Mary E. Blackmar from Moscow, Michigan; Captain Beckwith (Adjutant) from Watertown, New York; Mrs. Ruth

L, Mayhew; Miss Annie Gardner Bain of Glasgow, Scotland; and Major Robert Eden from Madison, Wisconsin, of the 37th Wisconsin Regiment.[28] Also attending the celebration was Reverend and Mrs. A—, Mr. Peck (USSC), and Hannah, Adelaide's trusted contraband.

As mentioned in Chapter 3 on contraband women, Hannah was a critical factor to the success of the operation. Hannah served as the eyes and ears of the wedding, recording and recalling information she had heard around the post, then bringing it back to Adelaide. On January 26, Hannah was on high alert, although nobody suspected her intentions. Nothing and nobody got past her. As the "wedding hour" approached, she made sure the situation looked perfectly normal so nobody would suspect that a bride, groom, Presbyterian minister, and wedding party were gathering inside their selected location. Hannah stood sentry at the door as if it were just another ordinary day. After the ceremony, she was invited to come inside and celebrate the joyous event of the most successful gawker of the month. Pleased with the news of the wedding, Aunt Becky received a visit on February 15 from the official couple so she could wish them the best in life after their wedding.[29]

Although not gawkers, it should be noted here, as in chapter three, there was another official wedding at Point of Rocks when Celia became a bride, with Martha and Amelia serving as bridesmaids.[30] According to Miss Adelaide Smith, the wedding she arranged was the only marriage performed at City Point during the year, making Annie the most successful gawker at City Point.

Crazy Old Lady

Another gawker that Mrs. Grant had to contend with was simply known as "nameless old woman." She was likely somewhat mentally ill or a clever spy, because she rambled on incoherently and followed the Army of the Potomac. Although she had limited belongings, she managed to move when the camps moved and stayed with the Army of the Potomac until the end of the war. How she survived remained uncertain. She probably slept on the ground, and when it grew dark or the weather turned nasty, she likely slept on the floor of someone's tent. Those who knew of her just ignored her. For those individuals who were new to the area, her rambling amazed and amused them. When the old woman could find someone to listen to her, she sang a simple verse over and over again. The verse or poem/song was as follows:

> In Sixty-one the war was begun.
> In Sixty-two "T" was half way thorough.
> In Sixty-three the blacks were freed.
> In Sixty-four the war will be over.

Her odd behavior and unique ability to find new people she could sing to was a source of amusement to the regular members of the City Point community and the command staff. She wandered in and out of the facilities like a gawker and periodically got in the way of the military but never caused a serious problem.[31]

Just Going Home

The last story is about neither a gawker nor a vivandière. There was a young soldier that the women really didn't have personal experience with but who provided great gossip. Known as Charley Anderson from the 69th Ohio, he came to City Point and appeared at the office of the provost marshal to see if he could get a pass to go home to Cleveland, Ohio. He then said he had been discovered in the ranks and was really a woman. However, she had no money and needed help getting back to Ohio. She said "Charley" had been mustered out of the 69th Ohio Regiment on January 18. The provost marshal was easily convinced of the gender mishap and ordered the captain of the guard to provide necessary papers and a pass. However, in exchange, the young woman was told never to return. She agreed to the terms and gathered more paperwork at the Second Brigade, First Division, 9th Corps before being sent back to Cleveland on January 22, 1865, with help from the Pennsylvania state agent. It was a sensational story for the rumor mills.

Together, these women of City Point provided a lot of interesting stories about what was happening during the course of a chaotic year in our country's history. Many of the women followed their husbands while they fulfilled their military careers. Others had unique responsibilities and experiences in their roles. Some women established unique friendships that lasted a lifetime, and some of the women just faded off into history while some went on to organizing or reorganizing future organizations. All made impacts on those who served at City Point. Their homeward bound journey provides glimpses into their lives after being at City Point in 1864 and 1865.

11

Homeward Bound Journey

The following information, an alphabetical list of women who were at City Point during the occupation and organized into five groupings, was compiled from a variety of primary and secondary sources, such as letters, military journals, historic newspapers, books relating to caregivers, and historians' job-related knowledge. The initial quest started with research put down primarily on paper. It was, however, also during the early computer days. This means that occasionally a website URL has changed, but I have done my best to ensure errors have been eliminated. Research is ongoing with the help of the Internet and periodical historical society visits, providing hindsight into the long-term impact of the war experience on women. Websites such as Ancestry, Family Search, and Find-a-Grave have been a significant resource for the later details about the women's lives. By cross-referencing the names with other sources, new details have emerged. However, many remain just fragments of information, with more to be discovered at another time. Occasionally the names appear in the earlier chapters along with a story or situation, but sometimes the context was vague, so the names are listed here as well. The author hopes that even though the information is occasionally just bits and pieces, the segments will help others and inspire new research on the many women who served, worked, or even passed through City Point during the years 1864 and 1865.

General information uncovered has been paraphrased during the research of the City Point area. Whenever a photograph of the woman could be located, regardless of if it was a grainy old newspaper image or a high-quality Library of Congress print, has been referenced to help provide a visual perspective on the women. Names have been listed as they were most frequently used—one has to remember the context of the period. Married women were generally referred to by their husband's position or rank, such as Mrs. General — or Mrs. Doctor —. Keeping with the propriety of the time, unmarried women or those whose marital status was unclear are listed as "Miss." However, some of the married women may have actually been unmarried at the time, and some of the women may have been widowed. Each name is keyed to a corresponding number from sources that are listed at the end. The women are divided into the following five categories:

1. Women who were at City Point as healthcare providers; i.e., government nurses, independent nurses, state relief agents, or with the United States Christian Commission (USCC) or the United States Sanitary Commission (USSC). Officers' wives who worked in this capacity are noted with an asterisk (*) after their names, although some also appear in the military wives' section. This section contains women from the City Point Hospital and Point of Rocks. The two groups went back and forth and on occasion socialized with one another. When pension information was found either in the application or the certificate, the numbers have been listed.
2. Primarily northern women who were military wives. They may have been residing at City Point or simply visiting the area because of their husbands. A few of the daughters who came with their mothers are also listed.
3. Women who had lived in the area prior to the war and now resided in the "safeguard" area. Many of the women remained committed to the Confederacy even though this situation was difficult and uncomfortable.
4. African American women who were contrabands or former slaves who were associated in a working capacity. Hopefully someone will recognize a long-lost relative and add real names to this section.
5. Women mentioned only in very brief passing. Frequently they arrived on one of the steamers such as the *Thomas Morgan*, or the *DeMolay,* or even the *Silver Star*, or had been seeking transportation north.

Healthcare Providers

Some officers' wives worked as nurses and are listed in this section (with an asterisk). Several of the women stayed with their regiments, moving from battle to battle or location to location, and they are listed here because they provided nursing care. An excellent compilation of some of the women and their tours can be found in *Women of Gettysburg* by E.F. Conklin. The focus on the women who came to City Point is somewhat fragmented, but frequent questions about what happened to them after the war have opened new possibilities. Information about their lives was included when it was available. The intent is to inspire other researchers to pick up the segments and add to the knowledge about the women.

11. Homeward Bound Journey

The numbered source or sources at the end of each entry refers the reader to the numbered source list that begins on page 225.

Mrs. Reverend A—*

Reverend A— was a Methodist minister who took part in Miss Bain's wedding (see Miss Annie Bain in the Officers' Wives section and Miss Adelaide Smith later in this section). His wife was with him at City Point and helped in the wards by distributing religious materials and paper. {Source 34}

Mrs. Ashe

Mentioned in a letter from Miss Pauline Bush. She was at City Point with Mrs. Lee, Mrs. Hart, Misses Willets, Hancock, and Polk. {Source 19}

Miss Ballard

Miss Ballard served with Miss Bucklin as a government nurse in 2nd Corps. {Source 3}

Mrs. Arabella Griffith Barlow*

Wife of Major General Francis Barlow. They were married on April 20, 1861, and left the next day for the war. Untiring in her labors as a nurse, she worked at many locations, including Gettysburg, Fredericksburg, White House Landing, and City Point. Arabella Barlow was associated with the USSC and 2nd Corps Hospital. She died on July 24, 1864, of typhus fever and exhaustion. She is buried in Sommerville, New Jersey. By March of 1865, her husband had met another young lady and was considering another marriage. {Sources 2, 7, 10, 11, 12, 16, 46, 231}

Miss Clara Barton

Well-known matriarch of the fledgling American Red Cross, she was born in Massachusetts. Prior to the war she had been a teacher but felt compelled to assist the soldiers who were in dire need of supplies while out in the field once the war began. Her focus was primarily on the delivery of logistical materials, but she offered nursing care when she could, such as at Fredericksburg and Antietam. She visited City Point and Point of Rocks in June/July and then returned to the area again in August of 1864. Her interest was not in providing nursing care in the hospitals but more on getting needed supplies to the front. When in the hospital area, she made sure the nurses had what they needed to care for the soldiers.

Her ability to touch the heart of the hardened soldier was remarkable. For example, she wrote in her personal notes at Sophia Smith College (pages 21–34) about the difficulties she had with some soldiers while out in the field:

> The leader George, whose coal black hair and eyes would have well befitted the chief of a Banditti—As they waited- I again invited them to sit by the fire. "No thank you" he replied "we didn't come to warm us- we are used to the cold"—"But"—he went on slowly as if it were a little hard to say—"But we come to tell you that were ashamed of ourselves"—I thought honest confession good for the soul—and did not interrupt him. The truth is"—he continued—"in the first place we didn't want to come." "There's fighten ahead- and we've seen enough o[f] that for men who don't carry no muskets— only whips—and then we never seen a train under charge of a woman afore—and we couldn't understand it and we didn't like it—and we thought we'd break it up,—and we've been mean and contrary all day—and said a good many hard things—and you've treated us like gentlemen.—We hadn't no right to expect that supper from you—a better meal than we've had in two years—and you've been polite to us as if we've been General and his staff. And it makes us ashamed—and we've come to ask forgiveness." "we shant trouble you no more." My forgiveness was easily obtained and I reminded them that as men it was their duty to go where their country had need of them. As for my being a woman—they would get accustomed to that—and [I] assured them that so long as I had any food. I should share it with them. That when they are hungry and supperless—I should be—that if harm befell them—I would care for them—if sick, I should nurse them—and under all circumstance, I should treat them like gentlemen. They listened silently—and when I saw the rough woolen coat sleeve drawn across their faces—it was one of the best moments of my life.

At the end of the war, she invested her energies in the resolution of the prisoners of war specifically at Andersonville. She became the first woman to head a government bureau known as the Missing Soldiers Office. With stacks of "missing soldier" letters, she felt compelled to locate the deceased who were often buried in the unmarked graves and to let their families know the fate of the soldier. Although dog tags had not come about yet, marked clothing, scraps of paper, and brass name coins were sometimes left on the bodies. Barton noted any identification she could find on the bones or in the grave before the body was reburied. She had the reburied soldier's grave listed and marked with a wooden marker. By 1868, she was able to track down about 22,000 soldiers.

After her work in the Civil War, she went to Europe and worked with the International Red Cross and became inspired to establish a similar organization back in the states. She confronted significant opposition, but the U.S. government finally ratified the Geneva Convention in 1882. Miss Barton also served at age 77 during the Spanish American War. Bold and assertive, she fell in and out of favor with the nascent American version of the Red Cross but was reabsorbed into their concepts of humanitarian caregiving. In 1912, the government appropriated $400,000 and the New York Military Order of the Loyal Legion appropriated another $300,000 for a memorial building to commemorate the service of women during the Civil War. That building became the headquarters for the American Red Cross in Washington, D.C., and cemented

Clara Barton's name and deeds with the organization. {Sources 2, 10, 34, 36, 89, 90, 91, 93, 143, 159, 242, 243}

Mrs. Ellen Janette Baxter*

Born in 1811, she became the wife of the Honorable Portus Baxter of Derby, Vermont, and mother of surgeon Jedediah Baxter. An elder member of the "ladies community," she helped members of the 2nd Regiment, Vermont Brigade, 6th Corps, with nursing care and distributing apples when they arrived. Janette had a total of eight children, although three died early. Jedediah (Jedediah the 2nd) was born in 1837. Janette passed away in 1882 and was buried in Derby Line, Vermont. {Source 30}

Miss Blackman

She came from Michigan, where she was appointed by Ms. Dix. She worked with the 2nd Corps Hospital under the umbrella of the USSC. One of her good friends was Sarah Palmer, aka Aunt Becky, and they would get together about once a week during February and March. At the end of the war, Miss Blackman was at Tenlytown Hospital, near Washington, D.C. {Source 34}

Miss Mary Blackmar (Brunson)

Mary worked in the wards filled with Confederate patients. At one point she stayed with an injured soldier 24 hours to keep pressure on a wound so he wouldn't bleed to death. She served at City Point for ten months. Along with Miss Smith, Mary served as one of the bridesmaids for Miss Bain during the City Point wedding.

After the war, she became a medical student at the Women's Medical College in Philadelphia and eventually practiced medicine in Florida. Her formal name became Dr. Mary Blackmar Brunson. She received a pension (#1138430). {Sources 2, 23, 34, 231. Image found in Smith, A. (1919). *Reminiscences of an Army Nurse During the Civil War*. New York: Greaves.}

Miss Amy Bradley

Born in 1823, she was originally from North Vassalborough, Maine, and is mentioned by Isabella Fogg in her recollections. Miss Bradley was the superintendent of the old hospital steamer *Knickerbocker* and served occasionally on the *Ocean Queen*. She had Miss Gilson and Miss Etheridge as part of her staff, with two contraband women and an Irish washerwoman who helped her. Dr. Swan was the surgeon in charge, so the unit was most likely the 5th Maine Regiment. At one point, she stopped to care for a wounded CSA soldier. When told of her error, she informed the individual that she cared for all the wounded, regardless of where they came from. A terrific reorganizer, part of her work included updating and activation of 150 soldiers from the classification of deserters to honorable discharge status after the war.

After the war reorganizing task, she took a brief rest in her home state, but by 1866 she was off on another adventure to Wilmington, North Carolina. Confronting the stereotypes of "the evil Yankee," or carpetbagger, she won people over with her sincerity and integrity. She focused on the education of the many poor by using nontraditional teaching methods (now known as experiential learning techniques) that brought success and then acceptance to the community. She died at the age of 81 in 1904 in Wilmington and was buried in the Oakdale Cemetery in Wilmington, North Carolina. {Sources 2, 10, 16, 19, 45, 52, 174, 231. Images at https://en.wikipedia.org/wiki/Amy_Morris_Bradley}

Mrs. Mildred S. Brooks

Born in Mauch Chunk, Pennsylvania, she grew up in Pawtucket, Rhode Island. When the war broke out, she headed south to help. She began nursing in Philadelphia and then moved to a hospital in Washington where she met Clara Barton. Mrs. Brooks was recruited to go to Gettysburg to nurse the wounded for three days. When she left Gettysburg, she joined the Army of the Potomac Hospital Corps, specifically the 1st Army Corps, and served in various locations, including Virginia.

After the war, she moved to Hartford, Connecticut, and raised a family. She remained a member of the King's Daughters in Pawtucket, Rhode Island. She passed away on April 12, 1916. {Sources 48, 49. Image at Obituary: Mrs. Mildred S. Brooks. (April 12, 1916). *The Hartford (CT) Courant*, p. 7}

Mrs. Mary A. Brown

Mary A. Berry Brown was the daughter of William and Lydia Berry of Kent's Hill, Maine. She met and married Ivory Brown in the fall of 1861. In 1864, he reenlisted with the 31st Maine Regiment and Mary went along as a cook, soldier, and nurse. They both engaged in active military campaigns during the war. While in Petersburg, she was right next to her brother-in-law when he was killed. After the war, they returned to Brownfield, Maine, where her husband became a minister until his death in 1902. Mary moved to Portland, working as a meeting planner and preacher until 1936. She received a pension and passed away in March of 1936. She is buried in the Brownfield Pine Grove Cemetery next to her husband. {Sources 132, 135. Image in Sudlow, L.L. (2000). *A Vast Army of Women: Maine's Uncounted Forces in the American Civil War*. Gettysburg, PA: Thomas}

Miss Sophronia Bucklin

Miss Bucklin worked at a variety of locations prior to City Point. She served with the 1st Div., 2nd Corps under surgeon F.M. Hammond of the 156th New York Volunteers. She mentioned working with Mrs. Spencer and Miss Smith and was one of the young ladies who got in trouble for going to the Point of Rocks with Miss Smith.

After the war, she moved first to Auburn, New York, and then to Ithaca where she retired to her home on the corner of Tioga and Falls Street in Ithaca, New York. She purchased her home with her pension money. She compiled *In Hospital and Camp: Official Papers of Sophronia Bucklin*. She died on November 28, 1902, and was buried in Lakeview Cemetery in Ithaca. Her estate remained unresolved in 1904. {Sources 3, 10, 13, 152–154, 231. Image in Bucklin, S. (1869). *In a Hospital and Camp: Official Papers of Sophronia Bucklin*. Philadelphia: J.E. Potter}

Mrs. Henrietta Bunnell

Wife of David S. Bunnell, 110th or 116th Pennsylvania in June of 1864 until April 1865. Henrietta had been commissioned by Governor Curtin of Pennsylvania, and most likely served as a nurse close to the front so she could be near her husband, who worked as an embalmer. Her pension application was #1150162 and listed as Nurse Med. Dept. U.S. Vol. Her husband passed away in December of 1898 in Philadelphia. She was an active member of the National Association of Civil War Nurses for many years. Henrietta continued to reside at 2006 N. 16th in Philadelphia until her death in 1910. {Sources 21, 165. Image in: Executive Committee of the National Association of Civil War Nurses. (1910). *In Honor of the National Association of Civil War Nurses: 44th Encampment Grand Army of the Republic*. Atlantic City: Yeakel}

Miss Cahoon

She worked with Miss Bucklin for a period of time at the Point of Rocks location. Miss Cahoon and Miss Larnard, along with Steward Compton, took a boat to Richmond at the end of the war and made a visit to Libby prison. Shortly after, Miss Leonard went north and Miss Cahoon remained at City Point, working in the hospital wards until May. {Sources 2, 3}

Mrs. Mary Cary

She was from Albany, New York. She came to City Point with her sister (no name) and both worked as nurses. {Source 2}

Mrs. Cynthia Case

Mrs. Case was from Newark, Ohio, and served on the hospital steamer *Connecticut* with Mrs. Hood, Miss Sharpless, and Miss Reifsynder. Provost Marshal Marsena Patrick referred to her as a shy person: "I had a quiet talk with her and drew her out," and "That she seemed to be a fine person." She was known to be quite bitter about the South, but she rose above her emotions and helped Mrs. Grant and Mrs. Baxter with work on the prisoner exchange. {Sources 2, 28, 46, 232}

Mrs. Ella Cole

Originally from Medway, Massachusetts, Mrs. Cole is listed in the rosters of the USCC as a manager of the diet kitchen. Unlike many of the six-week USCC stays, she served in Louisville, Washington, Memphis, and Nashville before coming to City Point. It is probable that she was the wife of Benjamin Cole, a shoe leather merchant in the greater Boston area and they had a son Edward who worked in the same area of Boston. {Sources 38, 195}

Mrs. Helen Brainard Cole

Helen Brainard was born in 1838 in Oneida, New York, and the family moved to Sheboygan, Wisconsin in 1846 where she married William Cole. In less than a year William died of tuberculosis. At age 21 Helen volunteered and became a Dix nurse. Mrs. Helen Brainard Cole is based on two different descriptions from the ladies who met her at City Point. She worked to the point of exhaustion at Fredericksburg and White House Landing as a Michigan state agent with Miss Wheelock before coming to City Point. By the time the Army of the Potomac crossed the James River, she was requested back in Washington. She had a brief stay of only one night at City Point. However, she crossed paths with Aunt Becky, who assumed she was USCC at the previous locations and was well thought of. When Mrs. Cole left City Point, she went to care for Tad Lincoln's children and went to the funeral of Willie Lincoln.

After the war, she moved to Boston for several decades. In 1893, she was appointed to serve on a Commission for the New Liberty Bell. She moved with her husband to Sheboygan, Wisconsin, where she became Department President for the Army Nurses Association for Wisconsin. She remained in Sheboygan and received a pension of twelve dollars per month (#1131667). She died in 1931 at the age of 93 and was buried in the Sheboygan Falls Cemetery. {Sources 20, 21, 148, 149, 165, 172. Image at https://www.findagrave.com/memorial/54439089/helen-cole}

Author's Note: It should be noted that there was a Mrs. L.C. Brainard who became the national chaplain of the G.A.R. National Encampment in 1902. Although the names are similar, they are most likely two different women or it could be an initial handwriting error. {Sources 23, 37}

Miss Harriett Dame

Born in North Barnstead, New Hampshire, on January 15, 1815, she remained there until 1836 when she moved to Concord and opened a hospital. When the 2nd New Hampshire was mustered into war service, she insisted she go with the regiment. The men called her "Mother Dame." She served all four years of the war, starting with the Peninsular Campaign. During the retreat of the James, she stayed with the sick and wounded to make sure they were cared for or at least buried if need be. Her attire during the retreat was "unique" because she wore heavy rubber boots and mosquito netting over her head, but she remained heathy. She was captured at Bull Run and given a pass by Stonewall Jackson when she was released. She was at Fredericksburg, Chancellorsville, and on the field at Gettysburg, as well as many other battles. She arrived at City Point before going to the Point of Rocks facilities. During the four years of war, she organized the New Hampshire Relief Association and help convince Surgeon General Barnes to convert the *Argo* and the *Fulton* into hospital transport ships. For her war service she was entitled to wear the diamond of the 3rd Corps, the cross of the 18th and the heart of the 12th and given a gold badge by the men of the 2nd New Hampshire. The New York State Odd Fellows made Harriett Dame and Clara Barton honorary members of the Rebekah Odd Fellows in 1904.

After the war, she went back to Washington to live. She worked in the currency division of the Treasury as a loan counter. In 1895, she fractured her hip, and then at the age of 70 she broke her leg when a woman on a bike ran into her. She was eventually granted a pension and given $500 by the New Hampshire Legislature and took her money to New Hampshire, where she built a large home for veterans on Lake Winnipesaukee. Her picture hangs in the New Hampshire Legislature. She died at her home in Concord, New Hampshire, in April of 1900. {Sources 7, 10, 157, 160–162, 186, 191, 231. Images at https://en.wikipedia.org/wiki/Harriet_Patience_Dame}

Miss Bridget Deavers (also Divers and Devers)

Bridget was born in Northern Ireland around 1839 and came to the United States in 1849 at about the age of 11. She was attached to the 1st Michigan Cavalry as a soldier and as their mascot/vivandière/daughter of the regiment. She worked as a liaison with the USSC and USCC. Periodically, she would come to City Point from the field to gather supplies or information and assistance.

When General Grant ordered that women would not be allowed with the regiments, she resided at the hospital area and worked as a housekeeper/staff assistant for Miss Hancock of 2nd Corps. For obvious reasons, Bridget preferred to help in the Cavalry Corps hospital. According to Mary Livermore, she married a private, but no record has been found at this time.

After the war, she went to Washington, D.C. for the Grand Review of the troops and reportedly joined a cavalry unit headed out west to fight the Indians. One has to consider what the "west" was at that point and look for clues in Texas, Missouri, and even Utah. The rest of her history remains elusive but intriguing. However, there are some interesting clues that need to be explored. {Sources 10, 12, 18, 19, 38, 227, 228, 229, 234. Illustration image in Livermore, M.A. (1889). *My Story of the War*, Hartford, CT: A.D. Worthington; or at https://en.wikipedia.org/wiki/Bridget_Diver}

Author's Notes: In 1898 for the month of May to June, there is a notice in the *Kansas City (MO) Journal* regarding the final settlement of the estate of Daniel Deavers with a Bridget Deavers listed as Administratrix. On the Will and Probate records (#3577–3608), the name Bridget Deavers appears on the cover page. There is also a listing for a Bridget Deavers on Find-a-Grave showing a woman who was born in 1834 and died on November 11, 1912, in Kansas City, Missouri.

One immigration listing for Daniel shows him arriving in 1853 when he was 24, coming from Liverpool and going into New York City. Furthermore, Daniel has a listing for a pension but it is filed in New York.

One "Civil War Nurse Dies" newspaper clipping listed Mrs. Bridget Murphy of Ashland, New York, passing away at 91. This was the only Bridget out of over 300 Union nurses followed. A marriage record may shed light to a possible connection with Bridget Deaver. {Source 63}

Additionally, there is a David W. Devers who died in November of 1897 who was listed as a private then promoted to corporal with the 15th Regiment of the Missouri Cavalry. This needs more investigation to see if he was married and who his wife might have been.

Miss Dorothea Dix

She was appointed superintendent of the highly controlled government nurses and had considerable power to hire or not hire the young women who applied for the position of nurse. Some of the ladies liked her while others avoided her. She was tall, very slender, and still vigorous in her sixties towards the end of the war. In the winter of 1864, she came to visit the nurses, quite confident she would be provided quarters. However, all spare spaces were occupied at the time so she ended up sharing a storeroom and sleeping on top of boxes with her good friend Mrs. Wittenmyer. Like Clara Barton, Miss Dix made her rounds of the facilities and staff but really did not participate in the hospital ward work.

In 1881, she organized the Ex-Nurse's Association for the District of Columbia and served as the president of the association in 1883. She died in 1887 before her dream of national organization could be completed. In 1892, the organization's named changed to the National Association of Army Nurses of the Civil War. {Sources 3, 7, 38, 117. Images at https://en.wikipedia.org/wiki/Dorothea_Dix and https://www.bestnursingmasters.com/10-greatest-nurses-of-the-american-civil-war/}

Ms. Lois Harding Dunbar

Originally hired by the Masonic Mission of Masons out of New York, Ms. Dunbar was attached to the 9th Corps hospital until late July or August of 1864. Later in the fall, she moved to help at the small Government Hospital at the Depot. After the war, she married George Dunbar and they moved to Salt Lake City, and Ogden, Utah, where they invested in real estate. In June of 1906, she suffered a massive stoke and died five hours later. {Sources 10, 23, 34, 217–219}

Miss Kate M. Duncan

A Scotch Canadian woman by birth, she managed the 5th Corps USCC diet kitchen. She also ran the USCC kitchen for the Corps d'Afrique Hospital. Like several of the other women, she had a contemptuous attitude, according to Rebecca Usher. Colonel Parker of the 32nd Massachusetts Regiment noted that Miss Duncan ran the diet kitchen—and the men who worked for her—like a tight ship. She was all business, and "no time was frittered away, [and] a perfect system was maintained" using a despotic attitude and manners. Like some of the other "seasoned" ladies, the soldiers never wanted to displease or disappoint her. Everything was clean and spotless. Cooking pots and pans had a specific order and her storerooms were well-organized and logical. Food supplies and rations were carefully calculated. Nothing went to waste. Every part of meat was used and what could not be served was boiled for soups and jellies, with any residual fed to the pigs. After the war, she became an active member of the National Association of Civil War Nurses. {Sources 22, 24, 27, 163, 165. Image in Nurses Famous on Many Battlefields. (August 16, 1903). *The San Francisco Call*, pp. 12–13}

Miss Mary E. Dupee

Originally from Portland, Maine, she worked as an assistant in the Maine State Agency with Mrs. Eaton, Miss Rebecca Usher, and Mrs. Ruth Mayhew. She had previously been in charge of thirteen wards at the Naval School Hospital in Annapolis, where many of the returning prisoners were sent. She served at City Point for only three months, from April until June of 1865. After the war, she married and moved to San Francisco, California. {Sources 2, 34, 45, 163. Image in Sudlow, L.L. (2000). *A Vast Army of Women: Maine's Uncounted Forces in the American Civil War.* Gettysburg, PA: Thomas}

Mrs. E—

Mrs. E— is mentioned briefly by Miss Smith as a woman representing the Masonic Mission. There was not a kind word from Miss Smith about her. Mrs. E— left Point of Rocks and went to City Point before returning to New York. This probably was Sarah Edson. {Source 34}

Mrs. Harriett Eaton

A widow of a Baptist minister, she left Portland, Maine, in 1862 to move wherever the Army of the Potomac went, representing the Maine Camp Hospital Association. During her field experiences, which included many critical battles, she often worked with Isabella Fogg. The two ladies did not share the same perspective on how the work should be done or when it should be done. As a result, they often locked horns and often had a not-so-silent cat fight that others noticed. In December of 1864, she was relieved by Mrs. Ruth Mayhew and was able to head back north. She passed away in 1885, and was buried in the Evergreen Cemetery in Portland, Maine. {Sources 2, 10, 45, 239}

Mrs. Sarah P. Edson

She was from Fleming, New York, married and moved to Pontiac, Michigan, before the couple moved to Marysville, Kentucky. She worked briefly with Miss Bucklin before she left. According to the papers, Mrs. Edson was with the Masonic Mission. However, General Grant revoked her permit to be in the army. She was arrested and sent back to the Washington area. In January 1865, she filed a suit against the Masonic Mission organization. According to the Mission, "All just bills are paid promptly by the society; but demands for service never rendered ... will be successfully resisted." The incident helps clarify why the women suggested Miss Smith removed her Masonic Mission badge when she came to City Point. {Sources 3, 150, 151}

Mrs. M.A. Ehler

She was from Lancaster, Pennsylvania, and was attached to the Cavalry Corps Hospital. She worked with Mrs. McKay and Mrs. Spaulding. {Source 18}

Mrs. Ruth Ellis

She came to City Point from Bridgewater, Massachusetts. {Source 2}

Mrs. Annie Etheridge

Attached to the 3rd Michigan Infantry, she was mentioned by Amy Bradley and Cornelia Hancock. Respected and well-liked by others, she could sweet-talk the other women into riding miles to deliver much-needed supplies to her Michigan units. Her friends on the post would help her acquire badly needed personal clothing replacements during the last stages of the war. Annie was only five feet, three inches tall and, like Bridget Deavers, she served as a vivandiere for the Michigan unit. On May 26, 1863, she was presented a medal for Brave and Meritorious Conduct on the field in the Battle of Chancellorsville. For her work during the Civil War, she received the Kearney Cross. After the war, she married Charles Hook and was employed in the Treasury Department in Washington, D.C. She resided at 116 Sixth Street until 1878. She died in January 1913, with services in Lee's chapel at Georgetown University Hospital. She is buried in Arlington National Cemetery. {Sources 2, 10, 12, 19, 37, 52, 117, 130, 191, 229. Images at Library of Congress and https://www.bestnursingmasters.com/10-greatest-nurses-of-the-american-civil-war/; and to Livermore, M.A. (1889). *My Story of the War.* Hartford, CT: A.D. Worthington}

Mrs. Amanda Colburn Farnham (Flech)

She was an appointed government nurse for Vermont units and 6th Corps. When she first met Miss Dix, Amanda was wearing bloomers so she could march better with her boys. Miss Dix was shocked and commented about how ugly her attire was, but allowed her to decide what she wanted to wear while working as a nurse. She had a long wartime career, starting with the Peninsula Campaign, then Gettysburg, Antietam, Fredericksburg, White House Landing, Cold Harbor and City Point. She is credited with establishing laundry procedures for the quartermaster. Her resourcefulness reduced the constant need for new clothing. She moved to City Point with the unit but transferred out about August 21, 1864, when the 6th Corps moved to the Shenandoah Valley. However, by December she had returned to City Point.

After the war, she married Marshall Flech, formerly of Company H, 4th Vermont. They moved to Denver, Colorado, where they built a hotel and did mining and farming. That led to their discovery of dinosaur bones and a reputation that was quite unique. As a paleontologist, she also became known as a gracious hostess and cook for those interested in dinosaurs. For her war service, she received a pension of $12 a month. She died on December 31, 1893, in

Denver and is buried at Greenwood Pioneer Cemetery in Canon City, Colorado. {Sources 7, 10, 225, 226}

Mrs. Annie Faxon (Foxon)*

She was the wife of Surgeon W. L. Faxon of the 32nd Regiment, Massachusetts Infantry. Surgeon Faxon was placed in charge of the Fifth Corps Hospital, and his wife served as a nurse within the Fifth Corps Hospital. She had been with them in earlier campaigns and added a touch of civility to the men's lives. Colonel F.J. Parker noted, "Surgeon Faxon of the 32d was placed in command of the hospital of the 5th corps, near City Point, and when the army had settled down to the siege of Petersburg, Mrs. Faxon was ordered to the front, and a description of the hospital and of hospital life from her point of view will not be uninteresting" (p. 232). After the war, they returned to Quincy, Massachusetts, where he worked as a physician and they raised their four children (John, Florence, Harold, and Randall). In 1916, there was a contested pension petition by a Mrs. Mary J. Faxon (#848065), also shown as a widow. {Sources 24, 27, 165}

Mrs. Delia Fay

Originally from Upper Jay, New York, she married Mr. Fay, who became the mayor of Chelsea, Massachusetts, and then superintendent with the USSC. She served through the war whenever and wherever she was needed. In 1864, she was at Point of Rocks to nurse the wounded.

An extended family member of John Brown, she felt compelled to attend his funeral. After the war, she became involved with the New York Association of Nurses and served as a president of the National Association of Nurses. {Sources 165, 205. Image in Executive Committee of the National Association of Civil War Nurses. (1910). *In Honor of the National Association of Civil War Nurses: 44*th *Encampment Grand Army of the Republic.* Atlantic City: Yeakel}

Miss Harriet C. Flagg

According to old census records, city directory records, and ancestry.com, she may have been born in Ohio in 1834. If so, her mother was Canadian and her father was from Connecticut. However, for most of her life she lived in the South Windsor area outside of Hartford, Connecticut. According to Provost Records #15523, she served with the USSC Kitchen #3 at Point of Rocks. With her was Mrs. E.H. Reeves from Sandusky, Ohio. There were many Flagg families in the Hartford area, and according to census records, she remained single until she met James Walker. In 1886, they were married in Paulding, Ohio. After their marriage, they moved to Ohio, where he became a resident of the Home for Disabled Soldiers while she became the assistant matron at the Protestant Orphans' Homes in Toledo. Her name appears in the city directories through 1906. {Sources 195, 244}

Mrs. Isabella Fogg

Mrs. Fogg was a widow and a mother of a soldier from Calais, Maine. She went off to war while representing the Maine Camp Hospital Association. Like Mrs. Eaton, she served as a field nurse during many of the critical battles of the war, such as Fredericksburg and Gettysburg, as well as in Louisville. While in Louisville, she was on the steamer *Jacob Strader* and fell through the hatchway. Her injuries disabled her for the rest of her life. Mrs. Eaton and Mrs. Fogg did not share the same perspective on how tasks should be done and they often locked horns over differing opinions. In November of 1863, she was released from the Maine Camp Hospital Association and decided to go to City Point under the umbrella of the USCC in August of 1864. The pontoon bridge was still in operation when she arrived at City Point and Mrs. Fogg was able to help Mrs. Harris, Mrs. Hall, Miss Etheridge, and Miss Bradley. Mrs. Eaton was working for the Maine State Agency at the time. The two remained distant and sometimes hostile toward one another.

After the war, she received a pension of eight dollars. However, due to her disability, her pension was increased to twenty dollars per month in 1867 and then thirty dollars in 1871. Mrs. Fogg died at the age of 49 on December 23, 1873, and is buried in Forest City Cemetery in South Portland, Maine. {Sources 2, 10, 16, 19, 20, 45, 231. Image in Sudlow, L.L. (2000). *A Vast Army of Women: Maine's Uncounted Forces in the American Civil War.* Gettysburg, PA: Thomas and Maine State Historic Society}

Mrs. Rebecca Frick

A regular "Dix" nurse, she served in Washington, Annapolis, Winchester, Hampton Roads, and City Point.

After the war, she continued to work in the caregiving profession and retired in West Conshohocken, Pennsylvania, near Philadelphia, where she ran a boarding house at 232 South 4th Street. The house was quite well-known for serving great luncheons for prominent financiers and officials of the Pennsylvania railroad. She was an active a member of the National Association of Nurses and frequently travelled to their conventions. She received a pension (#857703) of twenty dollars a month and passed away on September 28, 1911. {Sources 21, 165, 224. Image in Executive Committee of the National Association of Civil War Nurses. (1910). *In Honor of the National Association of Civil War Nurses: 44*th *Encampment Grand Army of the Republic.* Atlantic City: Yeakel}

Miss Gardner

She was mentioned by Amy Bradley as a USSC representative working on the hospital transports. An Irish girl by the name of Ellen was Miss Gardner's personal assistant. Miss Gardner could possibly be Mary J. Gardner, who married Mr. Doherty. If so, she applied for an invalid pension in 1892. Or she could possibly be Mary Fryer Gardner, who also married a soldier and served during the first years of the war with the 105th Pennsylvania. {Sources 2, 19, 165}

Miss Gibbs

She was referred to as a "dresser" of the soldiers' wounds by Mrs. Wheelock. {Source 37}

Miss Agnes Ann Gillis

Born in 1832, she came to City Point from Lowell, Massachusetts, where her mother had been a dressmaker. Little else is known other than she passed away in 1927 in Lowell. {Source 2}

Miss Helen Louise Gilson (Osgood)

Prior to the war, Helen Gilson had been a schoolteacher in the Boston area. She was rejected by Miss Dix for a government nurse position because she was attractive, so she became an independent nurse from the state of Massachusetts. Her service included Gettysburg, Antietam, Fredericksburg, Chancellorsville, White House Landing, and City Point. She served with the Third Corps with Mrs. Husbands and Mrs. McKay.

A gifted communicator, she worked with many of the contrabands and freed slaves. Appalled by the conditions of the contraband camp, Miss Gilson reorganized the facilities and worked in a special diet kitchen for the Corps d'Afrique Hospital. When President Lincoln came through the hospital area in April 1865, she was working in the Ninth Corps Hospital. She was considered one of the "most beautiful as well as the most faithful of nurse" by the soldiers. For her noble labors she commanded admiration, respect and gratitude from the soldiers.

In 1865, after the Union moved into Richmond, she went there as a teacher. She met and married Hamilton Osgood and was in Richmond working with a black orphanage in 1868. Always compassionate, she was one of the ladies who participated in the first Memorial Day in Richmond. When she found she was expecting a child, she returned to Newton, Massachusetts, only to die on Monday April 20, 1868, during childbirth at the age of twenty-two. She is buried at Woodlawn Cemetery in Chelsea, Massachusetts. After the war, many locations erected memorials to honor her. {Sources 2, 5, 10, 12, 13, 16, 17, 23, 34, 165–169, 174. Images at Library of Congress and https://www.bestnursingmasters.com/10-greatest-nurses-of-the-american-civil-war/}

Mrs. Rebecca Ellison Gray

Born in Ireland in 1840, she moved to America when she was 12. She met General Hooker when she tried to swim across the Potomac to see her husband. Little is known about her work while at City Point but it is known that she worked on the hospital steamer *Vanderbilt*.

After the war, she moved to Brooklyn, New York, where she had adjustment issues with one of her neighbors, a Mrs. Murphy. Their husbands defended their actions and ended up getting arrested by the police. Her earlier residence was 762 Bergan Street in Brooklyn and then 847 Pacific Street in Brooklyn. They never had children. Ultimately, she lost her sight, had a serious fall and became bedridden. One report mentioned that she received a disability pension. However, according to NARA, a pension application (#1399669) was filed but "was rejected because the War Department could find no record of federal military service" and her obituary stated she never received a pension. Her husband passed away prior to her death and the city gave her $50 a year as a destitute blind person. Eventually there was an appeal by the Board of Aldermen to provide her with $300 a year, but a unanimous consent was needed for the board to make it effective. The vote was not unanimous, so the consent was withheld. When she passed away, the Women's Relief Corps took over the funeral arrangements and provided a flag to drape over her coffin in January 1917. {Sources 21, 74, 147, 165, 171, 173}

Mrs. Mary J. Guest

She arrived at City Point from Buffalo, New York, to help as a nurse. Her husband was either Sam or Stephen Guest with the 77th New York Infantry and they returned to Buffalo after the war. {Source 2}

Miss Maria M.C. Hall (Richards)

Born in Washington, D.C., Maria was a "Dix nurse" who served at Antietam, Annapolis, and on a hospital steamer on the James River, moving the wounded and former prisoners north. She was the nurse called to special duty for three weeks to care for Tad Lincoln and would often tell schoolchildren about caring for the critically ill president's son until he passed away. While at

Annapolis, she wrote stories for *The Crutch*. She became a close friend of Mrs. Harris and Mrs. Husbands.

After the war, she married Mr. Lucas of Unionville and had two sons. Mr. Lucas retired to Wethersfield, Connecticut, where Maria became president of the local Robert O. Tyler Women's Relief Corps. She was an honorary member of the Ex-Prisoners of War Association and often spoke to the public about her experiences. At the twenty-first session of the Medal of Honor Legion, the women's auxiliary asked her to speak. She presented the following speech:

> I am always glad to see all the comrades, and today I suppose I look in the faces of those who must have been the bravest and the best. Were you all the best boys in the ranks? I used to hear so many stories from my soldier boys, I used to think a great many of them deserve medals of honor. Of course for a good while I saw many soldiers who have been in Andersonville and Libby and all those dreadful places; perhaps some of you know something about it. I am sure that the bravery that they showed, the courage and the patience that enabled them to live there and remain loyal, made them deserve medals of honor. I remember one day I was in a tent among a great many of those men who had recently been brought in, all skeletons and worn to the bone, looking as if they hardly had the breath of life left in them and they told me stories about the elections held there when Abraham Lincoln was elected. They told me how they used black beans and white beans secured from the authorities. I said to them, "Why, how in the world could you vote for Lincoln when he has been keeping you in prison all these for such a long time?" The exchange of prisoners had been delayed for an unusual time—and I said "How did you ever vote for Lincoln when he kept you down there starving all those months?" And one of the poor skeletons replied, "I don't think you know anything about it. Lincoln didn't do it and if he did it was all right if Lincoln did it." As we went on talking he told me about how they felt when they first saw the flag. Just then a little fellow who took care of my storeroom and did my errands came in the tent. I said to him "Johnny we are talking about what they thought when they first saw the flag. What did you think when you saw the flag for the first time?" He said "The first flag I saw was the one flying from your tent down here at Annapolis as we came up the bay, I was so starved and so weak I was down in the hold in the boat, and when I was brought up and laid on deck the first flag I saw was the one flying from your tent." I said "Yes, but what did you think when you first saw it?" "Oh" he said, "I thought, there's grub under that flag, that's what I thought." My friends, I never received a silver medal or anything except the days when I was a little girl in school, for spelling. Then I used to get silver medals I could keep for a week if I kept at the head of my class, and it then had to be given up. You have your medals for all time and you have the medal of happiness, of seeing your country saved by your efforts, which is the best medal of all. I am so glad to look into your faces again. September 21, 1911

Maria received a pension of twelve dollars a month. She died at her home in West Hartford at the age of 75 and was buried in New Rochelle, New York. {Sources 2, 10, 21, 51, 64–66, 146, 165, 231. Image at Library of Congress and http://john-banks.blogspot.com/2013/10/remembering-their-ancestor-civil-war.html}

Miss Cornelia Hancock

Raised in a comfortable Quaker home in New Jersey, she was twenty-five years old when the war began, and she went off to do good deeds. Cornelia worked at Gettysburg, Brandy Station, Fredericksburg, White House Landing and City Point. Mrs. Lee was her mentor, Mrs. Barlow and Mrs. Husbands her peers. She was extremely fond of several surgeons, especially one young doctor, Dr. Frederick Dudley, who had graduated from Yale. Dr. Dudley was captured at Hatchers Run, leaving her distraught and her psyche permanently damaged. After her love affair with Dr. Dudley, she decided to never marry. For her work at City Point, she earned sixteen dollars a month as manager of the First Division, Second Corps diet kitchen. For her diligent work with the Third Division, she received a silver medal.

Always deeply concerned about children, she went to South Carolina after the war and started a school for black children. In 1878, she moved to 120 North 19th Street in Philadelphia and started the Society for Organizing Charities. In 1882, she organized the Children's Aid Society and served as the National Secretary to the National Association of Army Nurse of the Civil War.

She died in Atlantic City in 1927 and is buried in the Cedar Hills Friends Cemetery in Harmesville, New Jersey. During the war, she wrote letters and a diary that were eventually compiled in *South After Gettysburg*, which was published in 1937. She received a pension (#1162959). {Sources 2, 10, 12, 19, 21, 50, 158, 165, 231. Images at https://www.bestnursingmasters.com/10-greatest-nurses-of-the-american-civil-war/ and http://www.wondersandmarvels.com/2016/02/what-civil-war-nurses-did-after-the-war.html}

Miss M.A. Happer

From Monongahela, Pennsylvania, she served in Base Hospital kitchen #2 at Point of Rocks with the USCC. She served with Miss Pettis and Miss Mary Houghton. According to genealogy and church records, she married John Beacom in 1868, who had served with the 6th Pennsylvania Heavy Artillery. Later, they were affiliated with the Mango Presbyterian Church in Pennsylvania. {Source 195}

Miss Eunice Hardenbrook

Originally from Wyandott City, Kansas, she served in Base Hospital kitchen #1 at Point of Rocks for the USCC. With her was Mrs. E.H. Jones and Mrs. T.H. Potter. According to a Nebraska City Directory, she resided in 1908 in Kearney, Nebraska. She may have then married Thomas Vipond, a Free Methodist minister and former soldier in Wet Mountain Valley. If so, she is the Eunice Hardenbrook Vipond buried in Lakeside Cemetery in Colorado in 1914 with a Civil War marker. {Source 195}

Mrs. John Harris

Mrs. Harris was the wife of Dr. Harris of Philadelphia. She worked at Gettysburg, Fredericksburg, and City Point, representing the Ladies' Aid Society. She was a close friend of Isabella Fogg. While at City Point, she spent most of her time on the hospital steamer *Vanderbilt* and some time on the *Nellie Baker*. At the end of the war, she worked in Virginia and North Carolina with the returning prisoners from Andersonville and Salisbury. Her health suffered from the years of constant exposure to the weather and bouts of sunstroke.

After the war, her husband was the attaché to the United States Consul in Italy. She died in Venice and was eventually buried in Florence, Italy. {Sources 2, 10, 12, 16, 19. Image at http://www.quazoo.com/q/Women_in_the_American_Civil_War}

Mrs. Hart (possibly Virginia Hart)

Mrs. Hart was mentioned in Pauline Bush's letter regarding the care of Mr. George Law, Company F, 109th Pennsylvania Volunteers, 5th Corps. She was probably at the 2nd Corps or Cavalry Hospital. She enjoyed her "off" time with Cornelia Hancock. Mrs. McKay referred to a Miss Virginia Hart, who may be the same person. There is also a Lucy Hart, from Spencer, Massachusetts, who served with the Army of the Potomac. She was the widow of Massachusetts infantry soldier Toby Hart. Together, they had 21 children. She passed away in January of 1919. {Sources 12, 18, 19, 136, 208}

Mrs. Fannie Titus Hazen

Fannie was born in Vershire, Vermont, on May 9, 1840, to Simon and Eliza Titus. She was DAR member #29891. She was not the wife of General Hazen. Fannie was the oldest of eleven children. She felt compelled to help with caregiving during the war. Three of her brothers joined the military and two died at Spotsylvania. She worked in Washington before heading to Virginia with the Army of the Potomac when her younger brother, Joseph, was wounded in the Battle of Cold Harbor. Later she met an army courier, Charles Hazen, who was from Vermont, and they married during the war years and had a daughter. She became manager of the 9th Corps Hospital and the USCC kitchen.

After the war, Fannie was persistently bothered by a shoulder injury and collected invalid's pension #847656. Charles and Fannie lived in Cambridge, Massachusetts, where they maintained a boarding house and had only the one child. In 1883, their daughter married Ernest Conant in Massachusetts. With more time to devote to a cause, she founded the Army Nurse Association for the state of Massachusetts in 1896. She served as president of the National Association of War Nurses from 1905 to 1906. She filed to collect an invalid's pension but also received a widow's pension (#858688) and died on January 16, 1930, at age 90 at her home in Cambridge, Massachusetts. {Sources 23, 47, 165, 174, 176, 201, 231. Images in Executive Committee of the National Association of Civil War Nurses (1910). In Honor of the National Association of Civil War Nurses: 44th Encampment Grand Army of the Republic, Atlantic City: Yeakel; and They Were Nurses During the Civil War. (April 15, 1922). *The Bridgeport Times and Evening Farmer* (Bridgeport, CT), p. 16}

Mrs. Mary Hill

Mrs. Hill went with Mrs. McKay and Miss Hart to Petersburg the day after it fell, on April 4, 1865. She lived in Washington, D.C., after the war at 1125 Twenty-fourth Street NW and received a pension.

Author's Note: There is also a Mary Hill Johnson affiliated with the 133rd Massachusetts Infantry, Second Massachusetts Heavy Artillery and it may be the same person. Her pension file was #1515263. {Sources 18, 117}

Mrs. Anna Holstein

Born in Upper Marion, Pennsylvania, Anna Morris Holstein was the great-granddaughter of Revolutionary War Captain Sam Morris and regent at Mount Vernon. She was the wife of Major Reverend William H. Holstein of Pennsylvania and made matron-in-chief by Dr. C.N. Chamberlain when Camp Letterman hospital was established at Gettysburg. At City Point, she was matron of the 2nd Corps Hospital and manager of the 2nd Corps kitchen USSC. She was at City Point when the explosion took place. Her husband often worked at Fort Monroe. According to Cornelia Hancock, Dr. Burmeister "boarded" with Mrs. Holstein. However, challenged by the task of maggot removal from the soldiers' wounds and the endless duties as a nurse, Anna Holstein left City Point to take on an easier public awareness cause. She spent a great deal of time touring and talking to the women back home about what they could do to help and about the conditions of the men returning from the war and prison camps. Towards the end of the war, she worked at Annapolis with the returning POWs. She wrote *Three Years in Field Hospitals*.

After the war, she received a pension (#1126339) for serving with the Pennsylvania Volunteers and became active in and Regent Emeritus of DAR's Valley Forge Chapter. In addition, she served as matron of the Pennsylvania Building at the World's Fair and was an active member of the local Grange. She passed away in early January of 1901 and is buried in Old Swedes Christ Church Cemetery in Bridgeport, Pennsylvania. {Sources 2, 10, 12, 14, 27, 163, 212, 231. Image at https://www.findagrave.com/memorial/15459924/ann-morris-holstein}

Mrs. Dr. Hood*

She was the wife of Surgeon in Chief Hood, from Newark, Ohio. She was stationed on the hospital steamer *Connecticut* with Mrs. Case, Mrs. Sharpless and Mrs. Reifsnyder. Provost Marshal Marsena Patrick found her to be "a rather peasant lady." {Sources 27, 46, 232}

Mrs. Mary Houghton

She was born around 1829 in Massachusetts. She was recruited to go with the USCC to represent Dorchester, Massachusetts. She served in Base Hospital kitchen #1 at Point of Rocks. She may have been married to either William H., Joseph B, or Moses B. Houghton. They were soldiers getting a pension with Mary E. listed as their spouse, but most probable is W.H., who served with 1st Massachusetts Infantry, or J.B., who served with 22nd Massachusetts infantry. {Source 195}

Mrs. Clara Hoyt

Mrs. Hoyt was from Maine and served in Base Hospital kitchen #1 at Point of Rocks. Her pension application (#1133681) was dated 1892. It is probable that she was married to James Hoyt, who was with 9th Maine. {Source 195}

Mrs. Mary F. Huron

Mrs. Huron was a representative for the Indiana State Relief Agent. She contacted typhoid fever while at City Point and almost died from the illness. She was part of the touring party to see Petersburg on April 4, 1865. She received a pension after the war (#1387619) and died in 1909. {Source 34}

Mrs. Mary Morris Husbands

Known as "Mother Husbands," this affluent Pennsylvania lady came from 18th and Spruce Street in Philadelphia. She was logistically supported by the Ladies' Aid Society of Philadelphia. She served at Gettysburg, Chancellorsville, Fredericksburg, White House Landing, and City Point with the 13th Ohio Cavalry regiment. For a while she worked with Hancock's Corps attached to the Second, Third, and Sixth Hospitals. At other times, she was with the USSC in charge of the Second Division diet kitchen. While at City Point, she created the modified apron with large pockets and would move between the beds "without inconvenience" and carry supplies the men had requested. She always had a kind word for everyone and was well loved by the men of the 2nd, 3rd, and 6th Army Corps who saw her as their protector and mother. When she was near the soldiers knew that everything would be all right.

After the war, she worked for the Freedman's Bureau in Florida. She received a pension of twenty-five dollars a month. She returned from Florida and lived a 1011 G Street NW in Washington, D.C. She passed away on March 6, 1894, at the age of 73. She was buried in Laurel Hill Cemetery in Philadelphia. {Sources 2, 10, 12, 19, 117, 178–180. Images at Moore, F. (1867). *Women of the War*. Hartford, CT: S.S. Scranton; and https://www.findagrave.com/memorial/28643187/mary-husband}

Mrs. Johnson

The name "Mrs. Johnson" was a catchall name, but there was a Mrs. Johnson who served as a representative of the Maine State Relief Agency and USCC. She reported to Dr. Dalton on June 17, 1864, and left on August 2, 1864. She probably worked with Mrs. Mayhew as one of the two assistants who helped in the mess kitchen. She also worked for six weeks with Mrs. Wheelock as a dresser in the wards. Her full name may never be known. However, there was a story of a Miss Mary Jane Johnson which may also be a mixture of rumors and blended Johnson stories. For example, Charlotte Johnson (later Mrs. McKay) was born in Watertown, Maine, and may have blended into the rumor mill (see Charlotte McKay later in this section). The rumor of Mary Jane Johnson was that she was young and followed the love of her life from the 16th Maine Regiment into battle. He was killed and she was captured and sent to Belle Island in Richmond, and, according to the Richmond paper, was then held in Castle Thunder. There is also Mary K. Johnson, formerly Hill, who was a nurse (see Mrs. Mary Hill in this section) and a Mary J. Johnson who was married to Noah Johnson from Brooks, Maine. (See last section.) {Sources 10, 37, 45, 54}

Mrs. H.E. Jones

She was the widow of a Presbyterian minister from Wellesley, Massachusetts, and worked for the USCC at Point of Rocks. She had a long career with the USCC and was a respected and loyal friend of Mrs. Wittenmyer. Mrs. Jones had a daughter who was the attending physician of the college in Wellesley. {Sources 38, 195}

Miss Hetty Jones

Mrs. Hetty Jones was the daughter of Reverend Horatio Jones. Hetty was from the Roxborough area in Philadelphia and represented the Ladies' Aid Society. She headed to City Point to be with the 3rd Division of 2nd Corps, about the first of November. She became ill right after Thanksgiving with typhoid fever. Dr. Painter watched over her medically while others helped find pillows for Hetty to sleep on in order to increase the comfort of a straw bed. However, she died of the fever at City Point on December 21, 1864. Her body was exhumed from the City Point Cemetery at her brother's request and taken to Philadelphia, where it was buried in the family plot. A Grand Army of the Republic Post in Philadelphia was named in her honor. {Sources 2, 34}

Miss Maria Josslyn

She was from Roxbury, Massachusetts, and came to work as a nurse. She may be Harriet Maria Joslyn/Josslyn who was born in 1828 and she may have served with one of the Massachusetts regiments. {Source 2}

Miss Agnes Le Clerq Joy

She was born in Baltimore on Christmas day in 1840 and worked as a young actress and circus performer. In 1862, she married Colonel Felix Salm-Salm who was a soldier of fortune from Austria serving with the Union. "Miss Joy," aka "Princess Salm-Salm" met and rubbed elbows with many people at Point of Rocks and City Point. She had quite a reputation at City Point and in Atlanta. After the war, they had adventures in Mexico with Maximilian forces and then the Prussian War, where he was captured. However, a good talker, she managed to get a pardon for him that required they leave the country for a while. Not totally giving up her quest for adventure, she managed to pass her examinations in surgery and was on the staff of the Prussian Surgeon General as a Directress of Camp Hospitals. After her husband's death, she remained in Germany. In 1876, she married an English man whose last name was Heneage in Stuttgart, Germany. Still called Princess, she was presented to President William McKinley in 1899 as Princess Le Clerq Salm-Salm by her cousin, Mr. Joy, who was then the representative from Missouri. She passed away in Karlsruhe, Germany, on December 21, 1912. {Sources 25, 193, 194, 200, 202, 222, 245, 276. Images at http://www.snipview.com/q/House_of_Salm; and https://en.wikipedia.org/wiki/Agnes_Salm-Salm}

Mrs. King

She was the wife of Nathan King who was a paymaster from Michigan. She moved wherever he moved. While at Point of Rocks, she helped in the hospital. {Source 25}

Mrs. Mary Roby Lacey

Married at age 15 to Benjamin Roby, she was turned down by Miss Dix, so she began by rolling bandages in the Refreshment Salon. Four weeks later, she became a nurse when she was only 17 years of age and served with the Army of the Potomac with Company E, 1st New Jersey. After the war, she became involved with the Association of Nurses and eventually moved to the Salt Lake City area. There are pension papers for Sgt. Benjamin Roby, Company E, New Jersey Infantry, showing Mary E. and a minor child John E. Lacey. It appears her pension was attained as a widow in 1871 (#158239). {Sources 159, 176. Image in Nurses Famous on Many Battlefields. (August 16, 1903). *The San Francisco Call*, San Francisco. CA. pp. 12–13}

Miss Anna Larnard

She was a seasoned regimental nurse (probably an independent nurse) from Michigan and escorted wounded soldiers from Point of Rocks to City Point, then escorted them onto one of the steamers bound for Washington. {Sources 3, 34}

Mrs. Anna Latham

This is probably Mrs. P.C. Latham, who was from Springfield, Illinois. If so, she worked at one of the Soldiers Homes in Springfield before heading to City Point just before the war ended. She became part of the Committee of Citizens to enter Richmond. {Sources 2, 203}

Mrs. Mary W. Lee

Mrs. Lee was not related to General Robert E. Lee. She worked with Misses Willetts, Hancock, Polk, Hart, and Ashe at the 2nd Corps Hospital and was a good friend and coworker of Dr. Aikens. She was mentioned by Mrs. Pauline Bush. She served at Gettysburg, Brandy Station, Fredericksburg, White House Landing, and City Point. Serving for considerable time, she was probably attached to the USSC, however, references to "cooking" could have been USCC. She was known for her excellent voice and often sang for the men. {Sources 2, 10, 12, 19, 231}

Mrs. Ellon McCormick Looby

Born in Ireland in 1834, she came to the states and married Rody Looby of Waddington, New York. They had three sons. Her husband enlisted with the 14th Heavy Arty and was eventually wounded at Petersburg. Upon hearing her husband had been wounded, she left the children with family members and went to City Point. She worked as a nurse from August of 1864 until the war ended. {Source 110}

Mrs. Lyons

She was a friend of Mrs. Spencer and accompanied Miss Bucklin from City Point to Camp Stoneman in Washington. She was a good riding companion to Mrs. Spencer and they would frequently ride out to deliver supplies to the rifle pits. {Source 3}

Mrs. Ruth Mayhew

Born in Orland, Maine, she grew up and married a reverend. He passed away before the war, so as a widow she became attached to the Maine Camp Hospital Association, otherwise known as the Maine State Relief Agency from Rockland and Portland, Maine. She had served with Mrs. Fogg earlier and then at Gettysburg with Mrs. Sampson. She came to City Point to relieve Mrs. Eaton in December when she needed a rest. Mrs. Mayhew had an outstanding soprano voice and was frequently asked to sing military and patriotic songs for the men and was part of a singing quartet with Miss Smith. At one point, she was in charge of the Maine State Relief Agency mess kitchen. Occasionally, she and her two assistants and Mrs. Sampson went to the front outside Petersburg to help deliver supplies to the Maine soldiers.

After the war, she went to help teach at an Indian school for a short while but then returned to Maine. She resided with her sister's family. She received a pension (#548311) and died in 1874. She is buried in Seaview Cemetery in Rockland, Maine. {Sources 2, 10, 34, 45. Image in Vintage Maine Images, item 5198, Maine Historical Society}

Mrs. Charlotte McKay

Mrs. Charlotte Johnson McKay was born in Watertown, Maine, but lived in South Reading, Massachusetts, as a widow when the war began. A well-respected caregiver, Mrs. McKay became an independent nurse during the war. At City Point, she was attached to the Cavalry Corps Hospital under Dr. Mitchell of the 8th Pennsylvania and she was manager of the diet kitchen and worked with Mrs. M.A. Ehler and Mrs. Spaulding. Mrs. McKay had a good working relationship with the provost marshal, which helped when she had a major disagreement with Mrs. Wittenmyer of the USCC. As a result, she was able to get a reassignment to Dr. Dalton's command.

After the war, Mrs. McKay stayed in Virginia for several years to help the freedmen. She became the recipient of the Kearney Cross and received a gold medal from the men of the 17th Maine, and in 1876 she wrote *The Stories of Hospital and Camp*. She never applied for nor received a pension and died in San Diego, California, in 1894. She is buried in Olivewood Cemetery in Riverside, California. {Sources 2, 18, 27, 28, 45, 46, 231, 235}

Mrs. Mary Merritt

Mrs. Merritt was born in Pennsylvania in 1834, but her family moved to Cleveland, Ohio, before the war started. She worked with the USCC at Point of Rocks. {Source 20}

Miss Margaret "Maggie" Mitchell

Maggie was attached to the 9th Corps Hospital. In November, she was with Mrs. McKay and Dr. Dalton when they ran into General Marsena Patrick. The provost marshal eventually developed concern for and a protective nature over Maggie. She left City Point on February 20, 1865, to return home. There is some doubt as to whether she was a caregiver or an actress or the Miss Mitchel (spelled with one l) listed in the next section. It is alleged that because she was an actress, she was a friend of John Wilkes Booth. {Sources 27, 28. Image at https://www.loc.gov/item/2016646123/}

Mrs. Moore and Daughters

The Moore women worked with the USCC in the Corps d'Afrique Hospital and in the Ninth Corps Hospital after the explosion in 1864. One of the daughters was referred to as a "screamer" due to her complaining nature. Mrs. Moore and Dr. Price complained directly to Generals Grant, Meade, and Patrick. Their comments were neither well-received nor appreciated. {Sources 28, 46}

Mrs. Mary Moore/Mrs. Mercy

One of the older women who worked at Point of Rocks until the end of the war, she was born in 1810 and was the wife of Thomas Moore of Hartford, Connecticut. After her husband died, she moved to Hinton, Texas, where she passed away in 1905. {Source 209}

Mrs. Matilda E. Moore

Born in 1835 in Germany, this lady came from Cleveland, Ohio, and served under Dr. Bliss while in Washington. She married Lewis Moore and they had two daughters. Later, she worked under direction of Sheridan and served as a nurse for three years. It is not known if she was also the Mrs. Moore listed previously. She passed away from pneumonia in 1923 and received a pension (#854939). She was buried in the Hargrove Cemetery in Cleveland, Ohio (Find-a-Grave #17262557). {Sources 165, 280}

Mrs. Murry

She was mentioned by Miss Bradley as one of the women who worked in the culinary department. {Source 2}

Mrs. Laura Mount Newman

Originally from Indiana, she was a Dix nurse until July 3, 1865. Her husband, Abraham Mount, was part of the 6th Maryland Regiment and was wounded at Petersburg. Consequently, she stayed at City Point while he was there. They divorced after the war. She married Frank W. Newman on February 16, 1891. She was active in the National Army Nurses Association and received a pension (#1158311) of twenty dollars a month in 1913 and lived in Lafayette, Indiana. {Sources 21, 118, 165. Image in Executive Committee of the National Association of Civil War Nurses. (1910). *In Honor of the National Association of Civil War Nurses: 44th Encampment Grand Army of the Republic* Atlantic City: Yeakel}

Miss Ney

Miss Ney was a representative of the New York State Agency. She had no love for the Mission of Masons group and advised Miss Smith to remove or conceal her identification pass for the organization when she arrived at City Point. After the war, she returned to school and became a doctor. She graduated from the New York Homeopathic School. She eventually married a former Confederate doctor whose last name was also Ney, thus becoming Mrs. Francis Ney or Dr. Ney. {Sources 34, 231}

Mrs. Mary Elizabeth M. Nolan

Mrs. Nolan came to America at about 9 years of age. She married Peter Nolan of the 10th New York and they had nine children. She was survived by fourteen great grandchildren and enjoyed her daily walks until shortly before her passing. Peter was a blacksmith as well as a letter-writer during the war. After the war, he invented the fire hydrant, and that provided substantial income. After Peter died, Mrs. Nolan moved to 63 Berkeley Place in Brooklyn and passed away at the age of 95. She was buried in Holy Cross Cemetery in Brooklyn. {Source 210}

Miss Hettie Noyes

She was a member of the USCC from Canton, Ohio. She spent most of her time at Point of Rocks. She had been stationed elsewhere earlier in the war and was a trusted friend of Mrs. Wittenmyer. She had a good voice and sang for the USCC and would occasionally join the other women at the Depot Complex when they got together. After the war, she married George Aucker (Aucher) from Athens, Ohio. He had served with the 28th Regiment, Ohio Infantry and 173rd Ohio Regiment. In 1906, she applied for a pension (#1353565). {Source 38}

Ohio State Relief Agent

The agent was a pretty young girl with long brunette curls and very dark, almost black, eyes. She became quite ill while at City Point and had to be hospitalized. All the agents helped to care for her and she was able to recover. {Source 34}

Dr. Ester Hettie Kersey Painter

Born in 1820 in Philadelphia, Dr. Painter was a state agent representative from both New Jersey and Pennsylvania. Dr. Painter was a petite Quaker lady who always wore a white nightcap and a shorter gown with multiple petticoats. She may have been a contract surgeon for New Jersey but would not have operated unless the situation was desperate, due to the fact she was a woman. She was the doctor who cared for Miss Hetty Jones before she died. She had two children. Her son, Jesse, was stationed at the telegraph station at Hatcher's Farm near Bermuda Hundred. She spent a significant amount of time mentoring Miss Adelaide Smith and Miss Cornelia Hancock. To demonstrate her pluck, she demanded that some green shutters on one of the houses at White House landing be removed and relocated to her quarter.

After the war, she moved to Nebraska with her husband, Joseph H. Painter (formerly 7th New Jersey Infantry), and became involved in the Relief Corps efforts. In 1888, she was elected as a delegate to meet and negotiate with the Public Board of Charities. She received a pension (#663929) and died in early January 1889 in Lincoln, Nebraska. She was buried in the Wyuka Cemetery. {Sources 17, 34, 79, 80. Images at Smith, A. (1919). *Reminiscences of an Army*

Nurse During the Civil War. New York: Greaves; and at www.findagrave.com/memorial/73669005/esther-painter}

Mrs. Sarah Palmer

Born in 1830 or 1832 in upstate New York near Ithaca, she was the only girl in a family of boys. Her real name was Annie Graham. She married Mr. Abel Palmer while she was a teen and they had two daughters. According to one source, she was 17 the war started, but it is likely she was much older. Envious of the boys who went off to war, she chose the option of being a nurse to the soldiers. She sought out Secretary of War Benjamin Tracy and appealed to his sense of duty. He was able grant her a permit to join the 109th New York Regiment. She left her children with family in Binghamton, New York, and was sworn in by Miss Dix in Beltsville, Maryland. After a long and eventful journey, she arrived at City Point with Mrs. Strouse. The soldiers gave her a difficult time when she first became a nurse, but they deeply loved her and called her "Aunt Becky." She survived the war with a very limited wardrobe that consisted of two sturdy bed ticking dresses, a small black hat, and shoes that were three sizes too large for her feet. She considered herself the "common nurse for the common soldier," never seeking better conditions or glory. She believed if the men could endure the conditions, so could she. She was attached to the 109th New York Volunteers in Ninth Corps at City Point. After City Point, she moved to Tenlytown, just outside of Washington, until the soldiers were sent home. She was offered transportation home on a passenger train but decided to stay with her men and rode in a cattle car back to New York.

After the war, she went back to Washington to serve as the matron of the Asylum of Orphans. In 1867, she married David C. Young, who was a carpenter and former Canadian soldier. They moved to Des Moines, Iowa, where they raised Aunt Becky's two daughters (Alice and Belle). She was the founder of one of the New York and the Iowa State Sanitary Associations. When Aunt Becky went back to the reunion for the 109th, she was always called upon to sit on stage with the dignitaries or to speak. At the 1890 reunion, she spoke in response to the loud "Aunt Becky" cheers. She:

> made a brief, humorous and entirely extemporaneous speech. She expressed her pleasure at looking over the old faces. She alluded to her going to the front, when she had rather to run away to do so, and briefly sketched her camp experiences. She told of the kindness of the soldiers to her in the West, attributing it, as she humorously put it, perhaps to her good looks. Her husband, she said, was a soldier and her son-in-laws were soldiers also. Her husband told her not to kiss every old soldier she met. She had not done it today, but felt that she wanted to just the same. Aunt Becky's speech was a good one, full of quiet humor, delivered in an unpretentious way and great effect, and it was received with unstinted applause. At the conclusion of her remarks she received three rousing cheers [*Oswego Gazette*, August 28, 1890].

She died on April 6, 1919, at the age of seventy-six, and is buried at Woodland Cemetery in Des Moines, Iowa. She wrote *The Story of Aunt Becky's Army-Life*. A bronze marker placed at the cemetery states, "On behalf of a Grateful Nation, and in Honor of the Service Rendered her Country during the American Civil War, 1861–1865, This stone is set at the final post of: 'Aunt Becky.' Sarah A. Graham Palmer Young 109th New York Volunteer Infantry Regiment United States Army Nurse this 11th day of November 2009 by General Grenville M. Dodge Camp 75 Sons of Union Veterans of the Civil War and Company "A" 49th Iowa Volunteer Infantry Regiment 'The Iowa Rifles' Honor Guard for the Department of Iowa." {Sources 23, 53, 68–73, 156, 231. Images at https://en.wikipedia.org/wiki/Sarah_Palmer_Young; and Palmer, S. (1868). *The Story of Aunt Becky's Army-Life*. New York: John F. Trow}

Ms. Pettis

Originally from Oswego, New York, Tryphena (Triphena) A. Pettis worked at Point of Rocks with the USCC. After the war, she married George W. Wilcox. They travelled briefly to Mexico before they returned and settled in Rockford, Illinois. They lived in Rockford for 60 years and had two children, Frances May and Howard. Tryphena collected a pension (#908227) and passed away in 1924. {Source 195}

Miss Jennie Pitkins

The Pitkins were a well-respected old family in Hartford, Connecticut. It is believed that Jennie was one of the daughters of the family. She went to City Point with the USCC and worked in the diet kitchen of the 3rd Vermont Regiment. After the war, in 1866, she married Edward F. Williams. According to cemetery records, Edward passed away in 1869 and Jennie passed away in 1908. {Sources 20, 195}

Mrs. Polk

Mrs. Polk worked with Mrs. Lee and was referred to in a letter from Mrs. Pauline Bush. {Source 19}

Mrs. Rebecca L. Price

Miss Pennypacker was born in 1837 in Phoenixville, Pennsylvania. In 1853, she married Edwin Price and became Mrs. Price. During the war she served as a volunteer or independent nurse. Mrs. Price came to City Point after working at White House Landing with Mr. Ritz and Miss Sayles. They all were agents from the state of Pennsylvania. While at City Point, she was often seen helping with the organization of the wounded onto the hospital steamers using a state agent's pass that Governor Curtin of Pennsylvania had issued to her. After the war, she returned to Lancaster, Pennsylvania, and became a member of the Association of Civil War Nurses, where she served two terms as president. At the fifteenth anniversary reunion of the Battle of Gettysburg in 1913, she met two Union soldiers and three Confederate soldiers whom she had nursed during the war. Much to her surprise and delight, they remembered her. She died in May of 1919 at her home in Pottstown, Pennsylvania. She received a pension (#1153922), which was verified by Mrs. Wittenmyer. {Sources 19, 37, 165, 184, 272. Image at https://en.wikipedia.org/wiki/File:Mrs._L._Price,_(aka_Rebecca_L.)_Pennypacker,_c._1910.jpg}

Mrs. Reading

Mrs. Reading was mentioned by Amy Bradley as helping in the wards as an "assistant dresser." {Source 19}

Miss Reeves

Originally from Sandusky, Ohio, she was at Point of Rocks working in Diet Kitchen #3 for the USCC. She may have been Eliza M. Braden, wife of Wilbur A. Reeves. If so, they married in December of 1865. She eventually received a widow pension (#540073) from Ohio. {Source 195}

Miss Harriett Reifsnyder

Cousin to Miss Sharpless, they both served on the *Connecticut* along with Mrs. Hood and Mrs. Case. She had a brother, George, who was with the 3rd Regiment Pennsylvania Heavy Arty at Point of Rocks. Lt. Marsden was quite interested in trying to socialize with her and would frequently come to visit, but her work interfered with any amount of social time. The two Harrietts (Reifsnyder and Sharpless) were always equally concerned about Confederate and Union soldiers. She was considered a Good Samaritan by many of the wounded rebels. At a fundraising event for the USSC in Catawissa, Pennsylvania, Miss "Hattie" Reifsnyder was voted, with a majority of 280 votes, to be the prettiest girl in town. After the war, she married one of her cousin's brothers in 1868 and took custodial charge of three her own brothers' children (Sarah, Ellen and George). There are conflicting reports as to when she died. One says she passed away on December 7, 1906, while another says March 22, 1912. As an Army nurse, she received a pension (#948154). {Sources 177, 232, 237, 238, 241, 282}

Carrie Robinson Mills

Carrie was the daughter of a physician. She began her nursing career working with Dr. Crosby of Concord, New Hampshire. Later, she became a Dix nurse and served for three months at Point of Rocks hospital before going to Harpers Ferry. She later married John E. Mills from Haverhill, Massachusetts, who served with the 17th Massachusetts band. John returned to his former profession of shoemaker after the war and Carrie became involved with the retired Nurses Association for Massachusetts. In 1899, she received a widow's pension and passed away after 1922. She was buried at Elmwood Cemetery, in Bradford, Massachusetts. {Sources 2, 165, 201, 205. Image in They Were Nurses During the Civil War (April 15, 1922), *The Bridgeport Times and Evening Farmer* (Bridgeport, CT), p. 16}

Mrs. Samples

She served as the state agent from Delaware. She was part of the touring party on April 4, 1865. {Source 34}

Mrs. Sarah S. Sampson*

Mrs. Sampson, from Bath, Maine, worked as a very bold and often outspoken state agent representing the Maine Camp and Hospital Association. Her husband, Charles Sampson, was a captain with Company D 3rd Maine Infantry Regiment (later LTC). She followed him from the start of the war to the end of the war, including to Gettysburg and Fredericksburg. She worked with Miss Hancock who considered her to be a slow individual to work with. Perhaps her pace was from her last assignment at Fredericksburg, perhaps it was for another unknown reason. She complained about being quite ill and skeleton-like as well as having to learn to walk all over again. Aware that she was not fulfilling her obligations, in November of 1864 she wrote to Mr. Hinds at the Maine agency asking if her sister Mary could take over her duties. At one point, Mrs. Mayhew and Mrs. Sampson went to the front at Petersburg to deliver necessary supplies. Recovering from her illness, she later appeared in New York with Mrs. Read, Moulton, and Arthurs to mix socially with Mrs. Maria Daly.

After the war, she established a home for the orphans of the Maine soldiers killed in the war. When her husband died, she went to Washington to work in the Pension Office and eventually received a pension (#293993) of twenty-five dollars a month. In 1906, she attended the last reunion of the 3rd Maine back in Maine before returning to Washington. She died in 1907 and was buried in site #1261 near several other Civil War Army nurses in Arlington

National Cemetery. {Sources 10, 11, 12, 19, 45, 163, 230, 231. Image at http://www.arlingtoncemetery.net/sarahssa.htm}

Miss Sayles

She was a state agent from Pennsylvania at City Point. She was often seen helping with the organization of the wounded on to the hospital steamers. She may have been Jane F. Sayles, who was married to David Sayles of the 52nd PA Infantry. {Sources 19, 37}

Miss. Harriet Sharpless

She was born in February of 1837 as the only daughter to Joseph and Mary Sharpless in Bloomsburg, Pennsylvania. In 1861, she helped establish a Ladies' Aid Society in the town and began her nursing work in Fredericksburg as an organizer, but not as a nurse. Affectionately called "Hal," by 1864 she was chief nurse on the steamer *Connecticut* with Mrs. Hood and Mrs. Case and her cousin Harriet Reifsynder. For almost a year and a half, they transported 33,000 patients.

After the war, she returned to her home of Bloomsburg. A considerate and kind individual to all she worked with, she was publicly recognized by Mrs. Grant in 1887 as having served with the Army of the Potomac as a nurse. She lived with her brother in Bloomsburg, Pennsylvania. She was 69 years of age when she died on December 8, 1906. She is buried in Rosemont Cemetery in Bloomsburg, Pennsylvania (Find-a-Grave #75734989). {Sources 2, 28, 77, 111, 176, 177, 211, 232. Images in Nurses Famous on Many Battlefields. (August 16, 1903). *The San Francisco Call*, pp. 12–13; and Find-a-Grave #757344989}

Ms. Mary and Sarah Shaw

These women were USSC representatives on the transport steamer *Sarah E. Brown* that was fired upon on April 5, 1864, when Chief Engineer John Hamlin was killed. Mary Shaw may have been Mrs. George Shaw from Boston. Although no other information has been verified yet, George received a pension (#425400) from Massachusetts. {Sources 2, 188}

Miss Adelaide Smith

Originally from Brooklyn, New York, she was born in 1831 to Willian Penn Smith and Sarah Cooke Smith. Miss Smith gained nursing and organizational skills with the returning soldiers on Bedlow's Island in New York (later renamed Liberty Island and home of the Statue of Liberty). At that point, she met people from the Mission of Masons who offered her work as an independent nurse at

Point of Rocks (just beyond the Depot complex). Being young and quite confident, she accepted the proposition and headed south. When she arrived, she found the organization to be deceitful and highly inefficient. As a result, she gathered several other women who had also been told they would have employment and headed back to City Point, where other adventures began. She became close friends with Dr. Painter and many of the Maine Agency personnel. However, she would periodically lock horns with officers and staff at City Point and was used in a fundraising scheme by the Masonic Mission in New York City. Adelaide decided she wanted the prime position of a state agent from New York and devised a way to attain the position. As the battle of personalities grew, so did her skills.

After the war, she remained in Norfolk, where she became superintendent of colored schools. She eventually returned to her home on Bedford Avenue in Brooklyn, where she was encouraged to write her story. She became an active suffragette in the New York area. In November of 1913, she rode in an open-air car at the head of the first suffrage parade and demonstration in Brooklyn with 5,000 women marching with suffrage banners. Her book took several years to complete and was called *Reminiscences of an Army Nurse During the Civil War*. It was published posthumously in 1919. She died in January of 1914 of a freak accident when a young driver, Lottie Wallum, 18, was driving her father's car and forgot to throw out the clutch when she got out of the car. This caused the car to lurch forward, jumping the curb and crashing into the Sterling Piano Company, where Adelaide was shopping. The car injured several people outside and came through the window and tossed Miss Smith several feet. She was 84 at the time and died within three hours of the accident.

Prior to that incident, she resided at the Home for the Aged on 101st and Amsterdam Avenue in Manhattan and was honored by many suffragists, like Mrs. Carrie Chapman Cait of the Brooklyn Women's Suffrage Party and Mrs. R.C. Talbot-Perkins, president of the Kings County Suffrage Party. She was buried in the family plot in Patterson, New Jersey. {Sources 3, 10, 27, 28, 34, 56–64, 213, 231, 246–249. Images in Smith, A. (1919). *Reminiscences of an Army Nurse During the Civil War*. New York: Greaves}

Mrs. Soyer

She was the wife of a USSC representative at City Point. She went to Petersburg with a group of the nurses and Miss Bucklin at the end of the war. She received a widow's pension in 1901. {Sources 2, 3}

Mrs. Spaulding

Mrs. Spaulding was a very kind and motherly woman from Springfield, Maine. She had four sons in the Union Army, two of whom survived the war.

She began working as a caregiver/nurse after she came to City Point to help one of her injured sons, who died five days before she arrived. Sergeant A.D. Spaulding was buried in the yard "East of the Railroad" near Patricks' Station. Mrs. Spaulding decided to stay and work with Mrs. McKay to help those who were in need of the motherly comfort she could provide at the Cavalry Corps Hospital. The men frequently remarked how much she seemed like their mother or how her hands felt like their own mother's hands. The family has a cemetery plot in Springfield and Mrs. Spaulding is buried with the rest of her family in the Springfield Cemetery. {Sources 18, 19, 45}

Mrs. R.H. (Elmira Keeler) Spencer*

She was born in a log cabin on September 15, 1819, near the village of Mexico, New York. At the age of ten, her family moved to Oswego, New York. She married R.H. Spencer in 1840 and followed him when he went to war with the 147th Regiment. Elmira started by working for the Maine State Relief Agency but changed to the New York State Agency, where she served for three years. She had the purveyor's steamer the *Planter* at her disposal, which brought about many unkind comments from other women, and she was eventually released due to showing partiality in supply distribution. While at City Point, she worked with the New York State Relief Agency that was attached to the 147th New York Regiment where her husband had become a surgeon. Mrs. Spencer had major altercations with Miss Smith over the charge of agents' duties. She seemed to believe she was invincible, but Mrs. Spencer was struck in her corset by a shell when the ordnance wharf exploded on August 9, 1864. The injury temporarily paralyzed her legs and left permanent sciatic nerve damage, which disabled her for life.

After the war, she became an ardent spokesperson for the Women's Relief Corps. As a speaker at the Round Lake, New York, veteran's convention in 1893, she spoke about her wartime experiences. She received a pension of twenty dollars a month, and a bust of her was placed in the capitol in Albany, New York on the west staircase. She died in 1912 and was buried in Rural Cemetery in Oswego, New York. {Sources 2, 3, 19, 21, 23, 25, 165, 176, 192, 273, 274. Image in Executive Committee of the National Association of Civil War Nurses (1910). *In Honor of the National Association of Civil War Nurses: 44th Encampment Grand Army of the Republic*. Atlantic City: Yeakel; and Brockett, L.P. & Vaughn, M. (1867). *Women's Work in the Civil War*. Philadelphia: Zeigler, McCurdy}

Mrs. Sperry

She was with the USSC at Point of Rocks. {Source 20}

Mrs. Sarah Jane Milliken Sprague

She worked as a nurse from Massachusetts. She was the wife of William N. Sprague, who was a 1st Massachusetts Cavalry soldier of Lynn, Massachusetts. After the war, she applied for her own pension (#1138696) in 1892 but they probably lived on his pension. She passed away in 1924 and is buried in Pine Grove Cemetery in Lynn, Massachusetts. {Sources 3, 45}

Ms. Elizabeth Stenton

She was with the USCC 2nd Corps and at Point of Rocks. {Source 20}

Mrs. Stretch

She went to White House Landing and then City Point with Miss Bucklin and Mrs. Strouse on the *Lizzie Baker* and was seen on the Massachusetts Sanitary Commission boat. Mrs. Stretch was probably attached to the 2nd Corps. {Source 3}

Mrs. Rebecca Strouse

Little is known about Mrs. Strouse other than she arrived with Aunt Becky on June 18, 1864. She was probably born in Pennsylvania in a Quaker household in York, but this needs more clarification. Before the war, she married Dennis Strouse of New Jersey. Dennis was with Co. H of the 138th Pennsylvania Infantry, so like many of the other women, she followed her husband into the war zone. {Source 23}

Mrs. Emily Thorpe

Raised in Reynoldsville, New York (near Ithaca), she petitioned President Lincoln for permission to take care of her seriously wounded husband, S. Chauncey Thorp (note spelling difference) after the battle of Cold Harbor. Permission was granted and Mr. Thorpe eventually recoverd. When her husband headed home, Mrs. Thorpe remained with the Army of the Potomac as a nurse. Chauncey received a pension of $30 per month. She passed away at the age of 91 in 1927. {Sources 3, 67, 283}

Mrs. Captain Townsend*

She was the mother of Eddie Townsent. While at City Point, she stayed with Dr. and Mrs. Brinton onboard the *Planter*. Her husband acquired a pass for her in February of 1865 to enter the City Point complex, where she was able to work as a nurse on the steamer *State of Maine*. She remained at the complex until the end of the war. {Source 28}

"Two nurses who returned with me"

All that is known is that Miss Dix sent two women to City Point on the same boat Sophronia Bucklin was on. All three reported to the surgeon in charge and one of the nurses was ordered to Dr. Mitchell's command in October 1864. {Source 3}

Miss Rebecca Usher

Rebecca Usher was from Hollis, Maine, and part of the Maine Camp and Hospital Association. She was a representative for the Maine State Relief Agency at City Point and resided with Mrs. Mayhew and Mr. Eaton. Miss Usher was a good friend of Bridget Deavers and watched as Bridget strapped the body of a young captain, who had been killed in a skirmish, to a horse and delivered it to the hospital. Miss Usher met Mrs. Lincoln while receiving her on the ward during the March presidential visit. Mrs. Mayhew found Miss Usher an individual with a "warm interest in the cause" and a young woman who had a "highly cultivated mind." After the war, Miss Usher returned to Bar Mills, Maine, and received a pension (#1132597). She died in 1912 and is buried in the Tory Hill Cemetery in Buxton, Maine. {Sources 10, 12, 19, 45, 164, 231. Images in Sudlow, p. 201; and Maine Historical Society}

Miss Mary Vance

Miss Vance had worked as a missionary prior to the war but was appointed by Miss Dix to be a USSC nurse. She was also a member of the USCC when she was at the hospital in Madison, Indiana. During the earlier experience, she helped Mrs. Wittenmyer uncover a corrupt doctor who resigned when he found out about the investigation. At City Point she was attached to the 2nd Corps Hospital and assisted in the Confederate wards. {Sources 2, 23, 34, 38}

Dr. Mary Walker

Born in 1832, Mary Walker was a graduate of the Syracuse Medical College in 1855 and was married to Dr. Miller. She practiced her medical profession in Columbus, Ohio, and Rome, New York. Mary was a creative thinker and visionary way beyond her generation and she was a suffragette long before the movement took hold. For example, she devised the internal neck band on a shirt to stop chafing on the neck of the collar buttons, and often wore trousers. Not always a radical, she did wear dresses at home. During the war and while travelling, she found hoop skirts difficult and confining while trousers simply made sense. Dr. Walker joined the 52nd Ohio Volunteers and was with the Army of the Potomac in Fredericksburg in September of 1863. She was later arrested and sent to Richmond, where she was incarcerated in Castle Thunder prison for four months. While in Richmond, she shook up the southern citizens and caused much discussion about a woman who wore men's pants. *The Richmond Examiner* on June 29, 1864, wrote:

> Miss Walker, The Yankee Surgeoness— Miss Doctoress—
> Miscegenation, Philosophical Walker, who has so long ensconced herself very quietly in Castle Thunder, has loomed into activity again. Recently she got mad, pitched into several of her roommates in long clothes, and tore out handfuls of auburn hair from the heads of one of them.... She is very fond on listening to the thuds of Papa Grant's pop-gun below, and when they sound, her favorite song is "The Camels are coming, hie oh, hie oh," and it is said she has a Yankee Major lover among the prisoners at Libby prison, which is one square below the Castle

She was released under the flag-of-truce in August of 1864 with the exchange location being City Point. After the war, she continued to advocate for liberties and clothing rights for women. At one point, she appeared at the Secretary of the Interior's office in Washington and took off her Prince Albert coat but had a second coat underneath. She also wore pink-striped trousers with her outfit. She challenged President Grant over a Treasury position and the difficulties the Treasury Department placed in front of her. She was granted the Medal of Honor, only to have the medal later taken from her. In 1887, she advocated for the passage of the Giegerich bill to allow probate of the last will during the life of a testator. In 1917, she had a serious accident when she slipped and fell on the steps of the U.S. Capitol building. She returned to Oswego and stayed at a dear friend's home hoping to recover. She had been left monies from two members of her regiment that would have made her last days comfortable, but the bequests were held on a technicality. She died in poverty in 1919 at age 87 at her home on Bunker Hill in Oswego, New York. {Sources 1, 8, 10, 17, 34, 81–88, 170, 214, 215, 231, 275. Images at Library of Congress and https://en.wikipedia.org/wiki/Mary_Edwards_Walker}

Author's Note: A news story on April 13, 1864, in the *Washington Republican* (p. 1), it was reported that Dr. Walker apparently had met the female soldier Francis Hook and described her as having "dark hazel eyes, dark brown hair, rounded features and a feminine voice."

Miss Julia Wheelock

A Michigan state relief agent but not a state agent, she served in Washington, Fredericksburg, and White House Landing prior to arriving at City Point.

She served only three months before exhaustion set in and she became incapacitated. After her recovery, she returned to the Washington area. She was paid five dollars a week from the people of Michigan for helping feed soldiers, write letters home for them, and offer moral support when she could.

After the war, she wrote about her experiences and the many boys who had died and were covered by a white sheet, in the aptly titled 1870 book *The Boys in White*. In 1873, she married Porter C. Freeman from Michigan. They had two sons, one of whom died early. She was eventually granted a pension of twelve dollars a month. She died on June 7, 1900, and is buried in Hazelwood Cemetery in Springfield, Missouri. {Sources 27, 37, 155, 231. Image at http://www.michiganwomenshalloffame.org}

Mrs. Lydia K. White

Limited information is available other than she was at Point of Rocks and received a pension (#495510) after the war. {Source 25}

Miss Georgiana Willets

Georgiana served at Gettysburg, Fredericksburg, and White House Landing before arriving at City Point. She arrived with Miss Hancock and Mrs. Lee and was there about the same time Mrs. Swisshelm arrived. Miss Willets was attached to the 2nd Corps Hospital, where she supervised eleven wards and the diet kitchen. At one point, she helped Mrs. Price load 250 wounded onto hospital transports. Quite exhausted and ill, she left City Point in September of 1864. Abbie Gibbons took her place. {Sources 12, 19}

Mrs. Wilson

Mrs. Wilson is known to have worked for the USSC. {Source 27}

Mrs. Annie Wittenmyer

She carried considerable clout with the USCC and often locked horns with the ladies of the 9th Corps diet kitchens. She worked between the Point of Rocks facilities and the Depot complex.

After the war, she compiled a recipe book called *A Collection of Recipes for the Use of the Special Diet Kitchen in the Military Hospital*, which revealed the magnitude of the preparation of food for the recovering solders. In 1863, she helped establish the Iowa Soldier's Orphans Home Association, and in 1865 she opened a second facility in Cedar Falls, Iowa. Then she negotiated with the War Department to use Camp Kinsman in Davenport, Iowa, as a state orphans' home. She became the first president of the National Women's Christian Temperance Union, and in 1895 she wrote *Under the Guns*, detailing her wartime experiences. She received a pension under Special Act #220. Mrs. Wittenmyer died at her home in Saratoga, Pennsylvania, at the age of 73 on February 2, 1900. {Sources 10, 20, 28, 38, 78, 142, 176, 231. Images available at https://humanrights.iowa.gov/annie-wittenmyer and https://en.wikipedia.org/wiki/Annie_Turner_Wittenmyer}

Military Wives

Mrs. Caroline Ames

Mrs. Ames was from Hartford, Connecticut. She was killed while visiting her husband Charles Ames, who was with either the 22nd Connecticut Regiment or the 1st Connecticut Cavalry. Their son Carlos was with the 6th Connecticut Infantry. She was buried near the Perkin's House towards Reams Station. Their youngest son, Frederick, apparently served with a New York Infantry. {Source 233}

Charlotte "Charley" Anderson

This unique woman was born in Hamburg, Germany. Charlotte came to the United States at age 15 and lived with her/his mother in Erie, Pennsylvania. Slight in build and feminine in features, she/he was good at cross-dressing and moved through the lines. At Petersburg, Charley was a "female soldier" from Cleveland, Ohio, who was discovered in the ranks. She was about 20 years of age, fluent in three languages, a dead shot and great horseman. She was sent to the provost marshal's office on January 18, 1865, and mustered out of the 60th Ohio Regiment, Second Brigade, First Division, 9th Corps and sent back to Cleveland on January 22, with help from the Pennsylvania state agent. However, in February, Charlotte was arrested with another woman by Commissioner Kikpatrick after being reported by the Soldiers Aid Society. Using the names Charlotte and Emma, the two women were applying for transportation to Washington. Emma had no idea that Charlotte had previously been a soldier and periodically posed as a man. When asked about the situation, Charlotte grew very indignant. After a military physical investigation, she turned out to really be male. Charley was then locked up in the city prison under the suspicion of being a rebel spy. Apparently, when Charley appealed to Provost Marshal Patrick in January, being a woman justified the disguise and played on a man's heart. Charley now expressed interest in returning to his unit as soon as he could to get transportation to Washington, D.C. According to Hall, the question remains: were Charlotte and Emma really soldiers or were they spies? Perhaps they were simply scam artists using the military transportation and benefits for their own good. {Sources 10, 28, 140}

Miss Annie Bain (Eden)

Miss Bain was born in Dumbarton, Scotland, although some records, like her wedding certificate, show she was born in Glasgow, Scotland. She was a very graceful, young, blond Englishwoman who finessed entry into City Point without a pass. She caused quite a stir wherever she went. Her good friends were the New York and Maine state agents. At one point she was visiting the Dutch Gap area with Miss Smith when they were caught under fire. Their option was to risk the shelling and possible drowning while escaping or staying with the officers overnight. They proclaimed they would rather face the shells or drown than spend the night in such "evil" circumstances. They escaped across the river with shells screaming overhead, having grown wiser from the experience.

Determined in her pursuit, Miss Bain arrived at City Point about three months before her marriage to Major Eden on January 25, 1865. Major Eden, an Oxford graduate, was the son of Rev. William Eden and Baroness Grey du Buttyn of Bishops Bourne, Kent. He had come to America after graduation and lived in Oshkosh, Wisconsin. At the start of the war, he raised Company A of the 37th Wisconsin Volunteers.

After the war, he was promoted to colonel and they lived in several locations, including back in England for a few years and then Rhode Island before moving to Wisconsin, where he was engaged in an international electrical engineering profession. Annie and the colonel had three sons and three daughters. {Sources 23, 34, 100. Images in Smith, A. (1919). *Reminiscences of an Army Nurse During the Civil War*. New York: Greaves}

Mrs. Surgeon-General Barnes

She came with the Stanton family in March of 1865 on the *River Queen*. {Source 138}

Mrs. Barr

She came down to visit from Washington with her husband. They lived on 9th Street in Washington, D.C., and had met other Presbyterians while at church who suggested they should go to City Point and see for themselves what life there was like. {Source 232}

Mrs. Sally Barrett

She was the wife of a prominent Washington lawyer named Oliver D. Barrett. Mrs. Barrett came to City Point on April 10, 1865, to visit the former Confederate capitol. As she toured the two-mile area near the James River, she found a small brown and white terrier and took the dog home with her. She named the dog "Richmond" in honor of the city she had visited. Born in 1837, she would have been 28 at the time of her visit. She died in 1905 and was buried in the Congressional Cemetery in Washington, D.C. {Sources 9, 279}

Mrs. Beck

Mrs. Beck is mentioned as part of the party going on a "special train" to visit the front with Annie Nelson on Tuesday March 7, 1865. {Source 28}

Mrs. Bell

She came with her husband in March on board the *River Queen* with Miss Stanton. {Source 138}

Miss Bidgood (Bitgood)

An older lady at age forty-four, she was arrested in Washington, D.C. and sent to Old Capitol prison until a trial could be arranged for the accusation of smuggling goods back to Richmond. After taking the oath, she was released and sent from Washington, D.C., to the exchange location at City Point and then sent home without any of her possessions. (See Chapter 2.) {Sources 141, 269}

Mrs. Colonel Bowman

She came to visit her husband with her child and servant while he was with the Army of the Potomac. They returned home on the USS *Blackstone*. {Source 187}

Mrs. Breed and Daughter

Doctor Breed and his wife came to City Point on three occasions and brought their daughter Menah with them. They first arrived on October 25, 1864, then again in December, and February 1865. They were good friends with the Owens and with Josiah Wilson, who headed the Freedman's Committee. The Breeds lived in Washington, D.C., across the street from the Stantons. They were part of the board for the Home for Infirm Women and Children of Color in Washington, D.C., that later locked horns with Mrs. Swisshelm after the war. {Sources 28, 138, 240}

Mrs. Burgess

She left City Point on a boat on November 26, 1864. She was assisted on board by Provost Marshal Patrick. {Source 28}

Lady Guests of Mr. Burnley

They arrived on board the *Northerner* with the Sewards and Spanish Minister Don Gablele Garcia Tassara. Mr. Joseph Hume Burnley was the interim English minister and they had come for three or four days to pay a visit to General Grant. {Source 132}

Mrs. Cadwallader

She arrived in early January of 1865 and stayed until the end of March. She became a close associate with Mrs. Grant and Mrs. Rawlins. {Source 4}

Miss Cameron

She was the daughter of former Secretary of War Simon Cameron. She had arrived at City Point with the party visiting on March 8, 1865. (see Mrs. Stanton). {Source 1}

Mrs. General Septima M. Collis

Septima was from Charleston, South Carolina, and the wife of General H.T. Collis. She contributed to the "pleasant social calls" to the other ranking officers and their wives. She enjoyed having oysters with the Grants while they all "sat on the floor."

After the war, she made trips to London and Paris with her husband and their son Charles and became involved in the woman's movement spearheaded by Elizabeth Cady Stanton. Her husband was a commissioner of public works in New York City and became embroiled in a financial dispute. She joined the Daughters of the Confederacy. In 1889, she published *A Woman's War Record*. Her son Charles married Miss Frances Williamson in Poughkeepsie, New York on January 15, 1922. {Sources 6, 10, 28, 94–97. Image at https://docsouth.unc.edu/fpn/collis/collis.html}

Mrs. Rosco Conkling

Mrs. Conkling went with her husband and son via boat to Richmond on April 5, 1865, to "view" the conquered city. {Source 28}

Pleasant Cooke

Travelling with the military units often placed women in danger. Pleasant Cooke was probably a cook or simply a wife who was killed or died and buried at City Point near the Railroad lines in 1864. {Source 233}

Mrs. and Miss Cox

Mrs. Cox and her daughter were called to be witnesses for the case of Colonel Ketchem while at City Point. Miss Elliott was also called to testify. Mrs. Cox apparently was considered a rather outspoken individual for the time period. {Source 28}

Mrs. General Elizabeth Custer

Born in 1854, Elizabeth Bacon of Monroe, Michigan, was the daughter of Judge Daniel Bacon. She married and became the wife of General George Armstrong Custer. When she came to City Point, she stayed with Mrs. French on the *Baltimore*. On April 10, 1865, she went to Richmond to stay with her husband.

After the war, she followed her husband to Texas and then to Colorado, New Mexico, Nebraska, and Wyoming. She was alive in 1930 and spent much of her time collecting data for Civil War records. She collected pension #178408 as a widow. {Sources 2, 9, 29, 98. Image at https://kshs.org/kansapedia/elizabeth-bacon-custer/12030 or at https://www.geni.com/people/Elizabeth-Custer/6000000002964077359}

Mrs. Dr. Dalton

The wife of Dr. Ned Dalton, she arrived on a boat on December 28, 1864. She was a very lively and pleasant lady who was not afraid to speak her mind. As a result, she would occasionally lock horns with Dr. Mitchell. While she was on the post, an old family friend, Professor Horsford, came to visit City Point. They had known one another while living in Cambridge, Massachusetts, and were considered on equal social ground. {Source 28}

Mrs. Frederick Dent

Mrs. Margaret "Madge" Dent was the daughter of Major Lynde of 5th Corps and the wife of Lieutenant Colonel Frederick Tracy Dent, aide-de-camp (ADC), who served with General Grant until April 5, 1865. She socialized with Mrs. Grant (Julia Dent Grant), Miss Hyde, and Miss Steele. They all were at the party onboard the steamer *Martin* on December 14, 1864.

After the war, she participated in many of the Grant household activities. {Sources 33, 46, 101}

Mrs. Derby

Mrs. Derby was the wife of topographer Mr. Derby of Washington, D.C. They came to visit and party on the *River Queen* at City Point on March 7, 1865. Mrs. Derby also came with Mrs. Webb and she was considered to be a "superior woman" by Provost Marshal Patrick. On March 10, 1865, Mrs. Derby and her entourage left on the *Colyer* to return to Washington, D.C. {Source 28}

Mrs. Doane

She was the wife of Chief Engineer Doane. They were from New York and came to visit in July of 1864. {Source 232}

Captain Dod's Mother

On August 26, 1864, Captain Dod's mother arrived at City Point. She had been notified that the captain was dying and being treated in Miss Hancock's quarters because the Hancock and Dod families were old friends. Mrs. Dod was there for one day before her son passed away. Touched by the kindness and compassion shown to the soldiers, she gave Miss Hancock one hundred dollars to be used for soldiers who were in dire need and then returned back home with her son's body. {Source 12}

Mrs. and Miss Elliott

Mrs. Elliott was called as a witness on the Colonel Ketchem case. (See Mrs. and Miss Cox in this section.) {Source 28}

Cora Fox

Having caught the eye of a reporter, she appeared as "a women of fine appearance but questionable repute." She appeared at the front with passes from

General Grant that allowed her quarters and the freedom to go wherever she wanted and to use military transports. General Parker was most concerned about the woman, and it was rumored that General Grant went to see her on occasion. After the war, she resided at the Platt Hotel in Baltimore. {Source 268}

Mrs. Mary Ellen French

The wife of Mr. French, she toured the area aboard various steamers in April of 1865. She spent significant time with various congressmen when they were in the area. On April 10, 1865, she was aboard the *Baltimore*.

After the war, she engaged in charity work and applied for a pension. She was in Oyster Bay, New York, in September of 1909 when she fell down some stairs and fractured her skull and sustained multiple injuries. She passed away shortly thereafter. {Sources 9, 92, 99}

Mrs. G— (possibly Mrs. Rosemary G—)

They were at City Point on March 8, 1865, with a large party. Mrs. G— was the wife of Dr. G—, whose sister was Mrs. Smith (very slight possibility that it may have been Miss Adelaide Smith). {Source 1}

Miss Gibbons

Miss Gibbons was the sister of General John Gibbons. The family started out in Pennsylvania but then moved to North Carolina. As a result, three of the brothers had joined the Confederate Army. Young Miss Gibbons was in Richmond trying to get a pass to go north. Finally, on November 12 or 13, she was able to board a flag-of-truce boat and come down the James River to City Point. General Gibbons was there to help expedite her pass to and out of City Point. {Source 1}

Mrs. Julia Dent Grant

Born in St. Louis, Missouri, in February 1826, she became the wife of General Grant and sister to Lieutenant Colonel Dent. She travelled in and out of City Point at times alone and other times with her youngest son, Jesse. When she socialized, it was with the high-ranking officers' wives, such as Mrs. Rawlins, Mrs. Webb, Mrs. Cadwallader, Mrs. Collis and also with Mrs. Wittenmyer, who supervised all the USCC diet kitchens. When necessary, she would entertain Mrs. Lincoln. On February 5, 1865, she arrived to help with various duties, such as overseeing the prisoner-of-war exchange on February 19.

After the war, Grant became president of the United States and Mrs. Grant became the first lady. She travelled extensively, forgetting and forgiving many she had met during the war. She even had a friendship with Mrs. Davis two decades after the war. Mrs. Grant received $150,000 for *Personal Memoirs of U.S. Grant* in October of 1886. She died of Bright's disease in December of 1902 and was buried next to her husband in Riverside, New York. {Sources 29, 33, 46, 102–106, 144, 252–258. Images at https://www.alamy.com/stock-photo/julia-dent-grant.html}

Miss Nellie Grant

Nellie was the younger daughter and sister to Jesse Grant. She came to visit her father and her brother and mother in August of 1864. She married Algernon Satoria in 1874 while her father was still president. They had four children together. {Sources 29, 33. Image at https://www.pinterest.com/christinax65/nellie-grant/}

Mrs. General Charles (Sally) Griffin

Born and raised in an affluent family, Sally (or Sallie) was the daughter of William T. Carroll of Carrolleton, Maryland. She married General Charles Griffin and they had several children, one who was named Charles. Their son lived only a few months. The general died in 1867 and she married Hungarian Ambassador Count Ezterhazy. They moved to Hungary and not much is known about their lives. Along with Mrs. Mary Ord, she had a reputation for being a skilled equestrian. Her riding abilities helped upset Mrs. Mary Todd Lincoln by riding too close to the president instead of riding in the carriage with Mrs. Lincoln. {Sources 4, 33, 144}

Mrs. Josephine E. Griffins

Mrs. Griffins was a social reformer from Washington, D.C. Her platform was the care and development of the newly freed slaves. She wanted to put order in the disorder. On April 10, 1865, she was with the group from Washington who came down to City Point to tour the area. After the war, she became a commissioner of the Freedman's Bureau. {Sources 2, 9}

Clara Haxall Grundy

Clara Haxall was the daughter of Dr. Robert Haxall and was born in April of 1830 in the Richmond, Virginia, area. In 1853, she married Thomas Grundy. When the war started, her husband joined the Confederacy and Clara learned to fend for herself. She found entertaining officers also had benefits, which annoyed Mary Chestnut. After her home was broken into and cash items such as barrels of sugar were taken, Clara decided there had to be other opportunities. Gathering information was a skill she utilized. The best place to gather information was at a local gathering spot, so she moved to the hotel in City Point. The location provided her access to many Union officers and significant intelligence. The nurses despised her and that was fine with Clara. After the war, she returned to Richmond and married twice, first to Colonel Beirne until he passed away and then to W.J. Leaky. She died in March of 1916 and was buried at Shockoe Hill Cemetery, in Richmond, Virginia (Find-a-Grave #14949293). {Sources 196–199}

Mrs. H—

She was with her husband for the party on the *River Queen* on March 8, 1865. They were referred to as "Lady Patroness Mrs. H— and Noble Patron Mr. H—." {Source 1}

Mrs. Ann Harlan

Originally from Kentucky and married in 1846, Mrs. Harlan was the wife of Senator Harlan of Iowa. The Harlans came down as part of Mrs. Lincoln's special group and were at City Point the day Petersburg fell. Mrs. Harlan helped with the wounded at Shiloh and was particularly interested in the soldiers from the state of Iowa, but would assist with whatever was needed when it came to the care of the sick and wounded. (See Chapter 10.) {Sources 2, 19, 33, 112. Image at https://civilwartalk.com/threads/ann-e-harlan-who-ministered-to-union-soldiers.140795/}

Miss Mary Harlan

Born in 1846, she was the daughter of Senator Harlan of Iowa. On April 5, 1865, she was socializing at City Point.

After the war, Mary married President Lincoln's son, Robert Lincoln, in 1866. They had two daughters and one son. Mary died at the age of 90 on March 31, 1937, and is buried in Arlington Cemetery (Find-a-Grave #7186237). {Sources 33, 107, 108. Image at https://en.wikipedia.org/wiki/Mary_Harlan_Lincoln}

Mrs. Anne Sturgis Hooper

Born in 1813 in Barnstable, Massachusetts, she married Samuel Hooper. He became a senator. In March, the senator and Anne came on board the *River Queen*. They had one daughter. After the war, they returned to Boston, where

Anne passed away on August 28, 1884, at the age of 70, and was buried in the Mount Auburn Cemetery in Cambridge. {Source 138}

Mrs. Horton

Mrs. Horton came to City Point October 16, 1864, and stayed until the 19th. She had come to care for her dying son, who died on the 18th. The surgeon-in-charge said the "injudicious treatment" (by the mother) caused the soldier's death. {Source 28}

Miss Humphrey

She was the daughter of General Humphrey and arrived at City Point with her escort, Mrs. Seten, via one of the boats on December 20, 1864. {Source 28}

Mrs. Huntington

Wife of ___ Huntington, she was a friend to Captain Beckwith. On March 19, 1865, she was socializing with Mrs. Grant and Mrs. Rawlins. They rode to church together with Provost Marshal Patrick. {Source 28}

Miss Hyde

Miss Hyde was on the steamer *Martin* with Mrs. Grant, Mrs. Dent, and Miss Steele on December 14, 1864, for an evening of socialization. {Source 28}

Miss Jenkins

Miss Jenkins was the daughter of General Summer. On March 7, 1865, she travelled to City Point to participate in a dance onboard the *River Queen*. On March 9, she took a tour of the front and left on the *Colyer* (sometimes spelled *Collyer*) on March 10. {Source 28}

Mrs. Cora W. King

Mrs. King was on the *Baltimore* with other members from Washington, D.C., on April 10, 1865. (see Mrs. Mary Ellen French in this section.) {Source 9}

Mrs. Arthur Leary

She came for the victory tour with Mrs. and General Stoughton. {Source 6}

Mrs. Frances Levy

She was 33 years of age and picked up in March 1864 for having excessive baggage and contraband goods and having no pass. She was sent to Carroll and the Old Capitol prison until a trial could be arranged (see Miss Bidgood in this section). After taking the Oath, she was permitted to return home with only the clothes she wore. She crossed into Confederate territory at City Point and went on to Richmond. She was probably the wife of Myer Levy. {Source 141}

Mrs. Mary Todd Lincoln

The wife of President Lincoln came to City Point on several occasions, either alone or with a host of associates, and sometimes with her youngest son Tad. She was difficult to socialize with due to her jealous actions and thoughts. On one occasion, she went through the wards escorted by many officers' wives and was noted by one solider as dressed in rich black silks, looking quite dignified. Mrs. Grant, Rawlins, and Mrs. Collis tread very lightly while Mrs. Lincoln was at City Point.

After the war, she found life difficult to deal with and her eldest son had her institutionalized due to her inability to comprehend reality. {Sources 5, 24, 28, 29, 112, 144, 145, 259, 260. Images at https://www.biography.com/people/mary-todd-lincoln-248868}

Mrs. Colonel Mary A. Logan

The wife of Colonel Logan, she visited Petersburg with the touring party on April 4, 1865. After the war, she became invested in community activities and resided in a home at 16th and K Street in Washington, D.C. She was a member of the National Women's Relief Corps and the Executive Committee of the Garfield Hospital. When her husband passed away, she benefited from the income of the sales of his book and the publication of the *Home Magazine* she initiated. In addition, she published brief biographies of Civil War nurses. {Sources 34, 113–116, 231. Images at https://www.senate.gov/artandhistory/history/common/image/LoganJohnAMrs.html and http://ian.macky.net/expo1893/personnel.html}

Mrs. Louisa Lord

Mrs. Lord was the wife of photographer William Blair Lord. William was also known as someone who transcribed information from phonetic shorthand. She was with the group that toured the area after the war on April 10, 1865 with Mrs. French. {Source 9}

Mrs. Lyman

On March 29, 1865, she was part of the larger party that visited with Mrs. Meade. {Sources 1, 2, 12}

Mrs. Martin

Wife of Major Martin, she resided in the Cook home on Prince Street during the occupation of City Point. If you look closely at the National Park Service image of the house, you will notice two women seated and one in the doorway. A personal communication from 1994 with a local resident indicated that the women on the porch may have been the refugees Emma Wood Richardson and Old Mary Nelson, but it's more probable was that the women were Mrs. Martin and family. {Sources 15, 207}

Mrs. General Meade

The wife of General Meade, she had a large party that came to tour and visit the area on March 22, 1865. Mrs. Lyman and J.W. Nye were part of the group. Later, they all wanted to go up to the front but were delayed by bad weather. As a result, they went up the river for a special party tour. {Sources 1, 27, 29}

Mrs. Dr. Miller

The wife of Dr. Miller, she helped take care of Dr. Dudley of the 14th Connecticut Regiment when he had a severe fever on August 21, 1864. By September 2, 1864, she was quite ill. Her illness lasted for several days. {Source 12}

Miss Mitchel

Miss Mitchel was the sister of Captain Mitchel of Company K, Ninth Corps. She was at City Point in mid to late August as one of the women residing with Aunt Becky. According to Aunt Becky, "A certain Doctor from 2nd Corps..." was visiting Miss Michel "rather often." {Source 23}

Mrs. Dr. Mitchell and Two Sisters

She was the wife of Dr. Mitchell (occasionally spelled Miteball) who was attached to the Cavalry Corps Hospital but wanted to leave the service to become a contract surgeon. However, Dr. Dalton blackballed the vote. Mrs. Mitchell had various ailments while at City Point and the ladies periodically made social calls. One of her sisters was Maggie Mitchell (see Miss Margaret "Maggie" Mitchell in Healthcare Providers section.) {Source 28}

Mrs. Judith P. Morgan

She was the wife of breveted General Michael Ryan Morgan. He was born in 1832 in Halifax, Nova Scotia. Judith was born in Charlestown, Massachusetts, in 1837. They were married in 1860 and resided in Fort Monroe, where he was chief commissary officer. Judith brought her maid, Nancy, with her when travelling to military locations. Judith and Nancy were at City Point when General Grant met General Lee at Appomattox Court House. As part of the party for their husbands, Mrs. Grant, Rawlins and Morgan all waited for the men's arrival for a celebration. The men were delayed until four a.m. and the ladies had to be awakened upon their husbands' arrival. Mrs. Morgan had a son who died early. She died in 1877. {Sources 29, 33}

Miss Annie Nelson

Miss Nelson was part of a tour group that went to see the front on March 7, 1865, with Mrs. Beck on what they considered a "special" train. {Source 28}

Mrs. General Mary Ord and Daughter

Mary Mercer Ord was the daughter of a judge and member of the Virginia Congress. She was the wife of General Ord. She and her daughter came to City Point as visitors at the end of the war. Mrs. Ord was an excellent equestrian and rode "much too close" to the president, according to Mrs. Lincoln. There were actually four women riders, but Mrs. Lincoln harbored great anger at Mrs. Ord. She died in 1894 and was buried in San Antonio National Cemetery in San Antonio, Texas. {Sources 4, 29, 33, 261. Image at https://en.wikipedia.org/wiki/Edward_Ord}

Mrs. Georgy P. Admiral Porter and Another Lady

Born in 1819, she married her naval hero in 1836. A devoted wife, she came to visit City Point on October 19, 1864, and traveled as far as the Hancock's headquarters. They ran into several of the staff officers who commented on their presence. She was known to have "boundless hospitality."

After the war, she became a celebrity along with Mrs. General Logan. They summered at Jamestown, Rhode Island, and in June, the midshipman at Annapolis hosted a ball in her honor. Along with Clara Barton, she served on the executive committee for the Daughters of the Revolution in Washington, D.C. {Sources 1, 119–121, 277}

Mrs. Mary Hurlburt Rawlins

Mary Emma Hurlburt was the second wife of John Rawlins. She was on the post much against her husband's wishes and much to the wishes of Mrs. Grant. Having previously served as a governess and private tutor for the Lam family in Vicksburg, Mississippi, she came to the marriage to care for the young Rawlins daughter, Emily Smith Rawlins. Her social circle included Mrs. Grant, Mrs. Webb, and Mrs. Huntington.

After the war, she traveled with General Rawlins until he died in 1869 of tuberculosis. Then she returned to her hometown of Danbury, Connecticut. She was facing difficult financial times after General Rawlins' death, so President Grant went to Danbury to assist her with funeral arrangements. Emily then became a ward of General Grant. Shortly thereafter, President Grant offered to purchase a home for Mary and Emily in Danbury where they could remain comfortable while Mary cared for the Rawlins daughter.

Before long, Mary had met another man and married Charles Daniels. They moved to Cheyenne, Wyoming. The Rawlins daughter, Emily, was sent to live with other family members and several boarding schools but eventually returned to the original family home in Goshen, New York. Mary Hurlburt Rawlins is buried in Wooster Cemetery, in Danbury, Connecticut. {Sources 27, 29, 33, 39, 46, 122–129, 204, 277, 278. Images of General Rawlins at City Point with wife and daughter at Library of Congress https://www.loc.gov/item/2006691865/; Rawlins house on Balmfourth Avenue in Danbury, *Images of America- Danbury*, at Danbury Historical Society, Danbury, Connecticut}

Miss Reed

She visited the area with Mrs. Stoughton, Mrs. Steven, Collis, and Miss Van Buren. {Source 6}

Mrs. Russell

The wife of General Russell who was the "end stop" for Miss Smith's ride. It was probably Orilla Mason Russell, the wife of Henry S. Russell. Henry was the colonel in charge of the USCT in the attack on Baylor's Farm in June of 1864. He was wounded in the arm, which would have prompted his wife to go to City Point. Orilla died in September of 1929 at the age of 90 and was buried at Saint Peters Cemetery in Vergennes, Vermont. She may also be the women sitting in the wagon in front of the former Collis residence with Miss Smith on the horse. It should be noted that there is a very minute possibility that it may have been Mrs. E.J. Russell of Plattekill, New York, who was working as a Dix nurse, although she worked primarily in Baltimore with the returning prisoners. She would only have been visiting the area on the transports to help with more returning soldiers. If so, after the war she lived in Newburgh, New York. {Sources 2, 34. Image at www.findagrave.com/memorial/15203127/orilla-russell; wagon image with Adelaide Smith at Smith, A. (1919). *Reminiscences of an Army Nurse During the Civil War*. New York: Greaves, p. 235}

Mrs. Seten

Mrs. Seton went to City Point as a chaperone for General Humphrey's daughter. {Source 28}

Miss Seward

She went to City Point with her father, Secretary Seward, on the *Northerner*. {Source 132}

Miss Eleanor Adams Stanton

Miss Stanton was the attractive and properly schooled daughter of Secretary of War Stanton. She was part of the group to visit and tour the area on March 8, 1865, and participated in the big ball on board the *River Queen*. She later married a West Point graduate, Major James Clark Bush, from Waterbury, Connecticut. He was seven years older and she supported his military career. She passed away in Berkeley, California, on September 26, 1910, and was buried at Oak Hill Cemetery in Washington, D.C. (Find-a-Grave #41560484). {Sources 34, 133, 144, 262}

Mrs. Ellen Stanton and Friends

The wife of Secretary of War Stanton, she came down to visit after Lincoln's first visit to City Point. She arrived at City Point with her son Edwin, and a young lady, Miss A—. The young lady, who was from Columbus, Ohio, was the sweetheart of General P—, and they were married after 1865. Mrs. Stanton skillfully skirted around Mrs. Lincoln and refused to even call on her while Mrs. Lincoln was in the White House. {Sources 34, 133, 138, 144. Image at http://civilwaref.blogspot.com/2013/12/edwin-stanton-born-december-19-1814.html}

Miss Steele

Miss Steele was the daughter of John B. Steele. She was on board the steamer *Martin* on December 14, 1864, with Mrs. Grant, Mrs. Dent, and Mrs. Hyde. {Sources 28, 46}

Mrs. Surgeon Steven

She was the wife of the surgeon of the 1st Maine Cavalry. They called on Miss Usher on January 27th and asked her to call on them at their quarters. {Source 163}

Mrs. Paren Stevens

Mrs. Stevens resided in her posh Fifth Avenue address or in her Belleview Avenue mansion in Newport, Rhode Island. As a socialite, she came down to visit the area and spent time with Mrs. Stoughton. {Source 6}

Mrs. Stoughton

She was the wife of General Stoughton. They had arrived to do a tour or "the victory visit" on April 4, 1865. They came with Mrs. Arthur Leary, Mrs. Paren Stevens, and Miss Redd. They all rode to Richmond together. {Source 6}

Mrs. Jane Grey Swisshelm

An outspoken advocate for the rights and equality of women, Mrs. Swisshelm went to City Point as a journalist to learn about the difficult situations she could write about. She was born in 1815 and married James Swisshelm in 1836, then moved to Louisville, Kentucky. She struggled with an excessively controlling husband who interfered with her personal rights, and the marriage ended. Her second marriage was to an editor of the *Pittsburgh Saturday Visitor*. She worked on the paper from 1848 until 1852. In 1857, she purchased another paper, *The St. Cloud Minnesota Advertiser*, and shortened it to *The St. Cloud Visitor*. By 1862, she had changed the name once more to *The St. Cloud Democrat* and eventually sold the paper to her nephew but continued to contribute articles based on her wartime experiences. Her particular platform pertained to the brutal treatment of slaves, women's personal health issues (specifically bathing needs), the prohibition of corporal punishment of children, and equality of education and religion regardless of gender. Visiting the City Point complex gave her significant fuel for her political firestorms.

After the war, she continued to advocate for women's rights and education, specifically the right of a woman to obtain credible medical education. On January 11 and May 5, 1865, she was called as a witness of behalf of the Home for Infirmed Women and Children of Color regarding the allegations of abuse by one of the teachers, a Miss Maria Mann from Massachusetts. After much "fire and lightning," the subject was tabled, but Mrs. Swisshelm had made herself well known.

By 1866, she found her ability to sustain her interests difficult. With guidance from Secretary of War Stanton, she was able to sue her first husband, who was known as a "cheat and a liar and perjurer." She became the focus in the 1868 Pennsylvania Supreme Court case, Swisshelm vs. Swisshelm, dealing with women's property rights. She won the case and was able to gain the property known as "Swissvale." She wrote *Half a Century* in 1880 and died of intestinal cancer on July 22, 1884, at the Swissvale homestead near Pittsburgh. {Sources 12, 19, 35, 75, 76, 189, 190, 231, 240, 263–265. Image at http://education.mnhs.org/portal/mrs-jane-grey-cannon-swisshelm; and https://en.wikipedia.org/wiki/Jane_Swisshelm}

Mrs. General Taylor (later Mrs. Dr. Brinton)

Mrs. Emma Southwick Taylor Brinton was born in 1824 in Peabody, Massachusetts. When the war began, she served at the Mansion House hospital with her husband, General George W. Taylor. After his death, she continued working as a nurse. She lived onboard the *Planet*, which was moored at the dock in City Point. The boat was most likely the same one mentioned under Mrs. Spencer, as the *Planter*. Both *Planet* and *Planter* appear in Marsena Patrick's diary and in the Quartermaster's 1863 report under number 18, List of Vessels, a side-wheeled steamer listed as the *Planter* is shown. In 1880, Emma became the second wife of Dr. Jacob Brinton. In 1890, she received a pension, #550213. In 1894, Dr. Brinton passed away and Emma moved to 1313 11th Street NW in Washington, D.C. In April of 1921, she celebrated her 87th birthday with her friends. She was buried in Arlington National Cemetery in Washington, D.C. {Sources 28, 250, 251. Image at https://www.findagrave.com/memorial/49129787/emma-brinton}

Miss Anna Van Buren

Daughter of "Prince" John Van Buren, she came down with the Stoughtons, Stevens, and Miss Redd. They did the victory tour of the area and rode into Richmond at the end of the war. {Source 6}

Mrs. Von Hoffman

She came with her husband in March aboard the *River Queen*. {Source 138}

Mrs. Caroline Rosecrans Wade

She was the wife of Senator Benjamin F. Wade, and part of the touring group on April 18, 1865, on board the *Baltimore*. {Source 9}

Mrs. Andrew Webb and Children

They were part of the group that went down to City Point for the events and party on March 7, 1865. Mrs. Webb and Mrs. Derby went with others on the *Colyer*. On March 10, she tried to convince General Meade to allow her to stay with her husband, but Meade was firm about his position of not having ladies around. On March 27, she was quite agitated by an insult General Meade imposed on her. She associated with Mrs. Grant, Mrs. Rawlins, and occasionally Mrs. Lincoln. {Sources 1, 28, 46}

Miss ____ of Kentucky

This young lady was part of the March 8, 1865 group and party attendees. {Source 1}

Miss ____, Fiancée of Major Hemlock

Major Hemlock had lost his leg during the war and wrote to his fiancée releasing her of their obligations. She, however, refused to break the engagement and arrived at City Point to accompany him back home. They were married in Philadelphia. {Source 34}

300 Gentlemen and Ladies

Ambiguous as this may seem, the large group contained a significant number of women who left Washington, D.C., on March 9, 1865, and arrived at City Point for the social tours of the area. {Source 131}

Wife of an Officer with a Four-Year-Old Child

They spoke with Miss Smith, who had procured an ambulance and pass to take then down towards the front. The roads were extremely muddy and rough, but the lady found her husband and the wife and child remained with him near the front. {Source 34}

Residents

This section includes some of the women who had lived in the area prior to the war and continued to reside in the "safeguard" area. Many of the women remained committed to the Confederacy even though the situation was difficult for them. The list is alphabetical by last name, though if a woman was referenced without a name ("a very agreeable Southern Woman" or "weary women and children"), she appears at the end of the list.

Mrs. Baylor

This woman was a true resident of the area, but more than likely her name was chosen by the spy and blockade runner Mrs. Nettie Slater. Nettie had come to City Point on the flag-of-truce ship and was listed by Marsena Patrick as the daughter of Mrs. Baylor, who had married a Mr. Slater. {Sources 10, 28}

Miss Bidgood

See Miss Bidgood in Military Wives section

"Mrs. Botts"

She was a safeguard resident who lived near Petersburg and on whom Mrs. Collis frequently called to purchase fresh eggs. Mrs. Catherine Botts was the elder and very respected wife of Dr. Botts, but she died in 1853. Before her death, she had moved to the home of her sister, a Mrs. R—. This may have been the home where Mrs. Collis purchased the eggs. Mrs. Collis referred to the "house of Mrs. Botts." {Sources 6, 40, 44, 205}

"Family of Rebel General Dearing"

Cornelia Hancock and Dr. Miller were out riding one Sunday morning. They ended up spending the day with Dr. Potter at the "splendid house of rebel General Dearing." At some point, they noticed that part of the Dearing family was still residing in the house. The women were probably Mary Ann Lynch Dearing and Susan Lynch Dearing. {Source 12}

Mrs. Hatcher and Three Children

Miss Adelaide Smith was out touring with Dr. Hettie Painter and they travelled from City Point to Bermuda Hundred and then to Point of Rocks. At one point in the afternoon, they stopped at the Hatcher farm, "a former elegant plantation," where the owner had taken the Oath of Allegiance. The residents had sent their slaves south, so they lived quietly on the farm. Because they had taken the oath, their property and family had been given a house guard. Dr. Painter's son was a telegraph operator in what had once been the Hatchers' slave quarters. Miss Smith and Dr. Painter had a fine lunch with the young men. {Source 34}

Mrs. Levy

See Mrs. Frances Levy in Military Wives section

Mrs. Humphrey Marshall and Two Daughters

Originally from Louisville, Kentucky, the women were probably headed to Richmond. They disembarked at Aiken's Landing, which was also known as Mrs. Grover's house. {Source 28}

Old Mrs. Mary Nelson

She lived in Weston Manor with her husband, Captain Nelson, until General Hincks (Hinks) required that they move in June of 1864. It was the start of the occupation of the area by General Grant and the Nelsons and Woods were allowed to reside in a portion of the house for a short while. {Sources 30, 205}

Mrs. Emma Wood Richardson and Children

They were civilian refugees who moved into Weston Manor with old Mrs. Nelson. Shortly thereafter, General Hincks came into the area and confiscated part of the house for the military but allowed the residents to remain in the other part of the house. When General Sheridan moved in, the refugees had to find another place to live. {Source 30}

Mrs. Roberson

This woman accompanied Mrs. Stiles when she testified against the two men who had violated Mrs. Stiles on June 25, 1864. The 1863 map for the appropriate neighborhood of the incident shows a Robinson resident. According to the 1860 census, Mrs. C. Robinson, age 66, and three other women from the Williams family, who ranged from age 46 to 21, resided at the next numbered dwelling. Robinson is another spelling of Roberson. (See Mrs. Stiles in this section.) {Sources 28, 46}

Mrs. Slater

Sarah Antoinette "Nettie" Gilbert Slater was a spy, courier, and blockade runner who travelled under various names such as the "French Lady," the "Lady in the Veil," "Mrs. Howells," among other aliases. She was born in Middletown, Connecticut, on January 12, 1843, to the Gilbert family. Mr. Gilbert was the son of a Revolutionary War soldier and an old member of the Connecticut community. His son sailed to Martinique and eventually married. When the younger Mr. Gilbert and his new wife arrived back in Connecticut from Martinique, there was concern because of the West Indies blood. Over the next few years, they had several children. Fluent in French, the family offered language lessons to the Middletown community. Sarah had a reputation for being feisty as a young woman. In 1861, the oldest sister married a man in North Carolina, so part of the family went down for the wedding. Her mother, however, remained in New York due in part to the recent birth of a son. When the war broke out, the visiting family members were stuck behind Confederate lines and struggled to find an alternative way home. Sarah and two of her brothers moved to New Bern, North Carolina, where she met Rowan Slater, the local dance instructor. Shortly thereafter they were married. Rowan enlisted in the Confederate Army and went off to war and she never saw him again. Sarah's father and one brother died in North Carolina and her two other brothers went into brief CSA service. Savvy and alone, Sarah packed her bags and headed back to her original point of entry into North Carolina. She was arrested trying to get through the lines. Using her French- speaking charm and the fact her husband and two brothers were Confederates, she was able to get to Virginia. In Richmond, she investigated her options and was tapped to become a courier working through New York and then to Canada for the St. Alban's Raiders. Her dear friend, mentor, and ultimate protector was Judah P. Benjamin. They shared many commonalities, such as West Indies background, fluency in French, local Connecticut connections, bold, confident dual-hat personalities, plus the fact that Judah's wife shared similar features. Feminine and impeccably French, Sarah passed easily through the lines and used transports when needed. She often worked with Gus Howell and John Surratt and stayed at the Surratt home on her way north or while heading back south to make a report. She may have been one of the individuals who informed the Union forces about the potential kidnapping of Lincoln. Her last trip north was right before the Lincoln assassination when she disappeared and was never found ... until 2010.

Although a Mrs. Slater was brought in for the assassination trial, it was the wrong woman and she was released. Sarah Slater was the only one connected with the Surratts that was never pursued for the assassination, and it is probable she was a double agent. Sarah moved to New York City for a brief period of time and divorced Rowan. Later, she married one of her deceased sister's husband and changed her name to Spencer. About the same time, one of her brothers, who was close to Sarah, went from being a local jeweler to that of a well-connected and affluent real estate owner in the Jacksonville, Florida, area. Something in the family had changed and there was significant wealth. Sarah moved to Poughkeepsie and maintained a low profile. She died in 1920, leaving considerable money, jewelry, and investments. Her most confident "advisor" in New York City was the son of a Yale classmate of Judah P. Benjamin. Sarah was buried in Poughkeepsie, New York, next to her sister Josephine Lofton and her mother Antionette Gilbert. (See Mrs. Baylor in this section.) {Sources 10, 134, 236}

Mrs. Mary E. Stiles

Mary was a 29-year-old seamstress who lived in the area with her husband Benjamin, son C.A., and daughter Nancie, until the occupation. Her story is detailed in Chapter 2. After the war, Mrs. Stiles was still residing in the same location with her husband, daughter Nancie, and another child named Lizzie. In the 1870 census the name changes from Stiles to Styles. {Sources 28, 43, 46}

Miss Lucy Williams

Miss Williams was a cousin to Mrs. Stiles and key witness at the court-martial trial since she was in the next room during the incident with the soldiers. After the war, her name was no longer listed in the 1870 Prince George County census. Where she moved or when she passed away is not known. {Source 43}

Miss Mary Catherine Wiseman

There were several Wiseman families in the City Point area. The family patriarch had come from Germany. Mary Catherine was a local young lady born in 1845 who met and fell in love with a Yankee soldier named Frederick Belch. They were married in 1865, right after the war. He worked as a fisherman and keeper of a lighthouse. She bore six children and passed away in 1916. She was buried in St. John's Episcopal Cemetery in Hopewell, Virginia. {Sources 15, 266, 267. Image at City Point's Wiseman Family Marker, HMdb.org/Marker.asp?Marker=41498}

"Few ladies in the street"

On an April 4, 1865, visit to Petersburg, Mrs. McKay, Mrs. Hill, and Miss Virginia Hart noticed there were a few ladies out on the streets. They also noted that the women wore garments that had been in style four years earlier. {Source 18}

A Lady

On June 16, 1864, Chief Engineers Barnard, Comstock, and Kautz rode down to the Birchetts' house. The house was "large and fine," located "straight south of the Jordon Point Road about four miles." Inside the house was a "lady" (probably one of the Birchetts) and her husband. The husband was paralyzed, having been shot through the spine. Kautz treated the husband, and in turn the wife fed all a humble dinner of fruit, greens and pieces of cornbread, which was all they had to eat. {Source 44}

"One elderly lady"

On April 4, 1865, "one elderly lady" who was richly dressed walked along the street of Petersburg with a white handkerchief held over her eyes so she did not have to witness the fall of her beloved area. {Source 18}

"A pretty little girl"

The little girl lived in the home of Colonel Watts of Church Street in Petersburg. She raised her window so she could see the Union soldiers as they marched into the town. {Source 1}

"A pretty young girl, Confederate Officer, and two or three women"

Adelaide Smith went out with supplies in order to exchange them for fresh milk. She rode into the safeguard area to make the trade. Seeing women and soldiers on a front porch, she stopped at the house. She offered medical care and confirmed her only intent was to exchange supplies for milk. She was able to establish a relationship that allowed her to repeatedly return for fresh milk in trade for other supplies. {Source 34}

"Some young women on a piazza"

Several young ladies made faces and gestures at the twenty-four Union Officers and ladies touring the Petersburg area on April 4, 1865. {Source 34}

"A very agreeable Southern Woman"

The Soyers (USSC) and several nurses went to view Petersburg in May of 1865. They stopped at a residence of a woman who extended the hospitality of her home to them. She had a lovely garden with fruit trees in her yard. {Source 3}

"Weary women and children"

These were the women and children who were seen going in and out of the "gopher holes" in Petersburg. They hid for safety during the day and came out at night to go home and sleep. {Source 34}

"Woman in a shaker bonnet"

Mrs. McKay encountered the woman near Ford's Station. She had lost everything during the occupation, yet she allowed Mrs. McKay to stay in what was left of her home. When Mrs. McKay left, she gave the woman some cooking utensils and supplies. {Source 18}

Contraband or Former Slaves

Women who were contrabands or former slaves who were associated in a working capacity and were actually written about in other individuals' diaries are listed here. They are presented alphabetically by last name, if known; first name or nickname if not known. Women who were not mentioned by any sort of name (such as "one excited old woman" and "a perfect slave") are listed at the end.

"Aunty"

Aunty was a black woman who wore a bright red turban and a white apron and stayed with Adelaide Smith after the 2nd Corps Hospital left. She remained at City Point after the war ended. {Source 34}

"Aunty"

Another Aunty was mentioned as residing at the Eppes house near Bailey Creek. She was old enough to have "had double children, but had none." {Source 1}

Aunty Adeline

She was identified as a former slave of Rev. Jack Strong. {Source 15}

Aunty Miranda

She worked with Mrs. Collis during the winter of 1864. She was an older woman whom Mrs. Collis found living in the area. According to Mrs. Collis, "she was an excellent cook and maid." {Sources 6, 206}

C. Barney

Listed as a washerwoman in the 1860 census, C. Barney may have been Celia the laundress at Point of Rocks in 1864. The record indicated that she was not able to read or write at that time. {Source 270}

Martha Batte

She was born in 1836 and listed in the 1860 census as a washerwoman who could not read or write. She was the mother of a nine-year-old girl. She remained in the area after the war. {Source 270}

Eliza Bonnell

Eliza is listed as buried at Jones Landing near the neck. Her name is in the middle of many of the USCT. {Source 233}

"Old Aunty Cook"

She waited on Miss Bain and Miss Smith when they visited the Dutch Gap area. Old Aunty Cook had been hired by the officers stationed there and may have been one of the Hatcher family slaves. {Source 34}

Paulina Ruffin Eppes (Epes)

Paulina was the wife of former slave Henry Eppes (Epes). Henry eventually served as a sailor in the Union Army. Paulina was one of the many former slaves of Dr. Richard Eppes, the owner of Appomattox Manor. Paulina's father was James Madison and her mother was Harriet Ruffin. James (referred to as Madison) had been one of the Eppes' most trusted slaves.

After the war, some of the family returned to the area. Paulina and Henry had four children—two girls and two boys. The oldest daughter, Mary Elizabeth, tragically died of poisoning at age eleven in 1882, leaving Harriet (Hattie), Robert Henry, and William Henry. The couple resided in a small house on the bluff at the end of Prince Street in City Point. Paulina's husband Henry died of consumption in 1889. In 1938 at age 90, Paulina completed a WPA interview and lived almost another decade. She died on January 8, 1946, at the age of 98 and is buried in the Saint John's Episcopal Church grounds in City Point. {Sources 41, 42, 44, 183}

Hannah Evans

She lived in the area prior to the occupation and would have been about 40 years old in 1864. There was also Hannah Ruffin, who would have been about the same age. Either of them would have become a cook or skilled servant for the military or private citizens during the occupation. {Source 270}

Georgiana

She was the wife of Douglas. Together they helped William Barnes, who worked directly for General Grant. {Source 206}

P. Hamblin

This was most likely Parcila Hamblin, who was a seamstress in the City Point area. Her spouse was listed as a sailor named W. Hill. {Source 270}

Hannah

Hannah was a contraband woman that Adelaide Smith hired even though she thought Hannah was "rather incompetent." Hannah apparently helped in one of the kitchens of New Jersey, Pennsylvania, or even New York. There were several women called Hannah that appeared on Dr. Richard Eppes' "list of slaves" prior to the war. One was Hannah Slaughter, age fifty-six, who was known to have stayed in the area when the Union forces came in. {Source 34}

Harriet Jackson

Harriet was a mulatto woman and the former slave of P.H. Jackson of Prince Edward County, Virginia. As a young teen, she had been sold or hired out to a family that allowed her to work as a nurse to General Fitzhugh Lee when he was a child. In 1865, she was a middle-aged woman. She worked as the chief cook onboard the *Prince Albert*. On April 12, 1865, she defied the authorities and gave food to a Confederate prisoner named Lucien Hall. He was deeply touched by her kindness and remembered her enough to write her name and the incident into history. {Source 26}

Diley James

She was the wife of William James. They had had a small farm prior to the occupation but lost everything when the military came in August of 1864. Along with their daughter, Emma, the family moved to City Point and worked for the Quartermaster Department. After the war, they returned to their home and started over again. {Source 206}

Mary Jones

Mary worked as a laundress and personal servant for some of the officers in the Ninth Corps. She applied for subsistence rations in 1865. She had several children, and by 1880 she had relocated to the Richmond area. {Source 271}

Nancy Lewis

Born in 1844, she was a slave of Dr. Richard Eppes until he left for Petersburg. {Sources 41, 42}

"Nancy"

Nancy was a private maid/servant to Mrs. Judith Morgan. {Sources 29, 33}

Rachel

Rachel was the personal servant of Harriet Eaton, from Maine. {Source 239}

Sally Rives

Born in 1835, she was listed on the 1860 City Point Census as the wife of Peter Rives, who was a ships hand. They had a five-year-old daughter who would have been about nine when the military came to the area. {Source 270}

"One excited old woman"

A black woman was watching the Confederate prisoners being marched into City Point after the battle of Hatchers Run. She recognized some of the men. {Source 34}

"Perfect old slave"

On July 10, 1864, this woman and a young boy began working for Cornelia Hancock. The former slave called Cornelia "Honey" and resided with her in the tent. She slept in a regular bed, which amazed many of the women in camp. {Source 12}

Unknown Woman with the 29th Connecticut Infantry (Colored)

She was serving with the regiment and was discovered to be a woman only when she had a child in March of 1865. After the discovery, she was forced out of the unit and into the hospital. {Source 10}

Visitors

This section consists of women who were just passing through the City Point area. For example, five women are mentioned only in passing who would have arrived on one of the steamers such as the *Thomas Morgan*, or the *DeMolay*, or even the *Silver Star*, but were barely known. These women generally came to care for their wounded or sick husbands. For the most part, there were no names or identifiable information available, but the nurses would frequently mention that a wife was in the hospital ward or a wife and a child waited at an unidentified soldier's bedside, so they are included here. In addition, the newspapers referred to groups of women passing through City Point while heading north or heading south because City Point was a passenger point of debarkation or embarkation. Limited attempts have made to locate their names. For the women whose names are known, they only had a brief stay at City Point. Where they slept or what they ate remains unknown, but life must have been difficult for them.

When a woman's name is known, it appears alphabetically in the following list; if only a descriptor was used ("female political prisoners," "a lady with six children," "unknown woman"), she appears alphabetically by the descriptor.

Miss Bradley

She took the USS *Blackstone* north from City Point. She was probably Amy Bradley. {Source 187}

Mrs. Pauline Bush

In April of 1865, she came to collect her deceased son who served with Co. F, 190th Pennsylvania Volunteers. {Source 19}

Mrs. C—

Mrs. C— was a widow from Houlton, Maine. She had previously lost one son in the war and came to locate her second son who had been wounded. Her son was not at any of the City Point hospitals, but Miss Usher found him in a field hospital closer to Petersburg. While at City Point, she was fortunate enough to stay with Miss Usher. {Source 19}

Mrs. Lieutenant Dupree

She arrived from Rhode Island around August 15–19, 1864, with her brother to pick up the body of Lt. Dupree, who had died of a leg wound. {Source 23}

Mrs. Emery

Mrs. Emery took the USS *Blackstone* north from City Point. {Source 187}

Mrs. Jane Ferguson

Jane was quite young and was with her husband John, who was in the 1st New York Cavalry at the front. The previous year, she was in Kentucky dressed in male attire and arrested as a spy. She was court-martialed and sent to the military prison in Lexington, but she was considered incapable of being shrewd enough to be a spy and was released. {Sources 10, 139}

Mrs. John Ferguson

Probably a different woman than the previous entry, she went to war with her husband in the 1st New York Cavalry, 5th Corps and often served as a cook and a nurse to the wounded when in the hospital area. When she was at Antietam, she was slightly wounded in the knee by a shell fragment. After the war they lived in Brooklyn, New York. She died on or about December 6, 1906. {Sources 137, 139}

Mrs. Galbraith

From Ohio, she was alone and confused while searching for her son in the hospitals. She made friends with Mrs. Holstein, who assisted her. {Source 14}

Mrs. Johnson and Child

On July 24, 1864, Mr. Phiny Sanborne of the USCC ran into the mother and daughter at Fort Monroe. Mrs. Johnson had left City Point the day before. {Source 30}

Mrs. Martin

Mrs. Martin was a POW from Mobile, Alabama. She was referred to as a "lady." She had been at City Point for a short time while the military tried to figure out what to do with her. Who she was billeted with remains unknown. {Source 28}

Author's Note: There was another Mrs. Martin who may have gone through City Point because the boats had direct access to New York City. She was the wife of Confederate Colonel Robert Maxwell Martin, who caused subversive problems in New York during the war. His wife was Mrs. Caroline Martin. {Source 220}

Miss Mason

Headquarters requested Miss Smith to billet a woman in her quarters. She was a southern woman on her way home via the flag-of-truce boat. She stayed at City Point for several days and was sent on to Richmond with a detachment of paroled Confederate prisoners. {Source 34}

Miss E.L. Morey

She took the USS *Blackstone* to the north. {Source 187}

Mrs. Matilda E. Morris

On May 18, 1865, this former nurse passed through City Point on her way back home. She had procured a pass but got on the wrong steamer. It proved to be a humorous and memorable event for all concerned. (See Chapter 9.) After the war, she and her husband returned to the home of her parents and children at 112 Harbor Street, Cleveland, Ohio. {Sources 13, 280, 281. Image at http://schliessmann.blogspot.com/2010/05/civil-war-nurses-forgotten-heroes-of.html}

Mrs. Parr

She arrived at City Point with her husband (Joel Parr) and their children. They had been living about fifteen miles southeast of Petersburg when the war started. The Confederate authorities found them to be Yankee sympathizers and sent Joel Parr to prison. When released, they sought passage through the Union lines. {Source 182}

Mrs. Mary Seizgle (Seigle or Sickle)

Mary was a German woman who followed her husband, Frederick, who was in the 41st New York Regiment. She was detained for wearing a man's uniform but was released so she could return home to gather appropriate attire because she said she had no other clothes to wear. {Source 221}

Miss Sorton

She was from New York and managed to avoid or charm various provost marshals between Baltimore and City Point in order to find her brother. By the time she arrived, the brother had been dead for two weeks. Miss Sorton claimed the body and returned back to New York with it. {Source 109}

Bouncing Baby Boy

Hospital records at Point of Rocks indicated that a "Sergeant" from the 10th New York Heavy Artillery was ill and taken to the hospital. On March 6, the sergeant—either a woman disguised as a solder or a camp follower who had attached herself to the 10th NYHA—delivered a healthy baby boy. {Source 216}

Female Political Prisoners

Even though it was after the war, on or about November 16, 1865, Robert G. Eggling and Eugenia Harmmermister were released and sent through City Point for points north. The agent of exchange, Robert Ould, requested to send any other female political prisoners from the Richmond area as well. {Source 175}

Female Spy

A woman was caught trying to pass through the lines on December 26 while attempting to board the mail boat headed to Washington. She was wearing a colonel's uniform, but when asked for the required pass, she lost her composure and was detected as a woman. {Source 181}

Great Fat Irish Woman

Aunt Becky had to share her bed with this woman, who came to visit her husband. She left on April 1, 1865, on board the steamer *Connecticut* with the wounded soldiers. {Source 23}

"A Lady"

On February 8, 1865, a train returning from Petersburg stopped at Yellow House Station, where an officer and his lady got on. The couple was going to City Point. {Source 31}

A Lady with Six Children

All that is known is that she boarded the mail steamer *Colyer* and arrived at City Point for a trip north. {Source 223}

Old Father and His Daughter-in-Law

They came to City Point to get the remains of their family member. {Source 23}

"A Pennsylvanian woman"

She came to City Point seeking the bones of her son, who was to have been buried at White House Landing. Dr. Hettie Painter helped her by getting a transport and crew to search for the body. Unsuccessful, they returned to City Point, where the distraught woman was persuaded to go home and come back another time. It was on this trip that Dr. Painter procured the shutters for her own accommodations. {Source 30}

"Two Women"

Captain Oliver went to Richmond on the *Silver Star* to see Colonel Mulford. He picked up the women, who had been at City Point for some time wanting to go through the lines with a pass from the president. They may have been Miss Bidgood and Mrs. Levy, waiting to catch the flag-of-truce boat back to Richmond. {Source 28}

Unknown Woman and Child, Winter of 1864

The wife of a deserter came to plead for her husband's life. First, she went to Cadwallader, who then passed her on to General Bowers. General Bowers instructed her to go see General Meade, who sent her on to see General Grant. Grant passed her on to President Lincoln. Through dogged persistence and the ability to wear the men down, she won a limited release/reprieve for her husband. She returned the next day to Washington, D.C., via the ten o'clock mail boat. {Sources 4, 29, 33}

Woman from Pennsylvania and Her Baby

She came to City Point to see her husband, who had been wounded in the head. He died three days before she arrived. {Source 23}

Sources for Homeward Bound Journey

The numbered sources following relate to the five sections in the Homeward Bound Journey. When research was first begun, numbers were assigned as new material was found. Consequently, several numbers are missing in this sequence because they relate to other topics and not the women in this chapter.

1. Agassi, George (Ed.). (1922). *Meade's Headquarters: Letters of Colonel Theodore Lyman*. Boston: Massachusetts Historical Society.
2. Brockett, L.P. & Vaughn, M. (1867). *Women's Work in the Civil War*. Philadelphia: Zeigler, McCurdy.
3. Bucklin, S. (1869). *In a Hospital and Camp: Official Papers of Sophronia Bucklin*. Philadelphia: J.E. Potter.
4. Cadwallader, S. (Ed.). (1980). *Three Years with Grant*. Westport, CT: Greenwood.
5. Cambum, M.A. *Personal Recollections of Lincoln*. City Point files, Petersburg National Battlefield Park, Petersburg, VA.
6. Collis, S. (1889). *A Woman's War Record*. New York: G.P. Putnam & Sons.
7. Conklin, E.F. (1993). *Women at Gettysburg*. Gettysburg, PA: Thomas.
8. Fizen, L. (April 1994). The Lady's Carrying a Scalpel. *Civil War Magazine*, XXLII.
9. French, B.B. (1989). Cole, D.B. & McDonough, J.J. (Eds.). *Witness to a Young Republic: A Yankee Journal, 1828–1870*. Hanover, NH: University Press of New England.
10. Hall, R. (1993). *Patriots in Disguise: Women Warriors of the Civil War*. New York: Paragon House.
11. Hammond, H.E. (1962). *Diary of a Union Lady*. New York: Funk &Wagnalls.
12. Jacquette, H.S. (Ed.). (1937). *South After Gettysburg: Letters of Cornelia Hancock*. Philadelphia: University of Pennsylvania.
13. Holland, M.A.G. (1895). *Our Army Nurses*. Boston: Wilkerson & CO.
14. Holstein, A. (1867). *Three Years in the Field Hospital of the Army of the Potomac*. Philadelphia: J.B. Lippincott.
15. Hopewell (1985). *Our Share of Honour: Hopewell and Prince George County Women, 1600–1985*. Hopewell, VA: Hopewell Tourism Bureau.
16. Johnson, R. (1894). *Campfire and Battlefield*. New York: Bryan, Taylor & Co.
17. Maxwell, W.Q. (1868). *Lincoln's Fifth Wheel: The Political History of the United States Sanitary Commission*. New York: Longman, Green & Co.
18. McKay, Mrs. C.E. (1876). *Stories of Hospital and Camp*. Philadelphia: Claxton, Remsem & Haffelfinger.

19. Moore, F. (1867). *Women of the War.* Hartford, CT: S.S. Scranton.
20. Moss, Rev. L. (1868). *Annals of the United States Christian Commission.* Philadelphia: J.B. Lippincott.
21. Executive Committee of the National Association of Civil War Nurses. (1910). *In Honor of the National Association of Civil War Nurses: 44th Encampment Grand Army of the Republic.* Atlantic City: Yeakel.
22. O'Hall, J. (June 25, 1975). Lady in the Veil. *The Maryland Independent* (LaPlata, MD).
23. Palmer, S. (1868). *The Story of Aunt Becky's Army Life.* New York: John F. Trow.
24. Parker, Colonel F.J. (1880). *32nd Regiment Massachusetts Infantry.* Boston: C.W. Calkins.
25. Parker, M.G. (1922). *Moses Greeley Parker M.D.* Lowell, MA: Privately printed.
26. Perkins, H.M. (December 1992). Lucien Hall's Prison Sketchbook. *Northern Neck of Virginia Historical Society,* XXLII, 483–485, 498–506.
27. Pfanz, D. (transcriber). (1988). *The Depot Hospital at City Point.* Petersburg, VA: Petersburg National Battlefield Park.
28. Pfanz, D. (transcriber). (1987). *The Diary of Marsena Patrick, Provost Marshal of the Army of the Potomac: June 15, 1864, to April 18, 1865.* Petersburg, VA: Petersburg National Battlefield Park.
29. Porter, General H. (1897). *Campaigning with Grant.* New York: The Century.
30. Richardson, Mrs. E.W. *Notes on the Civil War: From Colonel Kingston Winger.* Hampton Center for the Arts and Humanities. City Point files, Petersburg National Battlefield Park, Petersburg, VA.
31. Rosenblatt, S. (Ed.). (1983). *Anti-Rebel: The Civil War Letters of Wilber Fisk.* Croton-on-Hudson, NY: Haddon Craftsman.
32. Sanborne, Pliny Fiske. *USCC Civil War Chaplin Daily Extracts from June 7 to August 15, 1864.* City Point files, Petersburg National Battlefield Park, Petersburg, VA.
33. Simon, J.Y. (Ed.). (1975). *The Personal Memoirs of Julia Dent Grant.* New York: G.P. Putnam's Sons.
34. Smith, A. (1919). *Reminiscences of an Army Nurse During the Civil War.* New York: Greaves.
35. Walker, P.F. (1978). *Moral Choices: Memory, Desire, and Imagination in the Nineteenth-Century American Abolition.* Baton Rouge: Louisiana State University.
36. Personal Notes of Clara Barton, Sophia Smith Collection. Sophia Smith Library, Hatfield, MA.
37. Wheelock, J. (1870). *The Boys in White: Experiences of a Hospital Agent in and Around Washington.* New York: Lange & Hillman.
38. Wittenmyer, A. (1895). *Under the Gun: A Woman's Reminiscences of the Civil War.* Boston: E.B. Stillings.
39. Wilson, J.H. (1916). *Life of John Rawlins.* New York: Neala.
40. Van Zandt, A.B. (1857). *The Elect Lady: A Memoir of Mrs. Catherine Bott.* Philadelphia: Presbyterian Board Publication.
41. Baptism, confirmation, marriage and death records of St. John's Church, Hopewell, VA.
42. City Point files on Dr. Richard Eppes. Petersburg National Battlefield Park, Petersburg, VA.
43. Court Martial Files #MM1481. NARA, Washington, D.C.
44. Summer, M.E. (*Transcribed notes) from the diary of Cyrus Ballou Comstock.* City Point files, Petersburg National Battlefield Park, Petersburg, VA.
45. Sudlow, L.L. (2000). *A Vast Army of Women: Maine's Uncounted Forces in the American Civil War.* Gettysburg, PA: Thomas.
46. Sparks, D.S. (Ed) (1964). *Inside Lincoln's Army: Diary of Marsena Rudolph Patrick, Provost Marshal General of the Army of the Potomac.* New York: Thomas Yoseloff.
47. Mrs. Fannie T. Hazen. (January 16, 1930). *The New York Times,* p. 23.
48. Obituary: Mrs. Mildred S. Brooks. (April 12, 1916). *Hartford (CT) Daily Courant,* p. 7.
49. That He Who Runs May Read. (April 11, 1916). *The Evening Telegraph* (NY), p. 9, col. 2.
50. Nurse Tells of Meeting Lincoln in a Hospital. (February 4, 1923). *New York Times,* p. 12.
51. Relief Corps Inspection. (October 30, 1899). *Hartford (CT) Courant,* p. 7.
52. Conquering a Rebel. (November 16, 1866). *Hartford (CT) Daily Courant,* p. 6.

11. Homeward Bound Journey 227

53. Battlefield Angels. (August 25, 1899). *Democrat and Chronicle* (Rochester, NY).
54. A Female Soldier from Maine. (December 31, 1863). *Richmond Examiner* copied to the *Hartford Courant*, p. 2.
55. Obituary. (February 11 or 12, 1865). *The Republican Advocate* (Batavia, NY), Tuesday Morning.
56. Civil War Army Nurse Relates Her Experiences. (October 14, 1911). *Brooklyn Daily Eagle*, p. 4, col. 1.
57. Planning to Help Soldiers. (Saturday, June 11, 1898). *Brooklyn Daily Eagle*, p. 7, col. 3.
58. Honor Miss Smith's Memory. (January 16, 1915). *Brooklyn Daily Eagle*, p. 1.
59. Miss Smith Seeks Trace of the Last of the Preston. (January 4, 1903). *Brooklyn Daily Eagle*, p. 1.
60. Dr. Brundage Called to Side of Dying Woman. (December 31, 1914). *Daily Democrat and Recorder* (Amsterdam, NY), p. 1, col. 5.
61. Suffragists March to Show Brooklyn. (November 2, 1913). *The (NY) Sun*, p. 12, col. 3.
62. Wild Auto Kills Civil War Nurse. (December 31, 1914). *Hudson (NY) Evening Register*, p. 1.
63. Civil War Nurse Dies. (June 24, 1939). *Schenectady (NY) Gazette*, Saturday Morning, p. 1, col. 4.
64. W.J. Bray Is the New Commander. (September 21, 1911). *Hartford (CT) Courant*, p. 7.
65. Mrs. Maria M.C. Richards. (July 22, 1912). *Hartford (CT) Courant*, p. 2.
66. Letters from the People. (July 23, 1912). *Hartford (CT) Courant*, p. 8.
67. Civil War Nurse Dies at Corning. (January 12, 1927). *Amsterdam (NY) Evening Record*, p. 3, col. 5.
68. A Woman's War History. (December 20, 1901). *Perrysburg (OH) Journal*, col. 1, image 7.
69. Of Interest to Women and Home. (February 9, 1902). *Buffalo (NY) Courier*, p. 8, col. 2.
70. Noted War Work of Mrs. Sarah Young. (February 9, 1902). *Rochester (NY) Democrat and Chronicle*, col. 6–7.
71. "Aunt Becky" Dies in Iowa. (April 23, 1908). *Owego (NY) Gazette*, p. 1.
72. The 109th Regiment. (August 28, 1890). *Owego (NY) Gazette*, p. 1.
73. Death Claims Aunt Becky Young. (April 6, 1908). *Des Moines (IA) Tribune*, p. 1, col. 7.
74. A Neighborly Feud. (March 9, 1881). *New York Times*, p. 5.
75. Hoffert, S.D. (2004). *Jane Grey Swisshelm*. Chapel Hill: University of North Carolina Press.
76. The St. Cloud Democrat. (August 1858). *St. Cloud (MN) Democrat*, p. 1.
77. Civil War Nurse Dies. (December 09, 1906). *The Washington (D.C.) Herald*, p. 5, col. 1.
78. Saturday's News. (February 4, 1900). *Daily Leader* (Marietta, OH), p. 1, col. 4.
79. Department of Nebraska. (January 02, 1890). *The National Tribune* (Washington, D.C.), p. 6, col. 5.
80. Relief Corps News. (December. 27, 1888). *The National Tribune*, p. 6, col. 4–5.
81. Miss Walker. (May 29, 1864). *The Richmond Examiner*, Civil War Richmond. #785447, www.mdgorman.com
82. Freedom Trail and Dr. Walker Exhibits. (January 22, 1949). *Daily Sentinel* (Rome, NY), p. 2, col. 3–5.
83. Dr. Walker Is Dead at 87. (February 23, 1919). *Hartford (CT) Courant*, p. 2.
84. Dr. Mary Walker. (February 07, 1902). *Hartford (CT) Courant*, p. 7.
85. Dr. Walker and Her Claim. (July 11, 1876). *Hartford (CT) Courant*, p. 1.
86. Dr. Mary Walker Ill in New York. (May 18, 1912). *Hartford (CT) Courant*, p. 1.
87. Local Notes. (January 27, 1906). *Oswego (NY) Daily Times*, no page, col. 6.
88. Pants for the Women. (March 1, 1917). *Oswego (NY) Daily Palladium*, p. 3, col. 5.
89. Wooley, Captain R.W. (1988). A Short History of Identification Tags. *Quartermaster Professional Bulletin*, December, Fort Lee, VA.
90. Clara Barton and Andersonville, Andersonville National Historic Site, http://www.nps.gov/ande/historyculture/clara_barton.htm.
91. Civil War@Smithsonian Identification tags. http://www.civilwar.si.edu/soldiering_id_tag.html.
92. From All Parts of Long Island. (September 1, 1904). *The Newtown Register* (Jamaica, NY), p. 2.

93. House Favors Memorial for Civil War Women. (August 13, 1912). *Hartford (CT) Courant*, p. 1.
94. Trip of General Collis. (December 27, 1896). *New York Times*, p. 15.
95. Prominent Women Dine. (December 23, 1896). *New York Times*, p. 16.
96. Public Works Scandal: Comments of the Charges. (October 4, 1898). *New York Times*, p. 14.
97. Col. Collis Marries Miss Williamson. (January 15, 1922). *New York Times*, p. 22.
98. Day of Memories for Custer's Widow. (June 25, 1930). *New York Times*, p. 22.
99. Society News and Chat. (May 31, 1891). *The Sunday Herald and Weekly National Intelligencer* (Washington, D.C.), p. 1.
100. National Archive File #1340181 and #862851, RG 15, NARA Civil War Files.
101. Frederick Tracy Dent, Arlington Cemetery. http://www.arlingtoncemetery.net/ftdent.htm.
102. Mrs. Grant Critically Ill. (December 14, 1902). *New York Times*, p. 1.
103. Arrival of Mrs. Grant. (August 5, 1885). *New York Times*, p. 2.
104. Received by Mrs. Grant. (October 14, 1886). *New York Times*, p. 2.
105. Mrs. Grant's Funeral. (December 17, 1902). *New York Times*, p. 9, col. 4.
106. Mrs. Grant and Mrs. Davis. (June 26, 1893). *New York Times*, p. 2.
107. Mary Eunice Harlan Lincoln, Find a Grave, #7186237.
108. Mary Eunice Harlan, http://en.wickipedia.org/wiki/Mary_Eunice_Harlan.
109. *Diary of Judson B. Andrew, Assistant Army Surgeon, 6th Corps*. City Point files, Petersburg National Battlefield Park, Petersburg, VA.
110. Women in the Civil War: Five Nurses from St. Lawrence County. Association of University Women, http://stlawrence.aauw-nys.org/nurses.htm.
111. Entertained by Mrs. Grant. (August 07, 1887). *The (NY) Sun*, p. 1.
112. Gone to City Point. (April 05, 1865). *Washington (D.C.) Evening Star*, p. 2, col. 5.
113. Widows of Heroes. (July 27, 1890). *Pittsburgh Dispatch*, p. 16, col. 1.
114. Garfield Hospital Officers. (January 17, 1888). *The Washington (D.C.) Critic*, p. 4.
115. W.R.C. Convention. (August 29, 1889). *Los Angles Daily Herald*, p. 4.
116. Mrs. General Logan's Home Magazine. (February 11, 1892). *The Record-Union* (Sacramento, CA), p. 2, col. 2.
117. The Nurses. (May 16, 1883). *National Republican* (Washington, D.C.), p. 2, col. 2.
118. Pension file #1158311, RG 15, NARA, Washington, D.C.
119. Daughters of the Revolution. (October 12, 1890). *The Sunday Herald and Weekly Intelligencer* (Washington, D.C.), p. 8, col. 1.
120. Social News. (May 31, 1894). *The Sunday Herald and Weekly Intelligencer* (Washington, D.C.), p. 12, col. 2.
121. By Telegraph. (June 04, 1869). *Public Ledger* (Memphis, TN), p. 4, col. 1.
122. General Rawlins as a Soldier—Mrs. Rawlins and Her Confederate Lover. (September 26, 1868). *San Francisco Daily Bulletin*, in Rawlins file and personal papers, Danbury Historical Society, Danbury, CT.
123. Death of General Rawlins. (September 9, 1869). *Daily Arkansas Gazette*.
124. Intelligence and Express. (September 20, 1869). *Daily National Intelligence and Washington Express* (Washington, D.C.).
125. When Mrs. Rawlins Was a Maiden. (September 23, 1869). *Gallipolis Journal*, Danbury Historical Society file.
126. General J.A. Rawlins. (September 11, 1869). *The Jeffersonian* (Danbury, CT), p. 2.
127. General Grant to Visit. (September 11, 1869). *The Jeffersonian* (Danbury, CT).
128. The Burial of the Dead. (November 18, 1874). *The Jeffersonian* (Danbury, CT).
129. Obituary, Mrs. Major General Rawlins. (November 11, 1874). *The Jeffersonian* (Danbury, CT), p. 2.
130. Crotty, D.G. (1874). *Four Years Campaigning in the Army of the Potomac*. Grand Rapids, MI: Dygert Bros.
131. General News. (March 9, 1865). *Hartford (CT) Courant*, p. 2.
132. Pleasure Trip from Washington. (March 31, 1865). *Hartford (CT) Courant*, p. 3.
133. From the Army of the Potomac. (March 20, 1865). *Hartford (CT) Daily Courant*, p. 3.

11. Homeward Bound Journey

134. Christie, J.M. (April 14, 2012). *Sarah Slater: The Spy Who Got Away*. Popular and American Culture: Civil War and Reconstruction Conference. Boston, MA.
135. Woman Who Marched with Sherman Is Dead. (March 16, 1936). *New York Times*.
136. Mother of 21. (January 20, 1919). *The (NY) Sun*, p. 7, col. 5.
137. Obituary, Mrs. John Ferguson. (December 6, 1906). *New York Times*, p. 7, col. 5.
138. From City Point. (March 19, 1865). *New York Times*, p. 1.
139. Female Spy Mrs. Jane Ferguson. (July 3, 1864). *New York Times*, p. 6.
140. Arrest of a Supposed Rebel Spy. (February 14, 1865) *Cleveland Ledger*, in the February 19, 1865, *New York Times*.
141. Miss Bidgood and Mrs. Frances Levy, #3738, Turner Baker Papers, RG 94, NARA.
142. Carroll, J.M. (1983). *Collection of Recipes Special Diet Kitchen in Military Hospitals*. Mantituck, NY: The Virginia Historical Society Library.
143. Barton, Clara. Personal Notes and Papers, Sophia Smith Collection. Sophia Smith Library, Smith College, Hadley, MA.
144. Badeau, A. (January 19, 1887). Was Mrs. Lincoln Insane? *Fredonia (NY) Censor*, p. 1, col. 2.
145. Mrs. Lincoln Rebukes Mrs. Grant. (January 9, 1887). *New York World*, p. 12, col. 1–2.
146. Letter to the Editor. (August 2, 1883). *National Tribute* (Washington, D.C.), p. 6, col. 6.
147. Personal communication concerning Rebecca Gray with NARA, June 29, 2003.
148. The New Liberty Bell. (April 10, 1893). *Oswego (NY) Daily Times*, p. 3, col. 5.
149. Woman Aged 92, Who Attended Tad Lincoln Tells of the Simple Kindness of the Great Emancipator. (February 12, 1902). *Geneva (NY) Daily Times*, p. 14.
150. The Mason Mission. (January 16, 1865). *New York Herald*, p. 5, col. 3.
151. Untitled. (April 18, 1865). *Auburn (NY) Citizen*, p. 10.
152. Noble Woman Dies. (December 6, 1902). *The New Clown* (Ithaca: NY), p. 1, col. 6.
153. Untitled. (May 14, 1904). *Ithaca (NY) Daily News*, p. 3, col. 2.
154. Sophronia Bucklin, Find-a-Grave #71159852.
155. Biography of Julia Susan Wheelock 1833–1900. http://www.whelockgeneology.com/WheelcokWeb/pages/juliabio.htm.
156. A Woman's War History. (March 01, 1902). *Richmond (VA) Planet*, p. 2.
157. Harriet P. Dame. (March 28, 1895). *The Norfolk Virginian*, p. 4.
158. Miss Cornelia Hancock. (September 22, 1906). *Cook County Herald* (Grand Marais, MN), image 5.
159. Salt Lake Woman Lauds Clara Barton. (April 13, 1912). *The Salt Lake (UT) Tribune*, p. 14.
160. Famous Army Nurse: Career of Harriett Dame Who Served Through the Entire Civil War. (October 12, 1900). *Perrysburg (OH) Journal*, image 6.
161. An Eventful Career. (November 30, 1895). *The Evening Post* (New York), p. 2, col. 4.
162. The Woman of the War. (July 16, 1890). *Fredonia (NY) Censor*, p. 1, col. 9.
163. Cheered the Sick and Dying. (June 26, 1898). *The Philadelphia (PA) Inquirer*, p. 34.
164. Rebecca Usher Diary January 10, 1865–March 1865. Maine Historical Society. MMN#1451. www.MaineMemory.net.
165. Logan, Mrs. John L. (1912). *The Part Taken by Women in American History*. Wilmington, DE: Perry-Nalle Pub.
166. At Third Army Corp Reunion. (December 31, 1868). *Rutland (VT) Weekly Herald*, p. 2, col. 1.
167. Mrs. Helen Gilson Osgood. (December 24, 1868). *Brooklyn Daily Eagle*, no page, col. 2.
168. Memorial Day. (May 30, 1895). *The Standard Union* (Brooklyn, NY), p. 1.
169. The Third Army Corps of the Potomac. (December 25, 1868). *Philadelphia (PA) Inquirer*, p. 1.
170. Josiah Allen's Wife. (1879). *My Opinions and Betsy Bobbet's*. Hartford, CT: American Publishing.
171. Permits Bond Company's Fine. (February 4, 1917). *New York Call*, p. 4, col. 5.
172. Experiences as a War Nurse Are Related. (June 15, 1931). *La Crosse (WI) Tribune*, p. 1.
173. Mrs. R.E. Gray, Nurse in the Civil War, Dies. (January 7, 1917). *Brooklyn Daily Eagle*.
174. Other Organizations. (August 18, 1904). *Hartford (CT) Courant*, p. 10.
175. City Point. (November 16, 1865). *Gallipolis (OH) Journal*, p. 1, col. 6.

176. Nurses Famous on Many Battlefields. (Aug. 16, 1903). *The San Francisco Call*, pp. 12, 13.
177. Turner, George A. Harriet Reifsnyder Sharpless, Civil War Nurse from Bloomsburg, http//colcohist-gensoc.org.
178. Kensington. (March 6, 1894). *Evening Star* (Washington, D.C.), p. 12, col. 2.
179. How She Descended from Robert Morris. (October1, 1886). *Evening Star*, Washington, D.C.: p. 4, col 2.
180. Memorable Event for the Year. (December 31, 1894). *Rock Island (IL) Argus*, p. 3, col. 2.
181. The Quiet Along the Lines. (December 26. 1864). *New York Times*, p. 1.
182. Army of the Potomac. (July 8, 1864). *New York Times*, p. 8.
183. Memorial Stone to Be Placed on the Grave of Ex-Slave Paulina Ruffin Eps. *Diosova News*, March 19, 2015. http://diosovanews.blogspot.com/2015/03/memorial-stone-to-be-placed-on-a-grave-of.html.
184. Woman Who Served as Civil War Nurse Dies at Pottstown. (May 31, 1919). *Harrisburg (PA) Telegraph*, p. 2, image 2.
185. Funeral of Mrs. Annie E. Hooks. (January 27, 1913). *Evening Star* (Washington, D.C.), p. 3, image 3.
186. Famous Army Nurse. (October 18, 1900). *Phillipsburg (KS) Herald*, image 5.
187. Passengers Arrived. (August 6, 1864). *New York Times*, p. 8.
188. From General Grant's Army: All Quiet at the Front. (August 7, 1864). *New York Times*, p. 1.
189. Mr. Lincoln's White House. Notable Visitors. http://www.mrlincolnswhitehouse.org/inside.asp?ID=710&subjectID=2.
190. Queries and Answers: Romantic History of Mrs. Jane Swisshelm. (January 30, 1909). *New York Times*, p. BR67.
191. Obituary. (April 25, 1900). *The (NY) Sun*, p. 2, col. 5.
192. E.K. Spencer. (December 30, 1912). *The Day Book* (Oswego, NY), image 32.
193. The Princess at the White House. (April 18, 1899). *New York Daily Tribune*, p. 9, col. 5.
194. Princess Salm-Salm. (September 16, 1876). *National Republican* (Washington, D.C.), p. 1.
195. List Ladies Employed in Special Diets Kitchens under the Directions of the USCC. #15523, March 13, 1865, M416, NARA.
196. Clara Caroline Haxall Grundy, Find a Grave #24949293.
197. Richmond. (December 2, 1881). *The Daily Dispatch* (Richmond, VA), p. 1.
198. Staunton. (December 2, 1881). *Staunton Spectator*, January 28, 1891, image 4.
199. Society at Home and Abroad. (October 18, 1908). *The Times Dispatch* (Richmond, VA), p. 2.
200. Princess Salm-Salm Is Here. (April 17, 1899). *The Evening Times* (Washington, D.C.), p 3, image 3.
201. They Were Nurses During the Civil War. (April 15, 1922). *The Bridgeport Times and Evening Farmer* (Bridgeport, CT), p. 16, image 16.
202. Princess Salm-Salm Dead. (December 22, 1912). *New York Times*.
203. WVA. (June 1, 1865). *Daily Intelligence* (Wheeling, VA), p. 1, col. 2.
204. Cotton, G. (2009). *Like a Hideous Nightmare: Vicksburg Women Remembered the Horrors of the War*. Vicksburg, MS: The Print Shop.
205. Vet and Nurses. (August 16, 1906). *The Minneapolis (MN) Journal*, p. 6, image 6.
206. Dabney, E. Afro Americans at City Point. National Park Service. Petersburg National Battlefield Park, Petersburg, VA.
207. Micklem, James. Personal communication. October 24, 1994. Hopewell, VA.
208. Mother of 21 Dead. (January 21, 1919). *Democratic Recorder* (Amsterdam, NY), p. 8, col. 1.
209. Sang at Lincoln's Funeral. (April 28, 1905). *Lawrence Democrat* (Lawrenceburg, TN), image 1.
210. Civil War Nurse Dies at 96 Years. (March 17, 1895). *Brooklyn Daily Eagle*, p. 5, col. 5.
211. Harriett Sharpless, Find-a-Grave #75734989.
212. The Days Dead: Mrs. Anna M. Holstein. (January 03, 1901). *The San Francisco Call*, image 9.
213. Nurse for the Army. (July 19, 1864). *New York Times*, p. 1.

11. Homeward Bound Journey

214. Dr. Mary Walker Dies at 87. (February 22, 1919). *Evening Public Ledger,* Philadelphia: image 1.
215. Oswego, N.Y. (February 27, 1919). *The Butler (MO) Weekly Times and County Record,* image 6.
216. Point of Rocks. www.chesterfieldmonthly.com/community/point-of-rocks.
217. Real Estate Transfers. (December 27, 1889). *The Salt Lake City (UT) Herald,* image 8.
218. Exchange of Real Estate. (April 04, 1885). *The Salt Lake City (UT) Herald,* image 7.
219. Was a Nurse in the Civil War. (June 22, 1906). *The Salt Lake City (UT) Herald,* p. 5.
220. Fearless Confederate Died Mysteriously in NYC. (February 15, 2009). *Murphreesboro (TN) Post.*
221. Forgotten Romance and Adventure of the Civil War. (July 13, 1913). *New York Times,* p. 2.
222. A Kiss from Princess Salm-Salm, and How to Forgive Dan Sickles, *Civil War Daily Gazette,* http://civilwardailygazette.com/a-kiss-from-princess-salm-salm.
223. Passengers. (November 15, 1864). *Evening Star* (Washington, D.C.), p. 2.
224. Mrs. Rebecca E. Frick Kept Famous Philadelphia House. (September 29, 1911). *New York Tribune,* p. 7.
225. Vermont Patriot or Union Angel of Mercy. (June 28, 2013). *Civil War Bummer.* http://www.civilwarbummer.com/vermont-patriot-or-union-angel-of-mercy/.
226. Amanda Colburn Farnham, http://cwnurses.tripod.com/afarnham.html.
227. Notice of Final Settlement. (May 31, 1898). *Kansas City (KS) Journal,* p. 9.
228. Bridget Deaver, Wikipedia.
229. Livermore, M.A. (1889). *My Story of the War.* Hartford, CT: A.D. Worthington.
230. Maine Memory Network, Sanitary Commission Business, Maine Historical Society. http://www.mainehistory.org.
231. Schultz, J.E. (2004). *Women at the Front.* Chapel Hill: University of North Carolina Press.
232. Recker, S.J. (2016). *Shadowing Grant: Reminiscence of the United States Hospital Transport Service in the Civil War 1864–1865.* Privately printed.
233. Rodgers, J.B. (1865) *Record of Federal Dead Buried from Libby, Belle Isle, Danville, and Camp Lawton Prison and at City Point, and in the Field before Petersburg and Richmond.* Philadelphia: United States Christian Commission, J.B Rodgers.
234. Bridget Diver: Custer's Female Wolverine, http://irishamericancivilwar.com/2012/08/16/bridget-diver-custer-female-wolverine/.
235. On the trail of the Kearney Cross and Charlotte McKay. (March 11, 2016). *Civil War News,* http://segtours.com/blog/archives/category/civilwar.
236. Last Will and Testimony, Sarah Spencer. File #26753. Dutchess County Records, Poughkeepsie, NY.
237. Orphan's Court. (December 18, 1868). *The Columbian* (Bloomsburg, PA), image 2.
238. A New Idea. (August 4, 1864). *The Jeffersonian* (Stroudsburg, PA), image 1.
239. Schultz, J.C. (2011). *The Birth Place of Souls: The Civil War Nursing Diary of Harriet Eaton.* New York: Oxford University Press.
240. Local News. (May 5, 1865). *Evening Star* (Washington, D.C.), image 1.
241. Columbia County Historical and Genealogical Society, http//colcohist-gensoc.org/search by-name/search=Harriet%20Reifsnyder.
242. Clara Barton, America's Angel. (1898). *New York Historic paper* (Ogdensburg, NY), col. 3–4.
243. Old Records Reveal Clara Barton's Role as a Sleuth. (December 2, 1997). *New York Times,* p. 22.
244. U.S. Union Provost Marshal Papers, 1861–1867. H.C. Flagg #15523, NARA.
245. Prince Salm-Salm. (September 8, 1870). *The Sweetwater (TN) Enterprise,* image 1.
246. Funeral of War Nurse. (January 3, 1915). *Brooklyn Daily Eagle,* no page.
247. Social News. (August 20, 1912). *Auburn (NY) Semi-Weekly,* p. 7.
248. Great Parade on Today. (November 1, 1913). *New York Tribune,* p. 1.
249. Bureau of Charities. (June 11, 1898). *New York Herald,* p. 7, col. 2.
250. Civil War Nurse Bids Others Emulate Her. (June 8, 1918). *Evening Public Ledger* (Washington, D.C.), p. 9, image 9.

251. Civil War Army Nurse to Celebrate Birthday. (April 3, 1921). *Evening Star* (Washington, D.C.), p. 4.
252. Mrs. Grant's Estate Goes to Her Children. (September 9, 1930). *New York Times*, p. 29.
253. Mrs. Grant's Illness. (May 14, 1887). *New York Times*, p. 5.
254. Mrs. Grant Unable to Attend. (August 9, 1894). *New York Times*, p. 4.
255. Mrs. Grant and the Veterans. (March 14, 1888). *New York Times*, p. 4.
256. Honors to Mrs. Grant. (April 28, 1897). *New York Times*, p. 5.
257. Mrs. Grant's Body Sealed in the Tomb. (December 21, 1902). *New York Times*, p. 2.
258. From the Headquarters of the Army of the Potomac. (April 6, 1865). *The Statesman* (Yonkers, NY), p. 1, col. 1–2.
259. Lincoln and "Tad" Visit Grant's Army. (March 28, 1865). *Washington Herald*, image 23.
260. From City Point. (March 25, 1865). *New York Times*, p. 1.
261. Mary Mercer Ord, Find-a-Grave #41560484.
262. Eleanor Adams Stanton Bush, Find-a-Grave #42143797.
263. Was Mrs. Surratt Kept in Irons? (April 2014). *The Surratt Courier* (Clinton, MD). Vol. XXXIX #4, p. 1.
264. Mrs. Swisshelm. (June 23, 1859). *Danbury (CT) Times*, p. 2, col. 3.
265. A Staunch Foe of Slavery. (July 23, 1884). *New York Times*, p. 5.
266. City Point's Wiseman Family Marker, HMdb.org/Marker.asp?Marker=41498.
267. Oath of Allegiance, Mary Wiseman, September 22, 1864. U.S. Provost Marshals' Papers, 1861–1867, for Mary Wiseman, NARA.
268. Some Old and New Facts Concerning Grant's Record. (November 18, 1876). *The (NY) Sun*, image 2.
269. Miss Bidgood, MO346, roll 64, NARA.
270. Slave Census Record, 1860 Prince George County, NARA.
271. U.S. Union Provost Marshal Papers. Ninth Corps, February 1 and March 1, 1865. NARA.
272. Major Vignos to Meet Nurse of Gettysburg After Two-Score Years. (August 25, 1907). *Canton (OH) Repository*.
273. The Likeness of Mrs. Elmira Spencer Will Be Cast in the Albany Capitol Staircase. (June 16, 1989). *The National Tribune* (Washington, D.C.), p. 2, image 2.
274. Round Lake U.S. Provost Soldiers Convention. (August 24, 1893). *The (NY) Sun*, p. 5, image 5.
275. Notice about Mary Walker and Giegerich Bill. (May 20, 1887). *Alma (MI) Record*, image 2.
276. Then a Princess. (May 07, 1899). *The San Francisco Call*, p. 20, image 20.
277. Georgy Porter. (Posted November 7, 2009). Civil War Women, Maggie McLean (ed.), http://www.civilwarwomenblog.com/georgy-porter/.
278. *Images of America Danbury*. (2001). Danbury Historical Society, Arcadia.
279. Sally Barrett, Find-a-Grave, #49373913.
280. Matilda Morris, Find-a-Grave #17262557.
281. Civil War Nurses, The Forgotten Heroes of the Great Rebellion. (May 29, 2010). http://schliessman.blogspot.com/2010/05/civil-war-nurses-forgotten-heros-of.html.
282. Harriett Reifsnyder or Jackson, www.familysearch.org/ark:/61903/1:1:K6HS-KX8.
283. United States National Homes for Disabled Volunteer Soldiers, 1866–1938. https://familysearch.org.

Appendix: Weather for 1864–1865

The following are weather comments recorded for the period of June 1864 through April 1865. Not all dates are listed because they were not all present in diaries or correspondence. The weather conditions help one understand not only the working conditions in the area, but also the psychological happiness for those at City Point in addition to the difficulty or ease of military movements for the soldiers.

June 1864

June 7—Strawberry season.
June 10—Sunny and cool.
June 13—Fine day.
June 14—Cold like winter, some thought it beautiful weather.
June 15—Warm like summer, a fine day.
June 16—Hot.
June 17—Weather continues to be splendid.
June 18—Dust flying everywhere like a cloud. Others thought it beautiful and very warm.
June 19—Quite warm.
June 20—Clear and fine, very warm.
June 21—Hot, 95 degrees.
June 22—Warm.
June 24—Excessively hot and no rain for weeks.
June 25—Very dry, fearfully warm.
June 26—Excessively hot, very warm with no breeze.
June 27—Rained a little, pleasant afternoon shower.
June 29—Cool to moderately cool.
June 30—Very dry.

July 1864

July 1—Dust is shoe high. Hot, 92 degrees.
July 2—No rain yet, fearfully hot.

July 3—Hot dry and dusty.
July 4—Hot in the evening.
July 5—The weather this morning is delightful.
July 6—Pleasant.
July 7—Delightful but fair.
July 8—Hot, sultry, dusty, no rain in a long time, very warm.
July 9—Warm and dry.
July 10—Very warm and dusty.
July 11—Hot day, more sultry, lots of mosquitoes.
July 12—Warm.
July 13—Warm.
July 14—Pleasant.
July 15—Hot and dusty.
July 16—Intensely hot, dry and warm, but night was chilly.
July 17—Pleasant.
July 18—Delightful day.
July 19—Rain, rain all day, rained very steady.
July 20—Rain continues off and on.
July 21—Delightful day, pleasant.
July 23—Beautiful, pleasant, foggy night.
July 24—Little rain, the wind blew very hard.
July 25—Storm, wind and rain.
July 26—Cool breeze.
July 27—Very warm, hot day.
July 28—Very hot.
July 29—Hot.
July 30—Very hot.

August 1864

August 1—Hot and sultry, the flies are biting.
August 2—Weather much cooler.
August 3—Refreshing shower.
August 4—Very warm, sultry and extremely hot.
August 5—Hot day.
August 6—Melting warm, rain in the pm, extremely hot.
August 7—Warm
August 8—Warm.
August 12—Oppressively hot and dead calm.
August 13—Hot and rain.
August 14—Awful hot day.
August 16—Warm.
August 17—Terrible wind and rain. Thunderstorm and lightning. Hot and rain.
August 18—Calm and beautiful.
August 19—Cloudy and rain.
August 20—Hot and warm.
August 21—Cloudy and light rain.
August 22—Cloudy and rain in the afternoon.

August 23—Cloudy but warm.
August 24—Hot, hotter and hottest.
August 25—Cool in the morning.
August 26—Very warm day.
August 29—Lovely cool day.
August 31—Pleasant.

September 1864

September 2—Weather nice and cooler.
September 3—Much cooler.
September 6—Cloudy and damp.
September 7—Bright and cool.
September 8—Cool in the morning.
September 9—Weather cooler.
September 10—Cool and rainy.
September 11—Cold damp evening.
September 12—Splendid morning.
September 13—Cool cloudy and clearing.
September 15—Pleasant, bright and lovely.
September 16—Glorious cool.
September 17—Wonderful am.
September 18—Rain in the afternoon.

October 1864

October 1—Drizzle in the morning.
October 2—Pleasant.
October 4—Heavy rains.
October 7—Burning midsummer.
October 8—Weather fine and dry, roads becoming passable.
October 9—Colder.
October 11—Fine day.
October 12—Jack Frost is upon us, very cold and bitter.
October 13—Beautiful and cool.
October 14—Lovely day.
October 15—Warm.
October 17—Weather is delightful.
October 19—Lovely, lots of moonlight.
October 20—Fine day.
October 21—Clear and beautiful.
October 22—Cloudy wind and rain.
October 23—Beautiful day.
October 24—Beautiful.
October 25—Clear and cold.
October 26—Fair.
October 27—Cloudy all day.

October 28—Beautiful morning.
October 29—Beautiful day.

November 1864

November 1—Rains of November.
November 3—Last night it began to rain and continued all night. The wind blew.
November 4—Morning fog.
November 6—Killing frost.
November 7—Rained.
November 8—Misty morning.
November 9—Rain.
November 13—Cold and windy.
November 14—Nasty storm.
November 18—Splendid day, Raining about dark.
November 19—Excessively stormy.
November 20—Rain continues.
November 21—Still raining.
November 23—Clear and cold.
November 24—Delightful and beautiful.
November 25—Clear and fine, not a cloudy obscured the sky.
November 26—Beautiful and cold.
November 27—Delightful weather, Indian summer.
November 28—Cheerful morning.
November 30—Fine days, delicious nights.

December 1864

December 1—Lovely day, beautiful morning.
December 4—Beautiful sabbath.
December 6—Beautiful day.
December 8—Pleasant day, cold but pleasant.
December 9—Cold, began to snow, clear and cold.
December 10—Snow and hail.
December 11—Very cold and clean.
December1 2—Very cold.
December 14—Warm and cloudy.
December 16—Warm.
December 17—Too warm for winter.
December 19—Mild.
December 20—Damp, cold winds.
December 21—Stormy and windy.
December 22—Chilly cold day.
December 23—Cold heavy snow turned to rain.
December 25—Most beautiful day, intensely cold but dry.
December 26—Misty and foggy.
December 27—Some rain and some sun.

December 29—Snowed quite hard.
December 31—Very stormy and heavy gales.

January 1865

January 1—Cold, clear, ground frozen.
January 2—Clear and cold.
January 3—Cold and cloudy.
January 4—Cold clear, ground covered in snow.
January 5—Clear and cool.
January 6—Rain, warm and cloudy.
January 7—Mud awful. Cool and blustery.
January 8—Clear and cold.
January 9—Splendid day, clear and cold.
January 10—Rainy day, cloudy.
January 11—Clear and cool.
January 12—Clear and cold.
January 13—Clear and cold.
January 14—Mild and pleasant.
January 15—Beautiful day, clear and cold.
January 16—Fine day, spring like, clear and pleasant.
January 17—Clear and cold.
January 18—Clear and cold.
January 19—Quite cold, cloudy.
January 20—Clear and cold.
January 21—Rain, hail and sleet.
January 22—Fog and mist, cloudy and drizzle.
January 23—Rain.
January 24—Clear and cold.
January 25—Clear and cold.
January 26—Clear and cold.
January 27—Clear and cool.
January 28—Coldest day, clear and cold.
January 29—Clear and cold.
January 30—Clear and cold
January 31—Beautiful warm, clear and cool.

February 1865

February 1—Clear and pleasant.
February 2—Warm, clear and pleasant.
February 3—Snow and rain.
February 4—Bright and beautiful, cloudy and cold, wild and windy.
February 5—Beautiful day, cool and cloudy.
February 6—Very cold and clear, very muddy.
February 7—Sleet and rain, mud, cold sleet heavy snow.
February 8—Clear and cold, muddy and windy. The weather yesterday was awful for the wounded. Heavy snow.

February 9—Clear and cold.
February 10—Clear and cold.
February 11—Cold miserable, clear and cold.
February 12—Intensely cold, cold and cloudy.
February 13—Cold and windy, bitter cold, the weather is intensely cold.
February 14—Clear and cold.
February 15—Rainy, cloudy, rain and sleet, sunshine.
February 16—Warm and cloudy.
February 17—Rain, cloudy and cool.
February 18—Clear and beautiful.
February 19—Beautiful and warm, clear and pleasant.
February 20—Clear and pleasant, birds singing.
February 21—Clear and cold.
February 22—Clear and pleasant.
February 23—Rainy and damp, cloudy and rain.
February 24—Cold and cloudy.
February 25—Rainy, cloudy and snow, and sunshine.
February 26—Warm and cloudy.
February 27—Clear and pleasant, mud, impassable mud.
February 28—Cloudy and rain.

March 1865

March 1—Cold and stormy.
March 2—Cold and stormy, rain, last night we had severe rain.
March 3—Rain and miserable, Cloudy and rain.
March 4—Rain in the am, clear in the afternoon, cloudy and stormy.
March 5—Glorious sunny day, clear and cool.
March 6—Cool and pleasant.
March 7—Clear and pleasant, beautiful weather, bright moonlight.
March 8—Wet day, clear and cloudy, raining.
March 9—Warm and cloudy.
March 10—Cool, rain in the evening, close and sultry rain, pelting rain continues.
March 11—Warm and pleasant, clear and pleasant.
March 12—Clear and cold, weather is still fickle and capricious.
March 13—Clear and very wintry.
March 14—Cool and cloudy.
March 15—Cloudy and cold.
March 16—Warm and sultry, stormed all night, beautiful morning, very windy and rain.
March 17—Clear and windy, clouds in every direction.
March 18—Clear and pleasant, clouds in every direction.
March 19—Clear and pleasant, unusually warm for the season, roads drying up.
March 20—Clear and cool and windy, rain gone, sun is out.
March 21—Warm and clear and windy, pleasant day.
March 22—Clear pleasant windy at night, rain all night, rainy all morning.
March 23—Clear cool and windy.

Appendix: Weather for 1864–1865

March 24—Windy, warm and rain.
March 25—Warm and sultry.
March 26—Clear and cool.
March 27—Clear and pleasant.
March 28—Clear and pleasant, lovely day.
March 29—Warm and sultry, nice and pleasant.
March 30—Rained all night, cloudy and rain.
March 31—Warm and rain.

April 1865

April 1—Clear and pleasant, sunny and windy.
April 2—Lovely day, clear and pleasant.
April 3—Cloudy with rain.
April 4—Sultry and warm.
April 5—Rain in the afternoon, clear and pleasant.
April 6—Warm and rain.
April 7—Clear and pleasant.
April 8—Clear and pleasant, sunshine.
April 9—Clear and pleasant.
April 10—Rain, cloudy with rain.
April 12—Warm and sultry, some rain.
April 13—Very pleasant.
April 14—Cold rain.
April 24—Weather is beautiful, trees in full foliage.

Chapter Notes

Chapter 1

1. Pudner, H.P. (1971). People Not Pedagogy. *The Georgia Review*, XXV(3), p. 275.
2. Buckley, S.J. I Have Found That Happiness Consists Not in Riches. *Virginia Cavalcade*, 51(4), 180, Autumn 2002.
3. Boucher, Jonathan, 9 March 1767, folder 1:3, Special Collections, Earl Gregg Swem Library, College of William and Mary, Williamsburg, VA.
4. Harrison, C.C. (1898). *The Well Bred Girl in Society*, Virginia Museum of History and Culture.
5. Parker, W.W. (1892). *Women's Place in the Christian World*. Richmond, J.W. Fergusson & Son. The Virginia Historical Society.
6. Hartley, F. (1860). *True Politeness: A Ladies Hand Book of Etiquette*. New York: Levitt & Allen.
7. *A Manual of Politeness: Comprising the Principles of Etiquette, and Rules of Behaviour in Genteel Society, for Persons of Both Sexes*. (1842). Philadelphia: J.B. Lippincott.
8. Rosa Cohn and William Flagenheimer Family Box, Beth Ahabah Archives, Richmond, VA. Rosa and William would be married in 1861 and have eight sons and two daughters. He would run a small confectionary business, but was better known for his beautiful penmanship and was hired as a clerk in the Quartermasters Department while Rosa remained at home raising the children.
9. Abbott, J.S.C. (1833*). The Mother at Home*. New York: American Tract Society. The Virginia Museum of History and Culture.
10. Marshall, K.M. (1987). *In a Combat Zone*. Boston: Little, Brown.
11. Jacquette, H.S. (Ed.). (1937). *South After Gettysburg: Letters of Cornelia Hancock from the Army of the Potomac 1863–1865)*. Philadelphia: University of Pennsylvania Press.

Chapter 2

1. Van Zandt, A.B. (1857). *The Elect Lady: A Memoir of Mrs. Catherine Bott*. Philadelphia: Presbyterian Board Publication. According to Mrs. Collis, she would purchase eggs from Mrs. Botts (or Bott). Although the Botts residence was in the Safeguard area, it was not the elder Mrs. Botts who was selling eggs; she passed away in 1853. The spelling of the Bott(s) last name is unclear. The 1850 and 1870, census records show Botts, but the 1860 census record shows Bott. The 1905 City Directory shows Botts and Births and Christenings show Bott.
2. Sparks, D.S. (Ed.) (1964). *Inside Lincoln's Army: The Diary of Marsena Rudolph Patrick, Provost Marshal General, Army of the Potomac*. New York: Thomas Yoseloff. p. 396.
3. Comstock, C.B. (M.E. Summer Ed.). (1864). *Diary of Cyrus Ballou Comstock*, Library of Congress #1MSS 17650, Petersburg National Battlefield Library.
4. From City Point. (October 24, 1864). *New York Times*, p. 1.
5. Eppes, Account book of Richard Eppes, Mssl, Ep734d343, Virginia Museum of History and Culture.
6. The Rape of Mary E. Stiles, Turner Baker Papers, Record group 94, File #MM1481, NARA.
7. Pfanz, D. (1988). *The Diary of Marsena*

Patrick, *Provost Marshal of the Army of the Potomac: June 15, 1864 to April 18, 1865.* Petersburg, VA: Petersburg National Battlefield Park. p. 5.
  8. *Ibid.,* p. 12.
  9. *Ibid.*
  10. Parker, H.F. (July 15, 1864). Personal diary, September 1863–June 1, 1866, City Point files. Engineer files, private papers Chris Caukins, Petersburg National Battlefield Park, Petersburg, VA.
  11. Sparks, D.S. (Ed.) (1964). *Inside Lincoln's Army: The Diary of Marsena Rudolph Patrick, Provost Marshal General, Army of the Potomac.* New York: Thomas Yoseloff. p. 399.
  12. *Ibid.,* p. 392.
  13. *Ibid.,* p. 419.
  14. Pfanz, D. (1988). *The Diary of Marsena Patrick, Provost Marshal of the Army of the Potomac: June 15, 1864 to April 18, 1865.* Petersburg, VA: Petersburg National Battlefield Park. p. 477. Between 1861 and 1866, 267 men were executed for crimes they had committed. The Court Martial at City Point was presided over by a board comprised of the following men: Brigadier General E.W. Hincks (Hinks), New York Volunteers; Col. C.T. Collis, 114th Pennsylvania Volunteers; Lt. Colonel E.R. Warner, 1st New York Arty; Captain J.S. Crawford, 114th Pennsylvania Volunteers; and Major General G.R. Platt, Judge Advocate.

  Additional files on violations in the area at the National Archives on violations in the area:

  William Jackson, Company G USC Infantry, case #1984, roll 2, GCMO #194, War Department, AGO July 1864.
  Washington Jackson, Private, Battery E, 1st USCT, Heavy Arty. Proceedings of the trial have never been found.
  William Henry Johnson, Company E 23rd Regiment USCT, executed on June 20th, in front of the Jordon Court House for violating a young lady at New Kent Court House. According the provost marshal, Johnson was hung at 0900 on the 20th near Bailey's outside of Petersburg (Sparks, 1964). Library of Congress image 4721, Brady collection (B815-789).
  Jackson, [first name unknown], USCT. Executed for the plunder, pillaging and rape of Mrs. Fanny Crawford (writing unclear), file #1523, roll 2. Mrs. Crawford lived near Richmond, about three miles from the city on Deep Run Road. The court martial was held in the field at Headquarters, 1st Division, 25th AC, on April 1, 1865. Jackson was executed on April 11, 1865. The court martial board consisted of Lt. C. Prall, 36th Infantry USCT; Major Johns, 115th USCT; Captain Rolf, 114th USCT; Captain James Blakely, 19th USCT; 1st Lt. Short, 22nd USCT; 2nd Lt. Wasson, 43rd USCT; and Captain March, 43rd USCT.

  15. Historical Markers (Mdb.org), Hopewell, VA.
  16. Micklem, J. (October 24, 1995). Personal communication, Hopewell, VA. Historical Markers (Mdb.org), Hopewell, VA.
  17. Miss Bidgood, in the 1860 census records, was an affluent single woman living in a boarding house in Richmond Ward 2, Henrico. In the Turner Baker papers, she was listed as Miss. However, Jackson Hospital payment forms from the Engineers Bureau list a George Bidgood, who may have been her husband or a relative. For the sake of convivence or relationship, there are times when Miss Bidgood was called Mrs. Bidgood. Engineer Bureau, 1861, file #M0346, roll 64, NARA.
  18. Bidgood and Levy, Turner Baker Papers, Record Group 94, File #3738, NARA.
  19. Sparks, D.S. (Ed.) (1964). *Inside Lincoln's Army: The Diary of Marsena Rudolph Patrick, Provost Marshal General, Army of the Potomac.* New York: Thomas Yoseloff. p. 458.
  20. Article 5. (December 31, 1864). *Hartford (CT) Courant,* p. 2.
  21. From City Point. (October 24, 1864). *New York Times,* p. 1.
  22. From City Point. (November 15, 1864). *Evening Star* (Washington D.C.), image 2.
  23. Find-a-Grave, Clara Caroline Haxall Grundy, #14949293.
  24. The Second State. (July 24, 1886). *The Auburn (NY) Bulletin,* col. 1.
  25. Reflections. (April 11, 1920). *The Call Magazine* (New York), p. 11, col. 2.
  26. Ten Years Ago. (September 26, 1872). *Corning (NY) Evening Journal,* p. 2, col. 3.
  27. From City Point. (October 24, 1864). *New York Times,* p. 1.
  28. Palmer, S. (1868). *The Story of Aunt*

Becky's Army Life, New York: John F. Trow. p. 175.

29. Smith, A. (1919). *Reminiscences of an Army Nurse During the Civil War*. New York: Greaves.

Chapter 3

1. U.S. Union Provost Marshals' Papers, 1861–1867, NARA.

2. *The War of the Rebellion: A Compilation of the Official Records of the Union and Confederate Armies,* Series 1, Volume 2, p. 761.

3. The Freedman's Bureau and the National Freedman's Relief Association. (June 11, 1865). *New York Times*, p. 2, image 2.

4. 1860 NARA, Federal Census Records, M653, roll 1396.

5. Dabney, E. (2009). *Civil War City Point: 1864–1865 Period of Significant Landscape Documentation*, Petersburg National Battlefield Park.

6. Holstein, A. (1867). *Three Years in the Field Hospital of the Army of the Potomac.* Philadelphia: J.B. Lippincott. p. 79.

7. Pfanz, D. (transcriber). (1987). *The Diary of Marsena Patrick, Provost Marshal of the Army of the Potomac: June 15, 1864 to April 18, 1865*. Petersburg, VA: Petersburg National Battlefield. p. 23.

8. General Order No. 30. (January 25, 1864). War Department, By Order of the Secretary of War, E.D. Townsend, Assistant Adjutant-General.

9. Trammel, J. (2012). *The Richmond Slave Trade: The Economic Backbone of the Old Dominion.* The History Press.

10. Pryor, S.A. (1904). *Reminiscences of Peace and War*. New York: Grosset & Dunlap, p. 282. Eliza Page was the daughter of Sucky Page, one of Dr. Richard Eppes' slaves. She was one of the few slaves who did not run away when Dr. Eppes moved to Petersburg. Eliza was very loyal to Mrs. Sara Pryor.

11. Mayors Court: Hannah Lynch. (October 5, 1864). *Daily Dispatch* (Richmond, VA), p. 1.

12. Mayors Court: Martha. (July 30, 1864). *Daily Dispatch* (Richmond, VA), p. 1.

13. Mayors Court: Catherine. (July 22, 1864). *Daily Dispatch* (Richmond, VA), p. 1.

14. Mayors Court: Henrietta. (July 1, 1864). *Daily Dispatch* (Richmond, VA), p. 1.

15. Mayor's Court: Unlawful Assembly. (October 5, 1864). *Daily Dispatch* (Richmond, VA), p. 1.

16. Mayors Court: Martha Henley. (July 30, 1864). *Daily Dispatch* (Richmond, VA), p. 1.

17. Pfanz, D. (transcriber). (1988). *The Depot Hospital at City Point.* Petersburg, VA: Petersburg National Battlefield Park. p. 24.

18. Bucklin, S. (1869). *In a Hospital and Camp: Official Papers of Sophronia Bucklin.* Philadelphia: J.E. Potter. p. 350.

19. Gilland, L. (2013). Sisterhood of Courage: African American Women and Their Efforts to Aid the Union Forces in the Civil War. *Saber and Scroll,* vol. 2, issue 3, Summer, article 6.

20. Pfanz, D. (transcriber). (1988). *The Depot Hospital at City Point.* Petersburg, VA: Petersburg National Battlefield Park.

21. The Rector's Office of St. John's church at 505 Cedar Lane, in Hopewell, VA, has slave marriages and baptism records for those residing in the City Point area. See Baptism, confirmation, marriage and death records of St. John's Church, Hopewell, VA.

22. Hopewell. (1985). *Our Share of Honour: Hopewell and Prince George County Women, 1600–1985*. Hopewell, VA: Hopewell Tourism Bureau. George Lewis, www.nps.gov/subjects/ugrr/discover_history.

23. Marion, J. (July 17, 1864). *Personal Letters of James Marion*, City Point files. Petersburg, VA: Petersburg National Battlefield Park.

24. NPS, http://.nature.nps.gov/views/Sites/PETE/HTML/ET_CP.htm.

25. Agassi, George (Ed.). (1922). *Meade's Headquarters: Letters of Colonel Theodore Lyman.* Boston: Massachusetts Historical Society.

26. Eppes Diary, Mss5:1Ep735:1, Virginia Museum of Historical and Culture, Richmond, VA.

27. Perkins, H.M. (December 1992). Lucien Hall's Prison Sketchbook. *Northern Neck of Virginia Historical Society*, XXLII, pp. 483–485, 498–506.

28. Hackett, H.B. (1864). *Christian Memorials of the War,* Boston: Gould & Lincoln. p. 215.

29. Lebsock, S. (1984). *The Free Woman of Petersburg: Status and Culture in a Southern Town, 1784–1860.* New York: W.W. Norton.

30. Jacquette, H.S. (Ed.). (1937). *South After Gettysburg: Letters of Cornelia Hancock from the Army of the Potomac 1863–1865).* Freeport, NY: Libraries Press. p. 32.
31. *Ibid.*, p. 120.
32. City Point files on Dr. Richard Eppes. Petersburg, VA: Petersburg National Battlefield Park.
33. Smith, A. (1919). *Reminiscence of an Army Nurse during the Civil War.* New York: Greaves.
34. Palmer, S.A. (1868). *The Story of Aunt Becky's Army Life.* New York: John F. Trow. p. 101.
35. *Ibid.*, p. 100.
36. *Ibid.*
37. Smith, A. (1919). *Reminiscence of an Army Nurse during the Civil War.* New York: Greaves. pp. 111–121.
38. Collis, S. (1889). *A Woman's War Record.* New York: G.P. Putnam & Sons.
39. Smith, A. (1919). *Reminiscence of an Army Nurse during the Civil War.* New York: Greaves.
40. Emma Stephenson, Find-a-Grave #125608677.
41. City Point as a Base of Supplies. (June 22, 1864). *New York Times*, p. 1.
42. Bucklin, S. (1869). *In a Hospital and Camp: Official Papers of Sophronia Bucklin.* Philadelphia: J. E. Potter. p. 351.

Chapter 4

1. Our Wounded and Sick Soldiers. (December 11, 1864). *New York Times*, p. 1.
2. Jacquette, H.S. (Ed.). (1937). *South after Gettysburg: Letters of Cornelia Hancock from the Army of the Potomac 1863–1865.* Philadelphia: University of Pennsylvania Press. p. 114.
3. Zinnen, R.O. (1991). City Point: The Tool That Gave General Grant Victory, *Quartermaster Professional Bulletin,* Spring, http//www.qmfound.com/citypt.html.
4. Christie. J.M. (1997). Performing My Plain Duty: Women of the North at City Point. *Virginia Cavalcade*, vol. 46 (5).
5. "From the Army of the Potomac," The Hospital at City Point—A Village of Tents—Admirable Working of the Sanitary Commission. (September 10, 1864). *New York Times*, p. 1.
6. Zinnen, R.O. (1991). City Point: The Tool That Gave General Grant Victory,

Quartermaster Professional Bulletin, Spring, http//www.qmfound.com/citypt.html.
7. Bucklin, S. (1869). *In a Hospital and Camp: Official Papers of Sophronia Bucklin.* Philadelphia: J.E. Potter. pp. 287–289.
8. Burnham, E. (May 21, 1864). CO A, 7th CT Heavy Artillery: Letters to His Wife. Wood Memorial Library, South Windsor, CT. The first two weeks in June of 1864 were sunny but pleasant. Strawberries were in season. By mid-June, the temperature vacillated from pleasant to hot by the end of the week. The lack of rain had caused considerable dust to fly about like clouds. The following week was in the mid 90s and still no rain. By the last week of June, the breeze from the river picked up and there was a modest amount of rain that held the dust down. By July, the temperatures were once more in the mid to upper 90s and the dust was shoe-deep. There was very little to no moisture. The weather grew even warmer, with a few nights having a drop in temperature. However, it grew hotter. Finally, by the week of the 17th, rain appeared and changed all the dust into cement-like mud. The last week of July was recorded as oppressively hot, although there was a breeze from the water during the first part of the week.
9. Palmer, S.A. (1868). *The Story of Aunt Becky's Army-Life.* New York: John F. Trow.
10. Jacquette, H.S. (Ed.). (1937). *South after Gettysburg: Letters of Cornelia Hancock from the Army of the Potomac 1863–1865.* Philadelphia: University of Pennsylvania Press. p. 119.
11. Palmer, S.A. (1868). *The Story of Aunt Becky's Army-Life.* New York: John F. Trow.
12. Smith, A.W. (1911). *Reminiscences of an Army Nurse during the Civil War.* New York: Greaves Publishing. p. 123; Jacquette, H.S. (Ed.). (1937). *South after Gettysburg: Letters of Cornelia Hancock from the Army of the Potomac 1863–1865.* Philadelphia: University of Pennsylvania Press. p. 69.
13. Schultz, J.E. (2004). *Women at the Front.* Chapel Hill: University of North Carolina Press.
14. Hall, R.H. (2006). *Women on the Civil War Battlefront.* Lawrence: University of Kansas Press. p. 246.
15. Jacquette, H.S. (Ed.). (1937). *South after Gettysburg: Letters of Cornelia Hancock from the Army of the Potomac 1863–1865.* Philadelphia: University of Pennsylvania Press. p. 115.

16. *Ibid.*, p. 73.
17. Moore, F. (1867). *Women of the War.* Hartford, CT: S.S. Scranton.
18. *Ibid.*
19. Jacquette, H.S. (Ed.) (1937). *South after Gettysburg: Letters of Cornelia Hancock from the Army of the Potomac 1863–1865.* Philadelphia: University of Pennsylvania Press. p. 22.
20. Bucklin, S. (1869). *In a Hospital and Camp: Official Papers of Sophronia Bucklin.* Philadelphia: J.E. Potter. p. 296.
21. Palmer, S.A. (1868). *The Story of Aunt Becky's Army-Life.* New York: John F. Trow. p. 169.
22. *Ibid.*, p. 171.
23. *Ibid.*, p. 177.
24. Bucklin, S. (1869). *In a Hospital and Camp: Official Papers of Sophronia Bucklin.* Philadelphia: J. E. Potter. p. 65.
25. Palmer, S.A. (1868). *The Story of Aunt Becky's Army-Life.* New York: John F. Trow. p.150.
26. Christie, J.M. (1995). *No Place for a Woman.* Exhibit, Appomattox Manor, City Point, Petersburg National Battlefield Park.
27. Hall, R.H. (2006). *Women on the Civil War Battlefront.* Lawrence: University of Kansas Press. p. 231.
28. Palmer, S.A. (1868). *The Story of Aunt Becky's Army-Life.* New York: John F. Trow. p. 133.
29. Wilson, J.H. (1916). *The Life of John A. Rawlins.* New York: Neale.
30. Bucklin, S. (1869). *In a Hospital and Camp: Official Papers of Sophronia Bucklin.* Philadelphia: J.E. Potter. p. 30.
31. *Ibid.*, p. 48.
32. Conklin, E.F. (1989) *Women at Gettysburg 1863.* Gettysburg, PA: Thomas.
33. Bucklin, S. (1869). *In a Hospital and Camp: Official Papers of Sophronia Bucklin.* Philadelphia: J.E. Potter. p. 281.
34. *Ibid.*, p. 287.
35. *Ibid.*, p. 64.
36. *Ibid.*, p. 38.
37. *Ibid.*, p. 142.
38. *Ibid.*, pp. 300–303.
39. *Ibid.*, p. 64.
40. *Ibid.*, p. 168.
41. *Ibid.*, p. 171.
42. *Ibid.*, p. 48.
43. *Ibid.*, p. 328.
44. *Ibid.*, pp. 153–154.
45. *Ibid.*, pp. 157–158.
46. *Ibid.*, p. 159.
47. Gossip from the Army. (February 1, 1865). *New York Times*, p. 2.
48. Palmer, S.A. (1868). *The Story of Aunt Becky's Army-Life.* New York: John F. Trow. p. 16.
49. *Ibid.*, p. 108.
50. *Ibid.*, p. 165.
51. *Ibid.*, p. 110.
52. *Ibid.*, p. 87.
53. Sanborne, P.F. (1864). *Diary of Pliny Fiske Sanborne: USCC.* City Point files. Petersburg, VA: Petersburg National Battlefield Park. p. 11.
54. McPherson, D.G. (1963). Experiment at City Point. *Military Medicine, 128,* 242–244.
55. Palmer, S.A. (1868). *The Story of Aunt Becky's Army-Life.* New York: John F. Trow. p. 101.
56. *Ibid.*
57. Burnham, E. (May 21, 1864). *CO A, 7th CT Heavy Artillery: Letters to His Wife.* Wood Memorial Library, South Windsor, CT.
58. Palmer, S.A. (1868). *The Story of Aunt Becky's Army-Life.* New York: John F. Trow. p. 165.
59. *Ibid.*, p. 77.
60. *Ibid.*, p. 69.
61. *Ibid.*, p. 59.
62. *Ibid.*, p. 208.
63. *Ibid.*, p. 106.
64. *Ibid.*, p. 147.
65. *Ibid.*, p. 67. Aunt Becky was stressed when she witnessed the soldiers being kicked, hanging by their tied thumbs, or having to "ride a horse," which involved having a soldier straddle a log for long lengths of time, causing pain in the groin. She was known to go over and cut the ropes when soldiers were hanging by their thumbs.
66. *Ibid.*, p. 150.
67. McKay, C. (1876). *Stories of Hospital and Camp.* Philadelphia: Claxton, Remsen & Haffelfinger. p. 96.
68. *Ibid.*, pp. 92–95.
69. *Ibid.*, p. 120.

Chapter 5

1. The Third Army Corps of the Potomac. (December 25, 1868). *Philadelphia Inquirer*, p. 1.
2. Brockett, L.P., & Vaughn, M. (1867).

Women's Work in the Civil War. Philadelphia, PA: Zeigler, McCurdy. p. 136.
  3. Logan, Mrs. John L. (1912). *The Part Taken by Women in American History.* Wilmington, DE: Perry-Nalle Pub. p. 331.
  4. *Ibid.*, p. 332.
  5. Reed, W.H. (1866). *Hospital Life in the Army of the Potomac.* Boston: William Spencer. p. 85.
  6. Logan, Mrs. John L. (1912). *The Part Taken by Women in American History.* Wilmington, DE: Perry-Nalle Pub. p. 333.
  7. Reed, W.H. (1866). *Hospital Life in the Army of the Potomac.* Boston: William Spencer. pp. 85–87.
  8. *Ibid.*, p. 140.
  9. *Ibid.*, p. 87.
  10. Palmer, S.A. (1868). *The Story of Aunt Becky's Army-Life.* New York: John F. Trow. p. 64.
  11. Arrival of Wounded Soldiers from North Carolina. (August 26, 1862). *New York Times.* p. 8.
  12. Smith, A.W. (1911). *Reminiscences of an Army Nurse during the Civil War.* New York: Greaves. p. 126.
  13. The Masonic Mission. (October 25, 1864). *New York Times*, p. 1, col 7.
  14. The Masonic Mission of Masons. (January 4, 1865). *The New York Herald*, p. 4, image 6.
  15. Palmer, S.A. (1868). *The Story of Aunt Becky's Army-Life.* New York: John F. Trow. p. 165.
  16. Smith, A.W. (1911). *Reminiscences of an Army Nurse during the Civil War.* New York: Greaves. p. 133.
  17. *Ibid.*, p. 144.
  18. *Ibid.*, pp. 148–149.
  19. *Ibid.*, p. 144.
  20. *Ibid.*, p. 153.
  21. Jacquette, H.S. (Ed). (1937). *South After Gettysburg: Letters of Cornelia Hancock from the Army of the Potomac 1863–1865.* Philadelphia: University of Pennsylvania Press. p. 6
  22. *Ibid.*, pp. 4–6.
  23. *Ibid.*, p. 124.
  24. *Ibid.*, p. 32.
  25. *Ibid.*, p. 148.
  26. *Ibid.*, p. 124.
  27. *Ibid.*, p. 122.
  28. *Ibid.*, p. 94.
  29. *Ibid.*, p. 32.
  30. *Ibid.*, p. 141.
  31. *Ibid.*, p. 159.
  32. *Ibid.*, p. 30.
  33. *Ibid.*, pp. 151, 163.
  34. *Ibid.*, p. 164.
  35. *Ibid.*, p. 49.
  36. *Ibid.*, p. 80.
  37. Eliot, E., Jr. (1932). *Yale in the Civil War.* New Haven, CT: Yale University. In addition are the *Obituary Records of Graduates Deceased during the Year Ending July 1, 1924.* (1924). New Haven, CT: Yale University.
  38. Census 1850, Madison, New Haven County, October 8, 1850. p. 142.
  39. Palmer, S.A. (1868). *The Story of Aunt Becky's Army-Life.* New York: John F. Trow. p. 176.
  40. *Ibid.*, p. 73.
  41. Jacquette, H.S. (Ed). (1937). *South after Gettysburg: Letters of Cornelia Hancock from the Army of the Potomac 1863–1865.* Philadelphia: University of Pennsylvania Press. pp. 118, 122, 163.
  42. *Ibid.*, p. 136.
  43. *Ibid.*, p. 160.
  44. Miss Cornelia Hancock. (September 22, 1906). *Cook County Herald* (Grand Marais, MN), image 5.
  45. Nurses Meeting Lincoln in a Hospital. (February 4, 1923). *New York Times*, p. 12.
  46. civilwartalk.com/threads/vivandierre-assorted.89545/. Augusta M. Foster. (May 13, 1862). *National Republican* (Washington, D.C.), image 3. In addition, the site has added names that are familiar and some that need to be fully investigated but are worthy of mentioning. Federal vandieres included Susie Baker (33rd USCT), Sarah Beasley (1st Rhode Island), Molly Divver (7th New York), Hannah Ewbank (7th Wisconsin), Elizabeth Cain Finnan (81st Ohio), Martha Francis (1st Rhode Island), Ella Gibson (49th Ohio), Lizzie Clawson Jones (6th Massachusetts), Sarah Taylor (1st Tennessee U.S.), Mary Tepe (27th and 114th Pennsylvania) and Eliz Wilson (5th Wisconsin), as well as southern women such as Eliza "Lide" Carico (10th Kentucky Partisan Rangers), Lucy Ann Cox (13th Virginia), Lucina Horne (14th South Carolina), Jane Claudia Johnson (1st Maryland C.S.), Leona Neville (5th Louisiana), Mary Ann Perkins (Gardes Lafayette, Mobile, Alabama), Rose Rooney (15th Louisiana), Betsy Sullivan (1st Tennessee C.S.A.), and Lavinia Williams (1st Louisiana). See also Sudlow, L.L. (2000). *A Vast Army of Women: Maine's Uncounted Forces in the American Civil War.* Gettysburg, PA: Thomas.

47. Miscellany. (September 28, 1866). *Bellows Falls (VT) Times*, image 1.
48. Correspondence from Headquarters. (September 21, 1861). *Ashtabula (OH) Weekly Telegraph*, image 1.
49. The Vivandière of the Philadelphia Fire Zouaves. (November 22, 1861). *Watertown (WI) Republican*, image 1.
50. Livermore, M.A. (1889). *My Story of the War: A Woman's Narrative of Four Years Personal Experience*. Hartford, CT: A.D. Worthington. p. 116. Also, Bridget Diver: Custer's Female Wolverine, http://irishamericancivilwar.com/2012/08/16/bridget-diver-custer-female-wolverine/.
51. Moore, Frank. (1867). *Women of the War*. Hartford, CT: S.S. Scranton. p. 110–111.
52. McKay, Mrs. C.E. (1876). *Stories of Hospital and Camp*. Philadelphia: Claxton, Remsem & Haffelfinger, p. 125.
53. Palmer, S A. (1868). *The Story of Aunt Becky's Army-Life*. New York: John F. Trow. p. 109.
54. Jacquette, H.S. (Ed). (1937). *South after Gettysburg: Letters of Cornelia Hancock from the Army of the Potomac 1863–1865*. Philadelphia: University of Pennsylvania Press, p. 131.
55. The Civil War Fifty Years Ago. (May 26, 1903). *Buffalo (NY) Evening News*. p. 4, col. 1–3.
56. *Ibid*.
57. Some War Heroines. (March 1, 1893). *Commercial Advertiser* (Canton, NY), p. 1.
58. Jacquette, H.S. (Ed). (1937). *South after Gettysburg: Letters of Cornelia Hancock from the Army of the Potomac 1863–1865*. Philadelphia: University of Pennsylvania Press. p. 166.

Chapter 6

1. *The North West Branch of the Christian Commission*, http://www.nwuscc.org/OldUSCC.html.
2. General News. (March 26, 1865). *Hartford (CT) Courant*, p. 2.
3. Article Two: As Appeal. (December 22, 1864). *Hartford (CT) Daily Courant*, p. 2.
4. Sanborne, P.F. (1864). *Diary of Pliny Fiske Sanborne: USCC*. City Point files. Petersburg, VA: Petersburg National Battlefield Park. p. 17.
5. The Christian Commission. (July 28, 1864). *New York Times*, p. 1.
6. From San Francisco. (September 12, 1864). *Hartford (CT) Courant*, p. 3.
7. Information for Army Meetings: U.S. Christian Commission. (October 1864). Philadelphia, PA: James D. Rogers. City Point files. Petersburg, VA: Petersburg National Battlefield Park. p. 6.
8. Telegraphic Items. (September. 26, 1864). *Hartford (CT) Daily Courant*, p. 3.
9. Wittenmyer, A. (1895). *Under the Guns: A Reminiscence of the Civil War*. Boston: E.R. Stillings. pp. 221–222.
10. Information for Army Meetings: U.S. Christian Commission. (October 1864). Philadelphia, PA: James D. Rogers. City Point files. Petersburg, VA: Petersburg National Battlefield Park. p. 34–35.
11. Moss, L. (1866). *Annals of the United States Christian Commission*. Philadelphia: J.B. Lippincott. p. 410; The Christian Commission with the Army of the Potomac. (June 14, 1864). *New York Times*, p. 1.
12. The Christian Commission. (July 21, 1864). *New York Times*, p. 8.
13. Information for Army Meetings: U.S. Christian Commission. (October 1864). Philadelphia, PA: James D. Rogers. City Point files. Petersburg, VA: Petersburg National Battlefield Park. p. 10.
14. Fire Engine Sent to the Army of the Potomac. (July 3, 1864). *Chicago Daily Tribune*, image 3.
15. The Christian Commission. (July 21, 1864). *New York Times*, p. 8.
16. Information for Army Meetings: U.S. Christian Commission. (October 1864). Philadelphia, PA: James D. Rogers. City Point files. Petersburg, VA: Petersburg National Battlefield Park. p. 31.
17. Wittenmyer, A. (1895). *Under the Guns: A Reminiscence of the Civil War*. Boston: E.R. Stillings. p. 212.
18. Article 9. (August 4, 1864). *Hartford (CT) Daily Courant*, p. 2.
19. The Work of the Ladies. (September 6, 1864). *Utica (NY) Daily Herald*, col. 7.
20. General News. (March 26, 1865). *Hartford (CT) Courant*, p. 2.
21. City Intelligence. (February 23, 1865). *Hartford (CT) Daily Courant*, p. 2.
22. United States Christian Commission. (March 21, 1865). *New York Times*, p 5.
23. The Great Duty of the Hour. (June 27, 1864). *Hartford (CT) Courant*, p. 2.

24. Moss, L. (1866). *Annals of the United States Christian Commission.* Philadelphia: J.B. Lippincott. p. 651.
25. Information for Army Meetings: U.S. Christian Commission. (October 1864). Philadelphia, PA: James D. Rogers. City Point files. Petersburg, VA: Petersburg National Battlefield Park. p. 15.
26. Billingsley, A.S. (1872). *From the Flag to the Cross or Scenes and Incidents of Christianity in the War.* Philadelphia, PA: New World.
27. Moss, L. (1866). *Annals of the United States Christian Commission.* Philadelphia: J.B. Lippincott. p. 543.
28. "Minute Men" of the Christian Commission. (June 1, 1864). *Brooklyn Daily News,* p. 2.
29. Moss, L. (1866). *Annals of the United States Christian Commission.* Philadelphia: J.B. Lippincott. pp. 682–683.
30. *Ibid.,* pp. 602–638.
31. Article Two: As Appeal. (December 22, 1864). *Hartford (CT) Daily Courant,* p. 2.
32. A Volunteer Nurse (1871). *The Bugle Call: A Summons to Work in Christ's Army.* New York: American Tract Society. pp. 8–11.
33. Information for Army Meetings: U.S. Christian Commission. (October 1864). Philadelphia, PA: James D. Rogers. City Point files. Petersburg, VA: Petersburg National Battlefield Park. p. 11.
34. Smith, E.P. (1871). *Incidents of the United States Christian Commission.* Philadelphia: J.B. Lippincott. p. 483.
35. Information for Army Meetings: U.S. Christian Commission. (October 1864). Philadelphia, PA: James D. Rogers. City Point files. Petersburg, VA: Petersburg National Battlefield Park. p. 13.
36. *Ibid.,* p. 18.
37. Moss, L. (1866). *Annals of the United States Christian Commission.* Philadelphia: J.B. Lippincott. p. 408.
38. Bucklin, S. (1869). *In Hospital and Camp.* Philadelphia: John E. Potter. pp. 286–288.
39. Palmer, S. (1868). *The Story of Aunt Becky's Army-Life.* New York: John F. Trow. p. 115.
40. Warman, Dr. D. (April 4–September 20, 1864). Contract Surgeon. http://homepages.dsu.edu/jankej/civilwar/warman.htm. p. 9.
41. Books for the Line. (December 26, 1864). *Cleveland (OH) Morning Leader,* image 1.
42. Smith, E.P. (1871). *Incidents of the United States Christian Commission.* Philadelphia: J.B. Lippincott. pp. 324–371.
43. Untitled. (June 30, 1864). *Daily Courier* (Lowell, MA), no page, col. 4.
44. Hackett, H.B. (1864). *Christian Memorials of the War: Or, Scenes and Incidents Illustrative of Religious Faith Principle, Patriotism and Bravery in Our Army. With Historical Notes.* Boston: Gould and Lincoln. p. 245.
45. Information for Army Meetings: U.S. Christian Commission. (October 1864). Philadelphia, PA: James D. Rogers. City Point files. Petersburg, VA: Petersburg National Battlefield Park. p. 21.
46. Professor A.W. Farnham Dead. (December 11, 1919). *Oswego (NY) Daily Palladium,* p. 5. col. 6.
47. Smith, E.P. (1871). *Incidents of the United States Christian Commission.* Philadelphia: J.B. Lippincott. p. 435.
48. Moss, L. (1866). *Annals of the United States Christian Commission.* Philadelphia: J.B. Lippincott. p. 408.
49. Telegraphic Items. (September 26, 1864). *Hartford (CT) Daily Courant,* p. 3.
50. The Hospital Car. (November 3, 1864). *The Jeffersonian* (Danbury, CT), p. 1, col. 3.
51. Moss, L. (1866). *Annals of the United States Christian Commission.* Philadelphia: J.B. Lippincott. p. 59.
52. Billingsley, A.S. (1872). *From the Flag to the Cross or Scenes and Incidents of Christianity in the War.* Philadelphia, PA: New World. p. 77.
53. Hackett, H.B. (1864). *Christian Memorials of the War: Or, Scenes and Incidents Illustrative of Religious Faith Principle, Patriotism and Bravery in Our Army. With Historical Notes.* Boston: Gould and Lincoln. p. 212.
54. Wittenmyer, A. (1983). *Collection of Recipes Special Diet Kitchen in Military Hospitals.* Mantituck, NY: John M. Carroll. The Virginia Historical Society Library. p. 40.
55. Moss, L. (1866). *Annals of the United States Christian Commission.* Philadelphia: J.B. Lippincott. p. 662.
56. McKay, Mrs. C.E. (1876). *Stories of Hospital and Camp.* Philadelphia: Claxton, Remsem & Haffelfinger. p. 117.
57. A Volunteer Nurse. (1871). *The Bugle*

Call: A Summons to Work in Christ's Army. New York: American Tract Society. p. 30.

58. Local Intelligence. (August 5, 1864). *New York Times*, p. 3.

59. A Volunteer Nurse. (1871). *The Bugle Call: A Summons to Work in Christ's Army.* New York: American Tract Society.

60. Billingsley, A.S. (1872). *From the Flag to the Cross or Scenes and Incidents of Christianity in the War.* Philadelphia, PA: New World. p. 114.

61. Hackett, H.B. (1864). *Christian Memorials of the War: Or, Scenes and Incidents Illustrative of Religious Faith Principle, Patriotism and Bravery in Our Army. With Historical Notes.* Boston: Gould and Lincoln. p. 66.

62. A Volunteer Nurse. (1871). *The Bugle Call: A Summons to Work in Christ's Army.* New York: American Tract Society. p. 17.

63. Bristol, F.M. (1908). *The Life of Chaplain McCabe.* New York: Fleming H. Revell. p. 182.

64. *Ibid.*, p. 191.

65. General News. (March 29, 1865). *Hartford (CT) Courant*, p. 1.

66. *Sounds from the Battlefield.* Civil War music, File box 1, Dewitt Historical Society Library, Ithaca, NY.

67. General News. (March 26, 1865). *Hartford (CT) Courant*, p. 2.

68. Bucklin, S. (1869). *In Hospital and Camp.* Philadelphia: John E. Potter. p. 354.

69. Holstein, A. (1867). *Three Years in the Field Hospital of the Army of the Potomac.* Philadelphia: J.B. Lippincott. p. 71.

70. From City Point. (March 18, 1865). *New York Times*, p. 3.

71. From City Point. (January 30, 1865). *New York Times*, p. 3.

72. State Matters. (March 18, 1865). *Hartford (CT) Daily Courant*, p. 2.

73. Palmer, S. (1868). *The Story of Aunt Becky's Army-Life.* New York: John F. Trow. p. 165; Jaquette, H.S. (1937). *South After Gettysburg: Letters of Cornelia Hancock from the Army of the Potomac 1863–1865.* Freeport, NY: Book for Libraries. p. 87. Although others accepted the magnitude of death, dying, and the executions, Aunt Becky and Cornelia Hancock could not help writing about their feelings.

74. *Ibid.*, p. 116.

75. Moss, L. (1866). *Annals of the United States Christian Commission.* Philadelphia: J.B. Lippincott. p. 544.

When the initial aggregated group of women started to emerge, there was significant debate among several historians over which group of women was right in their "triage" behavior and if their decisions really made a difference to the other women. To test the preferred differences among the many woman who answered the drumroll in a crisis situation, a random sample of (n = 42) military, medical, and civilian woman who lived and worked in the coastal Virginia area were given a brief survey. The sample mirrored the mix of women that would have been at City Point in 1864–1865. Six of the women were older and had served in WWII, four women had served in Korea, sixteen had served in the Vietnam war zone as either military or civilians, five served with the military during the Vietnam era but had not been in the war zone, three women were wives of current military personnel, and eight were random civilians who were tourists in the area. They were asked to prioritize, without great deliberation, what they would do if faced with a mass casualty situation: Would they: Try to wash the blood and grime off the woundeds' face and hands; comb their hair; give the wounded food or fluids; or get the soldier's name and unit?

The results indicated that the first choice was to give the wounded soldier food or fluids, the second choice was to get the soldier's name and unit, third was to wash the hands and face of the wounded, and last was to comb his hair. Although the option to say a prayer for the wounded soldier was not asked, nine of the women voluntarily indicated that if a man was obviously dying, they would try and say some type of quick prayer for him because they felt time was critical and if he died, a clean face or food would not matter to their heavenly maker. This reaction surprised several in the initial research, making the actions of the USCC ladies become more relevant. From Christie, J.M. (1995). No Place for a Woman. Exhibit, Appomattox Manor, National Parks Service, City Point, VA.

76. Information for Army Meetings: U.S. Christian Commission. (October 1864). Philadelphia, PA: James D. Rogers. City Point files. Petersburg, VA: Petersburg National Battlefield Park. p. 20.

77. Letters from City Point. (February 15, 1865). *Hartford (CT) Courant*, p. 2.

78. General News. (March 26, 1865). *Hartford (CT) Courant*, p. 2.

79. General News. (April 12, 1865). *Hartford (CT) Courant*, p. 2.
80. No title. (July 24, 1885.) *NY Recorder* (Mount Kisco, NY). Other papers also ran the information, such as: General News. (April 12, 1865). *Hartford (CT) Courant*, p. 2.
81. Moss, L. (1866). *Annals of the United States Christian Commission*. Philadelphia: J.B. Lippincott. p. 671.
82. Wittenmyer, A. (1895). *Under the Guns: A Reminiscence of the Civil War*. Boston: E.R. Stillings. pp. 210–211.
83. Wittenmyer, A. (1983). *Collection of Recipes Special Diet Kitchen in Military Hospitals*. Mantituck, NY: John M. Carroll. The Virginia Historical Society Library. p. i.
84. Jaquette, H.S. (19737). *South After Gettysburg: Letters of Cornelia Hancock from the Army of the Potomac 1863–1865*. Philadelphia: University of Pennsylvania. p. 130.
85. Moss, L. (1866). *Annals of the United States Christian Commission*. Philadelphia: J.B. Lippincott. p. 678.
86. Palmer, S. (1868). *The Story of Aunt Becky's Army-Life*. New York: John F. Trow. p. 99.
87. Bucklin, S. (1869). *In Hospital and Camp*. Philadelphia: John E. Potter. p. 153.
88. Wittenmyer, A. (1983). *Collection of Recipes Special Diet Kitchen in Military Hospitals*. Mantituck, NY: John M. Carroll. The Virginia Historical Society Library. p. 10.
89. *Ibid.*, p.17.
90. *Ibid.*, p. 26.
91. *Ibid.*, p. 43.
92. Palmer, S. (1868). *The Story of Aunt Becky's Army-Life*. New York: John F. Trow. p. 73.
93. *Ibid.*, pp. 80–81.
94. McKay, Mrs. C.E. (1876). *Stories of Hospital and Camp*. Philadelphia: Claxton, Remsem & Haffelfinger. pp. 121–122.
95. Palmer, S. (1868). *The Story of Aunt Becky's Army-Life*. New York: John F. Trow. p. 98.
96. Rodgers, J.B. (1866). *Federal Dead Buried from Libby, Belle Island, Danville and Camp Lawton Prisons and at City Point, in the Field before Petersburg and Richmond*. Philadelphia. Reprinted (1990) Heritage Books.

Chapter 7

1. From the Army of the Potomac. (September 10, 1864). *New York Times*, p. 1.
2. Maxwell, W.Q. (1868). *Lincoln's Fifth Wheel: The Political History of the United States Sanitary Commission*. New York: Longman, Green.
3. Geisberg, J.A. (2000). *Civil War Sisterhood: The U.S. Sanitary Commission and Women's Politics in Transition*. Boston: Northeastern University Press.
4. Censer, J.T. (Ed.). (1986). *Defending the Union*. Baltimore: Johns Hopkins University Press.
5. Reed, W.H. (1866). *Hospital Life in the Army of the Potomac*. Boston: W.V. Spencer.
6. Hackett, H.B. (1864). *Christian Memorials of the War*. Boston: Gould and Lincoln. p. 242.
7. The Soldier's Aid Society. (June 10, 1864). *Daily Evening Standard* (Bridgeport, CT).
8. Comfort for the Soldiers. (July 5, 1864). *Daily Evening Standard* (Bridgeport, CT), p. 1.
9. *Ibid.*
10. No title. (August 17, 1864). *Jeffersonian* (Danbury, CT), col. 4. Danbury Historical Society.
11. From City Point. (January 29, 1865). *New York Times*, p. 5.
12. *Ibid.*
13. Richmond—Rebel Leaders Hopeless. (March 23, 1865). *Daily Ohio Statesman* (Columbus, OH), image 3.
14. Sanitary Party. (December 22, 1864). *Chicago Tribune*, image 2.
15. The Drum Beat, http://blogs.law.harvard.edu/houghtonmodern/2009/06/03/earlydickerson/.
16. Reed, W.H. (1866). *Hospital Life in the Army of the Potomac*. Boston: W.V. Spencer. p. 90.
17. From City Point. (October 12, 1864). *New York Times*, p. 1.
18. From City Point. (January 29, 1865). *New York Times*, p. 5.
19. Our Wounded and Sick Soldiers. (December 11, 1864). *New York Times*, p. 1.
20. Moore, F. (1867). *Women of the War; Their Heroism and Self-Sacrifice*. Hartford: S.S. Scranton & Co. Philadelphia: J.B. Lippincott. p. 529.
21. From City Point. (January 29, 1865). *New York Times*, p. 5.
22. *Ibid.*
23. The Sanitary Commission. (January 10, 1865). *Philadelphia Inquirer*, p. 4.

24. From City Point. (January 29, 1865). *New York Times*, p. 5.
25. Marine Intelligence. (September 3, 1864). *New York Times*, p. 8.
26. Naval Movements. (September 23, 1864). *New York Times*, p. 2.
27. *My Dear Cousin Elizabeth*. October 30, 1864, USSC. Mss2 Sh463 b., Virginia Museum of History and Culture, Richmond.
28. *The Sanitary Commission Bulletin*. (April 1, 1865). Philadelphia, number 35, p. 1101.
29. Explosion. (August 12, 1864). *Hartford (CT) Daily Courant*.
30. *My Dear Cousin Elizabeth*. October 30, 1864, USSC. Mss2 Sh463 b., Virginia Museum of History and Culture, Richmond.
31. Explosion. (August 12, 1864). *Hartford (CT) Daily Courant*.
32. Holstein, A. (1867). *Three Years in the Field Hospital of the Army of the Potomac*. Philadelphia: J.B. Lippincott. p. 84.
33. *Ibid.*, p. 12.
34. Palmer, S. (1868). *The Story of Aunt Becky's Army-Life*. New York: John F. Trow. p. 98.
35. Leaking Badly. (January 23, 1865). *Evening Star* (Washington, D.C.), image 2.
36. Hackett, H.B. (1864). *Christian Memorials of the War*. Boston: Gould and Lincoln. p. 242.
37. Holstein, A. (1867). *Three Years in the Field Hospital of the Army of the Potomac*. Philadelphia: J.B. Lippincott. p. 108.
38. The United States Sanitary Commission compiled documents and private papers. (1863) NYPL p 76
39. Moore, F. (1867). *Women of the War; Their Heroism and Self-Sacrifice*. Hartford: S.S. Scranton & Co. Philadelphia: J.B. Lippincott.
40. *Ibid.*, p. 527.
41. Famous Nurses on Many Battlefields. (August 16, 1903). *The San Francisco Call*, pp. 12–13.
42. Moore, F. (1867). *Women of the War; Their Heroism and Self-Sacrifice*. Hartford: S.S. Scranton & Co. Philadelphia: J.B. Lippincott. p. 429–430.
43. Made Less Hideous. (October 16, 1896). *Kansas Agitator* (Garnett, KS), image 2.
44. Christie, J.M. (1995). *No Place for a Woman*, exhibit and lecture, Appomattox Manor, City Point, VA.
45. Moore, F. (1867). *Women of the War;*
Their Heroism and Self-Sacrifice. Hartford: S.S. Scranton & Co. Philadelphia: J.B. Lippincott. p. 125.
46. *Ibid.*, p. 66.
47. Conklin, E.F. (1993). *Women at Gettysburg*. Gettysburg, PA: Thomas. p. 18.
48. From City Point. (January 29, 1865). *New York Times*, p. 5.
49. Brockett, L P. & Vaughn, M. (1867). *Women's Work in the Civil War*. Philadelphia: Zeigler, McCurdy.
50. Hammond, H.E. (Ed). (1962). *Maria Lydig Daly: Diary of a Union Lady: 1861–1865*, NY: Funk and Wagnalls.
51. Hall, R. (1993). *Patriots in Disguise: Women Warriors of the Civil War*. New York: Paragon House. p. 226.
52. Brockett, L.P. & Vaughn, M. (1867). *Women's Work in the Civil War*. Philadelphia: Zeigler, McCurdy. p. 287.
53. Moore, F. (1867). *Women of the War; Their Heroism and Self-Sacrifice*. Hartford: S.S. Scranton & Co. Philadelphia: J.B. Lippincott.
54. Hospital Scenes. (December 4, 1864). *New York Times*, p. 5.
55. Holstein, A. (1867). *Three Years in the Field Hospital of the Army of the Potomac*. Philadelphia: J.B. Lippincott. pp. 71–72.
56. Myron E. Lake, 109th NY Vol., folder 5, Muster roll file 13 USSC letter, Dewitt Historical Society, Ithaca, NY.
57. Holstein, A. (1867). *Three Years in the Field Hospital of the Army of the Potomac*. Philadelphia: J.B. Lippincott. p. 10.
58. *Ibid.* p. 66.
59. *Ibid.*, p. 70.
60. *Ibid.*, p. 77.

Chapter 8

1. In Hospitals and Camps. (July 3, 1917). *Harrisburg (PA) Telegraph*, p. 2.
2. Oswego County Historical Society. (1954). *Elmina Spencer, Heroine of the Civil War*. Oswego, NY. *Palladium-Times*. p. 39–47.
3. Phisterer, F. (1912). *New York in the War of Rebellion 1861–1865*. Albany, NY: J. D. Lyon Co. p. 42.
4. No title. (February 6, 1865). *Portland Daily Press*, Maine State Historical Society. Augusta, ME.
5. Sudlow, L.L. (2000). *A Vast Army of Women: Maine's Uncounted Forces in*

the American Civil War. Gettysburg, PA, Thomas. The book offers significant insight into the lives of the women who worked with the Maine agencies both on the home front and in the war zones.
6. Wheelock, J. (1870). *The Boys in White: Experiences of a Hospital Agent in and Around Washington.* New York: Lange & Hillman. p. 206.
7. *Ibid.*, p. 38.
8. *Ibid.*, p. 152.
9. *Ibid.*, p. 196.
10. Jacquette, H.S. (Ed.). (1937). *South After Gettysburg: Letters of Cornelia Hancock.* Philadelphia: University of Pennsylvania Press. p. 120.
11. *Ibid.*, p. 130.
12. Smith, A. (1919). *Reminiscences of an Army Nurse During the Civil War.* New York: Greaves. p. 121. The fact that Dr. Painter had a medical background was a controversial issue. In 1864, there were thirty female students at Bellview Hospital, which caused an uproar because the women were presenting a desire to become equal. Women like Dr. Painter felt the concern about a woman doctor was male jealousy and the denial of a woman in the medical profession was an attempt to keep women ignorant and degraded. As opposed to the radical and masculine-attired Dr. Mary Walker, Dr. Painter maintained a feminine persona to avoid the growing cultural firestorm. The Question of Lady Doctors. (January 8, 1865). *New York Times*, p. 5.
13. Smith, A. (1919). *Reminiscences of an Army Nurse During the Civil War.* New York: Greaves. pp. 120–121.
14. Jacquette, H.S. (Ed.). (1937). *South After Gettysburg: Letters of Cornelia Hancock.* Philadelphia: University of Pennsylvania Press.
15. Masonic Mission. (October 25, 1864). *The Jeffersonian* (Danbury, CT), p. 1, col. 7. Danbury Historical Society.
16. The War in Virginia. (October 9, 1864). *New York Times*, p. 1.
17. Explosion. (August 24, 1864). *The Jeffersonian* (Danbury, CT), p. 2, col. 4. Danbury Historical Society.
18. Dabney, E. (November 11, 2011). City Point During the Civil War. In *Encyclopedia of Virginia for Virginia Humanities.* http//www.encyclopediaVirginia.org/City_Point_During_the_Civil_War.
19. Good News Generally: The Explosion at City Point. (August 15, 1864). *Hartford (CT) Daily Courant*, p. 2. There is significant information about the reaction of individuals who were in the area. At first, the numbers of dead were not known, but eventually the totals grew. The gravediggers who had sufficient work on a normal day were put to the test trying to bury the bodies that could be buried. For many, there was not enough of a body left to bury. More details were in: Twelve Bodies and Twenty Bags of Fragments Interred. (August 16, 1864). *Daily Ohio Statesman*, p. 1, col. 3; and The Explosion at City Point. (August 13, 1864). *New York Times*, p. 2.
20. Sparks, D.S. (Ed.) (1964). *Inside Lincoln's Army: The Diary of Marsena Rudolph Patrick, Provost Marshal General, Army of the Potomac.* New York: Thomas Yoseloff. p. 142.
21. Warren, H.F. & Warren, E. (1871). *Letters: From Two Brothers Serving in the War for the Union.* Cambridge: Printed for private circulation. p. 140. The description by the brothers about the event provides a vivid account.
22. Good News Generally: The Explosion at City Point. (August 15, 1864). *Hartford (CT) Daily Courant*, p. 2.
23. Fun for the Soldiers. (February 11, 1865). *New York Herald*, p. 1, col. 6.
24. Rebel Sympathizers on Staten Island. (February 12, 1865). *New York Times*, p. 8.
25. Smith, A. (1919). *Reminiscences of an Army Nurse During the Civil War.* New York: Greaves. p. 188.

Chapter 9

1. Smith, A. (1919). *Reminiscences of an Army Nurse During the Civil War.* New York: Greaves. p. 144.
2. Jacquette, H.S. (Ed.). (1937). *South After Gettysburg: Letters of Cornelia Hancock.* Philadelphia: University of Pennsylvania Press. p. 80.
3. Smith, A. (1919). *Reminiscences of an Army Nurse During the Civil War.* New York: Greaves. p. 113.
4. *Ibid.*, pp. 145–147.
5. Palmer, S. (1868). *The Story of Aunt Becky's Army-Life.* New York: John F. Trow. pp. 81–83.
6. *Ibid.*, p. 117.
7. Dewitt Library civil war letter collection, Orange City, Iowa.

8. Smith, A. (1919). *Reminiscences of an Army Nurse During the Civil War*. New York: Greaves. p. 192.
9. Palmer, S. (1868). *The Story of Aunt Becky's Army-Life*. New York: John F. Trow. p. 7–8.
10. Brockett, L.P. & Vaughn, M. (1867). *Women's Work in the Civil War*. Philadelphia: Zeigler, McCurdy. p. 430.
11. Palmer, S. (1868). *The Story of Aunt Becky's Army-Life*. New York: John F. Trow. p. 105.
12. The Lady in Gray. (June 13, 1889). *The Weekly Expositor* (Brockway Center, MI), image 7.
13. Jacquette, H.S. (Ed.). (1937). *South After Gettysburg: Letters of Cornelia Hancock*. Philadelphia: University of Pennsylvania Press. p. 148.
14. Smith, A. (1919). *Reminiscences of an Army Nurse During the Civil War*. New York: Greaves. p. 133.
15. *Ibid.*, pp. 131–134.
16. Palmer, S. (1868). *The Story of Aunt Becky's Army-Life*. New York: John F. Trow. p. 95.
17. Moss, L. Rev. (1868). *Annals of the United States Christian Commission*. Philadelphia: J.B. Lippincott.
18. Parker, M.G. (1922). *Moses Greeley Parker, Dr.* Lowell, MA. p. 75.
19. *Ibid.*, p. 69.
20. Yankee Alphabet. (June 10, 1865). *Oswego (NY) Press*.
21. Soldier's Daily Prayer. (June 3, 1863). *Jeffersonian* (Danbury, CT), col. 7. Danbury Historical Society.
22. Nurse Matilda Morris, http://schliessmann.blogspot.com/2010/05/civil-war-nurses-forgotten-heroes-of.html.
23. Simon, J.Y. (Ed.) (1975). *The Personal Memoirs of Julia Dent Grant*. Carbondale: Southern Illinois University Press. p. 135.
24. Old Abe's Last Joke. (June 28, 1864). *Daily Ohio Statesman* (Columbus, OH), image 1.
25. Made Grant Laugh. (August 16, 1903). *The San Francisco Call*, image 13.

Chapter 10

1. From City Point (March 19, 1865). *New York Times*, p. 1.
2. Gossip from the Army. (February 1, 1865). *New York Times*, p. 2.
3. Palmer, S. (1868). *The Story of Aunt Becky's Army-Life*. New York: John F. Trow. p. 186.
4. Social News. (May 31, 1894). *The Sunday Herald and Intelligencer* (Washington, D.C.), p. 12, col. 2.
5. Widows of Heroes. (July 27, 1890). *Pittsburgh Dispatch*, p. 16, col. 1.
6. Vet and Nurses. (August 16, 1906). *The Minneapolis (MN) Journal*, p. 6.
7. Social News. (May 31, 1894). *The Sunday Herald and Intelligencer* (Washington, D.C.), p. 12, col 2.
8. Zinnen, R.I. (1991). City Point: The Tool That Gave General Grant's Victory. *Quartermaster Professional Bulletin*. Spring.
9. Collis, S. (1889). *A Woman's War Record*. New York: G.P. Putnam & Sons. p. 73.
10. *Ibid.*, p. 43.
11. Lincoln and Tad, Visit Grant's Army. (March 28, 1865). *Washington (D.C.) Herald*, Society Section, p. 23.
12. Cotton, G. (2009). *Like a Hideous Nightmare*. Vicksburg, MS: The Print Shop. p. 19.
13. Woodward, W.E. (1928). *Meet General Grant*. New York: Horace Liveright.
14. Hammond, H.E. (Ed.). (1962). *Maria Lydia Daly: Diary of a Union Lady: 1861–1865*. New York: Funk and Wagnalls.
15. Sight-seers. (March 18, 1865). *New York Times*, p. 3.
16. City Point as a Base of Supplies. (June 22, 1864). *New York Times*, p. 1.
17. The President's Visit. (June 28, 1864). *Daily Ohio Statesman* (Columbus, OH), p. 1.
18. From Fortress Monroe. (August 15, 1865). *Hartford (CT) Courant*, p. 3.
19. General News. (March 9, 1865). *Hartford (CT) Courant*, p .2.
20. From City Point. (October 12, 1864). *New York Times*, p. 1.
21. From Fortress Monroe. (July 19, 1864). *The Brooklyn Daily Eagle*, p. 3.
22. Gossip from the Army. (February 1, 1865). *New York Times*, p. 2.
23. Washington. (April 26, 1865). *Daily Courier* (Syracuse, NY), col. 3.
24. Army of the Potomac. (October 8, 1864). *New York Times*, p. 1.
25. Sanborne, Pliny Fiske. *USCC Civil War Chaplain Daily Extracts from June 7 to August 15, 1864*. City Point files. Petersburg, VA: Petersburg National Battlefield Park. pp. 4, 9–10.

26. Jacquette, H.S. (Ed). 1937. *South after Gettysburg: Letters of Cornelia Hancock*. Philadelphia: University of Pennsylvania Press. pp. 89, 122.

27. Palmer, S. (1868). *The Story of Aunt Becky's Army-Life*. New York: John F. Trow. p. 153.

28. Smith, A. (1919). *Reminiscence of an Army Nurse During the Civil War*. New York: Greaves. p. 167–184. Regarding Rev. Henry Houghton: Dr. Reverend Henry Houghton served as the chaplain and was well-respected and liked by the nurses. He participated in the wedding ceremony for Miss Bain and Major Eden. He was also a driving force as chief of the Individual Relief Department in recording the many graves around the area. There were four main City Point cemeteries: Depot Field Hospital, Near Lepsey's house, The Cavalry Corps hospital and the line of the Railroad. Additional graves were located at the many forts in the area, at private homes, and in private gardens of Peters Burchard and Mrs. Cummings, as well as along the banks of the Appomattox River, etc. The magnitude of his work can be found in the *Federal Dead Buried from Libby, Belle Island, Danville and Camp Lawton Prisons and at City Point, in the Field before Petersburg and Richmond*. As a driving force, he organized many assistants around Virginia. At City Point, he had two delegates who helped with the arduous task. Those who specifically helped at City Point were Rev. J.B. Clark and Thomas Charters, Esq.

29. Palmer, S. (1868). *The Story of Aunt Becky's Army-Life*. New York: John F. Trow. p. 153.

30. Bucklin, S. (1869). *In a Hospital and Camp: Official Papers of Sophronia Bucklin*, Philadelphia: J.E. Potter. p. 351. Although the incident and their first names are known, there has been no other information thus far about who they were. Perhaps another researcher will start by consulting M 1875 Marriage Records of the Office of the Commission Washington HQ, of the Bureau of Refugees, Freedman and Abandoned lands, 1861–1869. www.archives.gov/files/research/microfilm/m1875.pdf.

31. Crazy Women. (January 27, 1864). *Danbury Times* vol. IV, number 203. Arrest of Supposed Rebel Spy. (February 14, 1865). *Cleveland Ledger* copied to *New York Times*, February 19, 1865. p. 6.

Bibliography

Primary Sources

Andrew, Judson B., Assistant Army Surgeon, 6th Corps. Diary. City Point files, Petersburg National Battlefield Park, Petersburg, VA.
Barton, Clara. Personal notes. Sophia Smith Collection, Sophia Smith Library, Hatfield, MA.
Boucher, Jonathan. (9 March 1767). Special Collections, folder 1:3, Earl Gregg Swem Library, College of William and Mary, Williamsburg, VA.
Burnham, E. (May 21, 1864). CO A, 7th CT Heavy Artillery: Letters to His Wife. Wood Memorial Library, South Windsor, CT.
Butler, Lucy Woods. Diary. Virginia History and Culture Museum, MsslL8378a330.
Cohn, Rosa, and William Flagenheimer. Family box. Beth Ahabah Archives, Richmond, VA.
Comstock, C.B. Diary. Library of Congress #1MSS 17650.
Eppes, Dr. Richard. City Point files, Petersburg National Battlefield Park and the Virginia History and Culture Museum, Petersburg, VA.
Lake, Myron E., 109th NY Vol. Folder 5, Muster roll file 13 USSC letter, Dewitt Historical Society, Ithaca, NY.
List of Ladies Employed in Special Diets Kitchens under the directions of the USCC. (March 13, 1865). #15523, M416, NARA.
Marion, James. (July 17, 1864). Personal letters. City Point files. Petersburg National Battlefield Park, Petersburg, VA.
Micklem, James. (October 24, 1994). Personal communication. Hopewell, VA.
My Dear Cousin Elizabeth. (October 30, 1864). USSC. New York Public Library, Mss2 Sh463 b.
NARA #1340181 and #862851, RG 15, NARA Civil War files.
Parker, H.F. (September 1863–June 1, 1866). Personal diary. Engineer Files, Private Papers Chris Caukins, Petersburg National Battlefield Park, Petersburg, VA.
Personal communication concerning Rebecca Gray. (June 29, 2003). NARA.
Rawlins. Personal file. Danbury Historical Society, Danbury, CT.
Richardson, Mrs. E.W. "Notes on the Civil War: From Colonel Kingston Winger, Hampton Center for the Arts and Humanities." City Point files, Petersburg National Battlefield Park, Petersburg, VA.
St. John's Church, Hopewell, VA. Baptism, confirmation, marriage and death records.
Sanborne, Pliny Fiske. (June 7–August 15, 1864). USCC Civil War chaplin daily extracts. City Point files, Petersburg National Battlefield Park, Petersburg, VA.
Slave Census Record. (1860). Prince George County, NARA.
Spencer, Sarah A. Last Will and Testimony. Dutchess County Records, Poughkeepsie, NY, File #26753.
Summer, M.E. Transcribed notes from the diary of Cyrus Ballou Comstock. City Point files, Petersburg National Battlefield Park, Petersburg, VA.
United States Sanitary Commission documents and private papers. New York Public Library.

256 Bibliography

U.S. Union Provost Marshal Papers. Ninth Corps, February 1 and March 1, 1865. NARA.
Usher, Rebecca. (January 19, 1865–March 1865). Diary. Maine Historical Society, MMN#1451. www.MaineMemory.net.
Warren, H.F., and Warren, E. (1871). *Letters: From Two Brothers Serving in the War for the Union.* Cambridge: printed for private circulation.
Wiseman, Mary. (September 22, 1864). Oath of Allegiance. U.S. Provost Marshal's Papers, 1861–1867, for Mary Wiseman, NARA.

Courts-Martial Files

Miss Bidgood, MO346, roll 64, NARA.
Miss Bidgood and Mrs. Frances Levy, #3738, Turner Baker Papers, RG 94, NARA.
Rape of Mrs. Stiles/Styles, #1523, file #MM1481, NARA.

Primary Printed Sources

Agassi, George (Ed.). (1922). *Meade's Headquarters: Letters of Colonel Theodore Lyman.* Boston: Massachusetts Historical Society.
Billingsley, A.S. (1872 orig. edition). *From the Flag to the Cross or, Scenes and Incidents of Christianity in the War.* Birmingham, AL: Solid Ground Christian Books.
Brockett, L.P. & Vaughn, M. (1867). *Women's Work in the Civil War.* Philadelphia: Zeigler, McCurdy.
Bucklin, S. (1869). *In a Hospital and Camp: Official Papers of Sophronia Bucklin.* Philadelphia: J.E. Potter.
Cadwallader, S. (Ed.). (1980). *Three Years with Grant.* Westport, CT: Greenwood.
Cambum, M.A. *Personal Recollections of Lincoln.* City Point files. Petersburg National Battlefield, Petersburg, VA.
Collis, S. (1889). *A Woman's War Record.* New York: G.P. Putnam & Sons.
Crotty, D.G. (1874). *Four Years Campaigning in the Army of the Potomac.* Grand Rapids, MI: Dygert Brothers.
Edmonds, S.E. (1865). *Nurse and Spy in the Union Army: Comprising the Adventures and Experiences of a Woman in Hospitals, Camps, and Battle-fields.* Hartford, CT: W.S. Williams & Co.
Executive Committee of the National Association of Civil War Nurses. (1910). *In Honor of the National Association of Civil War Nurses: 44th Encampment Grand Army of the Republic.* Atlantic City: Yeakel.
General Order No. 30. (January 25, 1864). War Department, By Order of the Secretary of War, E.D. Townsend, Assistant Adjutant-General.
Hackett, H.B. (1864). *Christian Memorials of the War.* Boston: Gould & Lincoln.
Hartley, F. (1860). *True Politeness: A Ladies Hand Book of Etiquette.* New York: Levitt & Allen.
Holland, M.A.G. (1895). *Our Army Nurses.* Boston: Wilkerson & Co.
Holstein, A. (1867). *Three Years in the Field Hospital of the Army of the Potomac.* Philadelphia: J.B. Lippincott.
Information for Army Meetings: U.S. Christian Commission. (October 1864). Philadelphia, PA: James D. Rogers. City Point files. Petersburg National Battlefield Park, Petersburg, VA.
Jacquette, H.S. (Ed.). (1937). *South After Gettysburg: Letters of Cornelia Hancock.* Philadelphia: University of Pennsylvania.
Johnson, R. (1894). *Campfire and Battlefield.* New York: Bryan, Taylor & Co.
Livermore, M.A. (1889). *My Story of the War.* Hartford, CT: A.D. Worthington.
Logan, Mrs. John A. (1912). *The Part Taken by Women in American History.* Wilmington, DE: Perry-Nalle Pub.
A Manual of Politeness: Comprising the Principles of Etiquette, and Rules of Behaviour in Genteel Society, for Persons of Both Sexes. (1842). Philadelphia: Published by J.B. Lippincott.

Maxwell, W.Q. (1868). *Lincoln's Fifth Wheel: The Political History of the United States Sanitary Commission*. New York: Longman, Green & Co.
McKay, Mrs. C.E. (1876). *Stories of Hospital and Camp*. Philadelphia: Claxton, Remsem & Haffelfinger.
Moore, F. (1867). *Women of the War*. Hartford, CT: S.S. Scranton.
Moore, F. (1889). *The Civil War in Song and Story: 1860–1865*. New York: P.F. Collier.
Moss, Rev. L. (1868). *Annals of the United States Christian Commission*. Philadelphia: J.B. Lippincott.
Palmer, S. (1868). *The Story of Aunt Becky's Army Life*. New York: John F. Trow.
Parker, Colonel F.J. (1880). *32nd Regiment Massachusetts Infantry*, Boston: C.W. Calkins.
Parker, M.G. (1922). *Moses Greeley Parker, M.D.* Lowell, MA: Privately printed.
Parker, W.W. (1892). *Women's Place in the Christian World*. Richmond, VA: J.W. Fergusson & Son, The Virginia Historical Society.
Phisterer, F. (1912). *New York in the War of Rebellion 1861–1865*. Albany, NY: J.D. Lyon Co.
Porter, General H. (1897). *Campaigning with Grant*. New York: The Century.
Pryor, S.A. (1904). *Reminiscences of Peace and War*. New York: Grosset & Dunlap.
Recker, S.J. (2016). *Shadowing Grant: Reminiscence of the United States Hospital Transport Service in the Civil War 1864–1865*. Privately printed.
Reed, W.H. (1866). *Hospital Life in the Army of the Potomac*. Boston: William Spencer.
Rodgers, J.B. (1865) *Record of Federal Dead Buried from Libby, Belle Isle, Danville, and Camp Lawton Prison and at City Point, and in the Field before Petersburg and Richmond*. Philadelphia: United States Christian Commission, J.B. Rodgers.
Rosenblatt, S. (Ed.). (1983). *Anti-Rebel: The Civil War Letters of Wilber Fisk*. Croton-on-Hudson, NY: Haddon Craftsman.
The Sanitary Commission Bulletin. (April 1, 1865). No. 35. Philadelphia.
Simon, J.Y. (Ed.). (1975). *The Personal Memoirs of Julia Dent Grant*. New York: G.P. Putnam's Sons.
Smith, A. (1919). *Reminiscences of an Army Nurse During the Civil War*. New York: Greaves.
Sparks, D.S. (Ed.). (1964). *Inside Lincoln's Army: Diary of Marsena Rudolph Patrick, Provost Marshal General of the Army of the Potomac*. New York: Thomas Yoseloff.
The War of the Rebellion: A Compilation of the Official Records of the Union and Confederate Armies, Series 1, Volume 2.
Weld, S.M. (1979). *War Diary and Letters of Stephen Minot Weld, 1861–1865*. Boston: Massachusetts Historical Society.
Wheelock, J. (1870). *The Boys in White: Experiences of a Hospital Agent in and Around Washington*. New York: Lange & Hillman.
Wilson, J.H. (1916). *Life of John Rawlins*. New York: Neala.
Wittenmyer, A. (1895). *Under the Gun: A Woman's Reminiscences of the Civil War*. Boston: E.B. Stillings.

Internet Sources

Ancestry.com
Chronicling America Library of Congress
Connecticut State Archives
FamilySearch.org
Find-a-Grave.com
Fulton History.com

Hartford Courant Historical
Historicnewspaper.com
Mainehistory.org
New York Times Historical
Smithsonian.org
Wikipedia.org

Additional Sources

Abbot, Rev. (October 1868). *The Seminary Magazine* 1(1), Richmond, VA.
Abbott, J.S.C. (1833). *The Mother at Home, or The Principles of Maternal Duty Familiarly*. New York: American Tract Society.

Buckley, S.J. (Autumn 2002). I Have Found that Happiness Consists Not in Riches. *Virginia Cavalcade* 51(4): 180.
Bullis, R.K. (2011). *Images of America Hopewell and City Point*. Charleston: Arcadia.
Carroll, J.M. (1983). *Collection of Recipes Special Diet Kitchen in Military Hospitals*. Mantituck, NY: The Virginia History and Cultural Center.
Censer, J.T. (Ed.). (1986). *Defending the Union*. Baltimore: Johns Hopkins University Press.
Christie, J.M. (1995). *No Place for a Woman*. Exhibit, Appomattox Manor, City Point, Petersburg National Battlefield Park, Petersburg, VA.
Christie. J.M. (1997). Performing My Plain Duty: Women of the North at City Point. *Virginia Cavalcade*, vol 46 (5).
Christie, J.M. (April 14, 2012). *Sarah Slater: The Spy Who Got Away*. Popular and American Culture: Civil War and Reconstruction Conference: Boston.
"City Point." NPS, http:/nature.nps.gov/views/Sites/PETE/HTML/ET_CP.htm.
Conklin, E.F. (1993). *Women at Gettysburg 1863*. Gettysburg, PA: Thomas.
Cotton, G. (2009). *Like a Hideous Nightmare*. Vicksburg, MS: The Print Shop.
Dabney, E. (2009). *Civil War City Point: 1864–1865: Period of Significant Landscape Documentation*. Petersburg National Battlefield Park.
Dabney, E. (November 11, 2011). City Point During the Civil War. *Encyclopedia of Virginia*.
The Drum Beat. Modern Books and Manuscripts, Houghton Library, Harvard University.
Eliot, E., Jr. (1932). *Yale in the Civil War*. New Haven, CT: Yale University.
Fizen, L. (April 1994). The Lady Carrying a Scalpel. *Civil War Magazine*, XXLII.
French, B.B., Cole, D.B. & McDonough, J.J. (Eds.). 1989). *Witness to a Young Republic: A Yankee Journal, 1828–1870*. Hanover, NH: University of New England.
Geisberg, J.A. (2000). *Civil War Sisterhood: The U.S. Sanitary Commission and Women's Politics in Transition*. Boston: Northeastern University Press.
Gilland, L. (2013). Sisterhood of Courage: African American Women and Their Efforts to Aid the Union Forces in the Civil War. *Saber and Scroll*, vol. 2, issue 3, Summer, article 6.
Hall, R. (1993). *Patriots in Disguise: Women Warriors of the Civil War*. New York: Paragon House.
Hammond, H.E. (1962). *Maria Lydia Daly, Diary of A Union Lady*. New York: Funk & Wagnalls.
Historical Markers (Mdb.org), Hopewell, VA.
Hoffert. S.D. (2004). *Jane Grey Swisshelm*. Chapel Hill, NC: University of North Carolina Press.
Hopewell. (1985). *Our Share of Honour: Hopewell and Prince George County Women, 1600–1985*. Hopewell, VA: Hopewell Tourism Bureau.
Josiah Allen's Wife. (1879). *My Opinions and Betsy Bobbet's*. Hartford, CT: American Publishing.
Lebsock, S. (1984). *The Free Women of Petersburg: Status and Culture in a Southern Town, 1784–1860*. New York: W.W. Norton.
MacCaskill, L. & Novak, D. (1996). *Ladies on the Field: Two Civil War Nurses from Maine on the Battlefields of Virginia*. Livermore, ME: Signal Tree.
Marshall, K.M. (1987). *In a Combat Zone*. Boston: Little, Brown.
McPherson, D.G. (1963). Experiment at City Point. *Military Medicine*, 128, 242–244.
The North West Branch of the Christian Commission, http://www.nwuscc.org/OldUSCC.html
Obituary Records of Graduates Deceased During the Year Ending July 1, 1924. New Haven, CT: Yale University.
O'Hall, J. (June 25, 1975). Lady in the Veil. *The Maryland Independent*, LaPlata, MD.
Perkins, H.M. (December 1992). Lucien Hall's Prison Sketchbook. Northern Neck of Virginia Historical Society, XXLII.
Pfanz, D. (Transcriber). (1987). *The Diary of Marsena Patrick, Provost Marshal of the Army of the Potomac: June 15, 1864 to April 18, 1865*. Petersburg, VA: Petersburg National Battlefield Park.
Pfanz, D. (Transcriber). (1988). *The Depot Hospital at City Point*. Petersburg, VA: Petersburg National Battlefield Park.
Pudner, H.P. (1971). People not Pedagogy. *The Georgia Review*, XXV(3).

Schultz, J.E. (2004). *Women at the Front*. Chapel Hill: The University of North Carolina Press.
Sounds from the Battlefield. *Civil War Music*, File box 1, Dewitt Historical Society Library, Ithaca, NY.
Straubing, H.E. (1993). *In Hospital and Camp: The Civil War through the Eyes of Its Doctors and Nurses*. Harrisburg, PA: Stackpole.
Sudlow, L.L. (2000). *A Vast Army of Women: Maine's Uncounted Forces in the American Civil War*. Gettysburg, PA: Thomas.
Trammel, J. (2012). *The Richmond Slave Trade: The Economic Backbone of the Old Dominion*. Charleston, SC: The History Press.
Van Zandt, A.B. (1857). *The Elect Lady: A Memoir of Mrs. Catherine Bott*. Philadelphia, Presbyterian Board of Publication.
Walker, P.F. (1978). *Moral Choices: Memory, Desire, and Imagination in the Nineteenth- Century American Abolition*. Baton-Rouge: Louisiana State University.
Woodward, W.E. (1928) *Meet General Grant*. New York: Horace Liveright.
Wooley, Captain R.W. (1988). A Short History of Identification Tags. *Quartermaster Professional Bulletin*, Winter 1988, Fort Lee, VA.
Zinnen, R.O. (1991). City Point: The Tool that Gave General Grant Victory. *Quartermaster Professional Bulletin*, Spring 1991, Fort Lee, VA.

Historical Libraries

Beth Ahabha Archives, Richmond, VA.
Clements Library at the University of Michigan, Ann Arbor, MI.
Library of Virginia, Richmond, VA.
Museum of the Confederacy, Richmond, VA.
National Park Service, Petersburg and Richmond, VA.
Virginia History and Culture Center, Richmond, VA.
Wood Memorial Library, South Windsor, CT.
Yale University Library and Archives, New Haven, CT.

University Museums or Historical Societies

Andersonville, NPS.
Columbia County Historical and Genealogical Society, Bloomsburg, PA.
Connecticut Historical Society, Hartford, CT.
Danbury Historical Society, Danbury, CT.
Dewitt Historical Society, Ithaca, NY.
Godfrey Genealogical Society, Middletown, CT.
Iowa Historical Society, Des Moines, IA
New Haven Colony Historical Society, New Haven, CT.
Tioga County Historical Society, Owego, NY.
Western Michigan Historical Society, Lansing, MI.
Wisconsin Historical Society, Madison, WI.

Newspapers

Alma (MI) Record: May 20, 1887.
Amsterdam (NY) Evening Record: January 12, 1927.
Ashtabula (OH) Weekly Telegraph: September 21, 1861.
Auburn (NY) Bulletin: July 24, 1886.
Auburn (NY) Citizen: April 18, 1865.
Auburn (NY) Semi-Weekly: August 20, 1912.

The Bridgeport Times and Evening Farmer (Bridgeport, CT): April 15, 1922.
Brooklyn Daily Eagle: July 19, 1864; December 24, 1868; March 17, 1895; June 11, 1898; January 4, 1903; October 14, 1911; January 3, 1915; January 16, 1915; January 7, 1917.
Brooklyn Daily News: June 1, 1864.
Buffalo (NY) Courier, February 9, 1902.
Buffalo (NY) Evening News: May 26, 1903.
The Butler (MO) Weekly Times and County Record: February 27, 1919.
The Call Magazine (New York): April 11, 1920.
Canton (OH) Repository: August 25, 1907.
Chicago Daily Tribune: July 3, 1864.
Chicago Tribune: December 22, 1864.
Civil War News: March 11, 2016.
Cleveland (OH) Ledger: February 14, 1865.
Cleveland (OH) Morning Leader: December 26, 1864.
The Columbian (Bloomsburg, PA): December 18, 1868.
Commercial Advertiser (Canton, NY): March 1, 1893.
Cook County Herald (Grand Marais, MN): September 22, 1906.
Corning (NY) Evening Journal, September 26, 1872.
Daily Arkansas Gazette: September 9, 1869.
Daily Courier (Syracuse, NY): April 26, 1865.
Daily Democrat and Recorder (Amsterdam, NY): December 31, 1914.
Daily Dispatch (Richmond, VA): July 1, 1864; July 22, 1864; July 30, 1864; October 5, 1864; December 2, 1881.
Daily Evening Standard (Bridgeport, CT): July 5, 1864; June 10, 1865.
Daily Intelligence (Wheeling, VA): June 1, 1865.
Daily Leader (Marietta, OH): February 4, 1900.
Daily National Intelligence (Washington, D.C.): September 20, 1869.
Daily Ohio Statesman (Columbus, OH): June 28, 1864; March 23, 1865.
Daily Sentinel (Rome, NY): January 22, 1949.
Danbury (CT) Times: June 23, 1859; January 24, 1864.
The Day Book (Oswego, NY): December 30, 1912.
Democrat and Chronicle (Rochester, NY): August 25, 1899.
Democratic Recorder (Amsterdam, NY): January 21, 1919.
The Des Moines (IA) Tribune: April 6, 1908.
Diosova News: March 19, 2015.
The Evening Post (New York): November 30, 1895.
Evening Public Ledger (Washington, D.C.): June 8, 1918; February 22, 1919.
Evening Star (Washington, D.C.): November 15, 1864; January 23, 1865; May 5, 1865; October 1, 1886; March 6, 1894; April 18, 1906; January 27, 1913; April 3, 1921.
Evening Telegraph (New York): April 11, 1916.
The Evening Times (Washington, D.C.): April 17, 1899.
Fredonia (NY) Censor: January 19, 1887; July 16, 1890.
Gallipolis (OH) Journal: November 16, 1865; September 23, 1869.
Geneva (NY) Daily Times, February 12, 1902.
Harrisburg (PA) Telegraph: May 31, 1919.
Hartford (CT) Courant: December 31, 1863; June 27, 1864; August 15, 1864; September 26, 1864; December 31, 1864; February 15, 1865; March 9, 1865; March 26, 1865; March 29, 1865; March 31, 1865; November 16, 1866; July 11, 1876; October 30, 1899; February 7, 1902; August 18, 1904; September 21, 1911; May 18, 1912; July 22, 1912; July 23, 1912; August 13, 1912; April 12, 1916; February 23, 1919.
Hartford (CT) Daily Courant: August 4, 1864; August 12, 1864; August 15, 1864; September 26, 1864; December 22, 1864; February 23, 1865; March 18, 1865; March 20, 1865; March 21, 1865.
Hudson (NY) Evening Register: December 31, 1914.
Ithaca (NY) Daily News: May 14, 1904.

Bibliography 261

The Jeffersonian (Danbury, CT): June 3, 1863; August 24, 1864; August 17, 1864; October 25, 1864; November 3, 1864; September 11, 1869; November 11, 1874; November 18, 1874.
The Jeffersonian (Stroudsburg, PA): August 4, 1864.
Kansas Agitator (Garnett, KS): October 16, 1896.
Kansas City (KS) Journal: May 31, 1898.
La Crosse (WI) Tribune: June 15, 1931.
Lawrence Democrat (Lawrenceburg, TN): April 28, 1905.
Los Angeles Daily Herald: August 29, 1889.
Minneapolis (MN) Journal: August 16, 1906.
Murphreesboro (TN) Post: February 15, 2009.
National Republican (Washington, D.C.): September 16, 1876; May 16, 1883.
The National Tribune (Washington, D.C.): December 27, 1888; June 16, 1889; January 2, 1890.
National Tribute (Washington, D.C.): August 2, 1883; June 16, 1889.
The New Clown (Ithaca, NY): December 6, 1902.
New York Call: February 4, 1917.
New York Daily Tribune: April 18, 1899.
New York Herald: January 4, 1865; January 16, 1865; February 11, 1865; June 11, 1898.
New York Recorder: July 24, 1885.
New York Times: August 26, 1862; June 22, 1864; July 3, 1864; July 8, 1864; July 19, 1864; July 21, 1864; July 28, 1864; August 5, 1864; August 6, 1864; August 7, 1864; September 3, 1864; September 10, 1864; September 23, 1864; October 8, 1864; October 9, 1864; October 12, 1864; October 24, 1864; October 25, 1864; December 4, 1864; December 11, 1864; December 26, 1864; January 4, 1865; January 29, 1865; January 30, 1865; February 1, 1865; February 12, 1865; February 14, 1865; February 19, 1865; March 18, 1865; March 19, 1865; March 21, 1865; March 25, 1865; June 11, 1865; March 9, 1881; July 23, 1884; August 5, 1885; October 14, 1886; May 14, 1887; March 14, 1888; June 26, 1893; August 9, 1894; March 17, 1895; December 23, 1896; December 27, 1896; April 28, 1897; October 4, 1898; December 14, 1902; December 17, 1902; December 21, 1902; December 6, 1906; January 30, 1909; December 22, 1912; July 13, 1913; January 15, 1922; February 4, 1923; January 16, 1930; June 25, 1930; September 9, 1930; March 16, 1936; December 2, 1997.
New York Tribune: September 29, 1911; November 1, 1913.
New York World: January 9, 1887.
The Newtown Register (Jamaica, NY): September 1904.
The Norfolk Virginian: March 28, 1895.
Oswego (NY) Daily Palladium: March 1, 1917; December 11, 1919.
Oswego (NY) Daily Times: August 2, 1883; April 19, 1893; January 27, 1906.
Oswego (NY) Press: June 10, 1865.
Owego (NY) Gazette: August 28, 1890; April 23, 1908.
Perrysburg (OH) Journal: October 12, 1900; December 20, 1901.
Philadelphia (PA) Inquirer: January 10, 1865; December 25, 1868; June 26, 1898.
Phillipsburg (KS) Herald, October 18, 1900.
Pittsburgh (PA) Dispatch: July 17, 1890; July 27, 1890.
Public Ledger (Memphis, TN): June 4, 1869.
The Record-Union (Sacramento, CA): February 11, 1892.
The Republican Advocate (Batavia, NY): February 13, 1865.
Richmond (VA) Examiner: December 31, 1863; May 29, 1864.
Richmond (VA) Planet: March 1, 1902.
Rochester (NY) Democrat and Chronicle: February 9, 1902.
Rock Island (IL) Argus: December 31, 1894.
Rutland (VT) Weekly Herald: December 31, 1868.
St. Cloud (MN) Democrat: August 12, 1858.
The Salt Lake City (UT) Herald: April 4, 1885; December 27, 1889; June 22, 1906.
The Salt Lake (UT) Tribune: September 22, 1912.
The San Francisco Call: May 7, 1899; January 3, 1901; August 16, 1903.
San Francisco Daily Bulletin: September 26, 1868.

Bibliography

Schenectady (NY) Gazette: June 24, 1939.
The Standard Union (Brooklyn, NY): May 30, 1895.
The Statesman (Yonkers, NY): April 6, 1865.
Staunton Spectator: December 2, 1881.
The Sun (New York): November 18, 1876; August 7, 1887; August 24, 1893; April 25, 1900; November 2, 1913; January 20, 1919.
The Sunday Herald and Weekly National Intelligencer (Washington, D.C.): October 12, 1890; May 31, 1891; May 31, 1894.
The Sweetwater (TN) Enterprise: September 8, 1870.
The Times Dispatch (Richmond, VA): October 18, 1908.
Utica (NY) Daily Herald: September 6, 1864.
The Washington (D.C.) Critic: January 17, 1888.
The Washington (D.C.) Evening Star: April 5, 1865.
The Washington (D.C.) Herald: March 28, 1865; December 9, 1906.
Watertown Republican, November 22, 1861.

Weather References

Affairs Below Petersburg. (February 13, 1865). *Hartford Courant,* p. 3.
Afternoon Dispatches. (June 18, 1864). *Hartford Daily Courant,* p. 3.
Army of the Potomac. (July 7, 1864). *New York Times,* p. 4.
Army of the Potomac. (March 15, 1865). *New York Times,* p.1.
City Point. (August 24, 1864). *The Jeffersonian,* p. 1. Danbury Historical Society, Danbury, CT.
Civil War letters of Mack and Nan Ewing, Michigan State Archives.
Diary of John Baird. Sharpsburg, Pennsylvania. Hiller Family Papers, Historic Pittsburgh.
A Dispatch from City Point. (July 22, 1864). *Hartford Daily Courant,* p 2.
From a Christian Commission Delegate. (April 5, 1865). *Hartford Courant,* p. 2.
From City Point. (October 12, 1864). *New York Times,* p. 1.
From City Point. (March 3, 1865). *New York Times,* p. 5.
From City Point. (March 19, 1865). *New York Times,* p. 1.
From Fortress Monroe. (August 6, 1864). *Hartford Courant,* p. 3.
From Our Own Correspondent. (March 11, 1865). *New York Times,* p. 1.
General Grant's Army. (March 9, 1865). *New York Times,* p. 1.
H.F. Parker, Engineers file, Petersburg National Battlefield Park, Petersburg, VA.
Hallock, Armstrong. Library of Congress, lcweb2.loc.gov/service/gdc/scd0001/2010/2010_01/.
Jacquette, H.S. (Ed.). (1937). *South After Gettysburg: Letters of Cornelia Hancock.* Philadelphia: University of Pennsylvania.
Judson Andrew, Assistant Surgeon 2nd CVA. City Point file. Petersburg National Battlefield Park, Petersburg, VA.
Letter from City Point. (February 13, 1865). *Hartford Daily Courant,* p. 2.
Letters from Richmond. (April 24, 1865). *New York Times,* p. 2.
Life Among the Freedmen. (March 2, 1865). *Hartford Courant,* p. 2.
Lorin Jessie Aimes, Letters 3 (November 1864). Accession # 43654, Library of Virginia, public guides.
Manuscripts of the American Civil War, John M. Jackson Letters, http://rarebooks.nd.edu/digital/civil_war/letters/jackson.
Mr. Pryor in Washington. (November 30, 1864). *New York Times,* p. 1.
Palmer, S. (1868). *The Story of Aunt Becky's Army-Life.* New York: John F. Trow.
Parker, Colonel F.J. (1880). *32nd Regiment Massachusetts Infantry.* Boston: C.W. Calkins.
Pfanz, D. (Transcriber). (1987). *The Diary of Marsena Patrick, Provost Marshal of the Army of the Potomac: June 15, 1864 to April 18, 1865.* Petersburg National Battlefield Park, Petersburg, VA.
Right Wing. (March 25, 1865). *New York Times,* p. 1.

Bibliography

Sanborne, Pliny Fiske. USCC Civil War Chaplain Daily Extracts from June 7 to August 15, 1864. City Point files. Petersburg National Battlefield Park, Petersburg, VA.

Smith, A. (1919). *Reminiscences of an Army Nurse During the Civil War.* New York: Greaves.

War Diary and Letters of Stephan Minot Weld, 1861–1865 (1979). Boston: Massachusetts Historical Society.

Warman. David, Contract Surgeon, Fort Monroe, April to September 1864. City Point files. Petersburg National Battlefield Park, Petersburg, VA.

Warren, H.F. & Warren, E. (1871). *Letters: From Two Brothers Serving in the War for the Union.* Cambridge: Printed for private circulation.

Wilson, J.H. (1916). *Life of John Rawlins.* New York: Neala.

The Year 1864 from *Diary of Alonzo Clapp.* https://www.worldcat.org/title/alonzo-h-clapp-diaries-1852-1865/oclc/155455039, http//web.cortland.edu/woosterk/genweb/alonzoclapp/alonzoclapp1864.html.

Index

A., Mrs. Reverend 155
accommodations 19, 20, 21, 29, 35, 64, 65, 66, 95, 108, 141, 148, 149; transportation 37; USCC 81
Adams Express 120
Afro-Americans 3, 9, 10, 11, 28; census 23; contrabands 23, 64, 85; criticism 23, 49; death 30, 120; desire to learn 25, 26, 32; fear 56; food 23–24; General Order #30, 24; humor 24; illness 32; nurse attire 115; punishment 24; quarters 22, 25; regulations 24; roles 14; singing 84
Agency Row 96, 117
Aiken, Dr. 66
Aiken's Landing 90
Aldrich, Milly 94
American Red Cross 155
Ames, Caroline 193
Anderson, Charley 152
anger 14, 15; disdain 142; personal conflicts 64
Appomattox Manor 13, 14, 141
Appomattox River 12, 135
Army Nurse Association of Wisconsin 160
Aronson, Captain 117
Ashe, Mrs. 155
attire: social attire 141; *see also* clothing
Aunty 22
Aunty Miranda 22
awards: bronze plaque 183; buried in Arlington 165, 185, 201, 209; bust in New York state Capitol 188; Kearney Cross 179; Medal For Brave and Meritorious Conduct 165; Medal of Honor 191; monument 169; Third Corps badge 161

Baileys Creek 27
Bain, Annie 30, 31, 62, 150, 194
Ballard, Miss 155
Baltimore 139
Barlow, Mrs. Arabella 34, 108, 155

Barnes, Mrs. Surgeon General 141
Barnes, Surgeon General 141
Barnes, William 138
Barney, C. 217
Barr, Mrs. 194
Barrett, Sally 195
Barton, Clara 59, 60, 155
Batte, Martha 22, 217
"Battle Cry of Freedom" 83
"Battle Hymn" 83
Baxter, Ellen Janette Portus 157
Baylor, Mrs. 13, 19, 211
Beck, Mrs. 195
Beckwith, Captain 150
Belch, Fred 18
Bell, Mrs. 195
Bellows, Dr. 93
Benjamin, Judah P. 19
Bermuda Hundred 12
Bidgood, Miss/Mrs. 18, 19, 195, 211, 224, 241*n*17
Birchett 13
Blackman, Miss 157
Blackmar, (Brunson), Mary E. 131, 150, 157
Blackstone 195, 220, 221, 222
"Blessing on you" 90
Blydenburg, Miss 86
body retrieval 38, 41, 47, 77, 223
Bonnell, Eliza 31
Botts, Mrs. 13, 211, 240*ch*2*n*1
Bowman, Mrs. Colonel 195
Bowser, Mary 25
Bradley, Amy 103, 157
Bragg, Amanda 28
Brainard (Cole), Helen *see* Cole, Helen Brainard
Breed, Mrs. 23, 149, 195
Brinton, Dr. 119
Brinton-Taylor, Mrs. Dr. 209
Brooks, Mildred S. 158

265

Index

Brown, Mary A. 158
Brownell, Kady 69
Brunch, Susan 28
Brunnell, Dr. 119
Bucklin, Sophronia 25, 32, 40, 45, 88, 130, 159
Bunnell, Henriette 159
Burgess, Mrs. 196
burials 47, 80, 108, 109
Burnley, Lady Guests of 196
Burnside, Major General 56
Bush, Mrs. Pauline 221
Butler, General 12, 22

Cadwallader, Mrs. 147
Cahoon, Miss 196
Caitlan, Colonel 135
Cameron, Miss 196
Camp Jones 15
cannonading *see* sounds
caregivers 1, 2, 12, 26, 51, 53, 82, 140
Cary, Mary 159
Case, Cynthia 34, 102, 160
Castle Thunder 133
casualties 35, 40, 42, 51
Celia 151
chaos 36, 93, 112; docks 101; schedule 43–44
Charlotte Shaw 75
Child, Ellen 63
Child, Dr. Henry 63
children 12, 17, 53, 64, 75, 94; appropriate behavior 14, 20, 24; fleeing families 12; of officers 138, 141, 142, 146, 148
Children's Aid Society 171
City of New York 148
City Point 1, 2, 4, 6, 7, 10, 12, 19, 21, 34, 36, 92; accommodations 20, 23, 96; cemetery 80, 255; exchange 13, 35; residents 35; water 18, 25, 36
"Close His Eyes His Work Is Done" 84
clothing 44, 48, 55, 68, 82, 110, 114, 148
coffins: burials 51; transporting north 111
Cohn, Rosa 8
Cold Harbor 43, 189
Cole, Ella 88
Cole, Helen Brainard 117, 160
Collis, General 17
Collis, Septima 31, 140, 143
Colyer 20, 198, 202, 210, 224
compassion 23, 28, 31, 47, 48, 49, 51, 57, 77, 108, 118, 131
confidence 15, 26, 27, 31, 55, 61, 65
conflict 35, 46, 111, 163
confusion 13, 19, 75, 148
Conkling, Mrs. 197
Connecticut 100, 102, 103, 160, 174, 184, 186, 224
Contraband Relief Society 23

Cook, Old Aunty 31, 217
Cooke, Pleasant 197
Cooking 56, 66, 81, 117
Corn, Hannah 29
Corps: Cavalry Corps 178, 188, 204; Corps d'Afric 62, 179; 2nd Corps 63, 99, 109, 111, 157, 159, 173, 189, 192; 5th Corps 166; 6th Corps 45, 157, 165, 174; 9th Corps 37, 152, 163, 168, 179, 182, 193
Corps hospitals: Corps d'Afric 36; 2nd Corps; 36, 5th Corps 36; 9th Corps 36
"Cottage of Dear Ones Left at Home" 84
courage 14, 17
court martial 14, 15, 16, 109, 221, 241*n*14
Cox, Mis/Mrs. 197
Custer, Elizabeth 197

Dalton, Mrs., Dr. 197
Daly, Mrs. 142, 146
Dame, Harriett 161
dangers 62, 90, 100, 101, 127, 131, 132, 133; explosion 122; horses 98; incoming 13; transport accidents 106
Daughters of the Revolution Valley Forge 173
Dearing, Family of General 211
death 3, 51, 78, 80, 101, 105, 109, 119
Deavers, Bridget 64, 69, 70, 161
De Cordova, J. 123, 124
defense of homes 13, 14, 17, 22
Delegate, S.D.T. 79, 87
DeMolay 154, 220
Dent, Mrs. Frederick 198
Depot Hospital 12, 35
depression 85
Derby, Mrs. 198
Diet kitchens 86, 135, 145
Dix, Dorothea 39, 67, 161; appearance and qualifications 39
"Dixie" 2
Doane, Mrs. 198
Dod, Captain: mother of 198
"Doxology" 83
Drum Beat 35
Dudley, Dr. Frederick 67, 68, 119
Dunbar, Lois 58, 59, 163
Duncan, Kate M. 163
Dupee, Mary E. 116
Dupree, Mrs. Lieutenant 221
dust 25, 37, 74, 117
Dutch Gap 31, 62, 90, 118

Eaton, Harriett 116, 117, 164
Eden, Capt./Major Robert 30, 150, 194
Edson, Sarah P. 58, 59, 164
education 9, 22, 25, 63, 119

Index

Ehler, M.A. 53, 164
Elizabeth 98
Elliott, Mrs./Miss 198
Ellis, Ruth 165
embalmer 79; benefit of knowing 118, 119
Emery, Mrs. 221
empathy 38, 47, 68, 118; lack of 148
Eppes, Dr. 12, 26, 27
Eppes, Hannah 28
Eppes, Pauline Ruffin 26, 217
equipment 14, 35, 37, 65, 120
Etheridge, Annie 69, 71, 165
Evans, Hannah 218
executions 16, 53; death march 84; hanging 16, 17
exhaustion 16, 36, 43, 44, 106, 109, 132, 192
explosion 99, 120

Farnham (Fletch), Amanda Colburn 34, 39, 44, 64, 165
Farnham, Dr. 79
Faxon (Foxon), Annie 166
Fay, Delia 135, 166
Fay, General Superintendent 99
fear 14, 15, 17, 63
Fenton, Governor 123, 124
Ferguson, Jane 221
flag-of-truce 19, 101, 191, 199, 211, 222, 224
Flagg, Harriet 135, 166
Flegenheimer, William 8
Fogg, Isabella 102, 106
Fogg, Lieutenant 65
food 13, 14, 19, 24, 35, 48, 105, 112, 128, 129, 131, 143, 144, 148; cooking 38; recipes 89, 90
Foster, Augusta 69
Fox, Cora 198
Freedman's Bureau 23, 175; Relief Society 23; school 57
French, Mary Ellen 199
Frick, Rebecca 167
frustration 6, 11, 14, 37, 64, 83, 145; lice 45; mice 48, 66; officers 61

Galbraith, Mrs. 221
Gardner, Miss 168
Gawkers 141, 147
Gay, W.H. 98
Geary, Daniel 15, 16, 17
Georgiana 26
Gerrigan John 78
Gibbons, Miss 199
Gibbs, Miss 168
Gillis, Agnus Ann 168
Gilson (Osgood), Helen Louise 32, 34, 55, 56, 130, 149, 168; helping others 25, 56

"The Girl I Left Behind" 84
"God Bless America" 2
gophers 62
Gordon, Ranson 15, 16, 17
Grant, General 10, 12, 13, 26, 69, 133, 138
Grant, Julia 87, 138, 141, 144, 145, 199
Grant, Nellie 200
Gray, Rebecca 34, 102, 106, 169
Graybacks 44
Griffin, Sally 200
Griffin, William T., aka Bolter, George 84
Griffins, Josephine 200
Grover 100
Grundy, Clara H. 20, 200
Guest, Mary J. 169

Hall, Lucien 27
Hall (Richards), Maria C. 34, 104
Hall, Virginia 69
Hamblin, P. 22, 218
Hamilton, J.R. 96
Hamlin, 2nd Engineer 100
Hampton, VA 13, 27
Hancock, Cornelia 28, 34, 37, 38, 39, 55, 61, 64, 88, 114, 127, 134, 171
Hancock, General 133
Hannah 29, 30, 60, 150, 218
Happer, M.A. 171
happiness: free time 100; singing 84
harassment 16, 51; officers and 61, 67, 102, 127, 129
Hardenbrook, Eunice 135, 171
Harding (Dunbar), Lois *see* Dunbar, Lois
Harlan, Ann 141, 201
Harlan, Mary 141, 201
Harlan, Senator 141
Harris, Mrs. John 104, 172
Hart, Mrs. Virginia 172
Hatcher, Mrs. 13, 15, 118, 212
Hatcher's Run 31, 219
Hazen, Fannie Titus 88, 172
Hill, Mary 173
Holstein, Anna 46, 66, 173; personnel conflict 111
Hood, Mrs. Dr. 34, 102, 174
Hooper, Anne Sturgis 141, 201
Hooper, Judge 141
Hopewell 18, 23, 35
horseback riding 61, 65, 99, 107, 122, 134
Horton, Mrs. 202
hospitals: Cavalry Corps 53; Corps d'Afric 35, 56; Depot Complex 12, 35; Engineer's Hospital 35; Government Hospital 35; Pest hospital 36; Post Hospital 36; Railroad Hospital 36
hotel 20, 21

268 Index

Houghton, Mary 174
Houghton, Reverend 123, 150, 253n28
Hoyt, Clara 174
humor 24, 51
Humphrey, Miss 202
Huntington, Mrs. 202
Huron, Mary F. 117, 174
Husbands, Mrs. Mary 108, 174
Hyde, Miss 202

illness 3, 76, 155, 176; diarrhea 42, 67; typhoid 118
"I'm Going to Fight Mit Seigle" 84
"In 61" 151
incarceration 13, 19
independent nurses: accommodations 65, 66; clothing 55; cultural norms 60; foraging 55; listening 57; roles 55
intelligence gathering 20, 21, 25
Iowa Soldier's Orphans Home 192
"Is That Mother?" 107

Jackson, Harriett 26
Jackson Hospital 19
Jacob Strader 167
James, Diley 26, 219
James River 12, 62, 100, 101, 138
Jenkins, Miss 202
"John Brown's Body" 83
Johnson, Mary 28, 175, 222
Johnson, Mrs. 117
Jones, H.E. 135, 175
Jones, Hetty 176
Jones, Mary 87, 219
Josslyn, Maria 176
Joy, Miss *see* Le Clerq, Agnes Joy
"Just Before the Battle Mother" 57

Ketchem, Colonel 197
King, Cora 202
King, Mrs. Cora 136, 177
King's Daughters 158
Knickerbocker 157

Lacey, Mary Roby 177
Ladies Aide Society 37, 94, 95
Ladies Soldier's Aid Association 109
Lake, Myron 110
Langdon, Captain 78
Larnard, Anna 177
Latham, Anna 177
laundry 27, 34, 49, 61, 126; days 46; facility 24, 49; location 30; procedures 25; wedding 151
Le Clerq, Agnes Joy 136, 176
learning 3, 4, 6, 10, 16, 25, 37, 39, 50, 63, 64, 80, 92, 97, 100, 108, 142

Leary, Mrs. Arthur 202
Lee, Mary W. 34, 37, 38, 39, 108
"Let Me Kiss Him for His Mother" 84
Levy, Mrs. Frances 18, 19
Lewis, Nancy 219
Lincoln, Abraham 32, 68, 136; soldier connection 68
Lincoln, Mary Todd 141, 144
Lizzie Baker 189
Logan, General 141
Logan, Mrs. 141, 142, 144, 203
Looby, Ellen McCormick 178
Lord, Louisa 203
Louisville 102
Lyman, Mrs. 204
Lyons, Mrs. 178

Maltby House 21
"Marching Through Georgia" 83
Marshall, Amanda 28
Marshall, Mrs. Humphrey 212
Martin 198, 202, 208
Martin, Colonel Robert Maxwell 222
Martin, Mrs. 204
Martin, Mrs. (POW) 19, 222
Mason, Miss 58, 59
Maxwell, John 122
Mayhew, Ruth 100, 116, 117, 130, 150, 178
McCabe, Reverend 83
McKay, Charlotte 178
McLean, Reverend J.K. 78
Meade, Mrs. General 204
mentoring 37, 56, 109
Mercy, Mrs. 179
Merritt, Mary 179
Metropolitan Hotel 21
military units: Army of the James 12, 135; Army of the Potomac 6, 127; 9th Corps 22
Miller, Mrs. Dr. 204
Mills, Carrie Robinson 185
Miranda, Aunty 217
Mission of Masons 119, 120, 123, 124, 164
Mitchel, Miss 204
Mitchell, Mrs. Dr. 204
Mitchell, Maggie 179
Moore, Matilda 138, 180
Moore, Mrs. 179
Morey, E.L. 20, 222
Morgan, Judith 205
Morgan, Gen. Michael Ryan 205
Morris, Matilda 222
Moss, Reverend 76
"Mother Is the Battle Over" 84
Murry, Mrs. 180
music 32, 53, 57, 83, 84, 140

Index

Nancy 26, 219
National Association of Civil War Nurses 159, 163, 166, 167, 171, 173, 180, 184, 188
Nebraska Relief Corps 181
Nelson, Annie 13
Nelson, Mrs. Mary 13, 212
networking 35, 61
New York Association of Nurses 166
Newman, Laura 34, 69, 180
Ney, Miss 58, 59, 117, 180
Ninth Corps 22, 37
Nolan, Mary Elizabeth 180
norms, cultural 3, 4, 5, 7, 8, 9, 11, 15, 37, 45, 60, 81, 98, 107, 140, 142, 149
Northerner 196, 207
Noyes, Hettie 87, 181
nurses: City Point complex 35; independence 65; integrity 38; listening 57, 67; pay 40; relationships 35, 64; reliability 39; role 35, 47; sanity 35, 56; tricks 38, 44, 49, 60
Nurses Association for Massachusetts 185

Ocean Queen 157
Ohio, Agent 117, 117
Old Capitol Prison 19
Oliver, Captain 19
Olmstead, Frederick 93
Onondaga 62
Ord, General 141
Ord, Mary 134, 141
organizational skills 58, 61, 88, 99
"Our Father" 137

Page, Eliza 24
Painter, Dr. Hettie 117, 130, 150, 181; visiting her son 118, 251n12
Palmer, Sarah "Aunt Becky" 21, 30, 40, 47, 48, 51, 66, 100, 114, 128, 130–134, 148
Park Barracks 58
Parker, Colonel 226
Parker, General 199
Parker, Mr. 17
Parr, Mrs. 222
passes 19, 43, 127, 128
Patrick, Provost Marshal 15, 17, 23
Patterson, Georgy 142
Peek, Mr. 123, 151
pensions 32, 157, 158, 160, 161, 165–167, 171–174, 177, 178, 180, 181, 183
Petersburg 6, 12, 13, 14, 28, 106, 110
Pettis, Ms. 183
Pitkins, Jennie 88, 183
Planter 189, 209
Pocahontas Island 118

poetry: "In 61" 151; "Is That Mother?" 107; "Our Father" 137
Point of Rocks 12, 34, 73, 87, 120, 135, 151
Polk, Mrs. 183
Porter, Georgy 141, 205
Potter, T.H. 135
Pratt, Rev. A.L. 78
Prentice, Dr. 122
Price, Rebecca 104, 115, 183
Prince Albert 22, 27
prisoners 13, 18, 67; arrests 19, 223; CSA 27; exchange 19, 101
Pryor, Sara 24
public relations 79, 94, 97, 116

quartermaster 26, 35, 87, 120, 122, 139

Rachel 219
Rammel, Chaplain 16
Randolph, Hannah 28
Rawlins, Mary Hurlburt 141, 144, 145, 206
Reading, Mrs. 108, 184
Reed, Miss 206
Reed, William H. 93, 95
Reeves, Miss 135, 184
refugees 149
regiments: 1st Connecticut Cav. 193; 1st Massachusetts Cav. 189; 1st New York Cav. 221; 1st Rhode Island 69; 2nd Michigan Reg. 69; 2nd Maine 69; 2nd Vermont 157; 3rd Maine 185; 3rd Michigan Inf. 69; 4th Vermont 165; 5th Wisconsin 69; 7th New Jersey; 7th New York Vol.; 8th Pennsylvania Vol. 16; 14th New York Heavy 178; 17th Maine 179; 17th Massachusetts band 185; 22 Connecticut Cav. 193; 22nd Massachusetts Inf. 166; 28th Ohio Inf. 181; 32nd Massachusetts Reg. 166; 37th New Jersey 59; 52nd Ohio Vol. 191; 60th Ohio 193; 61st New York Inf. 39; 68th Pennsylvania Vol. 16; 109th New York Reg. 182; 114th Pennsylvania 16; 133 Massachusetts Inf. 173; 147st New York Vol. 120; 173rd Ohio Reg 181; Philadelphia Fire Zouaves 69
Reifsnyder, Miss, Harriet 40, 184
Richardson, Emma Wood 13, 212
Richmond 2, 6, 19, 20, 24, 25, 67, 100
River Queen 194, 195, 198, 201, 202, 207, 210
Rives, Sally 22, 219
Roberson, Mrs. 13, 212
Roberts, Rev. B. 79
Robinson, S.C. 136
Root, Newel, aka Harris, George 84
routine schedule: daily 146; hospital chaos

42–44; hospital normal 41–42; transport boat 120; USCC 83, 104
Ruffin, Harriett 26
Russell, General 135
Russell, Mrs. 206

St. John's Episcopal Church 26, 214, 242n21
Salm-Salm, Major 136, 176
Samples, Mrs. 117, 185
Sampson, Sarah 117, 185
Sanborne, Reverend 72
Sanitary Fairs 58, 95; *Drum Beat* 95
Sarah Brown 100
Sayles 117, 186
Scoville, Captain 122
Second Corps 30, 36, 39
Seip, T.L. 98
Seizgle, Mary 223
Seten, Mrs. 202, 207
Sewell, William A. 103, 104
Sharpe, Colonel 17
Sharpless, Harriett 40, 102, 103, 186
Shaw, Mary 100, 186
Shaw, Sarah 100, 186
Shenandoah Valley 45, 65
Sheridan, General 13
Sickles, General 136
Silver Star 19, 220, 224
Slater, Rowan 19
Slater, Sarah "Nettie" 19, 211, 213–214
Slaughter, Amy 27
Slaughter, Susan 26
smells 40, 43, 50, 102, 103; wounded 59, 64
Smith, Adelaide 21, 29, 34, 55, 57–59, 114, 127, 134, 186; agents appointment 117–119, 122–124
Society for Organizing Charities 171
Society for Women and the Civil War (SWCW) 2
"Soldier's Tears" 84
songs: "Battle Cry of Freedom" 83; "Battle Hymn" 83; "Close His Eyes His Work Is Done" 84; "Cottage of Dear Ones Left at Home" 84; "Dixie" 2; "Doxology" 83; "The Girl I Left Behind" 84; "God Bless America" 2; "I'm Going to Fight Mit Seigle" 84; "John Brown's Body" 83; "Just Before the Battle Mother" 57; "Let Me Kiss Him for His Mother" 84; "Marching Through Georgia" 83; "Mother Is the Battle Over" 84; "Soldier's Tears" 84; "Tenting on the Old Camp Ground" 83; "Tramp, Tramp, Tramp" 83; "The Union Wagon" 84; "When This Cruel War Is Over" 83; "Yankee Doodle" 83
Sorton, Miss 223

sounds: bugle call 36, 42; cannonading 12, 13, 46, 48, 53, 68, 130; cutting down trees 36; death march 110; drums 16, 443, 84, 85, 102; equipment 13, 14, 18; flies 50; lack of noise 14; moans 43, 49, 53; taps 36, 42, 62; whistles 102
Soyer, Mrs. 187
Spaulding, Mrs. 53, 187
Spencer, Elmira 117, 120, 122–125, 130, 188
Sperry, Mrs. 188
spies 13, 19, 20
Sprague, Sarah Jane Milliken 189
Stanton, Eleanor Adams 141, 207
Stanton, Secretary of War 141
state agents: accents 114; appearance 117; cooking 117; dock task 120; illness 118; role 114
State of Maine 100, 190
Steele, Miss 208
Stenton, Elizabeth 189
Steven, Mrs. Surgeon 208
Stevens, Mrs. Paren 208
Stevenson, Emma 32
Steverson, J.M. 79
Stiles, Benjamin 14, 17
Stiles, Mary E. 14, 15, 16, 17, 214
Stoughton, Mrs. 208
Strachan, Reverend, John 12
stress 13, 14, 15, 35, 244n65
Stretch, Mrs. 189
Strouse, Rebecca 189
strumpets 21, 102
Stuart, George 72, 73
suffrage 3, 63, 187
Swisshelm, Jane Grey 23, 149, 208

Talbots 13
Taylor, Mrs. General *see* Brinton-Taylor, Mrs. Dr
Taylor, Susie King 32
teaching 24, 32, 56
ten o'clock mail boat 41, 225
"Tenting on the Old Camp Ground" 83
Thorpe, Emily 189
tours 140; "special" 195, 205
Townsent, Mrs. 189
trains 77, 78, 80
"Tramp, Tramp, Tramp" 83
transport/boats 96, 161; *Baltimore* 139; *Blackstone* 195, 220, 221, 222; *Charlotte Shaw* 75; *City of New York* 148; *Colyer* 20, 198, 202, 210, 224; *Connecticut* 100, 102, 103, 160, 224; *DeMolay* 154, 220; *Elizabeth* 98; flag-of-truce 19, 101, 191, 199, 211, 222, 224; *Grover* 100; *Jacob Strader* 167; *Knickerbocker* 157; *Lizzie Baker* 189; *Louisville*

Index

102; *Martin* 198, 202, 208; *Northerner* 196, 207; *Ocean Queen* 157; *Onondaga* 62; *Planter* 189, 209; *Prince Albert* 22, 27; *River Queen* 194, 195, 198, 201, 202, 207, 210; *Sarah Brown* 100; *Silver Star* 19, 220, 224; *State of Maine* 100, 190; ten o'clock mail boat 41, 225; *Vanderbilt* 102, 104, 172
transport incidents 100
transport schedules 104, 105, 106
transportation 12, 58, 62, 99, 100, 130
trauma 14, 50, 84, 101, 126
triage 248*n*75
Tubman, Harriet 32

"The Union Wagon" 84
U.S. Christian Commission: attire 76; Baltimore Fire Department 74; chapel 78; conflicts 85; contrabands 85; cooking wagons 74; death/ burial 80; delegates 72; diet kitchens 76, 86; library 78; locations/sources 72, 73, 75; minute men 75; Pacific Christian Commission 73; public relations 79; recipes 89–90; role 73–79; rubber blankets 74; supplies 73–74; trains 77, 78, 80; transportation 68; water pump 25, 27; women's role 85
U.S. Sanitary Commission 37, 39; back pay 96; Brooklyn Fair 95; *Bulletin* 98; burial procedure 108, 109; depot locations 93; differences with USCC 92; feeding stations 101; hospital transports 45; loading 102; railroad cars 100, 106, 107; roles 96; *Soldier's Friend* 97, 98
Usher, Rebecca 116, 163, 190

Van Buren, Miss Anna 209
Vance, Mary 190

Vanderbilt 102, 104, 172
Van Ingen, Reverend 122
violations 15, 241*n*14
Virginia 2, 4, 6, 7, 94, 131
visitors, unwanted 141, 147; *see also* gawkers
Vivandièr 68
Von Hoffman, Mrs. 210

Wade, Caroline Rosecrans 141, 210
Wade, Senator 141
Wakeman, Reverend 150
Walker, Dr. Mary 133, 190–191, 251*n*12
Walker, Hannah 28
Washington, George 118
weather 233–239
Webb, Mrs. Andrew 210
wedding 29, 150, 151
weeping/crying/tears 53, 77, 108, 126
Weston Manor 13
Wheelock, Julia 116, 117, 191
"When This Cruel War Is Over" 83
White, Lydia K. 136, 192
Whitman, Walt 35
Whitmore, D.C.H. 78
Whitney, Captain 70
Willets, Georgianna 104, 192
Williams, Lucy 14, 15, 214
Wilson, Mrs. 100, 108, 192
Wiseman, Mary Catherine 18, 214
Wittenmyer, Annie 38, 73, 86, 192
women, Southern 13, 15, 20, 143
Women's Council of Boston 101
Women's Suffrage Party 187

Yankee alphabet 136, 137
"Yankee Doodle" 83

www.ingramcontent.com/pod-product-compliance
Lightning Source LLC
Chambersburg PA
CBHW021350300426
44114CB00012B/1154